SAGE was founded in 1965 by Sara Miller McCune to support the dissemination of usable knowledge by publishing innovative and high-quality research and teaching content. Today, we publish more than 850 journals, including those of more than 300 learned societies, more than 800 new books per year, and a growing range of library products including archives, data, case studies, reports, conference highlights, and video. SAGE remains majority-owned by our founder, and after Sara's lifetime will become owned by a charitable trust that secures our continued independence.

Los Angeles | London | New Delhi | Singapore | Washington DC

Evaluation in the Extreme

Thank you for choosing a SAGE product!
If you have any comment, observation or feedback,
I would like to personally hear from you.
Please write to me at **contactceo@sagepub.in**

Vivek Mehra, Managing Director and CEO, SAGE India.

Bulk Sales

SAGE India offers special discounts
for purchase of books in bulk.
We also make available special imprints
and excerpts from our books on demand.

For orders and enquiries, write to us at

Marketing Department
SAGE Publications India Pvt Ltd
B1/I-1, Mohan Cooperative Industrial Area
Mathura Road, Post Bag 7
New Delhi 110044, India

E-mail us at **marketing@sagepub.in**

Get to know more about SAGE

Be invited to SAGE events, get on our mailing list.
Write today to **marketing@sagepub.in**

This book is also available as an e-book.

Evaluation in the Extreme

Research, Impact and Politics in Violently Divided Societies

Edited by

Kenneth Bush • Colleen Duggan

 **SAGE** www.sagepublications.com
Los Angeles • London • New Delhi • Singapore • Washington DC

International Development Research Centre
Ottawa • Cairo • Montevideo • Nairobi • New Delhi

First published in 2015 by

 SAGE Publications India Pvt Ltd
B1/I-1 Mohan Cooperative Industrial Area
Mathura Road, New Delhi 110 044, India
www.sagepub.in

SAGE Publications Inc
2455 Teller Road
Thousand Oaks, California 91320, USA

SAGE Publications Ltd
1 Oliver's Yard, 55 City Road
London EC1Y 1SP, United Kingdom

SAGE Publications Asia-Pacific Pte Ltd
3 Church Street
#10-04 Samsung Hub
Singapore 049483

**International
Development
Research Centre**
P.O. Box 8500
Ottawa, Ontario
Canada, K1G 3H9
www.idrc.ca
info@idrc.ca

ISBN (e-book)
978-1-55250-584-7

Published by Vivek Mehra for SAGE Publications India Pvt Ltd, typeset in 10/12 Times New Roman by RECTO Graphics, Delhi and printed at Chaman Enterprises, New Delhi.

Library of Congress Cataloging-in-Publication Data

Evaluation in the extreme : research, impact and politics in violently divided societies / edited by Kenneth Bush and Colleen Duggan.
  pages cm
Includes bibliographical references and index.
  1. Evaluation research (Social action programs) 2. Social conflict. 3. Violence. 4. War. I. Bush, Kenneth, editor. II. Duggan, Colleen, editor.
  H62.E847547   303.6072—dc23   2015   2015029481

ISBN: 978-93-515-0394-1 (HB)

The SAGE Team: Shambhu Sahu, Sandhya Gola, Megha Dabral and Rajib Chatterjee

Contents

List of Illustrations

Tables

Figures

Boxes

List of Abbreviations

AEA	American Evaluation Association
AES	Australasian Evaluation Society
ART	Antiretroviral Therapy
CDA	Collaborative for Development Action
CES	Canadian Evaluation Society
CGD	Centre for Governance and Development
DAC	Development Assistance Committee
DE	Developmental Evaluation
DFID	Department for International Development, United Kingdom
IDRC	International Development Research Centre
INCORE	International Conflict Research Institute
LSE	London School of Economics
INGO	International Non-Governmental Organisation
NGO	Non-Governmental Organisation
NPO	Non-Profit Organisation
OECD	Organisation for Economic Cooperation and Development
OM	Outcome Mapping
PCIA	Peace and Conflict Impact Assessment
PLHIV	People Living with HIV
RCT	Randomised Control Trial
REF	Research Excellence Framework
RTE	Real-Time Evaluation
SLEVA	Sri Lankan Evaluation Association
SLIG	Suffolk Lenadoon Interface Group
SROI	Social Return on Investment
UFE	Utilisation-Focused Evaluation
UNEG	United Nation Evaluation Group
VDS	Violently Divided Societies

List of Abbreviations

Preface

This book emerges from an exploratory joint research project between International Conflict Research Institute (INCORE), a research centre housed within the University of Ulster in Northern Ireland, and the International Development Research Centre (IDRC), a Canadian public organisation that funds research in the developing world.

Our goal was to map out some of the most vexing challenges and promising avenues for improving research and evaluation practice in societies affected by violence and conflict. The project brought together representatives of four groups from the Global North and South who share a stake in improving evaluation and research practice in societies affected by violence and conflict: researchers, evaluators, practitioners and funders.

Our journey began with a series of conversations that became increasingly animated over time. The initial questions around which discussions revolved were: How do we know whether research is making a difference to the lives of people in violently divided societies (VDS)? What can we learn from current practice to better understand the positive and negative impacts that research and evaluation have on peace and well-being in the Global North and South? The academic interest in these questions was driven by INCORE's specific interest in the efficacy of applied research in peace and conflict studies. IDRC's support to the project was anchored in its commitment to building evaluation as a field of theory and practice in the developing world, and in its mission to support developing countries' use of knowledge and science to find practical, long-term solutions to social, environmental and economic problems.

As project members came together, we encountered a series of challenges, the biggest of which was to figure out how to manage differences in language, institutional cultures and world views between the four types of participants. This was addressed with patience, humour and a peer-to-peer learning process that was conspicuous in the two write-shops held in Northern Ireland. Further, the development of a shared language and a sense of common project were strengthened through the collegial conversations stimulated by a collective peer-review process whereby authors wrestled with theoretical, practical and terminological points of contention.

One of the particularly notable (and enjoyable) elements of this project was the way it unexpectedly created a number of parallel channels for engaging and exploring its core issues, and for expanding the number and diversity of those wrestling with these issues. Ideas generated through the book project formed the basis for the development of a summer school course for mid-level professionals on evaluation in conflict zones, which was offered and refined over three consecutive years at the INCORE Summer School. (This summer school now continues at the University of York, UK, under the auspices of the Post-war Reconstruction and Development Unit.) Relatedly, the applied nature of the book project led to the creation and piloting of a number of professional development workshops on evaluation ethics by the book's editors, which were delivered at conferences of the African Evaluation Association and South Asian Community of Evaluators. Also, the debates within the book project found their way into the curriculum of graduate courses in evaluation in conflict zones in Northern Ireland and England.

Acknowledgements

This book came about, thanks to the dedication and commitment demonstrated by the many people we worked with and the organisations which collaborated on the 'Evaluation in Violently Divided Societies' project. The book benefitted from invaluable comments from a number of experts and practitioners working in the domain of international development. Among them, we would like to thank Rick Davies and Fred Carden for reviewing earlier versions of chapters as well as the overall manuscript. They were unstinting in the time and support they committed to this project. Thanks also goes to the two anonymous peer reviewers commissioned by SAGE to review the final manuscript.

The authors would also like to thank the International Conflict Research Institute (INCORE) at the University of Ulster, UK, particularly its Director, Brandon Hamber, who initiated the VDS project and hosted the write-shops noted above. A number of interns at the Institute performed yeoman's duty on the manuscript and helped out with the myriad technical and organisational tasks associated with the research, logistics and production of this book: Sofia Stolke, Ignacio Marino and Spiros Chairetis.

Thanks also goes to the International Development Research Centre (IDRC) which provided the financial support for this project. Current and former members of IDRC's Evaluation Unit offered helpful suggestions, insights and encouragement throughout the lifetime of the project, particularly Sarah Earl, Tricia Wind and Amy Etherington. Jackie Strecker, a former IDRC research awardee, is a contributing author and also did initial editing of a number of chapters. Nola Haddadian of IDRC's Communications Division guided us through the process of publishing. And finally, we would like to thank the team at SAGE India for their support in publishing this book.

PART I

Introduction

1

Research, Impact and Politics in Violently Divided Societies

An Evaluative Lens for Small Scale Maps

Kenneth Bush and Colleen Duggan

Introduction

Research is essential for understanding and responding to economic, social and political problems which, if left unaddressed, can create or aggravate societal tensions and divisions. Conflicts can be violent and militarised or they can assume less visible—but no less devastating—forms of expression. As conflicts multiply, interact and escalate, the domestic knowledge infrastructure of societies is frequently targeted directly and indirectly. Schools and universities themselves may become sites for those conflicts raging beyond their walls: as curricula are politicised; as schools and libraries are attacked; and as university students, staff and researchers are targeted by conflict stakeholders. Typically, journalists, public intellectuals and critics are simultaneously and systematically undermined and silenced. The result is a knowledge-depleted environment, at those very moments when ideas, research and innovation are essential for combating socio-political forces which can be retrogressive and parasitic, and for generating the evidence base needed for human development. Such conditions inhibit local researchers from contributing to efforts to address the multifaceted forms of violence that the *World Development Report 2011* described as the 'main constraint to meeting the Millennium Development Goals' (World Bank, 2011, p. 62).

While media headlines highlight the corrosive impacts of intense conflict on research and knowledge infrastructure, much less attention is devoted to the consideration of the impacts of research on the dynamics of conflict, or peace, for that matter. This blind spot has persisted, somewhat paradoxically, despite the substantial increase in the funding of research in and on violently divided societies (VDS) over the past two decades. Thus, for example, there has been: a proliferation of specialised journals and books; the establishment of specialised research centres, units and programmes (governmental, non-governmental, anti-governmental, academic, practitioner-focused and policy oriented); the creation or expansion of peace-focused research grants; and an explosion of graduate and undergraduate programmes of peace and conflict studies.

But, how do we know whether a piece of research (or a programme of research) has made any difference in VDS—whether constructively *or destructively*? The honest response to this question is that we have only anecdotes, rather than answers. This book is the first attempt to bring together the major stakeholders to address this question; stakeholders include researchers, evaluators, funders and practitioners of international aid. The book harnesses the political, technical and methodological sensitivities and capacities of these groups to a critical interrogation of the impact of research in VDS.

As detailed further later, this book contains two types of chapters: (a) case studies, and (b) synthetic chapters which wrestle with the meta-level questions of the interconnections between research, evaluation, impact and politics in VDS. The range of cases contained in the book pushes us to broaden our understanding of the heterogeneity of violence that divides societies. Thus, while the book includes cases of militarised violence (Sri Lanka, Darfur, Pakistan and Northern Ireland), it also includes a case on the evaluation of HIV/AIDS research and the politics of policy-making in post-apartheid South Africa (Chapter 6). Similarly, it includes a study of child-focused interventions in communities of sex workers in South Asia (Chapter 7). The latter two cases push us to broaden our understanding of the nature of the violence that divides societies. The South African case raises questions about the chameleonising nature of violence in societies *in transition*. The South Asian case highlights the iatrogenic impacts of child protection interventions—that is, where development interventions to protect children have the opposite effect. The synthetic chapters include: one charting out the *constituent literatures* that underpin the conceptual and theoretical terrain of the book (Chapter 2), and one addressing the challenges of building this field of work systematically (Chapter 9).

In an effort to ensure that the reader is able to appreciate both the inductive (case-specific/bottom-up) and the deductive (nomothetic/top-down) dimensions of the book, each subsection is prefaced with a brief discussion tying the constituent chapters to the cross-cutting themes of the book. This is intended to avoid a problem common to edited books—compartmentalised chapters and the failure of chapters to aggregate into something greater than the sum of their parts.

Assessing the Societal Impacts of Research in Violently Divided Societies (VDS)

The need for the systematic evaluation of the societal impacts[1] of research is pressing and challenging in both non-conflict and conflict contexts. However, as we explore in the current chapter, and throughout this book, it is even more complex in VDS. The interplay of context, knowledge production and research utilisation is not easily untangled, let alone measured. The most obvious positive impact of research on a VDS is to increase the practical knowledge base of crucial development stakeholders—institutions, policy-makers and civil society—through analyses characterised ideally by methodological rigour, timeliness, relevance and usability. However, research (even methodologically sound and scientifically valid) may also *exacerbate* tensions, for example, if its implications or conclusions are perceived to be threatening to the interests of one or more groups.[2] As such, we need to understand the political and societal contexts within which research is embedded and through which impacts are mediated. We need to ask, therefore, how individuals and institutions appropriate (or misappropriate) research, and apply (or misapply) it, for the purposes of influencing policy and practice.

The evaluation of research, however, faces a number of particular challenges. First, conventional approaches to programme and policy evaluation, including the evaluation of research programmes, are largely linear. While such approaches are the mainstay of many funders, they are not designed to be applied to research, much less to research in violence-prone contexts. To the extent that evaluations are undertaken on initiatives in VDS, they focus on development, humanitarian and peacebuilding programmes rather than research per se. While research and research activities are often housed within projects and programmes that include multiple types of interventions such as training, education or service delivery (to name a few), mainstream approaches for evaluating these sorts of programme interventions are ill-suited for evaluating research. Similarly, these sorts of programmes are often funded by international aid agencies, rather than research funders. In these cases, research is but one component, embedded within a larger, multi-facetted package of interventions. Consequently, evaluations focus on the overall impact of the project/programme, rather than the *research* component per se.

Second, in the world of international aid, too often evaluation adopts an almost singular focus on accountability—typically accountability for resource efficiency. While accountability for resource use is of unquestionable importance, the learning function of evaluation is also essential. This tendency to eclipse the learning potential of evaluation inhibits prospects for the generation of knowledge in situations and contexts of deep complexity. It is precisely in these environments that we are most in need of innovative thinking and new ways of viewing old problems. Relatedly, standard approaches to programme evaluation also tend to place more emphasis on the tangible, short-term outputs of activities, rather than on the more subtle, and less easily measured, outcomes and impacts of research within a programme.

Third, conventional approaches to the evaluation of research have been dominated by two modes of assessment—peer review and bibliometric analysis. While these approaches have their strengths, one of the principal problems with both is that they tend to assess the merits of short-term research results (outputs such as papers, articles and books or research management processes) but tell us virtually nothing about research effectiveness—how research is used to influence social change and contribute to solving societal problems. Despite some advancements, bibliometrics and peer review dominate academic settings and, in the absence of viable alternatives, tend also to dominate the evaluation of extra-academic research—that is, research that is led by the broader policy research community and which includes think tanks, not-for-profit firms, governmental, non-governmental and inter-governmental actors. These approaches, while limiting enough in academia, are even less helpful in VDS settings where the social change objectives of much research are inextricably linked to, and influenced by, politics and the dynamics of violence.

Research institutes (inside and outside the walls of a university) and agencies that fund research have been involved in generating knowledge oriented towards policy and practice change. So too have they been involved in nurturing innovation in the theory and practice of evaluation. Nonetheless, our sense is that, to date, these two broad fields of peace research and evaluation have developed in isolation from each other. The current book attempts to bridge these divides by mapping out the most vexing challenges—and promising avenues—to understanding and evaluating the impact of research in VDS. The central concern of the book is to systematically examine how practice can be improved to better understand the difference that research makes in VDS. In tackling this issue, it quickly became apparent that the book and its contributors would need to explore largely uncharted intellectual terrain, answering two important questions: (a) Why is evaluating research so much more difficult in contexts affected by violence? and (b) What can we apply from current evaluation practice in the Global North and South to our assessment of the impacts of research in VDS?

To interrogate these questions, this book brings together four groups seeking improvements in the conduct and use of research and evaluation in VDS: those who undertake research of different types (*researchers*); those who commission research or the evaluation of research (referred to as *funders, donors* or *grant makers*); those who make use of research in the course of working in violence-prone environments (*practitioners*); and those who evaluate research and non-research interventions (*evaluators*). Of course, these groups are not mutually exclusive. For example, researchers may serve as evaluators; evaluators often undertake research; and decision-makers within donor agencies may be active or retired researchers.

These four groups work within VDS or on the issues that affect these societies. They are regularly called upon to make snap decisions in high risk, high stake contexts. It is hoped that this book will help to prepare them (and the students who will eventually take their places) to anticipate, identify and respond effectively in these kinds of environments. By assembling contributors from these groups, our intention is to draw on, and harness, the experience and expertise needed to bring distinct fields of professional and intellectual activity together, and to develop a more self-conscious and systematic understanding of, and approach to, the evaluation of research on and in VDS.

The result is an exploration of the ways that research, power and politics interact in VDS. The analytical lens used to explore these interactions is drawn from the field of evaluation. We believe that this is a novel and fruitful approach for understanding more clearly and systematically the positive and negative role of research—and indeed any intervention—in VDS. An evaluative lens offers the possibility of bridging theory and practice, and ideas and impact. This particular focus locates the book on the interface between evaluation research and peace and conflict studies.

The objective of this introductory chapter is threefold: first, to present the rationale and objectives of the book; second, to orient the reader to the central concepts, issues, debates and challenges related to the conduct and evaluation of research in and on VDS[3]; and lastly, to sketch out the principal themes of the book.

The Two Faces of Research: Positive and Negative Societal Impacts

In many ways, we have only a rudimentary understanding of the societal and political effects or *impacts* of research—whether the research is undertaken by think tanks, research institutes, non-governmental organisations or by individual researchers inside or outside the walls of a university.[4] Within university settings, there is increasing debate around how to assess the quality and *extra-academic* impacts of research (i.e., how research is used and contributes to larger goals of social and economic betterment). As discussed in the literature review undertaken in Chapter 2, the intensity and motivations of this debate are complex—and are tied as much to funding politics as to the desire to optimise impacts beyond the walls of the university. Outside the university setting, efforts are also being made to evaluate the spread, use and influence of social change-focused research on policy and practice. The fruits of these efforts and the advances made in thinking about *research effectiveness* (understood as research use, influence and extra-academic or societal impacts) are evident in the chapters that make up this book.

In orienting ourselves to the evaluation of research, we need to bear in mind that research may have both positive and negative effects. As a social good, research can increase opportunities for cooperation and collaboration within and between divided groups. It can inform public policy decision-making, particularly in settings where new spaces arise for dialogue, and where there is an increase in the receptivity of policy-makers to make use of research findings. The likelihood of this occurring increases when researchers themselves produce methodologically sound research that is both relevant and timely to potential users. Instructive examples may be culled from the immediate post-apartheid environment in South Africa when anti-apartheid activists and researchers saw their research being incorporated directly into the policies and legislation of the post-apartheid dispensation.

On the other hand, we cannot overlook the ways in which research has had profoundly negative social impacts. Extreme examples may be found in: the central role of scientists in the eugenics movement in the early 20th century; the role of anthropological research in support of the apartheid and Nazi regimes; psychological research employed in intelligence testing using culturally inappropriate measures; the use of archaeological and historical research to exert moral or legal claims to contested territory.[5] Even research without obvious political content or ideological motivation may have negative implications if it is misused. Further, research which raises legitimate methodological questions may provoke significant political and ethical debates—for example, new ways of measuring or assessing vulnerability, morbidity or poverty within a population. The extent to which researchers and research funders can predict or be held to account for how research is actually used is a subject of intense debate.

This book argues that the risk that research will have a negative impact is increased by the inherent characteristics of VDS: fluidity, unpredictably, complexity and volatility. If this is so, then there is an increased responsibility on evaluators, researchers and funders to reflect upon the implications and consequences—both positive and negative—of the work they are doing or supporting.

This book wades into a thicket of thorny practical and theoretical issues like an explorer entering a semi-charted jungle. Chapter 2 provides a sense of the sheer volume of material related to the interests of the current book. However, the chapter's framing of existing research into *constituent literatures* illustrates that while we possess some general small-scale maps of parts of the continent, we have nothing that focuses specifically on the sub-field we are exploring here. The book contains two important messages for readers: the importance of appropriate approaches to, and methods for, evaluating the effects or *impacts* of research; and the imperative of addressing and engaging with context as a means of improving the theory and practice of research evaluation.

This last message is of particular importance given that social science methodology has traditionally considered context as *noise*. Researchers, evaluators, and to a certain extent, funders, as stated by Coffman and Beer (2011, p. 3), generally 'seek to "control for context," treating it as a set of mitigating factors from which the "true" impact of an intervention must be delineated'. They further state, '[a]s a result, "context" is discounted in research and evaluation design, in project implementation, and to a certain extent, in the use of research and evaluations' (p. 3).

Context is a term used to mean many things. For evaluators and researchers, *context* is often used to explain 'that which surrounds an object of interest and helps by its relevance to explain it' (Schwandt, 2012, p. 76 citing Sharfstein). *Context* in this book includes all of the political, ethical, sociological and security dynamics of working on, and in, violence-prone settings.

If one thing has become clear from this discussion, it is this: The evaluation of research is the Rosetta Stone for understanding and strengthening the links between research generation and research effectiveness. Evaluation is not, however, a *silver bullet* any more than research is a silver bullet. Efforts to identify and understand these links are embedded in a tangle of political and economic interests that interact with the conceptual, methodological, ethical and practical challenges that define this area of inquiry. In the absence of a systematic approach to evaluation of research undertaken in VDS themselves, we have only anecdotes, or worse, empirically unsubstantiated assertions, about impact. The current book is intended to be a first step in the direction of changing this reality.

Towards a Lingua Franca

In the early phase of this project, we were guided implicitly by a mechanistic model—whereby we saw our principle challenge to be that of ensuring that the right people made it to the table, so that they could each place their pieces into our research jigsaw puzzle. However, we soon realised that there were multiple understandings of the nature and parameters of the field we wished to explore; different assessments of the essential issues to be addressed; diverse experiences in different areas of our evolving field of research and practice; and most clearly, different institutional–cultural frameworks within our group of contributors.

It soon became apparent that a more self-consciously organic model would be better suited to our project. Thus, the project came to be driven by a collective process of exploring the conceptual, methodological, political and social terrains within efforts to understand the interaction of research, politics and power in VDS. One of our first steps was to develop a lingua franca among ourselves, so that we could understand what we were saying to each other. Just as the project sought to bridge the gaps between participants in the project, likewise, this book seeks to bridge gaps between the constituent contributor groups (researchers, evaluators, practitioners and funders).

Evaluation

As a starting point, we developed shared understandings of some of the basic terms and vocabulary. The term *evaluation* was understood to correspond to the standard definition offered by Fournier, namely:

> [A]n applied inquiry process that collects and synthesizes evidence that culminates in conclusions about the state of affairs, value, merit, worth, significance or quality of a program, product, person, policy, proposal or plan. (Fournier, 2005)

However, while there was a shared understanding of the broad definition of evaluation, the use of the term was often focused, implicitly or explicitly, on the evaluation of projects, programmes or policies, rather than the evaluation of research per se. This is not surprising, as this tends to be the primary empirical default setting for most people working in the publicly funded or not-for-profit spheres. Further, as discussed in Chapter 2, all of the sub-fields of evaluation are genealogically related—often sharing approaches, sensibilities, methodologies and pools of evaluators. To ensure clarity and consistency in our discussions, we delineated the four categories of evaluation that would serve as the principal referents of the project:

- *Programme and policy evaluation* is the systematic application of research methods to assess programme or policy design, implementation and effectiveness, as well as the processes to share and use the findings of these assessments.
- *Evaluation of conflict prevention, peacebuilding and humanitarian assistance programmes* is a subset of programme and policy evaluation

applied initiatives that seek to prevent violent (typically militarised) conflict, to mitigate its negative effects upon human beings or to *build peace*.
- *Evaluation of research* is a sub-field of evaluation that measures the
  quality, use or impact of research.
- *Evaluation of research within VDS* is an even more specialised, emergent sub-field that looks at the ways in which violent context affects, and
  is affected by, research and its evaluation.

While this project is focused on building knowledge and practice, in the
last category, our conceptual road map needs to include each of these
analytical referents. In Chapter 2, when we turn our attention to a selec-
tive review of the evaluation literature, it becomes clear that there are
a number of sub-literatures that apply to each sub-field. Each offers
insights into how we should or could evaluate the impacts of research in
and on VDS. However, while each sub-literature offers suggestions and
clues, none of them provide full answers.

Violence Dividing Societies

In this book, the term 'violently divided societies' is used to refer to
plural societies which possess all of the following characteristics:
(a) they are characterised by heterogeneity—ethnic, religious, linguistic, economic and so on; (b) the boundaries between sub-groups within
society are politicised and antagonistically charged, for example, when
they affect the allocation of, or access to, public resources (employment, education, etc.), or benefit certain sub-groups over others; and
(c) cleavages between groups are created and sustained through implicit
or explicit structures and processes of violence which may be articulated
physically, socially, economically, culturally and politically.

This definition expands our empirical scope beyond militarised
conflicts. Non-militarised violence, in a multitude of forms, is equally
conspicuous in the active dividing of societies. Examples from the recent
past include: mob violence (by Hindu extremists in India and sectarian
rioting in Northern Ireland); pogroms (the 1983 anti-Tamil riots in Sri
Lanka); state-sanctioned intimidation (Mugabe's ZANU-PF attacks on
White Farmers and the Movement for Democratic Change); inter-party
violence (Kenya in the period December 2007 to March 2008); structur-
ally violent regimes that create and manipulate fear to control the civil-
ian population (archetypically manifest in apartheid South Africa or the
South American dictatorships spanning the mid-1970s to later 1980s);

and genocidal violence (Cambodia under the Khmer Rouge and Sudan under Omar al-Bashir).[6]

All of these cases are united by the dividing impact of violence. In other words, it is not the *form* of violence, but the *fact* of violence, and most importantly, its societally divisive effects that tie these diverse cases together. This particular understanding requires us to consider a very broad range of cases within our scope of inquiry. Thus, in the current study, we include cases of militarised *post-war* violence such as in Sri Lanka, alongside cases of class or caste violence in India and South Africa, and the *post-troubles* violence in Northern Ireland. In each of the examples cited earlier, we see the instrumental use of violence to delineate, divide and then consolidate groups on the basis of race, class, social identity, religion, ideology, ethnicity and so on.[7]

Research

Research is another term that requires definitional clarity in this book. While Chapter 2 offers further distinctions around research types, here it is sufficient to note that research can be divided roughly into two types: basic research and applied research. Basic research is a systematic process of intellectual inquiry that seeks to contribute to our understanding of the workings of the world around us. It is driven by the curiosity of the researcher and is usually motivated by an interest in expanding human knowledge, rather than an instrumentalist desire to create, invent or resolve something (Donaldson et al., 2009, p. 2).

Applied research, as the term suggests, refers to the systematic creation, collation or application of research to generate or catalyse solutions to practical problems (social, political, economic, epidemiological and so on) in *real-world* settings that affect *real* people, organisations, communities and societies across the globe—as opposed to research undertaken within highly controlled, scientific conditions (Donaldson et al., 2009, pp. 2–3). Whether applied research harnesses existing basic research or generates its own data, it is ultimately defined by the problem-solving logic that dictates the choice of research problem, the means by which it is addressed, and most importantly, the explicit objective of resolving a problem. The focus of the current book is on applied research which ultimately has the goal of catalysing or informing social change—what we call 'social change research'. Conceptually, this research objective is not stringently enforced for reasons addressed later in the discussion of the distinction between research *on* and research *in* VDS.

Applied research and evaluation have many similarities and some differences. Both rely on social science methods and examine multiple facets of a problem, often using multi-method approaches. Both collect and analyse data in order to come to conclusions, and both utilise theory to inform work. While the two processes of inquiry share more commonalities than differences, two important features set evaluation apart: *judgement*, or *valuing*, and *use*. The primary purpose of evaluation is to amass sufficient information to allow an evaluator to assess the value or worth of something against a set of criteria. Evaluation is not just about collecting and analysing information, it is supposed to use data to make evaluative judgements. These are fed back to a client in order to assist management and decision-making, most often within an organisation (Preskill, 2005). Without this additional valuing dimension an evaluation is only a research project that may increase knowledge but does not help in decision-making. Figure 1.1 is helpful in delineating the distinction between evaluation and research.

Figure 1.1
Distinguishing between Evaluation and Research

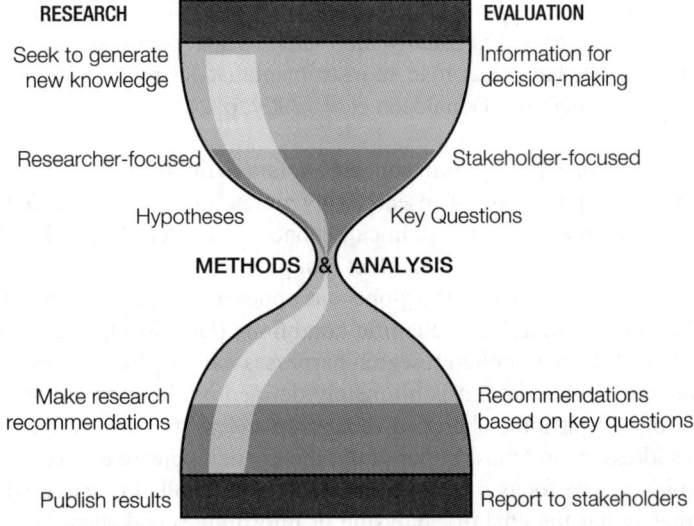

RESEARCH	EVALUATION
Seek to generate new knowledge	Information for decision-making
Researcher-focused	Stakeholder-focused
Hypotheses	Key Questions

METHODS & ANALYSIS

Make research recommendations	Recommendations based on key questions
Publish results	Report to stakeholders

Source: LaVelle (2010).

Research *on* and Research *in*

In this book, we distinguish between research *on* and research *in* VDS. This is more than a simple linguistic differentiation. Research *on* VDS explicitly examines the structures and processes of peace and conflict and generally is oriented to the investigation of the causes of violence and potential solutions. It is characterised by: the vastness of the scope of issues that fall within its analytical ambit; the multidisciplinary nature of the approaches it encompasses; the diversity and complexity of the cases that serve as empirical referents; and the micro-to-macro levels of analysis it employs. The locus of research *on* a VDS (its conceptualisation, conduct, communication and potential uptake and use) suggests a shift from inside to outside the immediately affected area. This shift of perspective from research *within* to research *from outside* influences how research is conceptualised, conducted and perceived. This may affect understandings of, or receptivity to, the solutions generated through research.

Research *in* VDS, however, encompasses an even broader swath of research activity because it includes *all* research undertaken in VDS *whether or not it possesses a peace- or conflict-specific focus*. It could thus include, inter alia, research in agronomy, physics or urban planning, if the goal is to catalyse or inform social change, and the research takes place within the setting of a VDS. It is essential to include this kind of research within the current study because the volatility of the environments within which it is undertaken ensures that research interventions will have positive or negative societal impacts, regardless of whether they are labelled as conflict prevention, peacebuilding, humanitarian, development, scientific, technological and so on. Consider as examples: a research study that increases the potential to extract minerals or geological materials from the land of marginalised (and already exploited) peasants in a conflict-prone region where militarised violence and repression are systemic; or a case where research leads to the introduction of an irrigation system that increases contact and common interests between divided communities, allowing for the evolution and expansion of cooperative and collaborative initiatives.

The inclusion of research *in* VDS in the current project expands its scope and increases its complexity. However, if we were to exclude it, we would be unable to learn from those initiatives whose impacts on the dynamics of peace or conflict are ignored because they were not labelled peace or conflict issues—even though such research is *far more common, if less overt, politically.* Similarly, the inclusion of 'research *in*' has implications that go beyond a simple expansion of the study scope. It also affects our evaluative analysis: It requires us to assess how individuals and institutions appropriate (or misappropriate) research, and apply (or misapply) it, for the purposes of accessing resources, influencing policy and practice, or shaping understandings that affect structures and processes of peace or conflict. The impact of research in VDS on social development is profoundly influenced by the peace and conflict context, both past and present. Prospects for knowledge generation, dispersion, translation and ultimately, use, are affected by the legacy, presence or threat of violence. This is what sets evaluating research in VDS apart from other contexts, the impact of violence on research conceptualisation and implementation, and on the human relationships and governance structures that will shape research receptivity.

The Importance of Building the Field of Research Evaluation in Violently Divided Societies[8]

The World Bank's (2011) *World Development Report 2011: Conflict, Security and Development* situates violence as a pivotal development challenge noting that repeated cycles of violence and instability have severely undermined prospects for global peace, development and prosperity. The same report points out that poverty rates are, on average, more than 20 percentage points higher in countries where violence is protracted than in other countries. When one looks at the needs of VDS, efforts to strengthen systems of research, or to build capacities to evaluate that research, may seem less pressing than other problems; this would also seem to be true when mainstream programme evaluation, itself, is relatively weak, and when critical sectors, such as health and education, are not being adequately evaluated.[9] However, these are false dichotomies and should be rejected as such. Rebuilding VDS requires a nuanced understanding of very complex and deeply politicised processes within highly volatile environments. Research plays a critical role in understanding the structures and processes of violence, and in developing effective responses to the most pressing social, political, economic and security challenges within VDS.

By and large, the international community is beginning to understand that it would be problematic to undertake, for example, an evaluation of a primary education programme in Afghanistan which did not take into consideration the violently contested environment within which that programme is nested. This is because the success or failure of the educational investments in that sector is as likely to be a function of their impact on narrowing or widening inequities, or their impact on peace or conflict dynamics, as of pedagogical impacts. Similarly, the achievement, scalability or sustainability of any social or pedagogical outcomes of the programme will inevitably be influenced, for good or bad, by concurrent shifts in the context or peace/conflict system.

Unfortunately, the same degree of understanding has yet to filter into the realm of VDS research evaluation. As discussed in more detail in the next chapter, in the absence of alternatives, the tendency has been to rely on two standard approaches to research evaluation: bibliometric analysis, which essentially consists of totting up of the number of citations or bibliographic references to the research output being *evaluated*;[10] and peer review, often undertaken by the gatekeepers of the academic industry.[11] The former relies on objective, quantifiable indicators. The latter relies on peer opinion. Both use acceptance and circulation within a community of peers (typically academic communities) as a proxy for research uptake, influence and use. This tells us something about how research is perceived within a community of scientific peers—but communicates next to nothing about the extra-academic or societal impacts of research, or the contribution it makes to solving *real-world* problems. Not surprisingly then, within the context of research on, or in, VDS, there is no systematic consideration of how research may affect, or is affected by, the structures and processes of violence and conflict (or peace).

Both the illustrative case of Afghanistan above and Colin Knox's chapter on integrated education in Northern Ireland (Chapter 5) demonstrate how a very broad variety of research (educational, cultural, psychological, historical and political) was essential *both* for the formulation and implementation of educational programmes and for evaluators trying to understand whether and how initiatives may have affected social change. Knox illustrates this by comparing the logical framework model of the programme he evaluated with competing theories of social change emerging from research on integrated education in Northern Ireland. This comparison provides a better sense of where, and how, to look for intermediate outcomes and longer term societal impacts. Knox's broad examination of two approaches to programme theory underscores the important role that research plays in programme creation and evaluation.

In the broadest terms, the question is: How will stakeholders— policy-makers, civil society and other interested parties—know whether or not research processes and findings are robust, and whether or not they are appropriate for informing changes or revisions to programmes, policies or practices? The answer seems self-evident: by evaluating the methodological, political and ethical integrity and impacts (broadly defined) of that research. However, in wide-ranging discussions throughout this project, we frequently heard from peace and conflict researchers that funders were unclear about what constituted credible evidence of the *extra-academic* influence of their research, or that such requests lacked conviction, coherence or follow-up. Typically, research council funders required confirmation that a specific research output had been produced—a book, conference paper, monograph, article, data set, a survey and so on.

On the other hand, research funded by bilateral or multilateral aid agencies or by private or public philanthropy was more likely to use traditional approaches to programme evaluation. However, in these cases evaluation focused not on the research per se, but on the hoped-for outcomes of the project or programme within which the research was undertaken—often development or humanitarian initiatives. In other words, the focus or unit of analysis was the administrative or operational mechanisms supporting the research (the project), rather than the societal impacts of the research itself. These colleagues, too, were quick to point out that these evaluations inadequately considered the unique contribution that research—its reach, use or influence—makes to larger outcomes or goals of social change. Unless we evaluate research through a broader societal lens, we have no systematic or empirical understanding of when, why and how it may inform programming, policy or practice.[12] Societally focused evaluation of research in contexts of violence and conflict is not a luxury—it is fundamental need.

A Dual Challenge

The Evaluation of Research

In addressing the impact of research in and on VDS, we face a daunting dual challenge: First, evaluating or *measuring* research impacts, particularly *extra-academic* or societal impacts—which are arguably more difficult than measuring other types of impacts. Second, VDS pose the most extreme operational, ethical and political challenges that any individual working for social change can expect to encounter—researcher, evaluator, development/humanitarian practitioner, funder and so on.

There are multiple methodological challenges that make it difficult to identify, delineate, assess and sort the contributions that research
makes to larger social, economic or political outcomes or impacts. In this
sense, it is often said that the impacts of research are less tangible, or that
they are tangled up with other factors or variables (the multiple pathways
problem).[13] Since the sort of social change that research often aspires
to influence is always the result of a multi-causal package of factors,
there is the perpetual problem of attributing specific changes to specific
pieces of research (the attribution problem). Research may be one of the
number of factors contributing to long-term social change. Further, an
ultimate impact such as social reconciliation or women's empowerment,
to which research contributes, may require considerable passing of time
to incubate or to bear fruit (the timeline to impact problem). However,
the accountability needs of the research funder are more likely to be
dictated by the requirements of considerably shorter institutional timeframes. Underpinning all of this is the ambiguity, or unquestioned acceptance, of theories about how social change actually happens (theory of
change). Oftentimes, such theories are immature, untested or not even
articulated by researchers, evaluators or funders. This is particularly true
for *peacebuilding* interventions which, according to some critics, are as
much about neoliberal social engineering as they are about stopping violence and achieving peace.[14]

The operational, ethical and political challenges of conducting
research and evaluation have been documented in the literature and in
discussions around practice (see ALNAP, 2005; Bamberger et al., 2006;
Bush and Duggan, 2013; Church and Rogers, 2006; Morris, 2008, 2010;
OECD, 2008). Indeed, throughout this project, we were continually
reminded of the need to straddle both the fields of evaluation research and
peace and conflict studies. Time and again, we returned to the question:
What is it about the particular contexts of VDS that makes the process of
generating, spreading and using research for social change different? We
came to the conclusion that the fluid, unpredictable and volatile contexts
that characterise VDS magnify existing research and evaluation challenges, rendering them more *extreme*. For example, the perennial problem of scarce or non-existent baseline data—an issue that plagues most
applied empiric research or programme evaluation—is more acute in
VDS where hard data has often been destroyed or is simply inaccessible
for a host of reasons related to security, censorship and control. But even
if data of some sort is available, deep contextual differences place limits
on the comparability of data within cases, across cases and across space

and time (a more extreme manifestation of problems of generalisability or external validity). This is true whether we are working in regions of militarised violence (Palestine or Afghanistan), social violence (favelas in Brazil) or criminalised violence (zones under the control of drug gangs throughout the Global North and South).

The Evaluation of Research in Volatile and Contested Contexts

During the course of this project, the *null hypothesis* arose as a methodological question in discussions.[15] It was observed that the evaluation of a research project needs to maintain the theoretical possibility that the research intervention may not *have an impact of any kind*—for a variety of possible reasons. While this may make sense methodologically— and while this is a possible outcome under normal conditions—there is something about the extreme-ness of a violently divided context that severely limits the possibility of a non-impact outcome. That is, the extremeness of the context itself magnifies and amplifies the destructive possibilities around the negative impacts of failure.

There is a tendency in evaluation to assess an initiative (whether it is a research project or a water and sanitation project) along a continuum between success and failure—where *failure* is framed as the *null hypothesis*, that is, the initiative had no effect, and where success is framed as meeting all the stated objectives. However, in VDS, the environmental conditions (volatility, zero-sum rationality, resource scarcity and insecurity) reduce the possibility that a project will have absolutely no effect. Failure in VDS is not the absence of effects or impact. It is the presence of outcomes that may be corrosive, explosive and lethal, for example, an increase in vulnerability, injustice, insecurity and so on for participants in the research or other intervention.

Examples of failure are not hard to find on the ground, although they rarely find their way into publicly available research or evaluation reports. Failure is the methodologically flawed hydrology study in a water-scarce region that leads to an attack on a village to secure the control of erroneously predicted water reserves. Failure is the pedagogical research supporting the building of a school in Gulu, Uganda, that resulted in the kidnapping of 20 children by the Lord's Resistance Army on the day it was opened because it was implemented with a blueprint logic that made students vulnerable to abduction; it is the misguided or premature application of Contact Theory[16] underpinning a cross-community youth project that results in increased tensions and scapegoating. Simply put, failed research produces unintended negative outcomes in contexts which researchers, funders and research evaluators ought to have known better. These stakeholder groups may not be able to foresee every obstacle or failure, but they can, through judicious monitoring and evaluation, think through more deliberately and systematically the risks and consequences of knowledge production and utilisation in the contexts and with the people they are often purporting to be helping.

Another challenge of working in violence-prone contexts is the short attention span of many funders. Because there are few, if any, *quick impacts* or visible short term pay-offs (financial or political) for funders, keeping them engaged over the long term is difficult. The slowness of long-term processes of reconstituting or building a new social, economic and political fabric and intellectual capital is especially conspicuous in the efforts to support and sustain research capacities—due to such issues as security risks to researchers, destruction of critical research/knowledge infrastructure, *brain drain* during periods of sustained violence and so on.

Figure 1.2 illustrates what we see to be the core domains of research and evaluation in VDS. More specifically, it identifies the domains

Figure 1.2
The Core Domains of Evaluation in VDS

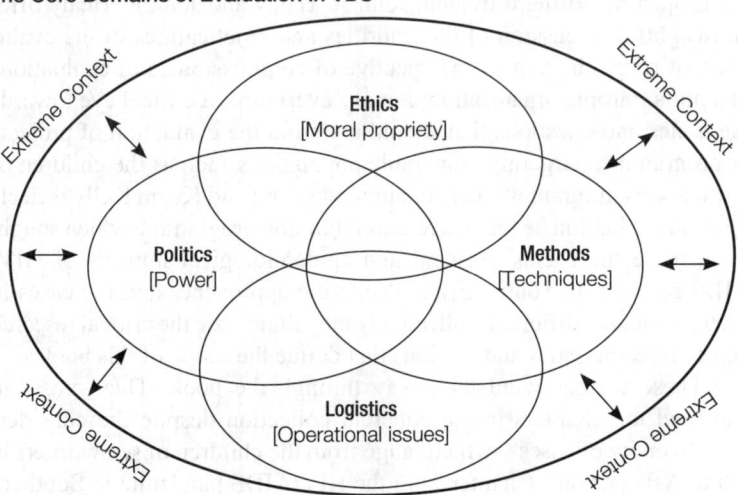

Source: Bush and Duggan (2013).

affected by the extreme contexts, which in turn, affect the work of evaluators and researchers, and in related forms, the work that funders support.

Efforts to understand the impact of research in VDS, through the use of evaluation, quickly confront one or more of challenges within these domains. The extreme environment may exercise a direct impact on each of these domains (in an almost endless number of ways), thereby affecting the ability of evaluators or researchers to undertake their work. As noted for VDS, similar pressures may be experienced in non-VDS contexts. However, the likelihood of this occurring, the diversity of the forms of challenges, and most conspicuously, the stakes are so much higher in VDS settings.

Overarching Themes of This Book

What has been the experience to date in our efforts to tackle the challenges outlined above?

There are a number of themes that emerged from discussions between the authors of this book and which illustrate the tensions that arise as the four core domains in the study framework interact. Different chapters examine specific dimensions of the evaluation of research in VDS. Thus, for example, in Chapter 5, Colin Knox analyses an evaluation which he undertook of a research component of a larger peacebuilding project in Northern Ireland; John A. Healy and John R. Healy offer an insightful discussion of the priorities and practicalities of the evaluation of research from the perspective of commissioners of evaluations in a philanthropic organisation; Sonal Zaveri turns a critical eye towards the issues and questions that should underpin the evaluation of projects or programmes targeting vulnerable populations such as the children of sex workers, migrant workers or slum dwellers; and Kevin Kelly reflects upon an evaluation he led of a research funding programme which sought to increase the social, political and epidemiological impacts of HIV/AIDS research in South Africa. While the approaches and the cases in each chapter are different, collectively they illuminate the critical research and evaluation issues and tensions that define the scope of this book.

These themes wind their way through the book. They cross-cut and bind the chapters into a coherent collection despite the considerable diversity of cases—which range from the children of sex workers in South Asia (Zaveri, Chapter 7) to the HIV/AIDS pandemic in Southern Africa (Kelly, Chapter 6), to integrated education policy in Northern

Ireland (Knox, Chapter 5), to accountability research in Nepal, Kenya and Argentina (Whitty, Chapter 3), to ethics and psycho-social interventions in Pakistan, Darfur and Sri Lanka (Jayawickrama and Strecker, Chapter 4). That such an array of cases may be integrated within a single book, demonstrates the applicability of the core debates of this study in VDS in the broadest sense. To orient the reader, a brief synopsis of the principal themes of the book is provided next.

Politics and Political Sensitivities

The authors in this book do not shy away from the deeply political dimensions that emerge for evaluation and research in VDS. Indeed, the cases illustrate the extent to which politics perforate both. The variety of ways in which this occurs is evident in every chapter. Politics are present at the very start of the process in the interests that motivate the decision to undertake, or evaluate, a body of research (Healy and Healy, Chapter 8; Kelly, Chapter 6). And, there are political implications in the choice of epistemological and methodological frameworks, particularly in the ways they implicitly legitimate some voices and realities, while de-legitimating and disappearing others (Jayawickrama and Strecker, Chapter 4). When the 'voices of the South' are no longer ignored, the systemically political nature of method becomes unavoidably clear (Jayawickrama and Strecker, Chapter 4).

This kind of thick politics is present in all research and evaluation though. It is the fact that all the cases in this book are set within VDS which makes it even more pressing to acknowledge and address the political. While the meanings and implications of the volatility and fluidity that characterise these environments need to be derived from the particularities of each case, the chapters remind us that they may be experienced differently by different individuals and groups. As for the evaluator in such environments, the political challenges are evident in operational constraints related to access and insecurity; the sensitivities around talking about certain topics; pressure to shape findings to suit political or financial interests; and the elevated risk that research or evaluation findings may be misused or harnessed to divisive political agendas. Indeed, as Knox points out in the case study of the evaluation of integrated education in Northern Ireland, politicians did not care about the details of research or evaluation, only whether it could be construed to support or refute policy decisions.

Evidence and Policy: When Good Research Is Ignored and When Bad Research Rules the Day

While evaluation may help us to understand the impacts research can have in VDS, there are a host of factors that need to be taken into consideration. As cases in this book demonstrate, even good research that meets criteria of scientific merit and integrity will not, on its own, affect sustainable change. Indeed, as Kevin Kelly points out in the case of HIV/AIDS research in South Africa (Chapter 6), the legitimacy and use of robust, quality research may be undermined by retrogressive political, social or economic forces—as with the refusal of the Mbeke regime to accept the scientifically-proven efficacy of anti-retroviral therapy. Conversely however, poor quality and methodologically dubious research may have a significant impact, particularly when it reinforces the dominant ideology or discourse, or when it serves the interests of powerful sub-groups.[17] The absence of *credible systems or approaches* to evaluate research can reinforce and maintain the dominant discourses, and obscure or render *suspicious* or *unreliable* the alternative analysis of experiences and realities that research can illuminate. Such a dynamic is as equally evident in the Global North as in the Global South.

Researchers and research funders, thus, know that *good* research can be ignored, and that *bad* research can be taken up and applied with gusto. Understanding how this could happen requires much more than an evaluation of the hermetically sealed impacts of research products on the research of other researchers [*sic*]. We need to look more systematically at how research interacts in context and with the structures and processes of power and politics at local, regional and international levels. When we explore more carefully and critically, we see that despite increased calls for *evidence-based decision-making* in science and public affairs, we are just as likely to find instances of *policy-based evidence making*.[18]

This recognition highlights the need for a repertoire of approaches to evaluation which include analytical flexibility, politically-sensitive critique and an awareness of democratisation processes at local and national levels so that research may be undertaken in ways that fundamentally change the systems and institutions of decision-making, the role of research within such systems and the ways that both connect with citizens. Research can be used to reinforce existing and dominant systems and agendas; or, it can be used to challenge and hopefully improve them. Power-sensitive, or conflict-sensitive, evaluation of research can play a crucial role in assessing whether research is doing either or neither.

For evaluation to play this role, evaluation as a field of theory and practice needs to be strengthened. The rationale for building a sub-field of evaluation in VDS is examined in more detail by Katherine Hay in Chapter 9.

Operational Difficulties

The following chapters demonstrate that the levels and types of operational difficulties affecting the evaluation of research in VDS vary according to the case. The dynamics of violence, the legacy of conflicts and the political and infrastructural context are all factors affecting the operational efficacy of research. However, as argued in the Healy and Healy chapter, effective research or programme evaluation may also generate the types of knowledge and information that may inform subsequent peacebuilding or development programmes *and may help to identify and overcome operational difficulties*. The chapters generate a long list of operational challenges. To name but a few: intransigent or suspicious government officials or community members; insecurity of evaluators, researchers and participants; cultural incommensurabilities; self-interest of stakeholders; destruction or manipulation of data; distrust; competing demands and expectations and so on.

Layers of Accountability and the Ethical Dimensions of Research and Evaluation

While ethics constitute the specific focus of the chapter by Jayawickrama and Strecker, it is a strong theme running throughout this book with many facets: the question of whether the evaluator or researcher can—or should—be independent in VDS settings; the management of the layers of (often competing) expectations; the question of how the evaluator should deal with negative findings; pressures to skew the findings of an evaluation; the relative absence in the practice of formal processes of ethical review of the work of evaluators; the bureaucratic nature of research ethics review processes within universities and the degree to which our approaches to evaluation and research are appropriate when applied within VDS.

Working in VDS implies working under conditions of considerable tension with the full spectrum of people, from the powerful to the powerless (though we need to remain attentive to the fact that competing forms of power coexist in VDS). Any work within such contexts raises ethical considerations—whether this research involves development, humanitarian, peacebuilding or research activities. As researchers, we are expected to do our utmost to ensure that our work does not compromise the physical, emotional, cultural or moral well-being of those involved in, or affected by, our research at all stages. These same requirements apply to those engaged in evaluating research in and on VDS. One of the challenges to achieving these objectives is the general tendency for both evaluation and research initiatives to be short term (often due to research funding timeframes) and extractive. Under such conditions, limitations of time and opportunity may inhibit the building of those reciprocal relationships of trust and understanding needed to be able to see, understand and assess the ethical implications of our research—at every stage of the research process, as projects are designed, undertaken, disseminated and operationalised.

Intimately related to ethics is accountability (Whitty, Chapter 3). Researchers and evaluators are accountable not only to local populations but also to funders, who often want findings that further their own intellectual agendas and institutional or political goals (see chapters by Zaveri; Healy and Healy; and Jayawickrama and Strecker). And, finally, researchers are also held to account by the wider research community and the research standards that undergird the legitimacy of research.

The multiple layers of motivations, obligations and accountability increase the complexity of evaluating research in and on VDS. But even when a researcher adheres to standard ethical principles and practice, there is no guarantee that s/he will produce research that is valuable, useful or acceptable to local stakeholders, funders or the academy (Fujii, 2008). On the other hand, research which does not *or cannot* adhere to the letter of institutionally prescribed standards (such as parental consent for orphaned or separated children) still has the potential to produce useful knowledge for any or all stakeholders. Moreover, research ethics guidelines are not designed with any consideration of the particular challenges that confront researchers in VDS, and consequently are often not appropriate or helpful. Indeed, they may constitute a hindrance to the research process—for example, where the requirement for written permission inhibits access to interviewers who view it (often correctly) as a potential threat to security.[19] The other side of this issue is the question of what a researcher/evaluator should do with information that reveals details about criminality, atrocities or war crimes. This raises issues about the trade-offs between confidentiality, security and justice.[20]

In the world of programme evaluation, there is an expectation that evaluators and commissioners of evaluation should be held accountable for universally accepted standards of evaluation (utility, propriety, feasibility, accuracy).[21] The propriety standard in particular is meant to address ethical dimensions that might emerge from evaluation design, implementation or use. The difficulty is that standards are of limited use when mechanisms are not in place to monitor and enforce them. Within the profession of evaluation, there is limited use of ethics review mechanisms similar to those that oversee university-based research.[22] In addition, because of the patron–client relationship existing between an evaluator and the commissioning entity, evaluators are vulnerable to being pressured by commissioners into changing negative evaluation findings (AES, 1998; Bamberger et al., 2006). This is a particularly marked risk in VDS where the consequences of a negative evaluation carry considerable costs (political as much as economic) if it becomes known that a programme did not unfold as planned or fell short of funder expectations.

Social Justice, Vulnerability and Power

Different chapters explore distinct facets of the themes of social justice, power and vulnerability through different case studies. So, for example, questions about vulnerability and power abound in the chapters by Jayawickrama and Strecker and by Whitty. However, they are conspicuous in each of the other chapters as well. The fact that the same theme finds its way into different chapters does not mean that it is understood or dealt with in the same way. Thus, while Zaveri probes the ways in which different forms of vulnerability condition the experience of social violence in red light districts (and indeed, how vulnerability reduction projects may actually *increase* vulnerability), Jayawickrama and Strecker examine a very different facet of vulnerability, observing that '[the] blanket labeling of whole groups as "vulnerable" pushes us from the methodological into the political.'

The consequences of this process for the interests of this book are powerfully articulated. Jayawickrama and Strecker note that despite the realities, problems and needs of researched communities,

> at the end of the day, it is the voice of the researcher, and her particular representation of the situation that will shape discourse in academic, policy, and practitioner circles. The particular question, within this

context, is: What are the implications—methodological, political, and ethical—for the evaluation of this kind of research?[23]

If knowledge is power, then research is inextricably involved in either empowering or disempowering individuals and groups by reinforcing or challenging structures of domination or liberation. To convey this idea, Foucault fuses the concepts of power and knowledge in his neologism, *power-knowledge*. In so doing, he underscores both the mutually reinforcing relationship between the two and his understanding that knowledge is never neutral. Rather, knowledge is generative and, thus, normative (Foucault, 1976). Because evaluation is a form of knowledge production, it is embedded within the same power/political context and carries the same power/political implications.

If there is one message that the editors of this book hope to leave with the readers, it is this: Research and evaluation are imbued with power and politics. In VDS, in particular, they are not technocratic or neutral exercises. They always have impacts—positive or negative—on the actors involved and bystanders. This is true for researchers, evaluators, funders and the ultimate beneficiaries of both research and evaluation. The extreme nature of VDS contexts amplifies the consequences of each decision made in the process. This means that researchers, evaluators, practitioners and funders must make efforts in good faith to tease out the inevitable peace, conflict or mixed impacts of any and all interventions in which they are involved.

Notes

1. Our use of the term 'impact' corresponds with the commonly accepted definition: 'Positive and negative, primary and secondary long-term effects produced by [an] … intervention, directly or indirectly, intended or unintended' (OECD DAC, 2002).
2. Examples are abundant; for example, the abduction and murder of academics illustrated in the cases taken up by such organisations as the Council for Academics at Risk.
3. As discussed further below, research *on* VDS refers to that which focuses on structures and processes of peace and conflict within a case, or set of cases. Research *in* VDS refers to *any kind of social change research* undertaken within VDS. Thus, research *on* VDS is defined by the nature or topic or research, while research *in* VDS is defined by the geographic location within which it is undertaken.
4. By research impacts, we mean the extra-academic influence of research: That is, the benefits that arise from academic research beyond the academic world (Donovan, 2009).
5. For a sampling of research in these fields, refer to Black (2008), Carlson (2001), Engs (2005), Gordon (1988), Schmit (1996) and Carey (2008).

6. The last two categories of examples illustrate the ways in which militarised and non-militarised forms of violence may be employed in tandem in the pursuit of absolute political, social and economic control.

7. In order to divide groups within society, it is first necessary to delineate that group from other groups. This has been done by treating groups differently economically, socially and politically (Horowitz, 1985). The instrumental application of violence—or the creation of conditions which permit or encourage violence to be inflicted on a defined group—is a particularly effective means of erasing affective ties of similarity, to replace them with politicised boundaries of difference (Horowitz, 1985).

8. Elements of this section are drawn from an earlier draft of Katherine Hay's chapter on field building for this book, Chapter 9. We thank Katherine for allowing us to include it in this introductory chapter.

9. For a South Asia-specific discussion of evaluation field building, see Hay (2010).

10. For a well grounded methodological critique of applying bibliometrics to social sciences and humanities research, see SSHRCC (2004).

11. According to Coryn (2008), few rigorous studies have been undertaking the 'workings of peer review', despite its 'importance as the basic mechanism for judging the merits of most research'. In one of the most complete and critical analysis of the peer-review system, Cicchetti (1991) found that 'the reliability of most reviews is no better than would have occurred by chance'; cited in Coryn (2008, p. 2).

12. While bibliometrics and peer review are the overwhelmingly dominant mechanisms to research evaluation, other approaches lend themselves to a more societally focused assessment. This would include: (social) network analysis, case studies, tracer methodologies, spillover analysis, data-mining and visualisation, econometric and other statistical modelling techniques. See Ruegg and Feller (2003) and Ruegg and Jordan (2007). While these approaches bring us closer to teasing out societal impacts, they nonetheless share the same myopic condition as the dominant approaches do to research evaluation—lack of a systematic consideration of the impact of violent context on these methods, and vice versa. See also Sumner et al. (2009).

13. For a recent review of these challenges with reference to development research, see Sumner et al. (2009).

14. For a stimulating and solitary discussion of theories of change in the field of peacebuilding, see USAID (2011).

15. I thank Rick Davies for bringing up this point, as well as for the critical intellectual rigour he brought to the project both in the final authors' workshop and by his trenchant comments as an external review of each of the chapters. His website offers a near-encyclopaedic offering of resources for monitoring and evaluation: http://mande.co.uk/

16. Gordon W. Allport is credited with the initial formulation of 'Contact Theory', which posits that, under appropriate conditions, face-to-face contact between individuals from divided groups is an effective means of reducing misconceptions, prejudice and scapegoating at an inter-group level.

17. An example of this phenomenon in South Asia can be found in the politically motivated archaeological research supported by religious extremists to justify the destruction, for example, of mosques on sites that are deemed to be historically Hindu—most obviously demonstrated in the history of violence in Ayodhya, India. So too is it evident in Sri Lanka, in the use of dubious archaeological research to justify *Sinhalese colonialism* in Tamil-majority regions, or to justify the National Sinhalese Buddhist status of the state and the country; see Kemper (1991).

18. Boden and Ebstein, the originators of the term 'policy-based evidence making' describe it as follows:

> This need [for evidence] has been reified in the UK and elsewhere, as routines of 'evidence-based policy-making' have been hardwired into the business of Government. Intuitively, basing policies that affect people's lives and the economy on rigorous academic research sounds rational and desirable. However, such approaches are fundamentally flawed by virtue of the fact that Government, in its broadest sense, seeks to capture and control the knowledge producing processes to the point where this type of 'research' might best be described as 'policy-based evidence'. (Boden and Epstein, 2006, p. 226)

19. Or the case of a graduate student in the Conflict Studies Programme of St Paul University who was required to ensure that the rural women selected as interviewees in a political empowerment study in Senegal would have access to a trained (Western) counsellor should they be adversely affected by discussing their political work— despite the inappropriateness of Western-style counselling to that context; the availability of existing effective local traditional methods of dealing with traumatising events developed during years of militarised conflict; and the fact that the only place for such counselling was a 14-hour bus ride away in the capital city. For a general discussion, see Kovats-Bernat (2002).

20. This particular tension is illustrated in the protracted legal battle between Boston College and the US Department of Justice. As part of an oral history project, the College was acting as the confidential repository for the transcripts of interviews with Northern Irish militants who had been promised that their stories would remain private until after their deaths. The US Department of Justice, on the other hand, subpoenaed the tapes from the university in connection with an investigation into an unsolved murder. For details on this story, see http://www.thedailybeast.com/articles/2012/07/10/boston-college-s-secret-tapes-could-bring-ira-exposure-and-retribution.html (accessed on 12 December 2012).

21. These particular criteria were formulated by the American Evaluation Association and are widely adopted by evaluation associations around the world. See also OECD-DAC evaluation quality standards and others at http://mande.co.uk/2011/lists/evaluation-quality-standards/on-evaluation-quality-standards-a-list/

22. As problematic as university ethics review processes may be in some cases (bureaucratised, innovation stifling, unenforced, secondary to financial needs of universities and so on), they still constitute one of the few institutionalised and operating mechanisms for ethics review.

23. This passage is culled from the unpublished research prospectus prepared by Janaka Jayawickrama for this project.

References

Active Learning Network for Accountability and Performance (ALNAP) in Humanitarian Action. (2005). *Assessing the quality of humanitarian evaluations: The ALNAP quality proforma 2005* (v. 02/03/05). London: ALNAP. Retrieved from http://www.alnap.org/pool/files/QualityProforma05.pdf (accessed on 5 June 2015).

Australian Evaluation Society (AES). (1998). *Guidelines for the ethical conduct of evaluations.* Australian Evaluation Society.

Bamberger, M., Rugh, J. and Mabry, L. (2006). *Real world evaluation: Working under budget, time, data, and political constraints.* Thousand Oaks, CA: SAGE Publications.

Black, Edwin. (2008). *War against the weak: Eugenics and America's campaign to create a master Race.* Westport, CT: Dialogue Press.

Boden, R. and Epstein, D. (2006). Managing the research imagination? Globalization and research in higher education. *Globalization, Societies and Education, 4*(2), 223–236.

Bush, K. and Duggan, C. (2013). Evaluation in conflict zones: Methodological and ethical challenges. *The Journal of Peacebuilding and Development, 8*(2), 5–25.

Carey, B. (2008). U.S. psychologists debate role in military interrogations. *New York Times.* Retrieved from http://www.nytimes.com/2008/08/16/world/americas/16iht-ethics.1.15349551.html (accessed on 27 April 2015).

Carlson, Axel. (2001). *The unfit: A history of a bad idea.* Cold Spring Harbor, New York: Cold Spring Harbor Laboratory Press.

Church, C. and Rogers, M. (Eds). (2006). Ethics in evaluation. In *Designing for results: Integrating, monitoring & evaluation in conflict transformation programs* (pp. 188–200). Washington, DC: Search for Common Ground. Retrieved from http://www.sfcg.org/Documents/dmechapter11.pdf (accessed on 22 April 2015).

Cicchetti, D. V. (1991). The reliability of peer review for manuscript and grant submissions: A cross-disciplinary investigation. *Behavioral and Brain Sciences, 14*(1), 119–135.

Coffman, J. and Beer, T. (2011). *Evaluation to support strategic learning: Principles and practices.* Washington, DC: Center for Evaluation Innovation. Retrieved from http://www.evaluationinnovation.org/publications/evaluation-support-strategic-learning-principles-and-practices (accessed on 22 April 2015).

Coryn, C. (2008). Editor's note. *New Directions for Evaluation, 2008*(118), 1–5.

Donaldson, S., Christie, C. and Mark, M. (2009). *What counts as credible evidence in applied research and evaluation practice?* Thousand Oaks, CA: SAGE Publications.

Donovan, C. (2009). *Demonstrating the public value of humanities and social sciences research: What should governments want?* (unpublished). Ottawa: SSHRC Congress.

Foucault, M. (1976). *The history of sexuality: An Introduction, Volume 1.* Toronto: Random House.

Fournier, D. M. (2005). Evaluation. In S. Mathison (Ed.), *Encyclopedia of evaluation* (pp. 139–140). Thousand Oaks, CA: SAGE Publications.

Fujii, L. A. (2008, December 4–5). *Ethical challenges of micro-level fieldwork.* Paper Presented at the Graduate Center of the City University of New York workshop on Field Research and Ethics in Post-Conflict Environments. Retrieved from http://www.statesandsecurity.org/sites/default/files/Fujii.FRE_.Wkshp_.pdf (accessed on 22 April 2015).

Hay, K. (2010). Evaluation field building in South Asia: Reflections, anecdotes, and uestions. *American Journal of Evaluation, 31*(2), 222–231.

Horowitz, D. L. (1985). *Ethnic groups in conflict.* Berkeley, LA and London: University of California Press.

Kemper, S. (1991). *The presence of the past: Chronicles, politics and culture in Sinhala life.* Ithaca and London: Cornell University Press.

Kovats-Bernat, J. C. (2002). Negotiating dangerous fields: Pragmatic strategies for fieldwork amid violence and terror. *American Anthropologist, 104*(1), 208–222.

LaVelle, John. (2010, February 26). *John LaVelle on describing evaluation* (AEA365 A Tip-a-Day by and for Evaluators). Washington, DC: American Evaluation Association. Retrieved from http://aea365.org/blog/john-lavelle-on-describing-evaluation/ (accessed on 17 April 2015).

Morris, M. (Ed.). (2008). *Evaluation ethics for best practice: Cases and commentaries.* New York, NY: Guilford Press.

————. (2010). Moral and ethical issues in evaluation. In P. Peterson, E. Baker and B. McGaw (Eds), *International encyclopedia of education* (3rd ed., pp. 622–628). Philadelphia, PA: Elsevier Ltd.

OECD. (2008). *Guidance on evaluating conflict prevention and peacebuilding activities.* Working draft for application period. Paris: OECD.

OECD DAC. (2002). *Glossary of key terms in evaluation and results based management.* Paris: OECD. Retrieved from http://www.oecd.org/dataoecd/29/21/2754804.pdf (accessed on 27 April 2015).

Preskill, H. and Russ-Eft, D. (2005). *Building evaluation capacity: 72 activities for training and teaching.* Thousand Oaks, CA: SAGE Publications.

Ruegg, R. and Feller, I. (2003). *A toolkit for evaluating public R&D investment: Models, methods, and findings from ATP's first decade.* Gaithersburg, MD: National Institute of Standards and Technology.

Ruegg, R. and Jordan, G. (2007). *Overview of evaluation methods for R&D programs: A directory of evaluation methods relevant to technology development programs.* Washington, DC: U.S. Department of Energy, Office of Energy Efficiency and Renewable Energy.

Schmit, B. (1996). *Creating order: Culture as politics in nineteenth- and twentieth-century South Africa.* The Hague: CIP-Gegevens Koninklijke Bibliotheek.

Schwandt, T. (2012). Political culture as context for evaluation. *New Directions in Evaluation, 135,* 75–87.

Social Sciences and Humanities Research Council of Canada (SSHRCC). (2004). *The use of bibliometrics in the social sciences and humanities.* Ottawa: SSHRCC.

Sumner, A., Ishmael-Perkins, N. and Lindstrom, J. (2009, November). *Making Science of Influencing: Assessing the Impact of Development Research, Volume 335.* Working Paper (Brighton, England: Institute for Development Studies).

USAID (Allan Nan, S. and Mulvihill, M.). (2011). *Theories of changes and indicator development in conflict management and mitigation.* Washington, DC: USAID. Retrieved from http://pdf.usaid.gov/pdf_docs/PNADS460.pdf (accessed on 2 April 2015).

World Bank. (2011). *World development report 2011: Conflict, security and development.* Washington, DC: World Bank.

2

Fundamental Issues in Evaluation and Research in Violently Divided Societies

An Analysis of the Literature

Philip McDermott, Zahbia Yousuf,
Jacqueline Strecker and Ethel Méndez

The evolution of evaluation is closely tied to the rise of publicly funded institutions and social programmes, primarily in North America and Europe. Respected evaluator Donna Mertens notes that evaluation, in its earliest form, appeared in the 19th century when 'the [US] government first asked external inspectors to evaluate public programs, such as prisons, schools, hospitals and orphanages' (Mertens, 2001, p. 367). However, most other commentators date the origin of evaluation (as we know it today) to the 1960s when more standardised forms and approaches to evaluation came to the fore (Georghious and Laredo, 2005, p. 1; McCoy and Hargie, 2001; Scriven, 2003).

Since this period, evaluation has established itself as a discipline in its own right. An important consequence of this has been a move towards *professionalisation* of evaluation as a field of theory and practice (Scriven, 2003; p. 7; Hay, Chapter 9 in this book). Thus, bodies such as the American Evaluation Association (AEA) and the European Evaluation Society have established quality standards and formal principles of practice for members and for the profession more broadly. These or similar standards of technical competency and integrity for evaluators have since been adopted by numerous national and regional evaluation associations in the Global North and South. Nevertheless, the field of contemporary evaluation theory and practice carries the legacy of the second half of the last century in its underpinning theories and methodologies, derived largely from government-driven desires to assess social programming, particularly in the areas of health and education (Rossi and Lipsey, 2004, p. 8).

Within the sphere of interest of this book, it bears noting that although the evaluation of academic and extra-academic research has also been going on since the 1970s (Luukkonen, 2002, p. 81), the debates and evolution in this field took place separately, albeit in parallel, to those taking place in the field of social policy and programme evaluation. As such, the evaluation of research was not a significant point of reference in the early evolution of the field of evaluation science (McCoy and Hargie, 2001; Rossi and Lipsey, 2004).

Indeed, contemporary evaluation research and practice have continued to be weighted towards social policy and programming, with a more specific focus on the evaluation of research, as interested stakeholders (research funders, users of research and researchers themselves) have come to understand that there is much learning that can be taken from the intersection of the fields of programme or policy evaluation and research evaluation. Fleshing out this learning has become increasingly important as those with an interest in producing actionable, social change research have realised that approaches to and methods for evaluating research uptake, use and impacts are imperfect and underdeveloped. As noted by Bush and Duggan in the introductory chapter to this book, this task is even more difficult in violently divided society (VDS) contexts that are characterised by volatility, complexity and non-linearity. In addition, the trajectories of research in these settings, from the moment of its conceptualisation through to it use for social change objectives, are highly politicised.

Overview

Given that the literature on social programme and policy evaluation and research evaluation is vast, this chapter reviews a selection of this literature in order to explore and ground the conceptual and theoretical foundations of the current book. It considers how the process of evaluation has evolved and developed historically, and highlights the main trends within the field. This will guide us to the relevant principles and concepts in the evaluation literature for use in subsequent discussions in this book of the evaluation of research in and on VDS. It will also allow us to identify missing components in the existing literature and potential gaps in theory and practice.

The sources included in this chapter were selected for detailed review from a larger set of references generated through searches on databases of peer-reviewed journals, Google and Google Scholar. The principal and secondary researchers involved in the VDS project (authors of this book) also provided articles and chapters which they considered to be of particular importance in influencing debates and forging trends in the fields of evaluation and of peace and conflict research in general.

The literature reviewed was selected on the basis of its potential to illuminate the primary question that forms the basis of this book: How can we improve evaluation practice to better understand the difference that research makes in VDS? Secondary questions that guided the review include: Why is evaluation so much more difficult in these contexts? What can we learn from the current evaluation practice in the Global North and South?

In order to organise learning around these questions, the chapter categorises sources reviewed around four constituent works of literature. The first body of literature is rooted in the evaluation of publicly funded social programmes and policies, a process which draws our analytical gaze back to the very origins of the field of evaluation. The second constituent literature brings to the fore, the important issue of violence and examines the much more recent, and still evolving, work on the evaluation of conflict prevention, peacebuilding and humanitarian assistance programmes. The third constituent literature is rooted in efforts to evaluate academic and extra-academic research. The final constituent literature is the most embryonic of all, and is explored throughout the chapters that make up this book—the evaluation of research in and on VDS. Debates and trends in the evaluation of international development aid programmes tend to cross-cut the four constituent works of literature and for this reason, this chapter also draws from this area of practice as needed.

In looking across these pieces of literature in the context of the VDS research project, it quickly became apparent that there are recurring themes, debates, problems and issues that absorb the attention of stakeholders involved in research and evaluation. We refer to these as fundamental issues, understood as 'underlying concerns, problems or choices that continually resurface in different guises throughout evaluation work' (Smith and Brandon, 2008, p. vii). By their very nature, these are issues that can never be finally resolved to the satisfaction of all stakeholders; this is especially true in VDS contexts where the ubiquitous presence or threat of violence renders these fundamental issues more extreme. Of the myriad fundamental issues that surface, the following are examined in varying degrees of depth across the works of literature as a means of deepening our understanding of the ways in which particular norms and values have become embedded in the field of evaluation, affecting the conceptual framing of the evaluation of research in VDS:

- The purpose of evaluation
- The role of the evaluator
- Who participates in evaluation
- Theoretical and applied approaches and methods
- The nature of evidence

Figure 2.1 illustrates the relationship and interaction in these four focus areas across the constituent pieces of literature, and also the nuanced differences between each area of evaluation. The purpose of the map is to show that, although there are many areas of evaluation in which there are coinciding interests, there are also numerous complexities which need to be borne in mind. Also, the map forms the basis for the structure of the rest of our chapter where we offer a more detailed explanation of the constituent pieces of literature and their fundamental issues.

Constituent Literature 1: The Evaluation of Programmes and Policies

As noted, the field of evaluation arose predominantly in the public administration domain in USA, Europe and Australia. It began in the fields of human, social and welfare services (including healthcare, social deprivation and poverty) with an early focus in the field of education. The intention of such evaluations was to assist in improving the quality of social programmes and policies. Much of the material written to date continues to focus on this particular area and, therefore, acts as the first port of call in our discussion. Box 2.1 provides a brief primer with basic evaluation terminology.

Figure 2.1
Constituent Literatures and Cross-cutting Themes in the Evaluation of Research in VDS

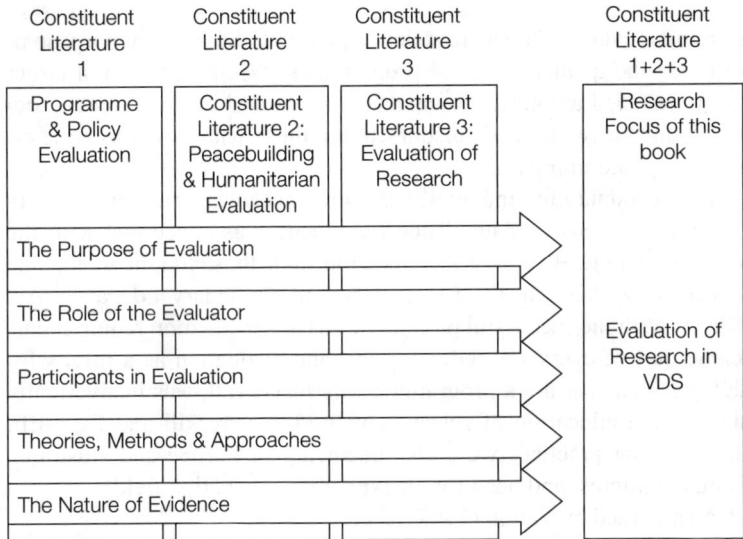

Source: Author.

Box 2.1
Key Evaluation Terms—Evaluation, Approach and Method

Evaluation Type: refers to whether the evaluation will be formative, summative or developmental.

Formative Evaluation: is intended to improve performance; most often conducted during the implementation of a programme.

Summative Evaluation: is intended to provide information about the merit or worth of a programme; most often conducted at the end of a programme.

Developmental Evaluation: positions the evaluator as a part of a programme's design and development process. It is done is real-time; has a series of short, rapid feedback loops; and allows the entity being evaluated to quickly adapt its strategies and activities.

Evaluation Approach: commonly called an evaluation theory, an approach describes the philosophy and process of evaluation.

Method: refers to the data collection strategy (qualitative, quantitative, mixed) tools and instruments used in an evaluation.

Source: Fournier (2005); Preskill and Russ-Eft (2005).

The Purpose of Evaluation:
Accountability versus Learning

Programme evaluation was first developed with the primary purpose of improving the quality of social programmes. Within this aim, a larger tension surfaced amongst proponents who viewed evaluation as a tool for accountability for funds disbursed and those who saw it as a means for learning and improvement.

The accountability model of evaluation became popular in the early 1960s. In the USA, Senator Robert Kennedy was concerned with the spending of federal money in education and, thus, fought to include an evaluation clause in the Elementary and Secondary Education Act (ESEA). With the successful passing of this act, evaluation requirements became part of every US federal grant, and evaluation as a means for judging whether or not a programme was successful, was inadvertently linked to the allocation of subsequent funding (Preskill and Russ-Eft, 2005). Similar practices were also occurring in Europe and Australia, raising the interest and need for an expanding evaluation field.

As affirmed by Patton (1997, p. 11):

> Programme evaluation as a distinct field of professional practice was born of two lessons: first, the realisation that there is not enough money to do all the things that need doing; and second, even if there were enough money, it takes more than money to solve complex human and social problems. *As not everything can be done, there must be a basis for deciding which things are worth doing.* Enter evaluation.

Consequently, the agencies and other bodies that fund public programmes have at times used evaluation findings to justify expenditure and future allocation of financial resources. In this respect, evaluation was charged with identifying flaws in a completed initiative in order to ensure that similar projects or programmes would not be funded in the future. Objective-based studies, pioneered by Ralph Tyler, Percy Bridgman and E. L. Thorndike were well tailored for this function, identifying the initial aims and objectives of the programme and then measuring whether or not these objectives had been met.

As the evaluation field developed, debates concerning the aim and purpose of evaluation broadened, and programme evaluation moved beyond a one-dimensional accountability approach, shifting the debate towards a wider discussion around the need to use evaluation as a learning tool rather than an end unto itself. Evaluation practitioners and scholars problematised the endemic power structures within the funder–client relationship, and identified the limitations of objectives-based approaches. For example, evaluators noted that in the course of a programme the initial goals may alter due to the nature of the programme, and, as a result, evaluating with these initial aims and objectives in mind may be detrimental to a fair and thorough judgement of the programme (Parlett and Hamilton, 1977). Others have similarly suggested that goal formation in many programmes is an ongoing process, with the major aims and objectives only becoming evident to leaders and managers once the actual programme is under way. Some evaluators have also advocated for goal-free approaches where the achievement of the initial aims and objectives is not a major concern with respect to the wider scale of the entire evaluation (Scriven, 1991). Instead, consideration is given to the wider context in which the programme has developed over time and what it has achieved.

In the light of these and other discussions, the field of evaluation has largely embraced evaluation to serve three broad functions:

1. Accountability: measuring and judging the merit and worth of programme results and accounting for use of resources;
2. Knowledge generation: creating new understandings about what works and what does not;
3. Programme planning or improvement: supporting clear, well-designed, feasible and measurable programmes with a view to increasing overall organisational effectiveness (Rutnik and Campbell, 2002).

Proponents of evaluation as a means for learning also contend that an evaluation should not just be viewed as the 'retrospective analysis of programme effects', but rather that it can play an important role in the design, implementation and ongoing monitoring of a programme (McCoy and Hargie, 2001, p. 319). These perspectives have led to increased investments into *formative evaluations*. Formative evaluations are episodic in nature, and are conducted during the development of a programme with the intent to improve or refine it (Scriven, 1991, p. 168). Formative evaluations are often contrasted with *summative evaluations,* which are conducted after stabilisation or completion of a programme, and are used to make a final evaluative judgement to determine the programme's merit, worth or value.

A third evaluation form, *developmental evaluation* (DE), was introduced by Michael Quinn Patton in the early 1980s. DE embeds the evaluator into the programme development process, so that the evaluator can provide regular and informed feedback to the programme team to assist with on-going refinements to design before a programme is tested and while a programme is underway. DE, and in particular the concept of the *embedded evaluator*, has raised further questions about what exactly the role of the evaluator is.

The Role of the Evaluator

The increased professionalisation of the field of evaluation has given rise to practitioner voices and created rich debates and discussions about the role of evaluators. There are some evaluators and commissioners of evaluation who maintain that evaluators should play only one role: providing arm's length, independent judgements about a programme's merit or worth (Scriven, 1991; Stufflebeam, 1994). In contrast, others have advocated for multiple evaluator roles, depending on the evaluation context. These include, but are not limited to: advocate, activist, change agent, collaborator, communicator, diplomat, external expert, group facilitator, information broker, internal colleague, methodologist, organisational analyst, politician, problem solver, trainer and technician (Greene, 1997; Love, 1991; Patton, 2008). The evaluator's role is often influenced by several factors including the epistemological and ontological view of the evaluator and those managing the evaluation; the type of evaluation being conducted; the situation and challenges present in the evaluation; and the type of evaluator (internal or external).

Conley-Tyler (2005) highlights that the internal–external debate is often underemphasised in evaluation practice. 'Given how common this scenario is, it is surprising that the choice between internal and external evaluators has not been the subject of much critical debate. Too often the issue is assumed either one way or the other without discussion of the issues involved' (Conley-Tyler, 2005, p. 3). Conley-Tyler further argues that there is a distinct separation between literature aimed at business and organisational audiences, which favours internal evaluators, and literature aimed at evaluation professionals, which privileges the external evaluator (Conley-Tyler, 2005).

External or *independent* evaluators are those not associated with the evaluated programme, and thus, in theory, have no stake in the evaluation outcomes (Molund and Schill, 2004, p. 17). Scriven (1991, p. 160) outlines the benefits of external evaluators stating that

> the external evaluator is less likely to be affected by personal or job-benefit considerations, is often better at evaluation; has often looked closely at comparable programs, can speak more frankly because there is less risk of job loss or personal retribution/dislike, and carries some cachet from externality.

The role of the external evaluator is often dependent on the type of evaluation selected and its methodology, but overall his or her role is to provide an external assessment of the programme as an outside observer. One limitation of external evaluation is that stakeholder participation is often limited out of a fear of jeopardising evaluation independence. As a result, stakeholders can feel removed from the evaluation process, and may dismiss or disregard the evaluation findings. In contrast, internal evaluators are organisationally attached to the programme being evaluated. According to Scriven, the internal evaluator

> knows the programme better and so avoids mistakes due to ignorance, knows the people better and hence can talk to them more easily, will be there after the evaluation is finished and hence can facilitate implementation, probably knows the subject matter better, costs less, and is sure to know of some other comparable projects for comparison. (Scriven, 1991, p. 160)

Internal evaluators are also at an advantage because they are familiar with the political and cultural factors which may be affecting the environment within which the programme is operating (Braskamp et al., 1987). Love (1991) cautions that the role of an internal evaluator is sometimes conflated with manager responsibilities, resulting in increased tension and poor evaluation quality.

While internal evaluators have been used in both formative and summative evaluations, a particular feature of formative evaluation is that it advocates a position whereby evaluation is something which need not be undertaken solely by a formal external evaluator. Instead, all actors may be encouraged to think about evaluation throughout the implementation of a particular programme. For example, if the programme staff is encouraged to think about evaluation issues throughout, this is viewed by many as having a positive impact on the project or programme as a whole. In other words, evaluation becomes an *in-built* feature of a pro-gramme itself (Scriven, 1991).

One assumption that often pervades the external–internal debate is the notion of objectivity. In 1988, Cummings et al. proposed rationales for why the objectivity of internal evaluators may be compromised by the underlying value systems of organisational policies. This position is not, however, supported by most current evaluation theories (Conley-Tyler, 2005). In contrast, evaluation scholars have continued to chal-lenge the objectivist approach arguing that every evaluator, regardless of whether he or she is internal or external, brings implicit values to an evaluation (House, 1980). As a result, the majority of scholars have since highlighted the importance of impartiality over objectivity. There are, however, a few remaining scholars (such as Scriven) who maintain that objectivity should remain the ideal.

While value can be found in both internal and external evaluator roles, the tendency to privilege one type over the other is representa-tive of the different worldviews at play. 'In one world view, evalua-tion is something that should be carried out primarily by professionals (external evaluators), while in the other world view, evaluation skills should be spread as widely as possible (such as to management and other staff)' (Conley-Tyler, 2005, p. 10). To help transcend these rigid distinc-tions, some practitioners and evaluation commissioners have started to advocate for combining internal and external evaluation, and thinking about evaluation relationships as existing along a continuum rather than as polarised extremes (Patton, 2008). Patton suggests, 'there are a good many possible combinations of internal and external evaluations that may be more desirable and more cost-effective than either a purely inter-nal or purely external evaluation' (Patton, 2008, p. 222). The combina-tion of internal and external evaluation reaps the benefits of the diverse types of evaluation roles, but proper execution can be difficult, as care is required to ensure that the responsibilities are appropriately divided.

The role of the evaluator is therefore variable and is often articulated and negotiated during the process of an evaluation. Although the increas-ing professionalisation of the field of evaluation has provided fuel for fiery and recurring debates about evaluator roles, little agreement has been reached as to whether evaluation should be viewed as a modality or as a profession. Increased desire for professionalisation is leading many evaluation practitioners to call for the strengthening of the field through training and accreditation.

Evaluation Approaches

Another prominent discussion that permeates evaluation is the approaches debate. Chambers defines an approach as, 'an orientation of behaviour, attitudes, and mindset associated with a method, methods or methodology' (Chambers, 2010, p. 10). There are two dominant approaches that have dominated evaluation practice: the positivist approach and constructivist approach. These approaches influence and shape the creation of knowledge paradigms in general, and by extension, the course of public policy discussion, discourse and practice. The duelling evaluation approaches are driven by different epistemologies rooted in contrasting worldviews, which are uniquely constructed from different values, assumptions, habits and beliefs.[1]

Programme evaluation was first governed by a positivist or post-positivist approach, which originated from experimental traditions in agriculture. Patton affirms, '[e]valuation was initially dominated by the natural science paradigm of hypothetico-deductive methodology, which values quantitative measures, experimental design, and statistical analysis as the epitome of "good science"' (Patton, 2008, p. 423).

As evaluation developed, the constructivist approach was established as an alternative, based on anthropological traditions, with a preference for using qualitative data, naturalistic inquiry and rich engagement with participants of the programme (Patton, 2008). Constructivism is premised on an understanding that social reality is rooted in the diversity of human experience, specifically the perceptions of those realities. Social reality is not a collection of unchanging, empirical facts, so much as a collection of subjective and inter-subjective experiences of events and conditions. Constructivists would view a *fact* to be both fluid and contingent upon social structures and processes. As such, the approach is advocated as being more responsive to the various characteristics of the programme as well as to the environment and issues that may be flagged by stakeholders.

Ultimately, the constructivist approach 'places the evaluators and programme stakeholders at the center of the inquiry process, employing all of them as the evaluation's "human instruments"' (Stufflebeam, 1999, p. 57). Constructivist evaluation has also provided the ontological foundations for the creation of additional approaches that emphasise certain facets of evaluation practice in order to ensure increased evaluation relevance and use. Some unique and prominent approaches born from constructivist ontology include DE, utilisation-focused evaluation (UFE) and participatory evaluation (McCoy and Hargie, 2001; Patton, 1997). These approaches will be further discussed later on in this chapter.

Two other distinct approaches that are rooted in both constructivist and positivist perspectives and which merit discussion here are goal-free evaluation and theory-driven evaluation. Goal-free evaluation was pioneered by Michael Scriven in the early 1970s, as an alternative approach to goal-based evaluations. Scriven argued that since most programmes either fall short or over-achieve the goals defined during initial planning, it does not make sense to restrict an evaluator to making judgements about achievement along these lines. Scriven (1972) noted that 'consideration of evaluation of goals was an unnecessary but also a possibly contaminating step... the less the external evaluator hears about the goals of the project, the less tunnel vision will develop, the more attention will be paid to looking for actual effects' (as quoted in Patton, 2001, p. 170). Goal-free evaluation, therefore, focuses not on preset goals and objectives, but on actual programme effects. Other practitioners have cautioned that this approach runs the risk of replacing the evaluator's goals with those of the programme and assumes the presence of both internal and external evaluators (Alkin, 1972; Patton, 2001).

Theory-driven evaluation assumes no direct ideological bias and can be traced as far back as the 1930s and Tyler's notion of testing programme theory. However, it was not until 1990, with the publication of *Theory-Driven Evaluation* by Chen, that this approach became prominent within evaluation practice (Coryn et al., 2011). Theory-driven evaluation is predicated on the use of an explicit theory or model to understand how a programme has caused the intended or observed programme outcomes (Rogers et al., 2000). This approach is based on a conceptual notion that an evaluation should explain programme theory, while empirically examining how programmes cause observed outcomes (Coryn et al., 2011). 'By developing a plausible model of how the programme is supposed to work, the evaluator can consider social science theories related to the programme as well as programme resources, activities, processes, and outcomes and assumptions' (Preskill and Russ-Eft, 2005, p. 121). As this approach grew in popularity, richer models were developed for understanding a variety of programme contexts. Coryn et al. (2011, p. 202) highlight that:

> In earlier conceptualisations, numerous theorists, including Weiss (1997; 1998) and Wholey (1979), among others, tended to favour

linear models to describe programme theories. In recent writings, others (e.g., Chen 2005; Rogers, 2008) have advocated for more contextualised, comprehensive, ecological programme theory models ... these types of models are intended to integrate systems thinking in postulating programme theory, taking contextual and other factors that sometimes influence and operate on programme processes and outcomes into account.

Despite the creation of these new approaches, Patton (2010) still questions their suitability for complex adaptive situations, which are constantly changing and unpredictable. This observation is of particular importance for evaluation practice in VDS situations which are characterised by fluidity, unpredictability and political complexity, as will be discussed further under constituent literature 2. Another weakness of the theory-driven approach is that it can be very time-intensive and, therefore, not feasible within certain evaluation timelines (Stufflebeam, 1999). Notwithstanding these critiques, theory-driven approaches continue to expand and accumulate their own debates and discourse.

With the creation of each new evaluation approach, longstanding debates on the worth of stakeholder participation, the types of methodologies used and what qualifies as evidence continue to re-surface as fundamental issues. These debates are ultimately influenced by differing ontological views, but many scholars have noted that the differing perceptivities actually help enrich and strengthen evaluation practice.

Who Participates

The merits of stakeholder participation are another important discussion that has permeated the programme and policy evaluation literature. Evaluation stakeholders are defined as individuals who have a vested interest in the evaluation findings (Patton, 2008) (see Box 2.2).

While different stakeholders each have a *stake* in the programme, their individual interests are often divergent, and can at times compete. For this reason, early positivist evaluation argued for limiting stakeholder participation, rationalising that the involvement of stakeholders would undoubtedly compromise the objectivity of the evaluation, and could bias the findings to suit personal interests. In the 1970s, however, studies started to emerge which showed a correlation between stakeholder involvement and evaluation uptake. Patton highlights that evaluations that had the 'presence of an identifiable individual or group of

Box 2.2
Key Evaluation Terms—Categories of Stakeholders

Evaluation Stakeholders: individuals who have a vested interest in the evaluation findings. Stakeholders can be clustered into the following five categories:

1. Individuals with authority to make programme decisions (policy-makers, funders, advisory boards, etc.)
2. Individuals with direct responsibility for the programme (developers, administration, managers, etc.)
3. Intended beneficiaries of the programme (individuals, families, communities, etc.)
4. Individuals who have been disadvantaged by the programme (those who lost in funding opportunities)
5. Individuals with indirect interest in the programme (journalists, taxpayers, etc.)

Source: Patton (2008).

people who care about the evaluation and the findings it generated' had an increased likelihood of long-term follow-through in getting evaluation findings used (Patton, 2008, p. 69).

Over time, evaluation practice has seen an increasing trend towards engaging stakeholders in evaluation across a wide variety of approaches (Christie, 2003). Today, stakeholder involvement has become an accepted practice in the evaluation profession, and has been noted as a hallmark of exemplary practice (Fitzpatrick, 2004; Patton, 2008). It is important to note, however, that there are prominent distinctions between how stakeholders engage. The degree, scope and nature of engagement differ significantly across evaluation practice, and have been theorised within a number of different evaluation approaches.

Participatory evaluation is one such approach which developed in the 1970s and 1980s to advocate for wider stakeholder involvement in the evaluation process. Advocates of participatory evaluation maintain that the process of evaluation needs to move outside of simple scientific frameworks towards approaches in which the target population is afforded a key role in shaping the evaluation plan (Drewett, 1997). Participatory evaluation ultimately presents a bottom-up approach that places engagement as a central focus. Cousins (2011) highlights that there are two streams of participatory evaluation: the practical stream, which is problem-solving and utilisation-oriented; and the transformative stream, which is emancipatory and empowerment-oriented. Both streams are similar in that they involve a partnership between the stakeholders and the evaluator, the parameters of which should always be discussed during the design of an evaluation.

Cousins and Whitmore (1998) highlight three dimensions of participation or collaborative inquiry. These include (a) who controls the technical decision-making in the evaluation process (a researcher–evaluator continuum); (b) stakeholder selection for participation (a continuum from all legitimate groups to just primary intended users); and (c) the depth of stakeholders participation (a continuum from consultation to rich involvement in all aspects of inquiry). How these different dimensions play out within an evaluation context determines the overall nature of participation and the benefits generated. Apart from increasing evaluation use, participatory approaches can assist stakeholders in building evaluation skills and knowledge; creating internal support-networks; and achieving a greater sense of self-efficacy (Whitmore, 1988).

The implementation of participatory evaluation can, however, add an additional level of complexity for the evaluator. Patton notes that 'participatory evaluation partnerships can be particularly challenging in part because of underlying fears, bad past experiences with evaluation, resistance to reality testing, and cultural norms that undercut openness and questioning' (Patton, 2008, p. 176 citing Podems, 2005). In spite of these barriers, the principles of participatory evaluation continue to inspire innovative approaches and methods which are all designed to incorporate stakeholders into the evaluative process.

Michael Quinn Patton's UFE approach is one example of an innovative, practical participatory evaluation approach. UFE is founded on the understanding that evaluations should be judged by their utility and actual use. The approach, therefore, focuses on the needs of the primary intended users, and considers how all aspects of the evaluation, from planning to dissemination, will affect use. Patton maintains that 'since no evaluation can be value-free, UFE answers the question of whose values will frame the evaluation by working with clearly identified, primary intended users who have responsibility to apply evaluation findings and implement recommendations' (Patton, 2012, p. 4). Similar to the majority of participatory approaches, there are no specific methods or theories advocated for within UFE. Instead, this approach suggests a need for situational responsiveness, whereby the evaluator and intended users work together to make decisions and source an appropriate evaluation design.

UFE is only one participatory approach, among many. However, it provides a prolific example of the polarised views regarding the merits of stakeholder participation. Evaluation practice has shifted significantly from the early positivist traditions that denied engagement to a flood of new constructivist approaches, which are built explicitly on stakeholder involvement. While discussions and debates still circulate on the ideal nature and degree of engagement, it is clear that involving stakeholders is beneficial to evaluation practice.

Methodological Practices

Another of the most prominent and important fundamental issues treated in the programme evaluation literature focuses on the appropriateness of methodological tools. While all evaluation approaches affirm that the key to evaluation is evidence-based research, there has been significant disagreement over whether quantitative or qualitative methods should be employed. In general terms, the collection of quantitative data is often supported by positivist arguments which hold that quantitative data yields more objective and accurate information because they are collected using standardised methods. These methods can be replicated and analysed using sophisticated statistical techniques and are based on hypothetico-deductive and quantitative models where an evaluator relies heavily on the use of statistics in order to measure the impact of a socially grounded programme. Quantitative measures focus on countable data that can be collected from information systems, official indicators, programme records, questionnaires, quasi experiments, rating scales, standardised observation instruments, norm-referenced tests, a posteriori statistical test and significance tests (Patton, 2008; Stufflebeam, 1999). The overall aim is to use statistics to facilitate comparisons and identify relationships between the programme and its outcomes.

In contrast, qualitative methods are generally supported by constructivist approaches and aim to capture personal meaning and participant perspectives on programme experience, by examining the diverse ways in which people articulate and express themselves. Qualitative data is, therefore, open-ended and not predetermined by imposed standardised choices. Qualitative methods include: 'ethnography, document analysis, narrative analysis, purposive samples, participant observers, independent observers, key informants, advisory committees, structured and unstructured interviews, focus groups, case studies, study of outliers, diaries, logic models, grounded theory development, flow charts, decision trees, matrices, and performance assessments' (Stufflebeam, 1999, p. 34). Advocates of qualitative methodologies highlight their ability to deepen understanding on how and why programmes work, and what outcomes mean (sense-making).

While both qualitative and quantitative methods have received support and criticism from their contrasting ontological camps, many scholars and evaluation practitioners have acknowledged that both contribute in important and differing ways to understanding a programme. Consequently, many evaluation approaches have encouraged the use of mixed methods. Stufflebeam suggests, 'by using both quantitative and qualitative methods, the evaluator secures cross-checks on different subsets of findings and thereby instils greater stakeholder confidence in the overall findings' (Stufflebeam, 1999, p. 34). From a practical perspective, it has been noted that much current evaluation practice routinely involves multiple types of data. For example, evaluations often use time series analyses of outcome monitoring or administrative performance data with interviews or surveys, together with case studies including participant observation (Datta, 2001).

Although there are infinite possibilities for applying mixed methods to technical aspects of evaluation, some such as Guba and Lincoln have argued that because the assumptions of different paradigms are incompatible, it is not possible to mix paradigms in the same study (Guba and Lincoln, 1989). Similarly, Patton suggests that even when mixed methods are used, 'one kind of data is often valued over the other' (Patton, 2008, p. 435). In contrast, other practitioners have suggested the possibility of applying mixed methods not only to technical procedures, but also to conceptual aspects of the evaluation process (Greene, 1997).

Methodological debate on evaluation has experienced significant ebbs and flows throughout the development of the field. Qualitative methodologies have gained relative acceptance, which is a significant change from early 1970s, which privileged quantitative methods (Patton, 2008, p. 421). Although disagreement about the relative merits of each has always existed, Mark (2003) suggests that the 'paradigm wars', which occupied the field during the 1970s and 1980s, quieted down at the turn of the century, settling into an uneasy peace. In 2003, however, these debates were refuelled when the US Department of Education's Institute of Education Science publicised their commitment to prioritising funding for quantitative approaches such as experimental and quasi-experimental designs. In response, hot exchanges and debates were reignited within the evaluation community, focusing attention on what counts as credible evidence and what method should be regarded as evaluation's 'gold standard'.

What Counts as Evidence:
Attribution versus Contribution

Although discussions about the merits of methodologies and evaluative design are entangled within the disputes about evaluation evidence,
Christie and Fleischer speculate that the credible evidence debate is more
likely rooted in 'how each "side" conceptualises "impact"' (Christie and
Fleischer, 2009, p. 20). Both positivists and constructivists recognise
that no method is infallible; however, disagreements arise on how to
approach strengthening evaluation evidence. These diverse perspectives
are once again supported by their underlying viewpoints about truth and
science and perceptions of the world (Christie and Fleischer, 2009).

A positivist or post-positivist approach views the world as something which is fixed and constant and, therefore, suggests that impact can
be determined by providing evidence of a causal relationship between
the intervention (e.g., the programme or other unit of analysis) and the
outcome generated. Davidson (2000) suggests that causation is critical
to determine; in its absence, financial and personal resources may be
wasted in expanding defective programmes. In order to determine causation, experimental or quasi-experimental approaches call for the use
of counterfactuals (a control or comparison group that allows the evaluator to establish what would have happened if the programme had not
taken place).

With the release of the Center for Global Development's 2006
report *When Will We Ever Learn* (Savedoff et al., 2006), Randomised
Control Trials (RCTs) were purported to constitute a fail-safe *gold standard* methodology for measuring the impact that a programme may have
had in relation to a particular established goal (Clinton et al., 2006).

Support for RCTs as a gold standard has since fluctuated over the
years but continues to be the 'design of choice' for some funders of international aid, who have dubbed this approach 'impact evaluation'. Many
evaluators have highlighted the limitations of RCTs noting that

> RCTs are not always best for determining causality and can be mis-
> leading. RCTs examine a limited number of isolated factors that are
> neither limited nor isolated in natural settings. The complex nature of
> causality and the multitude of actual influences on outcomes render
> RCTs less capable of discovering causality than designs sensitive to
> local culture and conditions and open to unanticipated causal factors.
> (AEA, 2003)

The feasibility of using experimental evaluation designs with RCTs for evaluating certain programmes including humanitarian relief, peace-building and democracy strengthening in contexts affected by violence and conflict has also been called into question given that these types of programmes are typically *emergent* and 'their impacts are often difficult to evaluate or measure using established tools' (Stern et al., 2012). It has also been noted that experimental and quasi-experimental approaches generally will have very limited utility because they cannot answer many important impact evaluation questions regarding how a particular intervention might exacerbate conflict drivers or enable structures and processes for peace (Chigas et al., 2014, p. iv). While researchers, evaluators and funders continue to argue the merits and demerits of experimental and quasi-experimental approaches, what is clear is that the debate has pushed actors in the worlds of evaluation and research to strive for improved evidence quality through the exploration of multiple approaches to *impact evaluation* (see Befani et al., 2014; Stern et al., 2012).

While all experimental methods have differing strengths and weaknesses, their reliance on counterfactual evidence is inconsistent with constructivist ontology. Constructivist worldviews suggest that it is impossible to distinguish cause and effect, since relationships are multidirectional and, therefore, everything is impacting everything at once (Christie and Fleischer, 2009). According to this perspective, providing evidence based on mere counterfactual claims is not inherently credible, since any number of factors present within a given context could have created the same result, even if the result was not produced by the intervention (Cook et al., 2010). Furthermore, it is suggested that 'evaluations need to recognise policy and programme interests of sponsors and yield maximally useful information, given the available resources and programme constraints' (Rossi and Freeman, 1989, p. 40). The assumption here is that there is a requirement for an evaluation to be designed in order to satisfy the information needs and particular agenda of stakeholders rather than be stifled through narrow adherence to abstract scientific norms (Stufflebeam and Shinklefield, 1985). Reliance on solely scientific means in the field of evaluation has, thus, been questioned and regarded as being somewhat restrictive in garnering a truly multilayered perspective on the impact of a particular programme.

Constructivists, therefore, maintain that credible evidence can be established in a number of diverse ways. Mathison (2009) suggests that evidence credibility is dependent on experience, perception and social convention. Rallis (2009) proposes that along with methodological rigour, characteristics of goodness, moral correctness and probity determine evidence credibility. From a similar perspective, Greene (2009) highlights that credible evidence 'needs to account for history, culture, and context; respects differences in perspective and values; and opens the potential for democratic inclusion and the legitimisation of multiple voices' (Donaldson, 2009, p. 15).

The differing perspectives of evidence creditability will be further expanded when this chapter discusses research quality or excellence. However, what is important to note here is that within the programme evaluation literature there no single agreed definition of credible evidence. In the epilogue of *What Counts as Credible Evidence in Applied Research and Evaluation Practice?*, Donaldson (2009) laments that, 'we are a long way from consensus and a universal answer to the question of what counts as credible evidence in contemporary applied research and evaluation' (Donaldson, 2009, p. 249). Instead of moving towards consensus, Donaldson suggests that the different understandings of evidence credibility are dependent on multiple characteristics including: the question(s) of interest; the context; assumptions made by the evaluators and stakeholders; the evaluation theory used to guide practice; and practical time and resource constraints (Donaldson, 2009, p. 250).

The programme evaluation literature has, thus, demonstrated the influence that ontology has on framing perspectives on the purpose of evaluation, the merits of stakeholder participation, what approaches and methodologies should be used and what qualifies as credible evidence. While these fundamental issues have not been resolved, a rich discourse from these opposing viewpoints has played a principle role in shaping practice outside of mainstream public social policy and programme evaluation.

Constituent Literature 2: Evaluation of Conflict Prevention, Peacebuilding and Humanitarian Assistance Programmes

The current section shifts its focus to the second constituent literature within which this chapter, and this book, is rooted: peacebuilding evaluation. This includes both the evaluation of self-labelled *peacebuilding projects* as well as the evaluation of the peacebuilding effects of development and humanitarian initiatives. The influence of fundamental issues in mainstream social programme, including the international development programme evaluation literature, is also evident in the literature on conflict prevention, peacebuilding and humanitarian programme evaluation. The peacebuilding and humanitarian evaluation sub-field has wrestled with, and learned from, the approaches, methods and debates discussed in the previous section. One of the main points of departure for this subset of literature is the distinctive violent and fragile settings in which these programmes are embedded.

Following the end of the Cold War, development and humanitarian agencies found themselves working in conflict (and *post*-conflict) zones, through levels of violence which would have spurred them to cease programming in the past. Within these contexts, a new kind of programming evolved which sought explicitly to support or build the social, economic and political structures, processes, and capacities for sustainable peace. It quickly became clear that the conventional approaches applied to the evaluation of development programmes would need to be revised, and adapted, before they could be effectively applied to initiatives in VDS settings.

At the same time, a related set of evaluation challenges began to loom large within the same violence or conflict-prone environments: consideration of the ways in which development, humanitarian and even peacebuilding interventions may positively or negatively affect the dynamics and structures of peace and conflict (Anderson, 1999, 2004; Bush, 1998, 2001, 2005). As noted by the Organisation for Economic Cooperation and Development (OECD) in its recently released guidelines for the evaluation of peacebuilding activities in settings of conflict and fragility, evaluation practice in these contexts poses real risks to both evaluators and those being evaluated. Understanding and adapting evaluation approaches and methods to violence, while mitigating the risk that evaluation itself might exacerbate violence or cause harm to those involved, forms the foundation upon which both research and evaluation practice should be built. Our analysis of the second constituent literature acknowledges the profound importance of understanding and making allowances for contexts affected by violence and conflict (OECD, 2012; Bush and Duggan, Chapter 1).

Purpose of Evaluation

Peacebuilding evaluation adopts a similar purpose and definition of evaluation as developed in the public programming literature. Evaluations

are heralded as mechanisms for contributing to learning and accountability. However, the peacebuilding evaluation literature tends to highlight process orientation over goal orientation. Church (2011), however,
maintains that in peacebuilding evaluation, the learning purposes can
remain unrealised, with other drivers relating to public relations, fundraising, justifying exiting programmes and/or predetermined decisions
taking their place. In practice, peacebuilding evaluation has failed to live
up to the ascribed purposes of learning and accountability. According
to Church, only a few evaluation processes actually catalyse learning,
and these exist outside of the norm (Church, 2011). She notes that there
are various reasons for these learning gaps, but the most common reasons include: a failure to integrate learning as a central pillar within the
organisational culture of most agencies; poorly designed evaluations
which do not support learning; and peacebuilding processes which rarely
capitalise on *process use* learning (Church, 2011). Duggan notes that one
important characteristic of conflict- and violence-affected settings is that
often the social capital of organisations and evaluation stakeholders has
been eroded. For this reason, more serious consideration should be given
to the development of evaluation approaches that embrace rather than
side-step the messiness of high-risk contexts; the purpose of evaluation
should be to revitalise rather than erode the social capital of those being
evaluated (Duggan, 2010).

The concept of accountability in evaluation has yet to be completely
unpacked by the peacebuilding field (Church, 2011; Whitty, Chapter 3).
Instead, accountability continues to be largely understood as upwards in
nature, responding to funders and governments, rather than to the communities being served (Church, 2011). While movement towards other
types of accountability has been made by humanitarian organisations,
until recently, accountability has tended to be a non-issue within peacebuilding programming, resulting in a lack of understanding from practitioners (Church, 2011). Church suggests that this failure to fully grasp
the concept of accountability poses a particular challenge for evaluators
attempting to develop systems to contribute to it, not least because of the
moral vacuum it creates for evaluation undertaken within environments
where ethical challenges are considerably more acute—and potentially
lethal—than in normal (non-conflict) conditions (Bush and Duggan,
Chapter 1).

While these challenges are not unique to peacebuilding evaluation,
they are rendered more extreme by the legacy or imminent threat of

violence to evaluation actors. For example, transparency and the provision of programming information are important dimensions of accountability, but these can present potential risks. For example, 'in highly volatile contexts, misused information could spark unrest or lead to local partners being threatened' (Church, 2011, p. 475). Evaluation in VDS must, therefore, not only seek to contribute to accountability and learning, but must also take particular care to not aggravate existing tensions in the process.

Evaluation within these particular contexts must, therefore, be sensitive to the structures and drivers of conflict and violence, and must ask what effect a programme, or an intervention, may have on actions, structures and processes that can support 'prospects for peaceful coexistence and decrease the likelihood of the outbreak, reoccurrence, or continuation, of violent conflict,' or on 'those structures and processes that increase the likelihood that conflict will be dealt with through violent means (Bush, 1998 as cited in USAID, 2008, p. 1). This focus on assessing drivers of violence and enablers of peace is unique to peacebuilding evaluation, a fact which sets it apart from other forms of international development programme evaluation (Chigas, 2014, p. iii).

This concept of *conflict sensitivity* has come to be understood as 'systematically taking into account both the positive and negative effects or impacts of interventions, in terms of conflict or peace dynamics, on the contexts in which they are undertaken, and, conversely, the implications of these contexts for the design and implementation of interventions' (Conflict Sensitivity Consortium, 2004 as cited in OECD, 2012, p. 11). It encapsulates the intricacies of undertaking any kind of intervention in a fragile and/or divided place, encompassing debates around power, gender, vulnerable groups and accountability, among others. This takes evaluation into murky operational territory.

The Role of the Evaluator

The conflict prevention, peacebuilding and humanitarian field evaluation literature also acknowledges the benefits of both formative and summative evaluations to assess the on-going progress as well as final achievements of programmes (Church, 2011). In response, many agencies have invested in in-house monitoring and evaluation expertise, to provide technical guidance to programme staff in charge of monitoring and formative evaluations. In situations which require quick evidence and feedback, humanitarian agencies often prefer the use of in-house staff to lead *real-time evaluation* (RTE) (see discussion later in the chapter), noting that it averts the lengthy recruitment procedures and start-up costs often associated with external evaluation (Jamal and Crisp, 2002 as quoted in Cosgrave et al., 2009).

The use of external evaluators, however, tends to be the dominant practice within this field, especially within longer term programmes. Since there is no accreditation process to distinguish *conflict/peacebuilding* evaluators, consultants and academics are often selected as evaluators on the basis of their credentials as subject matter experts who provide evaluative judgements by relying on the transference of their social science research skills and on-the-job learning (Church, 2011). Despite the expertise of these evaluators, they often remain outside of the larger professional programme evaluation community, and at times can conflate the role of the evaluator with that of the researcher, producing mini-research studies that are labelled evaluations (Church, 2011). Church highlights that, 'from the perspective of the evaluation discipline, these studies often fall short of the accuracy standard. Common accuracy gaps include a lack of contextual grounding and inadequate description of the evaluation purposes and procedures' (Church, 2011, p. 466). This is problematic since those who commission external evaluations require clarity of purpose in order to use evaluation findings to inform decision-making. Similarly, external evaluation should ensure credible methodological design that yields robust, contextually applicable evidence. Poor quality evaluations have been one impetus that has fuelled the professionalisation debate within this field, as well as strengthened the arguments for accreditation within the larger evaluation community.

While the variety of possible roles described in the first constituent literature on programme evaluation are applicable here, internal and external evaluators assessing conflict prevention, peacebuilding and humanitarian programmes are faced with myriad unique challenges including the high risk of violence, complex institutional contexts, multiple actors with shifting agendas, operational challenges to data collection and the politicisation and manipulation of evaluating findings (Bush and Duggan, Chapter 1). These evaluators are employed with the difficult task of assessing the effects of a programme both in terms of its stated aims or intentions and within the overall environment of fluidity and unpredictability. For this reason, evaluators are expected to possess deep peace and conflict contextual knowledge in addition to the subject matter and technical expertise required to assess the programme in question. Evaluators must also exhibit an acute degree of conflict sensitivity, to be able to anticipate potential positive and negative programme impacts, while also ensuring that the evaluation process itself has limited effects on the locality and people in which the evaluation is taking place.

As noted earlier, the responsibilities of evaluators are aligned with the growing discussion of conflict sensitivity within the peacebuilding, development and humanitarian fields which recognise that all assistance can, in effect, contribute to, and in many cases aggravate, the particular circumstances of a conflict and even lead to an upsurge in violence. This realisation has led to an expectation that evaluators have an understanding of the symbiotic relationship between the delivery of aid and its potential to do harm. In concrete terms, this translates into competencies that include conflict risk and analysis skills and a concurrent ability to mitigate negative risks and maximise, if possible, positive impacts (USAID, 2008).

Who Participates

Another important fundamental issue within this sub-field of evaluation is once again the question of participation. One of the particularities of peacebuilding and humanitarian evaluation is that stakeholders often come from vulnerable, traumatised, disenfranchised or otherwise disempowered populations. In these circumstances, who should participate, what form that participation should take, and most importantly, who, ultimately, is in control of participation matters immensely. Each of these questions is fraught with ethical, methodological, logistical and political considerations and implications.

Within this sub-field of evaluation, there are a variety of participatory approaches including practical stream approaches and transformative evaluation approaches, which offer potential for re-building and strengthening the social fabric often damaged by multiple forms of violence. For example, empowerment evaluation, a transformative approach stresses the active engagement of a diverse group of stakeholders, especially during decision-making processes (Weaver and Cousins, 2004 as quoted in Cox et al., 2009). Motivation for these approaches has grown as a response to evaluation's predominantly *Northern* roots, which have fostered push-back from Southern (e.g., developing country) and collectivist approaches. These approaches emphasise the need for a more active role for programme stakeholders, with local participation, capacity building and stakeholder empowerment at the heart of the evaluation process. Some empowerment approaches have even gone so far as to argue that interventions should be measured on their ability to act as a catalyst for social change (Bush, 2003).

Complementary debates have also focused on the need to expand the range of voices involved, and to acknowledge and address the unbalanced power structures in the evaluation process (Cousins and Whitmore, 1998; Chouinard and Cousins, 2009). Donna Mertens notes the importance of looking towards *Southern* methods as a potential way forward. According to Mertens, 'participatory models of evaluation that evolved in Latin America, India, and Africa provide guidance in ways to legitimately involve important stakeholders in an evaluation, especially those stakeholders who have been traditionally excluded from the corridors of power and decision making' (Mertens, 2001, p. 368). However, others argue that the concept of local ownership poses a dilemma on its own, since in some circumstances it has come to be perceived as a tokenistic gesture within peacebuilding and development initiatives (Schmelzle, 2005).

The question of whose voice counts in peacebuilding and humanitarian evaluations has been interrogated in multiple sources over the years. For example, in the Berghoff series, Paffenholz and Reychler ignore the more overtly political implications of this debate by advocating a technocratic approach that argues for the use of standardised procedures developed by Northern consultancy firms (Barbolet et al., 2005; Bush, 2005). Carl, on the other hand, warns against the potential of romanticising the local and indigenous capacities for peacebuilding. 'While these are vitally important, it is often overlooked that traditional capacities for conflict management have failed' (Carl, 2003 as quoted in Schmelze, 2005, p. 6). In the *Utstein report* Dan Smith also notes 'that in the context of violent conflict, local ownership becomes a more complex concept and needs to be handled with care. Local ownership can unintentionally come to mean ownership by conflict parties, or by the most powerful sectors of society' (Smith, 2004 as quoted in Schmelze, 2005, p. 6).

In evaluation practice, this once again raises the political implications of methodological choice, and whether linear models for programme management and evaluation, such as the logical framework approach, should uncritically remain the dominant tool-of-the-trade in peacebuilding, humanitarian and development practice. NGOs and practitioners, in particular, have been experimenting with the application of systems thinking to peacebuilding evaluation practice by development of practical tools that enable practitioners 'to exploit the insights of systems thinking, while avoiding the more arcane and complex methodological elaborations of the field' (Woodrow and Chigas, 2011, p. 205). Similarly, scholars have questioned the plausibility and utility of using standardised indicators across violence-affected contexts,[2] recognising that no two are the same and that external validity, thus, remains one of the principal challenges faced by evaluators for measuring results such as outputs, outcomes and impacts.

While each of these debates occupies a prominent and important place within this constituent literature, the realities on the ground often influence the degree to which participatory approaches can be used in VDS contexts. For example, the OECD (2012, p. 46) notes that

> Donors generally carry out their conflict prevention, peacebuilding and statebuilding actions in support of and in partnership with host governments. A logical extension of such cooperation is working together in evaluation. Such partnerships, however, may pose challenges where governments lack legitimacy or are primary actors in an ongoing conflict. The political context and its high stakes not only affect external partners, they are also likely to have very real impacts on how and why partners engage in an evaluation process.

In the light of the above, the OECD guidelines on evaluating peacebuilding activities highlight the critical importance of appropriately discussing and managing stakeholder participation for each evaluation context. Difficulties surrounding collaborative management are also apparent when working with programme beneficiaries or local community members. Church (2011) maintains that 'the current reality is that this constituency [programme beneficiaries] is called upon to be sources of information only. True participatory evaluation, where participants play a key role in every stage of the process, is exceedingly rare' (Church, 2011, p. 465). She notes that evaluation findings in peacebuilding programmes are often not even shared with this stakeholder group (Church, 2011). It would seem, therefore, that in spite of the rich discourse about the potential of participatory evaluation approaches within peacebuilding and humanitarian assistance programming, the participation of beneficiaries remains a largely theoretical discussion, with less practical experience currently contributing to the discussions.

What Counts as Evidence of Influence and Impact: Grappling with Volatility, Unpredictability and Risk

Within this sub-field, the primary question that tends to drive calls for *evidence-based* programming or policy-making (how do we know we are making a difference?) is accompanied by a second, equally pressing question: 'How do we know we are not causing harm or deepening conflicts and divisions?'

While this sub-field of evaluation faces many of the same obstacles faced in the evaluation of more traditional social policy or development programmes, VDS contexts generate several unique challenges. The attribution problem (ascribing a causal link from a particular programme to observed or expected social change on the ground) is more acute due to the fluidity and unpredictability of these settings and the frequently non-linear, multidirectional social change processes that take place within complex conflict systems. In addition, the presence or threat of violence does not only have implications for the safety of evaluation actors, it also poses thorny methodological challenges including the absence of baseline data, erratic access to data and stakeholders, and risks that data may be biased, incomplete and/or (voluntarily or involuntarily) censored (OECD, 2012, pp. 32–33). The often politicised nature of these settings also opens possibilities for strategic misinformation and the instrumentalisation of evaluation findings.

In the light of the above, there has been an increasing recognition that context is much more than a landscape or backdrop for evaluation; it must be the starting point of any evaluation (OECD, 2012, p. 34). In recent years, evaluation actors in this sub-field have been grappling with and reflecting upon the implications that contexts of violence and conflict will have upon evaluation practice. As a result, in its guidelines, the OECD recommends that conflict analysis should be built into the evaluation process noting that it 'may be used as the basis for assessing whether activities have been sufficiently sensitive to conflict settings, determining…what will be the evaluation questions…[and ensuring] that the evaluation itself is conducted in a conflict-sensitive way' (OECD, 2012, p. 35).

How this might be done in practice remains unclear. There is a conceptual and operational gap between what peace and conflict scholars and practitioners call conflict analysis (and the barrage of tools and frameworks articulated to categorise conflict and fragility), what humanitarian actors understand as 'do no harm' and what evaluation actors understand as contextual or situational analysis. In the world of international assistance, the last two decades has seen the rise of multiple tools and frameworks for analysing conflict dynamics. In general terms, these tools propose different methods to undertake a more 'systematic study of the profile, causes, actors, and dynamics of conflict' (International Alert et al., 2004) and exist to help practitioners better understand how particular causes and drivers of conflict—political, military, cultural, economic, etc.—might affect, either negatively or positively (but most often the former), their particular development, humanitarian or peace-building programme.

At the same time, there have also been concrete efforts to operationalise the principal of non-maleficence—or 'do no harm' in international aid. As noted, the Collaborative for Development Action's (CDA) 'do no harm' framework is one of the most widely used tools for conflict sensitivity in development and humanitarian practice and aims to assist organisations in identifying 'the conflict and peace potential of their programmes' (Anderson, 1999). The framework does this by identifying operational programme components which may affect a conflict and also puts forwards several agency behaviours that can reinforce conflictive or non-conflictive relations (as noted in OECD, 2012). The 'do no harm' framework has also played a pivotal role in expounding the nuances of conflict evaluation, serving as the catalyst for further discourse and the creation of diverse conflict evaluation tools.

The underlying concepts and motivations of conflict evaluation or analysis tools and the 'do no harm' framework resonate with the 'peace and conflict impact assessment' (PCIA) approach that was developed by Kenneth Bush (1998). PCIA focuses on assessing the actual or potential effects of initiatives on peace and conflict dynamics before, during and after their implementation. Proponents of PCIA see it as a process of mutual learning that can benefit local people living in conflict zones, and aid agencies who work in these settings (Anderson, 1999).

Moving these frameworks into peacebuilding evaluation and evaluation in contexts of violence and fragility has not been unproblematic. In a learning meeting organised by the OECD in 2011, practitioners, evaluators, commissioners and aid managers discussed the strengths and limitations of the OECD guidance. Evaluators cited a number of challenges in trying to incorporate conflict analysis into evaluations, including: lack of time or expertise to do a full socio-political, military, etc., analysis of the environment in which the programme was taking place;

and difficulty in moving from conflict analysis to evaluation framework questions (OECD, 2011), among others.

The difficulties encountered in efforts to incorporate conflict analysis frameworks into the evaluation process spring from two realities. First, existing conflict analysis tools have been developed to assist the analysis of aid practitioners or programme staff who may also be evaluation commissioners and managers—but not evaluators; and second, conflict analysis, PCIA and 'do no harm' frameworks focus upon how an intervention (project, programme) is affected by conflict, or how the intervention itself might affect peace and conflict dynamics (by either *doing harm* or *doing good*) in a given environment. In other words, the unit of analysis is the project or programme intervention—not the evaluation process which itself is also an intervention. Despite the expectation that evaluators should do or obtain a conflict analysis (OECD, 2012, p. 42), these frameworks are not meant to be used by evaluators whose main concern is how to determine which dimensions of violence or conflict will be relevant in influencing, either positively or negatively, prospects for planning and conducting *an evaluation*, and for articulating evaluative judgements that are underpinned by sound principles of ethical practice. While there is renewed interest among evaluators to incorporate a more explicit focus on context into evaluation inquiry,[3] evaluators disaggregate context in ways that are different from those of evaluation commissioners and managers. While conflict analysis can help evaluators navigate particular challenges that bubble up from conditions of violence, instability and tension, analysis around the drivers and causes of conflict must be part of, but cannot replace, good situational analysis for evaluation.

In reflecting upon how violence embeds unique challenges into the contexts in which evaluation must take place, the discussion that follows of approaches and methods will focus on how evaluation actors in this sub-field have been dealing with operational and logistical constraints and with the implications of dealing with non-linearity and complexity.

Approaches and Methodological Practice: Dealing with Non-linearity, Complexity and Emergence

The debates over qualitative or quantitative methodologies have also found a place in the conflict prevention, peacebuilding and humanitarian evaluation literature. However, due to the complexity and heterogeneity inherent in these contexts, the field has widely acknowledged that there is no single methodological blueprint for evaluation. Instead, evaluation practitioners reinforce the utility of qualitative and quantitative methods noting that 'the complex nature of interventions in fragile and conflict-affected situations generally makes it necessary to combine different methodologies in order to answer the evaluation questions. Many favour a mixed-method approach, using both qualitative and quantitative methods and data' (OECD, 2012, p. 50).

Church and Rogers' (2006) *Designing for Results* proposes a list of 14 considerations that assist in filtering suitable methodologies for specific environments. While the list is applicable for any programme evaluation situation, it highlights the nuances needed for conflict-affected settings. For example, the first consideration assesses a programme's level of complexity, highlighting that qualitative methods are often better suited to deal with the intricacies of increasingly complex environments (Church and Rogers, 2006). Another consideration examines the operational constraints of accessing data. For example if the respondents (or data sources) are in the bush fighting a war, direct observation or interviews may be required. In contrast, if respondents are located in city centres with access to the Internet, online questionnaires might prove to be the most efficient method (Church and Rogers, 2006).

In this sub-field of evaluation, methodological choice also needs to take into account issues of volatility. Church notes that in certain situations respondents are unable to articulate dissenting opinions without great personal risk. In these cases, methods that ensure the anonymity of sources should be selected over others.

> Any method that requires experiences to be documented, through the use of participant diaries or photographs, for example, deserves extra consideration in these contexts. If discovered by the wrong people, such as a paramilitary group or the army, these participants and sources might be in danger. (Church and Rogers, 2006, p. 213)

The examples put forward by Church allude to the diversity of settings that are all classified as situations of conflict or violence but which require drastically different evaluation methodologies. In order to ensure that appropriate methods are selected, many agencies and organisations operating in these settings have opted to produce their own evaluation publications to assist staff and consultants. As a result, there has been a proliferation of agency handbooks for practitioners and policy-makers responsible for managing or conducting evaluations.

Similar guides can also be found in the mainstream programme evaluation literature. One of the most notable examples that emerges from international development evaluation practice is Bamberger, Rugh and Mabry's *Real World Evaluation* (RWE) guide which was designed to assist evaluators who are confronted by budget, time and data constraints, as well as receiving pressure from government agencies, politicians, funding or regulatory agencies and stakeholders. RWE does not present new data collection or analysis methods, but rather provides a guide that evaluators can use to draw from a wide range of mixed methods and approaches to address the common evaluation constraints of the *real world* (Bamberger et al., 2006).

Although the RWE approach was not specifically designed for VDS settings, most evaluations required in the conflict prevention, peacebuilding and humanitarian fields are confronted by the constraints that RWE addresses. For example, RWE tackles the baseline challenge by providing measures that help reconstruct baseline data by using 'secondary data sources, recall, key informants, focus groups, construct mapping and participatory group techniques' (Bamberger et al., 2006, p. 4). Similarly, RWE suggests several steps for addressing time and budget constraints.

As evaluation actors come to grips with the need to adopt pragmatic approaches, aid agencies such as the UK's Department for International Development (DFID) have noted that evaluators need to be especially attentive to addressing methodological bias and unreliable data, particularly in situations of conflict where disinformation may be a tactic used by the combatants (DFID, 2010, p. 12). DFID's cautionary advice speaks to the fragility of environments affected by conflict and violence and the additional care needed for applying any evaluative approach. The nonlinear, dynamic and uncontrollable nature of many of these settings has pushed the evaluation community to look for alternative approaches that offer more flexibility and potential for tailoring and adaptation, as programmes evolve in response to contexts that are in flux.

In spite of the particular contextual complexities that characterise the evaluation of programmes in this sub-field, the dominant practice has been to adopt linear evaluation approaches that are often nested within complex conflict systems and which are subject to disruptions, shifts and change. Reina Neufeldt (2007, p. 8) maintains that the dominance of rigid, linear evaluation approaches is in part due to

> an optimism that is built into the belief that when we identify objective measures, this will lead to universal patterns and lessons to improve

our work in the future not only in one locale, but in many locales— an optimism that, just as we grow crops or markets, we can grow more peace.

In her 2011 publication, *'Frameworkers' and 'Circlers': Exploring Assumptions in Impact Assessment,* Neufeldt further examines this inherent optimism, along with the ontological orientations of peacebuilding practitioners, partitioning them into two archetypal camps. The *Logical Frameworkers* group which adheres to a more positivist approach, believing that programme design and evaluation should follow a linear, cause–effect trajectory. The nature of a programme's relationships are frequently visualised and tracked through detailed logical framework matrices. Frameworkers, therefore, believe that evidence should demonstrate 'the degree to which particular activities and their outputs contribute to larger or higher-order objectives and goals' and thus, 'indicators for activities, outputs, results or objectives are to be "SMART"', meaning specific, measurable, achievable, relevant and time-bound (Rouche, 1999 as quoted by Neufeldt, 2007, p. 3).

In contrast, Neufeldt's *Complex Circlers* group adopts a decidedly constructivist angle. Individuals in this group are characterised by their preference to work within a systems or complexity approach. This group approaches peacebuilding through a more elliptical lens; they are relationship focussed and have a desire to be flexible and responsive to each situation. Circlers generally do not believe that events in conflict environments can be predicted because they are part of a larger complex system made up of intermeshed forces over which peacebuilders or development agents have little (if any) influence. The assumptions that underpin this approach include the belief that every situation is unique, lessons are not transferable from one country or setting to another, planning has limitations and flexibility is always an asset.

In line with this thinking, there is a growing movement in the conflict prevention, peacebuilding and humanitarian sub-field towards the use of systems-based approaches in evaluation. While the move away from linear approaches is part of a larger trend in programme evaluation (particularly international development programme evaluation), evaluation practitioners in this sub-field have also recognised the analytical utility of systems thinking and complexity science for understanding developments and relationships in fast changing and unpredictable environments. This awareness is a prerequisite for ensuring that programmes are better able to adapt, and thrive, within conflict contexts (Ramalingam and Jones, 2008).

The discussion below provides a glimpse of some of the evaluation approaches that are anchored in systems and complexity thinking. These approaches are not necessarily unique to peacebuilding and humanitarian evaluation, nor do they serve as a comprehensive summary. Rather, what is presented is an acknowledgment of the range and diversity of approaches available and currently in use in this sub-field.

Real-time Evaluation

RTE was created in response to the particular needs of humanitarian assistance programming and is regarded as one of the most demanding types of evaluative practice. The primary objective of RTE is to 'provide feedback in a participatory way in "real time" (i.e., during the evaluation fieldwork) to those executing or managing a humanitarian response' (Cosgrave et al., 2009, p. 10). RTEs are most effective when they are conducted during the early stages of a humanitarian of conflict programme, as they are designed and executed to construct knowledge that can assist in the ongoing operational decision-making and programme adaptation. The primary audience for RTE is the staff of the implementing agency (at the various field, national, regional and global levels). One unique component of RTE is the rapid timeframe. Evaluation teams, often composed of one to four members, are expected to conduct 'light evaluation exercises' and deliver their report, or at least a substantive draft, before departing the field (Cosgrave et al., 2009). Evaluation practitioner Cosgrave notes that 'RTEs are well suited to the fast pace of decision making within the humanitarian sector, where they can bring a strong strategic focus at a critical stage of the response' (Cosgrave et al., 2009, p. 12).

Developmental Evaluation

While not specifically designed for application in conflict-affected settings, Michael Quinn Patton's DE is an approach that speaks directly to the complexity of conflict environments. The OECD Development Assistance Committee's (DAC) 2012 guidelines state that, 'few would dispute that settings of conflict and fragility are complex, combining high levels of unpredictability, a general lack of information, and potential strategic misinformation' (OECD, 2012, p. 32). Complexity is defined here, as contexts in which the relationships of cause and effect are fundamentally unknown, or only known in retrospect (Patton, 2010).

DE is informed by systems thinking, and addresses non-linear dynamics, enabling innovation and adaptive management (Patton, 2010). Patton specifies five contexts for DE: ongoing development and adaptation; pre-formative evaluation to support exploration and innovation; supporting local adaptation of general principles to navigate top-down and bottom-up forces for change; evaluating major systems change and evaluating in turbulent, disaster situations (Patton, 2011). While each of these situations could be present in conflict contexts, the last speaks directly to this field. Patton highlights that in turbulent and disaster situations, 'planned interventions must adapt and respond as conditions change suddenly' and, as a result, 'planning, execution and evaluation occur simultaneously' (Patton, 2011, p. 12).

DE was, thus, developed as an alternative to formative and summative evaluation, with the evaluator's primary function being to 'infuse team discussions with evaluative questions, thinking, and data, and to facilitate systematic data-based reflection and decision making in the developmental process' (Patton, 2010, p. 1). The DE evaluator is, therefore, embedded within the programme team helping to adapt programme strategies based on the data available and the changing circumstances.

Unlike other forms of evaluation, DE is not focused on accountability, but instead concentrates on adaptive learning. In this way the evaluator plays an active role in shaping the programme's development, while at the same time capturing innovative strategies and ideas. Although DE is a relatively new arrival in the evaluation community, it has been met with great enthusiasm. Patton (2011) is quick to caution, however, that DE is not meant for programmes that have a model, and are attempting to improve it, but rather for initiatives where there is no model in place.

Outcome Mapping

A final approach that has come to be applied to evaluation in complex settings is outcome mapping (OM)—although its origins and orientation were never peacebuilding or conflict-specific.[4] Rooted in contribution analysis thinking, OM is an integrated planning, monitoring and evaluation approach. It takes a learning-based and user-driven view of evaluation and is guided by principles of participation and iterative learning.

At the root of OM, is the notion of identifying strategic actors within a programme's sphere of influence, so that programme actors can credit their *contributions* to social change outcomes, rather than crediting the entire outcome to a single programme in isolation from the rest of the system. Results are consequently calculated by an analysis of 'the changes in behaviour, actions and relationships of those individuals, groups or organisations with whom the initiative is working directly and seeking to influence' (Smutylo, 2005 as quoted in Jones and Hearn, 2009, p. 1). Within the conflict prevention, peacebuilding and humanitarian sub-field, this means that peacebuilding or conflict prevention programmes can accurately acknowledge if their interventions contributed to resolving or preventing conflicts, rather than claiming that their programmes were solely responsible for the end of all violence.

Although OM has been applied in a multitude of contexts, it was originally born as a response to researchers' frustrations over inadequate ways of measuring the reach of research effects beyond a programme, particularly within development research programmes. The history, approaches and considerations of research evaluation are further explored in the next section, which focuses on this specialised sub-field of evaluation.

Constituent Literature 3:
The Evaluation of Research

Constituent literature 3 moves us away from the field of programme and policy evaluation and delves into questions that relate to the evaluation of research, which itself can be considered a specialised sub-field of evaluation. This section presents an overview of the literature on research evaluation and hones in on some of the unique challenges that evaluators of research face.

Evaluation of research has gained new importance in the last decade due to the increased pressure on governments and other funders of public research to allocate funds to researchers and institutions who produce high quality research. Much of the literature in this section stems from debates in the research council funding community in England, Australia and USA, and the controversies that have developed as they modify their research evaluation schemes. However, research evaluation is neither a new topic nor is it exclusive to funding councils and academia. According to Marjanovic, Hanney and Wooding, research evaluation blossomed during the 1960s and 1970s when several studies, particularly in USA, sought to understand, mostly through case studies, if and how research influenced innovation (Marjanovic et al., 2009).

Similarly, while much of the literature on research evaluation concerns academia or university-based research in the Global North and South, there are extra-academic research centres, think tanks, governmental and non-government research institutions that are also interested in research evaluation. These institutions often fund and/or conduct research that is meant to solve societal problems and the outputs may or may not be publishable articles that can be subjected to the traditional research evaluation mechanisms of peer review and bibliometric analysis (see discussion below for more detail on these mechanisms). A research-derived policy brief, for example, may be high quality but may not be considered under the traditional mechanisms of research evaluation. Similar to researchers conducting applied research within academia, these researchers and institutions have also raised concerns about the effectiveness of current research evaluation practices.

Before delving into the fundamental issues that surround research evaluation, two issues merit clarification and discussion. First, it is important to distinguish between the terms 'research' and 'evaluation'. As noted by Bush and Duggan in the introductory chapter of this book, evaluation is generally understood to refer to 'the process of collecting and analysing information in order to judge value, worth or impact' (Butcher and Yaron, 2006, p. 5). *Research* on the other hand has, as Mertens notes, been defined as, 'a systematic method of knowledge construction' (Mertens, 2009, p. 1). As noted by Patton (n.d.),

> because research is driven by the agenda of knowledge production, the standards for evidence are higher, and the time lines for generating knowledge can be longer. In evaluation, there are very concrete deadlines for when decisions have to get made, for when action has to be taken. It often means that the levels of evidence involve less certainty than they would under a research approach and that the time lines are much shorter.

The boundaries between research and evaluation can easily become ambiguous as evaluation may contribute to knowledge construction, and research may employ evaluative logic or analysis. However, while evaluation employs many of the same research techniques to gather empirical information, it is not accorded the status of research (Scriven, 2003, p. 7).

Second, and of equal importance, if we are to broaden our understanding of the value of research within and beyond the university research community, we need to understand how the intersection

Box 2.3
Research Approaches

> *Multi-disciplinary research:* refers to researchers from a variety of disciplines working together at some point during a project, but having separate questions, separate conclusions, and disseminating in different journals.
>
> *Inter-disciplinary research:* refers to researchers interacting with the goal of transferring knowledge from one discipline to another; allowing researchers to inform each other's work and compare individual findings.
>
> *Trans-disciplinary research:* refers to collaborative research in which exchanging altering discipline-specific approaches, sharing resources and integrating disciplines achieves a common scientific goal.

Source: Singh et al. (2013) citing TREC Centers at the Washington University School of Medicine at St. Louis.

of disciplines—that is multi-, inter- or trans-disciplinary research approaches (see Box 2.3)—influences approaches to research evaluation. The standards to which research will be held are influenced by the disciplinary bent of the researchers involved and the process by which a research interacts with and crosses disciplinary boundaries.

The literature discussed in this section focuses broadly on the evaluation of research, with no particular focus on research in VDS. In fact, review of the literature revealed that there is almost no literature about research on or in VDS informing the debates about research evaluation.

Purpose of Evaluation

Excellence in research is desirable in any type of research. However, if the purpose of social change research is to go beyond mere knowledge generation to the generation of knowledge that can be used to improve social and economic outcomes, one could argue that the stakes are higher when findings are meant to influence decisions that affect people's lives, the environment, governance and other areas of development (Méndez, 2012). Research findings gain credibility and chances for their uptake and use tend to increase if they derive from excellent research. Research evaluation, like programme evaluation, can help answer fundamental questions: Is the research effective? (e.g., is it being used for harm or for good?) Linked to this question is the principal question and rationale for research evaluation: How do we know the good research from the bad?

The purpose for evaluating research can vary depending on who is commissioning the evaluation. A funding agency may have different reasons for evaluating than a university research department or a local policy-maker who uses research findings to inform the creation of new policies and programmes. Roughly speaking, the literature groups the rationale for evaluating research into four main categories. The first, according to Marjanovic et al., is 'to increase the accountability of researchers, policy-makers and funding bodies, by making the research process, its outputs and impacts more transparent' (Marjanovic et al., 2009, p. 6). Similar to the evaluation of non-research projects, an evaluation process of this nature seeks to ensure that the researchers have done what they intended to do and that funds have been adequately spent.

Marjanovic et al. also explain that evaluation can help 'steer the research process towards desired outcomes' (2009, p. 6). This implies the type of learning that is usually associated with formative evaluations, where the research project is evaluated prior to its culmination and where the learning can lead to improvements, perhaps by adjusting research design, methods, mechanisms of analysis or management.

The third rationale also considers learning, albeit the learning occurs once a research project has concluded and lessons can be drawn to inform strategic or managerial decisions about future research. For example, evaluation findings about the relevance of a research topic can inform questions, hypotheses or even new lines of research that the institution may want to pursue in the future. Similarly, findings about the effectiveness or efficiency of the research process can inform managerial decisions.

The fourth and last suggested rationale has to do with evaluations that are conducted to prove research process or research output quality in order to advocate for the research team. This is the case of evaluations that are used to inform funding decisions. The evaluation signals the ability of a team to conduct good quality research, which determines future levels of funding (Marjanovic et al., 2009).

While these are the main recurrent research evaluation purposes, review of the literature also suggests others. Research funders across the board—public and private—are often interested (for different reasons) in evaluating the research they support to understand whether they are getting *value* for the money invested. This line of motivation is frequently pursued through the conduct of socioeconomic impact evaluation, a specific approach to evaluation that focuses on calculating, through the use of economic valuation methods, the 'social return on investment' (SROI) of interventions (including research). While SROI attempts to quantify and monetise the socioeconomic and environmental benefits of research are in many ways problematic and controversial, funder demands for *value for money* are pushing research evaluators to innovate and constantly question and improve practice.[5]

Review boards at peer-review journals evaluate research with the purpose of determining whether it meets the publication standards of a particular field, while there are others, like Van Raan who holds that the purpose of evaluating research is to 'to promote research quality' (Van Raan, 1996, p. 398). This preoccupation gives rise to an additional purpose for evaluating research, one that harnesses considerations of programme evaluation to research evaluation. As noted by Knox in this book, research is one of the fundamental building blocks of programme theory. Donors of peacebuilding and development projects and programmes use research to form the basis of the change theories that underlie the initiatives they fund. Evaluating the quality of that research—its relevance, methodological soundness, scientific merit, etc.—is essential for challenging assumptions and questioning the foundations upon which international aid initiatives are built.

Evaluation Approaches

Similar to programme evaluation, approaches in research evaluation depend largely on the purpose of the evaluation and the epistemological orientation of the evaluation commissioner and the evaluator. However, unlike programme evaluation, there are particularities about research that make selecting an approach more cumbersome. Deciding what approach to use when evaluating research is perhaps the most contested aspect of research evaluation. One reason for this difficulty is that there are various types of research and each one requires a nuanced approach to evaluation.

In 1997, Donald Stokes put forward the proposition that research can be classified along two dimensions: whether it advances human knowledge by seeking a fundamental understanding of nature; or whether it is primarily motivated by the need to solve immediate problems (see Figure 2.2; Ofir and Schwandt, 2012).

Stokes divides research into three distinct classes:

1.   Pure basic research (exemplified by the work of Niels Bohr, the early 20th century atomic physicist).

Figure 2.2
Research Classification

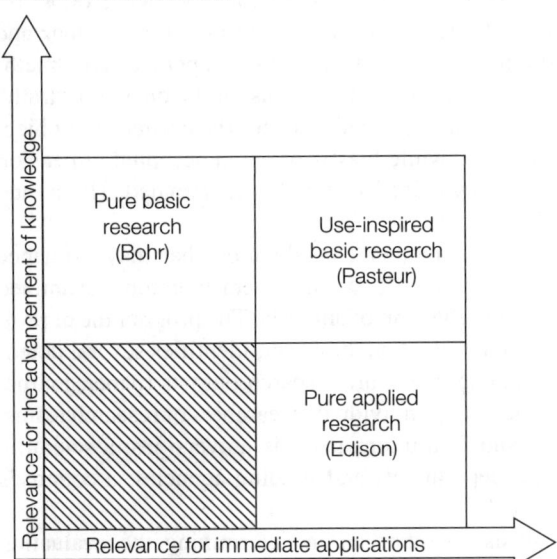

Source: Ofir and Schwandt (2012).

2. Pure applied research (exemplified by the work of Thomas Edison, inventor)

3. Use-inspired research (exemplified by the work of Louis Pasteur, pioneering 19th century chemist and microbiologist) (Ofir and Schwandt, 2012).

When determining the evaluation approach, the evaluator needs to consider whether it is applied or basic research that is under review since the approach used to evaluate applied research may consider the practical applications or use of that research, which may not be a consideration when evaluating basic research (Furlong and Oancea, 2005). Use-inspired applied research may require even further considerations.

The concern about research types extends to revolutionary research, which is generally understood to be research that moves beyond well-established fields and that is trying to break new ground by challenging basic assumptions or involving a paradigm shift (Andras, 2011). A similar concern emerges when evaluating interdisciplinary research. Most disciplines have their own standards for research quality. RCTs, for example, are considered the gold standard in healthcare research.

However, their value in the social sciences is increasingly questioned, among other reasons, because of the assumption that two groups living in a complex social environment can have parallel trends. Boaz and Ashby explain this problem from an epistemological perspective: 'methodological debates in the natural sciences focus on the quest for "truth" and the elimination of bias. In the social sciences the existence of objective truth is often contested, while bias is often an accepted dimension of knowledge, to be acknowledged rather than eliminated' (Boaz and Ashby, 2003, p. 9).

The unit of analysis is another consideration that may influence the evaluation approach. The first two constituent literatures examined included a clear and identifiable unit of analysis: The programme or project. Literature on research evaluation, however, identifies several potential units of analysis, among which are research outputs (paper, journal article, book, policy brief, etc.); individual researchers or research teams; scientific laboratories and institutions such as universities; a scientific discipline; government departments and funding agencies; a country's entire research base, etc.

The unit of analysis is important in determining the evaluation approach because it will determine what should and should not be considered in the evaluation. Take for example the new mechanism for research evaluation that the Higher Education Funding Council for England started to use in 2014, the Research Excellence Framework (REF). The REF considers departments within higher-level education institutions as the unit of analysis. The evaluation framework considers research outputs and impacts but given that the unit of analysis is research departments where researchers also have teaching and grant writing responsibilities, the framework must also consider things like doctoral degrees awarded, research income and research income in kind. Considerations of this nature have been grouped under a third aspect of the framework labelled 'research environment'. In a context where evaluation is conducted to inform funding, such as with the REF, such considerations become critical since omission of the research environment may incentivise researchers to focus strictly on research, therefore potentially compromising their teaching duties.

Methodological Practice

Although there are a variety of methods used to evaluate research, peer-review processes and bibliometric analysis are by far the most used and also the most controversial. Much of the discussion in this section will focus on those two methods with the recognition that due to their many shortcomings, several research evaluation exercises have used other methods such a self-evaluation, historical ratings, benchmarking, case studies, mixed approaches and even computerised semantic analysis. This wealth of different and sometimes new approaches suggests that research evaluators recognise the flaws of peer review and bibliometrics and are attempting to overcome them by complimenting them with creative and new methods. Be this as it may, peer review and biblometric analysis continue to dominate evaluation research practice.

Wooding and Grant (2003, p. 20) define peer review as

> a system in which experts make a professional judgment on the performance of individuals or groups, over a specified cycle, and/or their likely performance in the future. The groups could be research groups, departments or consortia. Assessment may be undertaken entirely by peers or may incorporate other experts such as representatives of user groups, lay people, and financial experts.

Peer review is often tied to publication since it is peer-review boards at journals and other publishing enterprises that determine what is publishable and what is not. Although peer review is the most commonly used method to evaluate research, a study that involved 142 research stakeholders in England noted that it also has the 'least good features and most bad features' in comparison to the other methods (Wooding and Grant, 2003, p. 25). Since peer review is based on people's opinion, it is criticised for its subjectivity and for the unhealthy competition that it generates among peers. Furthermore, since the review is often solely of research outputs, an evaluation based on peer or expert review often misses the research process, therefore missing potential learning opportunities.

Additional criticism comes from certain types of research, such as interdisciplinary and revolutionary research, which face several challenges including finding the right expertise for the review panels and overcoming the conservative tendencies of influential peers. Peer review can be time and resource intensive; it is sometimes unable to detect fraud and does not guarantee relevance to policy-making or compliance with methodological standards.

Despite the flaws, peer review continues to be the method of choice. After reviewing the benefits and challenges of peer review and other research evaluation methods, the 142 research stakeholders involved in the study cited earlier were asked to gather in groups to design their ideal method. Despite the many flaws they cited, 22 out of the 29 groups based their ideal system on an expert review process.

Bibliometrics, or arithmetical calculations of various publication rates, are the other dominant method used in research evaluation processes. Bibliometrics consist of

> publication count in a defined list of venues (journals, conference proceedings) by individuals, departments or universities, the citation count of these publications over a defined period of time, indexes calculated using these counts (e.g., h-index), metrics derived from citations and authorship graphs, and market share measures. (Andras, 2011, p. 90)

Bibliometrics offer various advantages over peer review: They are considered more objective, less burdensome and cheaper indicators of research quality.

However, despite the alleged benefits, even supporters agree that bibliometrics have many shortcomings and should not be used as sole indicators of research quality. The main problem with this type of measure is their validity, for they are not intrinsic indicators of quality but proxies that are generated after research outputs have gone through a peer-review mechanism and are then published. As Boaz and Ashby explain, 'it is a faulty assumption that all research that is published in journals or cited by others is accurate, reliable, valid, free of bias, non-fraudulent, or of sufficient quality' (Boaz and Ashby, 2003, p. 2).

Bibliometrics are also criticised because they generate negative incentives for researchers, especially in academia, to focus on publishing rather than on teaching or on producing outputs that may be more relevant to policy or other vehicles for social change. In addition, there is a strong bias favouring research produced in English or dealing with topics that are of interest to review boards in Northern-led, mostly English language journals. Researchers from the Global South are, thus, at a disadvantage because the research questions that are relevant in their context, in their language or the type of research output format they favour (i.e., policy or practice brief) may not be considered in the publication venues that calculate bibliometrics. This may generate the erroneous impression that research is of low quality when in reality, low citation or publication rates may be only a reflection of different languages, research priorities or indeed the purpose of the research in question (Tijssen et al., 2006).

Something similar occurs for researchers who are working on innovative or revolutionary research or science. This group may sometimes find it hard to get their research published because their ideas or findings may not interest journal review boards since they are considered unorthodox or ahead of their time. Publication or citation rates of these researchers may, therefore, not reflect the novelty, quality or importance of their research. Young researchers must also compete with more experienced researchers whose name may carry more weight in publication spheres, despite the quality of the research under consideration.

Another area of improvement for bibliometrics is in their uneven coverage of different disciplines. Coryn explains how the arts are at particular disadvantage since their work is usually expressed in forms, such as recital or painting, that are not publishable or citable (Coryn, 2006). Negative citations are also an issue with bibliometrics, given that a research paper may be heavily cited because of its many shortcomings. The same occurs with measures of paper downloads (as an indicator) since a paper may be deemed low quality after it is downloaded.

At the heart of the critiques that have been levelled against both peer review and bibliometrics is the concern that both of these mechanisms focus on one specific type of output: scholarly publications in journals with high impact factors. Implicitly, such an approach treats outputs as outcomes. The *success* of research is measured by publication within international peer-reviewed journals. This is taken to constitute evidence of both international esteem and good research practice. Additionally, it is assumed to constitute effective research communication and dissemination. In contrast to the evaluation practice under constituent literatures 1 and 2, there is little discussion of tangible outcomes in the way that programme evaluation would demand. In a nutshell, the main limitation of both of these methods is that they are primarily interested in the contribution that research makes to the advancement of scholarly knowledge—researchers influencing researchers.

This reality is particularly important for research for international development which may not be generated for the purposes of academic or scholarly advancement. This would include research for influencing policy and practice, undertaken by the broad research and policy-shaping communities that include think tanks, not-for-profit firms, and governmental, non-governmental and inter-governmental actors.

What Counts as Evidence?

Evaluating research excellence is vitally important in both academic and non-academic spheres. It is a simple fact that not all research is of the same quality. Without rigorous examination of research quality, a false equivalence is made between all research endeavours, leading to a poor understanding of the phenomena involved. When it comes to evidence based policy-making or decision-making, the inability to distinguish between good and bad research can lead to counter-productive policies and ineffective solutions.

It is necessary to evaluate research quality for any policy research/academic research organisation. That is because assessment of the quality of research can provide a very useful indication of whether the organisation is fulfilling its purpose or not, and what role is being played by research work of the organisation in this regard.

The two comments above, offered by two researchers located in the Global South under the umbrella of a study on perceptions of research excellence (Singh et al., 2013, pp. 11–12), demonstrate not only why considerations of quality and use are important, but also that *excellence* acquires meaning only in context. Defining quality or excellence in research is perhaps the most contentious fundamental issue in determining a research evaluation approach. As mentioned earlier, different disciplines have different quality standards, so it is a challenge to attempt to come up with a universal definition of research quality or excellence. In fact, these two terms, which are often used interchangeably, mean different things to different people. A useful distinction is provided by Grant, Brutscher, Kirk, Butler and Wooding who, referring to the REF, suggest that the distinction between quality and excellence is that excellence is a broader dimension comprising both quality and research impacts (Grant et al., 2010). However, this distinction in terms does not answer the questions of what is meant by research quality or research impacts. The following sections will address some of those questions.

Most definitions of research quality consider the methodological and technical aspects of research. For example, quality research has been described as comprising

> the scientific process encompassing all aspects of study design; in particular, it pertains to the judgment regarding the match between the methods and questions, selection of subjects, measurement of outcomes, and protection against systematic bias, non-systematic bias, and inferential error. (National Center for the Dissemination of Disability Research, 2005, p. 2)

However, a review of over 30 sets of research quality standards suggests that quality criteria can be grouped conceptually under five categories:

scientific merit, ethics, originality, relevance and purposivity. Under this classification, scientific merit comprises different forms for validity, soundness and rigour of methods and a logical interpretation of data (Méndez, 2012).

The ethical dimension of research, which is discussed by Jayawickrama and Strecker in this book and which is an area of particular importance in VDS, stems primarily from the principle of do no harm (as discussed under constituent literature 2). However, it is also related to the tension between the transparency required for accountability purposes and the need to ensure the safety and security of stakeholders. So too is it nested in the political sensitivities around the evaluation process (especially collaborative processes), as well as the volatile environment within which it is undertaken.

In a study with over 250 research stakeholders, it was found that originality as an element of research quality 'revolved around viewing existing issues, ideas or data in a new or different way, more so than generating new data or novel methods. Originality involved, also, the development of new theoretical and practical insights and concepts' (Becker et al., 2006, p. 12).

Relevance in research, as described by Boaz and Ashby refers to 'the extent to which the research addresses the needs of key stakeholders' (Boaz and Ashby, 2003, p. 12). Unlike impact, which occurs once the research is carried out, research relevance can be determined beforehand by looking at the research questions and determining whether it is significant for the discipline or for society.

Finally, purposivity speaks to the quality of research that Aagaard-Hansen and Svedin associate with having a well-formulated research question that is supported by relevant literature and that guides the research to meet a specific purpose (Aagaard-Hansen and Svedin, 2009).

Evidence of Impacts

In the introductory chapter of this book, Bush and Duggan emphasise that one of the key messages of this publication is 'the importance of appropriate approaches to, and methods for, evaluating the effects or "impacts" of research' (Bush and Duggan, Chapter 1). Research evaluation has indeed attempted to address the role of impact in determining research excellence. While there are no definite answers, much of the recent literature on research impacts has attempted to address three main questions: What is meant by research impacts? How do we measure research impacts? And, should research impacts be considered an element of research excellence?

While there is no clear consensus of what constitutes *research impact*, a number of researchers have explored this area in some depth. In a project launched by the London School of Economics (LSE) in 2011, research impact is understood to be 'an occasion of influence and hence ... not the same thing as a change in outputs or activities as a result of that influence, still less a change in social outcomes' (LSE Public Policy Group, 2011, p. 21).

In 2003, Nutley, Percy-Smith and Solesbury conducted a thorough literature review on research impact and distinguished between the conceptual and instrumental use of research, wherein conceptual use consists of 'changes in levels of understanding, knowledge, and attitude' and instrumental use includes 'results in changes in practice and policy making' (Nutley et al., 2003, p. 11). Similarly, the LSE project mentioned above makes a distinction between academic and external impacts. Academic impacts refer to instances when research influences actors in academia or universities and external impacts occur when research influences actors outside of academia, such as businesses, governments or civil society. Donovan refers to these distinctions as academic and extra-academic impacts (Donovan, 2008).

However, even if an evaluation clearly specifies the meaning and parameters of research impact, the path of research influence is typically erratic and unpredictable, making measurement and attribution of impacts a challenge. As discussed above, a few bibliometric measures, such as the journal impact factor and citation counts, have been used as indicators of impact. Non-bibliometric mechanisms have also been used, such as the case study approach used by the UK RAND/Arthritis Research Campaign Impact scoring system (RAISS), the self-evaluation approach used by the US Programme Assessment Rating Tool (Grant et al., 2010), and SROI approaches, as noted earlier. However, these too face the challenge of attributing causation.

Finally, there are authors who challenge the idea that research impacts should be considered an element of research excellence. Such criticism has emerged from circumstances in the UK where research evaluation is conducted with the purpose to inform future funding. Opponents argue that the focus on impacts that is promoted by such an *investment model* overlooks the primary value of research to produce new knowledge. That, in turn, can generate incentives that, according to Hammersley, may 'be at odds with any commitment to research informing public discussion of policy issues, since it frames inquiry within assumptions about predictable payoff' (Hammersley, 2008, p. 753).

In recent years, evidence of impact, as a fundamental issue in research evaluation, has expanded and come to focus more pointedly on research effectiveness, a notion that includes research use, influence and impact. The contribution that research can make to solving problems at a societal level is increasingly being questioned with a greater importance placed on the role of research within a knowledge-based economy as well as on the more overt demands from government and other funders for scientific contributions to the development and progression of society. As a result, there is increasing emphasis being placed on economic and social impacts, as well as on how funded research meets the needs of policy-makers and the broader population of stakeholders. Nowhere is this more evident than in the evaluation literature on policy-oriented research (see Boaz and Ashby, 2003; Carden, 2009; ODI, 2004).

The introduction of knowledge-for-action theories such as knowledge utilisation, implementation, diffusion, transfer or translation into evaluation practice has assisted research evaluators in developing more nuanced approaches to tracing impact trajectories and understanding how knowledge contributes to social change, including policy change (Ottoson, 2009). This evolution in evaluation practice reflects a growing recognition, among those who produce and use research, that research effectiveness should include some social change intent, highlighting the need for more integration between research uptake, policy and (presumably) practice.[6] Researchers are being asked more explicitly to demonstrate the relevance and utility of their work to solving *real-world problems*.

Towards a Literature on the Evaluation of Research in and on Violently Divided Societies

Figure 2.1, in the introductory section of this chapter, identifies the constituent literatures within which the current book is nested. The chapters which follow represent contributions to the development of a body of literature which is still at the earliest stages of formation. The diversity of themes, types of research, perspectives and cases in the following chapters are an accurate reflection of the heterogeneity and complexity of the sub-field we seek to explore. The current chapter is meant to demonstrate that, while we may be entering uncharted territory (Bush and Duggan,

Chapter 1), we are not without the tools and sensibilities that have been cultivated over the last 70 years of evaluation research and practice.

Notes

1. John A. and John R. Healy examine in further detail the implications that epistemology has on research funder evaluation practices in Chapter 8 of this book.
2. See http://www.berghof-handbook.net, 2005 for a discussion of standardisation.
3. See Conner et al. (2012) framework for context assessment in evaluation.
4. The OM manual is freely available online. A virtual collective of evaluation practitioners contributes and document the growth of OM, highlights synergies with other evaluation approaches and explores the applicability of OM in new fields; www.outcomemapping.ca
5. Unfortunately, a more complete examination of SRIO approaches to research performance and evaluation is beyond the scope of the current chapter.
6. Chapter 6 (Kevin Kelly) in this book includes an empiric case study which employs the influence frameworks emerging from the policy research literature.

References

Aagaard-Hansen, J. and Svedin, U. (2009). Quality issues in cross-disciplinary research: Towards a two-pronged approach to evaluation. *Social Epistemology*, *23*(2), 165–176.

Alkin, Marvin C. (1972, December). Wider context goals and goals-based evaluators. *Evaluation Comment: The Journal of Educational Evaluation*, *3*(4), 10–11.

American Evaluation Association. (2003). American Evaluation Association position on 'Scientifically based evaluation methods'. Retrieved from www.eval.org (accessed on 1 June 2015).

Anderson, M. B. (1999). *Do no harm: How aid can support peace—or war*. Boulder, CO: Lynne Rienner.

Anderson, M. (2004). *Experiences with impact assessment: Can we know what good we do?* Berlin: Berghof Research Centre for Conflict Management.

Andras, P. (2011). Research: Metrics, quality, and management implications. *Research Evaluation*, *20*(2), 90–106.

Bamberger, M., Rugh, J. and Mabry, L. (2006). *Real world evaluation: Working under budget, time, data, and political constraints*. Thousand Oaks, CA: SAGE Publications.

Barbolet, A., Goldwyn, R., Groenewald, H. and Sherriff, A. (2005). The utility and dilemmas of conflict sensitivity. In B. Bloomfield, M. Fischer and B. Schmelzle (Eds), *Dialogue series no 4—New trends in peace and conflict impact assessment (PCIA)*. Berlin: Berghof Research Center for Constructive Conflict Management.

Becker, S., Bryman, A. and Sempik, J. (2006). *Defining 'quality' in social policy research: Views, perceptions and a framework for discussion*. Lavenham, UK: Social Policy Association.

Befani, B. Barnett, C. and Stern, E. (2014). Introduction—Rethinking impact evaluation. *IDS Bulletin*, *45*(6). Retrieved from http://onlinelibrary.wiley.com/doi/10.1111/1759-5436.12108/epdf (accessed on 2 February 2015).

Boaz, A. and Ashby, D. (2003). *Fit for purpose? Assessing research quality for evidence based policy and practice*. ESRC UK Centre for Evidence Based Policy and Practice, Working Paper 11. Retrieved from https://www.kcl.ac.uk/sspp/departments/politicaleconomy/research/cep/pubs/papers/assets/wp11.pdf (accessed on 20 July 2015).

Braskamp, L. A., Brandenburg, D. C. and Ory, J. C. (1987). Lessons about clients' expectations. In J. Nowakowski (Ed.), *The client perspective on evaluation: New directions for program evaluation* (No. 36). San Francisco: Jossey-Bass.

Bush, K. (1998). A measure of peace: Peace and conflict impact assessment of development projects in zones of conflict. *Working Paper No. 1; The Peacebuilding and Reconstruction Program Initiative and The Evaluation Unit Ottawa: International Development Research Centre*. Retrieved from http://web.idrc.ca/uploads/user-S/10533919790A_Measure_of_Peace.pdf (accessed on 22 April 2015).

———. (2001). Peace and conflict impact assessment (PCIA) five years on: The commodification of an idea. In A. Austin., M. Fischer and O. Wils (Eds), *Dialogue Series No. 1—Peace and conflict impact assessment*. Berlin: Berghof Research Center for Constructive Conflict Management. Retrieved from http://www.berghof-handbook. net/documents/publications/dialogue1_bush.pdf (accessed on 27 April 2015).

———. (2003). PCIA five years on: The commodification of an idea. In Alexander Austin, Martina Fischer and Oliver Wils (Eds), *Berghof Handbook Dialogue Series No. 1: Peace and conflict impact assessment. Critical views on theory and practice* (pp. 37–51). Berlin: Berghof Centre for Constructive Conflict Management.

———. (2005). Field notes—Fighting commodification and disempowerment in the development industry: Things I learned about peace and conflict impact assessment (PCIA) in Habarana and Mindanao. In D. Bloomfield, M. Fischer and B. Schmelzle (Eds), *Dialogue series no. 4: New trends in peace and conflict impact assessment (PCIA)*. Berlin: Berghof Research Center for Constructive Conflict Management. Retrieved from http://www.berghof-handbook.net/documents/publications/dialogue4_bush.pdf (accessed on 22 April 2015).

Butcher, C. and Yaron, G. (2006). *Scoping study: Monitoring and evaluation of research communications*. Background paper produced for the Communications M&E Group Workshop, 5–6 September 2006, London.

Carden, F. (2009). *Knowledge to policy: Making the most of development research*. Ottawa and Delhi: International Development Research Centre and SAGE India. Retrieved from http://web.idrc.ca/openebooks/417-8/ (accessed on 27 April 2015).

Chambers, R. (2010). *Paradigms, poverty and adaptive pluralism* (IDS Working Paper 344). Brighton: The Institute of Development Studies, University of Sussex. Retrieved from http://www.ids.ac.uk/files/dmfile/Wp344.pdf (accessed on 22 April 2015).

Chigas, D, Church, M. and Corlazzoli, V. (2014). *Evaluating impact of peacebuilding interventions: Approaches and methods, challenges and considerations* (DFID Commissioned Report). London: Department of International Development. Retrieved from http://www.cdacollaborative.org/publications/reflecting-on-peace-practice/rpp-guidance-materials/evaluating-impacts-of-peacebuilding-interventions-approaches-and-methods,-challenges-and-considerations/ (accessed on 20 June 2015).

Chouinard, J. and Cousins, J. B. (2009). A review and synthesis of current research on cross-cultural evaluation. *American Journal of Evaluation, 30*(4), 457–494.

Christie C. A. (Ed.). (2003). What guides evaluation? A study of how evaluation practice maps onto evaluation theory. In *The practice-theory relationship in evaluation: New directions for evaluation* (pp. 7–36). San Francisco, CA: Jossey-Bass.

Christie, C. A. and Fleischer, D. N. (2009). Social inquiry paradigms as a frame for the debate on credible evidence. In S. I. Donaldson, C. A. Christie and M. M. Mark (Eds), *What counts as credible evidence in applied research and evaluation practice?* (pp. 19–30). Thousand Oaks, CA: SAGE Publications.

Church, C. (2011). Evaluating peacebuilding: Not yet all it could be. *Berghof Series.* Retrieved from http://www.berghof-handbook.net/documents/publications/ scharbatke_church_handbook.pdf (accessed on 23 April 2015).

Church, C. and Rogers, M. M. (Eds). (2006). Ethics in evaluation. *Designing for results: Integrating, monitoring & evaluation in conflict transformation programs* (pp. 188–200). Washington, DC: Search for Common Ground. Retrieved from http:// www.sfcg.org/Documents/dmechapter11.pdf (accessed on 22 April 2015).

Clinton, T., Nunes-Neto, B. and Williams, E. (2006). *Congress and program evaluation: An overview of randomized control trials (RCTs) and related issues.* Congressional Research Service, Library of Congress. Hauppauge, New York: Nova Science Publishers.

Conflict Sensitivity Consortium. (2004). An introduction to conflict-sensitive approaches to development, humanitarian assistance and peacebuilding tools for peace and conflict impact assessment (Chapter 2). *Resource Pack.* Retrieved from http://www. conflictsensitivity.org/publications/conflict-sensitive-approaches-development- humanitarian-assistance-and-peacebuilding-res (accessed on 20 June 2015).

Conley-Tyler, M. (2005, March/April). A fundamental choice: Internal or external evaluation. *Evaluation Journal of Australasia, 4* (new series, 1 and 2), 3–11.

Cook, T., Scriven, M., Coryn, C. and Evergreen, S. (2010). Contemporary thinking about causation in evaluation: A dialogue with Tom Cook and Michael Scriven. *American Journal of Evaluation, 31*(1), 105–117.

Coryn, C. L., Westine, C. and Schroter, D. (2011). A systematic review of theory- driven evaluation practice from 1990 to 2009. *American Journal of Evaluation, 32*(2), 199–226.

Coryn, C. L. S. (2006). The use and abuse of citations as indicators of research quality. *Journal of MultiDisciplinary Evaluation, 3*(4), 115–121.

Cosgrave, J., Ramalingam, B. and Beck, T. (2009). *Real-time evaluations of humanitarian action. An ALNAP guide.* London: Overseas Development Institute. Retrieved from http://www.alnap.org/pool/files/rteguide.pdf (accessed on 5 June 2015).

Cousins J. B. (2011, November 23). *Participatory evaluation: Theory, research, practice.* Presentation at IDRC, New Delhi.

Cousins J. B. and Whitmore E. (1998). Framing participatory evaluation. *New Directions for Evaluation, 80*(Winter), 5–23.

Cox, P. J., Keener, D., Woodard, T. and Wandersman, A. (2009). *Evaluation for improvement—A seven-step empowerment evaluation approach for violence prevention organisations.* Atlanta, GA: Centres for Disease Control and Prevention. Retrieved from http://www.cdc.gov/violenceprevention/pdf/evaluation_ improvement-a.pdf (accessed on 22 April 2015).

Datta, L. (2001). Mixed methods evaluation: The wheelbarrow, the mosaic and the double helix. *Evaluation Journal of Australasia, 1*(2), 33–40.

Davidson, J. (2000). Ascertaining causality in theory-based evaluation. *New Directions for Evaluation, 200*(87), 17–26.

Donaldson, S. I. (2009a). A practitioner's guide for gathering credible evidence in the evidence-based global society. In S. I. Donaldson, C. A. Christie and M. M. Mark

(Eds), *What counts as credible evidence in applied research and evaluation practice?* Thousand Oaks, CA: SAGE Publications.

Donaldson, S. I. (2009b). In search of the blueprint for an evidence-based global society. In S. I. Donaldson, C. A. Christie and M. M. Mark (Eds), *What counts as credible evidence in applied research and evaluation practice?* (pp. 2–18). Thousand Oaks, CA: SAGE Publications.

Donovan, C. (2008). The Australian research quality framework: A live experiment in capturing the social, economic, environmental, and cultural returns of publicly funded research. *New Directions for Evaluation, 2008*(118), 47–60.

Drewett, A. (1997). Evaluation and consultation. learning lessons. *Evaluation 3*(2), 189–204. Retrieved from http://evi.sagepub.com/content/3/2.toc (accessed on 22 April 2015).

Duggan, C. (2010). Guest editorial.Special issue: Transitional justice on trial: Evaluating its impact. *International Journal of Transitional Justice. 4*(3), 315–328.

Fitzpatrick, J. (2004). Exemplars as case studies: Reflections on the links between theory, practice and context. *American Journal of Evaluation, 25*(4), 541–59.

Furlong, J. and Oancea, A. (2005). *Assessing quality in applied and practice-based ducational research.* Oxford: Oxford University Department of Educational Studies.

Georghiou, L. and Laredo, P. (2005, September). *Evaluation of publicly funded research*: Report on the Berlin workshop, 26–27 September 2005. Paris: OECD.

Grant, J., Brutscher, P. B., Guthrie, S., Butler, L. and Wooding, S. (2010). *Capturing research impacts: A review of international practice.* Santa Monica, CA: RAND Corporation.

Greene, J. (1997). Advancing mixed-method evaluation. *The Evaluation Exchange, 3*(1). Retrieved from http://www.hfrp.org/evaluation/the-evaluation-exchange/issue-archive/methodology/advancing-mixed-method-evaluation (accessed on 20 June 2015).

Guba, E. G. and Lincoln, Y. S. (1989). *Fourth generation evaluation.* Newbury Park: SAGE Publications.

Hammersley, M. (2008). Troubling criteria: A critical commentary on Furlong and Oancea's framework for assessing educational research. *British Educational Research Journal, 34*(6), 747–762.

House, E. R. (1980). *Evaluating with validity.* Beverly Hills, CA: SAGE Publications.

International Alert et al. (2004). *Conflict-sensitive approaches to development, humanitarian assistance, and peacebuilding.* London: International Alert.

Jones, H. and Hearn, S. (2009). Outcome mapping: a realistic alternative for planning, monitoring and evaluation *ODI Background Notes.* London: Overseas Development Institute.

Love, A. (1991). Internal evaluation: Building organisations from within. *Applied Social Research Methods Series* (Vol. 24). Newbury Park, CA: SAGE Publications.

Luukkonen, T. (2002). Research evaluation in Europe: State of the art. *Research Evaluation, 11*(2), 81–84.

LSE Public Policy Group. (2011). *Maximizing the impacts of your research: A handbook for social scientists.* London: LSE Public Policy Group.

Marjanovic, S., Hanney, S. and Wooding, S. (2009). *A historical reflection on research evaluation studies, their recurrent themes and challenges* (pp. 7–12). Cambridge: RAND Corporation.

Mark, M. M. (2003). Toward an integrative view of the theory and practice of program and policy evaluation. In S. I. Donaldson and M. Scriven (Eds), *Evaluating social programs and problems: Visions for the new millennium* (pp. 109–141). Mahwah, NJ: Erlbaum.

Mathison, S. (2009). Seeing is believing: The credibility of image-based research and evaluation. In S. I. Donaldson, C. A. Christie and M. M. Mark (Eds), *What counts as credible evidence in applied research and evaluation practice?* Thousand Oaks, CA: SAGE Publications.

McCoy, M. and Hargie, O. D. W. (2001). Evaluating evaluation: Implications for assessing quality. *International Journal of Health Care Quality Assurance, 14*(7), 317–327.

Méndez, E. (2012). *What's in 'Good'?* Ottawa: International Development Research Centre. Retrieved from http://www.idrc.ca/EN/Documents/Lit-review-Final-English. pdf (accessed on 7 April 2015).

Mertens, D. (2001). Inclusivity and transformation: Evaluation in 2010. *American Journal of Evaluation, 22*(3), 367–374.

———. (2009). *Transformative research and evaluation.* New York: Guildford Press.

Molund, S. and Schill, G. (2004). *Looking back, moving forward: Evaluation manual.* Stockholm: SIDA Publications. Retrieved from http://www.oecd.org/development/ evaluation/dcdndep/47470919.pdf (accessed on 27 April 2015).

National Center for the Dissemination of Disability Research. (2005). *What are the standards for quality research?* (Focus: Technical Brief Number 9). Retrieved from http://www.ncddr.org/kt/products/focus/focus9/ (accessed on 23 April 2015).

Nutley, S., Percy-Smith, J. and Solesbury, W. (2003). *Models of research impact: A cross-sector review of literature and practice.* London: Learning and Skills Research Centre.

Overseas Development Institute (ODI). (2009). *Research and policy in development (RAPID): Toolkits.* Retrieved from http://www.odi.org.uk/RAPID/Tools/Toolkits/ index.html (accessed on 22 April 2015).

OECD. (2011). *Evaluating conflict prevention and peacebuilding activities. Lessons from the application phase. Chairman's summary.*Paris: OECD. Retrieved from http:// www.oecd.org/dac/evaluationofdevelopmentprogrammes/dcdndep/48092571.pdf (accessed on 22 April 2015).

———. (2012). *DAC guidelines and references series: Evaluating peacebuilding activities in settings of conflict and fragility—Improving learning for results.* Paris: OECD Publishing. Retrieved from http://dx.doi.org/10.1787/9789264106802-en (accessed on 23 April 2015).

Ofir, Z. and Schwandt, T. (2012). *Understanding research excellence at IDRC.* Ottawa: International Development Research Centre.

Ottoson, J. (2009). Knowledge-for-action theories in evaluation: Knowledge utilization, diffusion, implementation, transfer and translation. *New Directions in Evaluation 2009* (124), 7–20.

Overseas Development Institute, Research and Policy in Development (RAPID) programme. (2004, October). *Bridging research and policy in international development: An analytical and practical framework* (Briefing Paper). London: ODI. Retrieved from http://www.odi.org/sites/odi.org.uk/files/odi-assets/publications-opinion-files/198.pdf (accessed on 17 April 2015).

Parlett, M. and Hamilton, D. (1977). Evaluation as illumination. In M. Parlett and G. Dearden (Eds), *Introduction to illuminative evaluation: Studies in higher education.* Columbus, Ohio: Ohio State University Press.

Patton, M. Q. (1997). *Utilization focused evaluation: The new century text* (3rd ed.). London: SAGE Publications.

Patton, M. Q. (2001). *Qualitative research & evaluation methods* (3rd ed.). Thousand Oaks, CA: SAGE Publications.

———. (2008). *Utilization focused evaluation* (4th ed.). Thousand Oaks, CA: SAGE Publications.

———. (2010). *Developmental evaluation: Applying complexity concepts to enhance innovation and use.* NY: New York: Guildford Press.

———. (2012). *Essentials of utilization-focused evaluation.* Thousand Oaks, CA: SAGE Publications.

———. (n.d.). In conversation: Michael Quinn Patton. Retrieved from http://www.idrc.ca/en/themes/evaluation/pages/articledetails.aspx?publicationid=771 (accessed on 5 June 2015).

Podems. (2005). *Nonprofit evaluation in South Africa: A study of relationships between the donor and nonprofit organisation in the developing World* (PhD Dissertation). Union Institute at University, Cincinnati, OH.

Preskill, H. and Russ-Eft, D. (2005). *Building evaluation capacity: 72 activities for teaching and training.* Thousand Oaks, CA: SAGE Publications.

Rallis, S. F. (2009). Reasoning with rigor and probity: Ethical premises for credible evidence. In S. I. Donaldson, C. A. Christie and M. M. Mark (Eds), *What counts as credible evidence in applied research and evaluation practice?* Thousand Oaks, CA: SAGE Publications.

Ramalingam B. and Jones, H. (2008). *Exploring the science of complexity: Ideas and implications for development and humanitarian efforts* (Working Paper 285). London: Overseas Development Institute. Retrieved from http://www.odi.org.uk/sites/odi.org.uk/files/odi-assets/publications-opinion-files/833.pdf (accessed on 22 April 2015).

Rogers, P. J., Petrosino, A., Huebner, T. A. and Hacsi, T. A. (2000). Program theory evaluation: Practice, promise, and problems. *New Directions for Evaluation* (No. 87). San Francisco, CA: Jossey-Bass.

Rossi, P. and Freeman, H. (1989). *Evaluation: A systematic approach* (4th ed.). Newbury Park, CA: SAGE Publications.

Rossi, P. H. and Lipsey, M. W. (2004). *Evaluation: A systematic approach.* London: SAGE Publications.

Rutnik, T. and Campbell, M. (2002). *When and how to use external evaluators* (Briefing Paper I: Monitoring and Evaluation). Baltimore, MD: Association of Baltimore Grantmakers.

Savedoff, William D., Levine, R., Birdsall, N. et al. (2006). *When will we ever learn? Improving lives through impact evaluation.* Washington, DC: Centre for Global Development. Retrieved from http://www.cgdev.org/files/7973_file_WillWeEverLearn.pdf (accessed on 23 April 2015).

Schmelzle, B. (2005). New trends in peace and conflict impact assessment: introduction. In *Dialogue Series No. 4: Berghof handbook for conflict transformation.* Berlin: Berghof Research Center for Constructive Conflict Management. Retrieved from http://www.berghof-foundation.org/fileadmin/redaktion/Publications/Handbook/Dialogue_Chapters/dialogue4_pcianew_intro.pdf (accessed on 23 April 2015).

Scriven, M. (1972). Prose and cons about goal-free evaluation. *Evaluation Comment, 3*(4), 1–7.

———. (1991). *Evaluation thesaurus* (4th ed.). Newbury Park, CA: SAGE Publications.

———. (2003). Michael Scriven on the differences between evaluation and social science research. *The Evaluation Exchange, 10*(Winter), 7.

Singh, S., Dubey, P., Rastogi, A. and Vail, D. (2013). Excellence in the context of use-inspired research: Perspectives of the Global South. Ottawa: International Development Research Centre. Retrieved from http://www.idrc.ca/EN/Documents/Perspectives-of-the-global-south-Full-paper.pdf (accessed on 16 January 2015).

Smith, D. (2004). *Towards a strategic framework for peacebuilding: Getting their act together: Overview report of the joint Utstein study of peacebuilding* (Evaluation Report 1/2004). Oslo: Royal Ministry of Foreign Affairs. Retrieved from https://www.regjeringen.no/globalassets/upload/kilde/ud/rap/2004/0044/ddd/pdfv/210673-rapp104.pdf (accessed on 23 April 2015).

Smith, N. and Brandon, P. (2008). *Fundamental issues in evaluation.* New York, NY: Guilford Press.

Smutylo, T. (2005). *Outcome mapping: A method for tracking behavioural changes in development programs* (ILAC Brief 7). Retrieved from http://issat.dcaf.ch/ser/content/download/29484/414272/file/Smutylo_Outcome%20Mapping.pdf (accessed on 23 April 2015).

Stern, E., Stame, N., Mayne, J., Forss, K., Davies, R. and Befani, B. (2012). *Broadening the range of designs and methods for impact evaluations* (DFID Working Paper 38). London: Department for International Development.

Stufflebeam, D. L. (1994). Empowerment evaluation, objectivist evaluation and evaluation standards: Where the future of evaluation should not go and where it needs to go. *Evaluation Practice, 15,* 321–338.

———. (1999). Foundational models for 21st century program evaluation. In *Social Agenda/Advocacy Approaches. Occasional Paper Series.* The Evaluation Center, Western Michigan University.

Stufflebeam, D. L. and Shinkfield, A. J. (1985). *Systematic evaluation.* New York: Kluwer-Nijhoff Publishing.

Tijssen, R. J. W., Mouton, J., van Leeuwen, T. N. and Boshoff, N. (2006). How relevant are local scholarly journals in global science? A case study of South Africa. *Research Evaluation, 15*(3), 163–174.

USAID (Gunduz, C. and Klein, D.). (2008). *Conflict-sensitive approaches to value chain development.* Washington, DC: USAID. Retrieved from http://pdf.usaid.gov/pdf_docs/PNADY232.pdf (accessed on 12 April 2015).

Van Raan, A. F. J. (1996). Advanced bibliometric methods as quantitative core of peer review based evaluation and foresight exercises. *Scientometrics, 36*(3), 397–420.

Weiss, C. (1997). Theory-based evaluation: Past, present and future. *New Directions in Evaluation, 76,* 41–55.

———. (1998). Have we learned anything new about evaluation? *American Journal of Evaluation 19*(1), 21–31.

Whitmore, E. (1988). Participation, empowerment and welfare. *Canadian Review of Social Policy, 22,* 51–60.

Wooding, S. and Grant, J. (2003). *Assessing research: The researcher's view.* Leiden and Cambridge: RAND Europe. Retrieved from http://www.ra-review.ac.uk/reports/assess/AssessResearchReport.pdf (accessed on 23 April 2015).

Woodrow, P. and Chigas, D. (2011). Connecting the dots: Evaluating whether and how programmes address conflict systems. In N. Ropers et al. (Eds), *The non-linearity of peace processes: Theory and practice of systemic conflict transformation.* Berlin: Berghof Foundation.

PART II

Accountability, Ethics and Reflexivity

Introduction to Part II

The chapter by Brendan Whitty puts flesh on the much used (but under-examined) term 'accountability'. His chapter is an invitation for us to think more clearly, systematically and critically about the implications of accountability in our work. Not only does the term mean different things to different people but, as Whitty explains, there are multiple, often competing, entities to whom an evaluator and researcher is accountable. There is a natural connection between Whitty's work on accountability and the following chapter on ethics by Jayawickrama and Strecker. The connections, however, extend throughout the book, as each chapter includes cases of VDS characterised by competing sets of obligations and expectations among groups of stakeholders—all of which directly affect our evaluation and research within VDS. The challenge is to comprehend not only what a nuanced understanding of accountability means for our work, but also what it means for those with whom we are working inside and outside of VDS.

The choice of cases for this chapter is noteworthy: Nepal, Kenya, Argentina and a regional organisation in Latin America. Nepal and Kenya are nations where violence (militarised, criminalised and/or politicised) ebbs and flows in the lives of its inhabitants, while Argentina and the regional network live in the long shadows, and subsequent legacies, of military dictatorships and dirty war. Methodologically, then, the chapter includes cases of very different *conflict contexts*. We find similar heterogeneity in the sectoral activities of the projects in country cases, which range from participatory action research with a view to improving the equity of natural resource (Nepal) to '[mobilisation of] coalitions to conduct citizen monitoring of government activities, amongst other governance and development research activities'; to a Latin America regional network working through partnerships on rural development; and to a large policy research organisation working across a number of sectors in

Argentina. As Whitty examines the variations in the accountability *profiles* of each case, we also begin to get a glimpse at how variations in the conflict contexts and sectoral activities make a difference—or not—for our evaluation and research.

Methodologically speaking, Jayawickrama and Strecker offer a different approach to the examination of the themes that define this book. Bringing together expertise as both evaluators and researchers in VDS, their approach is characterised by an ethnographic reflexivity. They juxtapose (a) their evaluation and research experiences in conflict zones with (b) the basic principles articulated in the ethical frameworks for evaluators (notably, the Guiding Principles of the American Evaluation Association). In so doing, they point to tensions that may arise between principles and practice. While some of these tensions may be technical, many of the challenges are fundamentally political in the sense that they are rooted in power imbalances between *outsiders* and *insiders*. In a sense, the argument in that chapter teases out the politico-ethical tensions of imposing (largely) Northern ethical frameworks onto evaluators and researchers working in VDS.

Jayawickrama and Strecker try to do more than speak *about* Southern realities. Through this chapter, they are attempting to build a bridge whereby women and men in VDS are able to speak for themselves about their experiences as the *objects* of research projects or evaluations. Despite the increasingly clichéd use of the term, the inclusion of their voices and experiences genuinely 'speak truth to power'. This chapter offers a caution against assuming that the *outsiders* and *insiders* of evaluations shared the same ethical framework. More disturbingly, it suggests that evaluation, as a field of research and practice, may be a Trojan Horse of ethical orientations that clashes with *local* sensibilities. When read alongside Whitty's chapter, we become better able to tease out the connections between power/politics, methodology and ethics in the evaluation enterprise.

3

The Role of Accountability and Evaluation of Research on/in Violently Divided Societies

Brendan S. Whitty

Introduction

Research is assessed by—and the researcher is accountable to—a mix of different people, all with different criteria for their assessments. Funders, often the commissioner of the evaluation or research, will evaluate research according to criteria such as *impact* and research quality. The academic assesses his or her work according to its contribution to knowledge, or the insights it generates for the understanding of a particular phenomenon. The activist researcher is looking for the policy influence brought about by the work. The policy-maker values research according to its utility for creating or justifying solutions to policy problems, or for understanding or anticipating the consequences of particular policies. In these examples, each person has somewhat different criteria for their assessment of research, and this is informed by their particular set of perspectives, needs and interests. The researcher, no less than the evaluator and the research organisation, must balance all of these criteria.

The current chapter takes a step towards the development of a conceptual framework to help us understand how these different (and sometimes competing) perspectives, needs and interests intersect and affect evaluation in violently divided societies (VDS) through holding evaluators/researchers to account. The 'Fitting *Evaluation* within an *Accountability* Framework' section in this chapter assembles the base for the conceptual scaffolding by examining the links between accountability and evaluation. Accountability is defined as a characteristic of a relationship, based on shared norms or expectations; these should, ideally, be mutually re-enforcing. Understood as a part of accountability, evaluation is a critical tool for assessing the degree to which such shared norms exist and are respected (although evaluations are not only used for accountability purposes). The 'Profiling the Accountability of Research Organisations' section in this chapter examines the ways in which *research organisations* are accountable to the various stakeholders, by outlining the diverse forms of accountability that influence their work.

Collectively, the sum of these accountabilities constitutes what may be called the 'accountability profile' of an organisation. Empirically, this section draws on the experiences of four research organisations: two of them located in VDS, two not (or at least, less so). The accountability profile of each organisation is explored so that we might better understand how it may affect the evaluation of that organisation.[1]

The chapter argues that an organisation's accountability profile is formed by how it positions itself in the wider policy community. This is a process of constant negotiation, as organisations attempt to balance the external interests and expectations of multiple stakeholders, with the need for internal organisational sustainability and integrity. The final section of the chapter (Accountability and Evaluation in Violently Divided Societies) addresses the ways in which policy contexts, attitudes towards research and insecurity shape an organisation's operational decisions— all of which have implications for accountability.

In order to define this chapter conceptually and practically, two decisions were made. First, it was decided to focus analysis on the linkages between the evaluation of a piece of research and the broader set of issues concerning the accountability of the researcher him/herself. That is, the chapter will not consider the additional and separate question of the accountability of the evaluator of research. Second, it was decided to frame research as a process which is conducted, funded, evaluated and supported chiefly by individuals working within organisations, each of which possesses its own internal and external evaluation structures and processes, and maintains its own internal and external relationships of accountability.

Fitting *Evaluation* within
an *Accountability* Framework

This section develops a conceptual framework which outlines how the ideas of *accountability* and *evaluation* fit together. To do this, it is necessary first to identify what is meant by *accountability*. The term is often linked to particular identifiable forms of relationship, but is now often used as an *evaluative* term, suggesting broadly good governance and a generally appropriate use of power—and as a term indicating approval of the use of power, it is both 'contested and contestable' (Bovens, 2007, p. 450). This has led to the term being described as 'complex and chameleon-like' (Mulgan, 2000, p. 555), 'inherently ill-structured' (Kearns, 1994), 'malleable and often nebulous' (Newell and Bellour, 2002) or characterised by 'plasticity' (Goetz and Jenkins, 2004).

This vagueness and variability in the usage of *accountability* is a challenging starting point, either for linking evaluation to accountability or for analysing the specific challenges to researchers in VDS. A further challenge arises from the fact that there is not a single defined piece of literature or body of knowledge that sketches out the parameters of the field of accountability. Rather, different pockets of literature are produced by different stakeholder groups that reflect their particular sets of interests. So, for example, we see that the sub-literature on institutional legal forms of accountability is distinct from the literature addressing corporate social responsibility, which itself is distinct again from what we seek to explore in the current chapter: the subset of literature for researchers in VDS. While this last sub-literature may be tethered to the research ethics review protocols of universities, it may expand well beyond it as well.

The task is made more difficult by the context-specific and dynamic nature of accountability debates, which react to shifts in political power and give rise to contested areas where accountability gaps are created and negotiated (Newell, 2006; Newell and Bellour, 2002). In the 1990s, for example, scandals involving international development agencies, working in VDS and elsewhere,[2] triggered a vigorous debate on accountability, producing an operational shift in favour of participatory development and downwards accountability (Chambers, 1997; Chambers and Pettit, 2004). One result of this period was the establishment of numerous professional standards and self-regulatory initiatives (see Lingán et al., 2010 for an overview).

As a starting point, the current chapter draws on a narrow definition of accountability, which has specific characteristics linked to its traditional meaning as rooted in 'the rendering of an account'. More specifically, accountability here is defined as:

> a relationship where an actor is obliged to act in an established and identified way, and is responsible to give account to a stakeholder for discharging that obligation, with the actor facing consequences or redirection from the stakeholder in the event that they do not. (Bovens 2007, p. 450; Day and Klein, 1987)

This definition draws extensively on existing definitions and implies a framework of accountability with several dimensions. The discussion below will address these key dimensions.

Relational

First, accountability is fundamentally *relational* in that it describes a relationship between two kinds of agents: (a) the agent who is responsible for acting in a particular way, and (b) the stakeholder who will hold the agent to account. The agent and the stakeholder may be individual persons, or an organisation. This excludes the idea that accountability is an *internal* form of moral duty, instead linking accountability clearly to an external stakeholder, and is closely tied to the distinction between *responsibility* and *accountability*. A responsibility is a duty, but not every responsibility is accompanied by accountability to an external agent. Accountability is a composite of two responsibilities: first, the responsibility to behave in a particular way (which Wenar, 2004 describes as a *first-order responsibility*) and second, a second-order responsibility to render account. Thus, while all accountabilities entail responsibilities, not every responsibility is part of an accountability relationship. The difference in meanings is being eroded, as *accountability* increasingly occupies the semantic turf once occupied by *responsibility* (Jenkins and Goetz, 1999; Koppell, 2005; Mulgan, 2000, p. 556).

The distinction becomes important when considering the suggestion that a non-profit's accountability *to itself* to respect its mission is a form of accountability (Ebrahim, 2003, p. 199). Ebrahim criticises the agent–principal definition of accountability.[3] He argues that it excludes an NGO's accountability to its mission (Ebrahim, 2003, pp. 196–199), leading him to argue instead for an *integrated* definition of accountability which would allow accountability to mission (a purely internal form of accountability) to be included within the definition. This approach removes the second-order element of the stakeholder holding to account. With a definition containing only the first-order element, any socially justified twinge of conscience may constitute accountability.

However, following Bovens, an alternative understanding of the term is possible which maintains the useful distinction between responsibility and accountability. Insofar as accountability exists at this level, it ignores the fiction of legal personality of an organisation[4] and argues instead that the accountability happens within the organisations, but always between two people. Thus, the accountability mechanisms for the mission lie between the staff, management and governance (typically the board of trustees). This is, therefore, a form of accountability which exists between members or parts of the organisation but within a single (legal) person.

Shared Expectations or Norms

The second characteristic of accountability is that the agent and the stakeholder (holding him or her to account) share certain expectations.

> Accountability implies both a shared set of expectations and a common currency of justifications. There has to be agreement about the context, the reason why one actor gives explanation since it is precisely this sense of obligation which translates the giving of accounts into accountability ... If there is no such agreement ... we talk not about accountability, but about excuses, apologies or pretexts. (Day and Klein, 1987, p. 5)

Accountability, therefore, requires that both agent and stakeholder share a view of the responsibilities and the criteria against which the agent will be judged; the agent must be capable of explaining him or herself to the stakeholder against these criteria. Without shared understanding of the norms, sanctions imposed for failure to follow the order are the actions of external force. For example, the difference may be described as being between sanctions imposed by the court of an occupying power whose laws are illegitimate in the eyes of the local population, and the sanctions imposed by an arbitrator for a breach of contract between two business people. In the former, the local resident punished before the court does not share an understanding of the rules or their legitimacy, and is therefore not being held accountable but is only on the receiving end of illegitimate force; in the latter, both business-people are in understanding, and the remedies required of one for breaching the contract constitute the exercise of accountability for the breach.

Expectations fall into two categories. They may be created by the agents to govern that specific relationship in a form of *contract*; or they may arise from established norms. An example of a contractually based set of expectations is the case where a university researcher signs a grant agreement with a donor, and is thereby held to account for the implementation of agreed objectives. In most cases, in most universities, the same researcher will also be held accountable by a research ethics board. The first set of expectations is established and consolidated between the researcher and donor through the contract, while the second set is tethered to a research ethics review process rooted in an established set of norms. It should also be remembered that the expectations need not be formally articulated or institutionalised provided that they include a means of holding to account and an accompanying expectation that the agent will have to justify him/herself. In such contexts, expectations can be informal.

While this analytical definition does not address the practical implications of accountability for power dynamics, it is worth noting the shift in development discourse from *holding to account* towards *taking into account* as part of a desire to improve *downward* accountability. The formulation of shared expectations constitutes an important element for the role of accountability to address power differences. In the non-profit sector, for example, the operational-shift towards participatory definition of project activities and interventions at a local level is central to the push for *downward* accountability, and aims to redistribute power to communities by giving them voice and control over the development interventions done in their name and ostensibly for their benefit. Thus, literature in the NGO sector widens the focus from *holding to account* to *taking into account* characterised by the drive towards participatory development approaches, which seek to involve beneficiaries in the definition of project activities. This shift has been represented in the research field by an increased use of participatory action research methodologies, with their own standards of evidence quality, validity and applicability.

Our definition of accountability encompasses, but is not broader than, the agent–principal conceptual framework. This describes a relationship where the agent works for and on behalf of a principal. As such it meets our definition. Nonetheless, it is too narrow because it implies a relationship that is role-defining, formally identified and singular. It is role-defining because the character as an agent is defining of the agents' motivations. It is formally identified, because it is articulated in its particulars as part of the contract; and finally, it is singular because it requires a contract, a specific agreement, to bring it into being, and that this will be unique in form (see Ebrahim, 2003, pp. 196–199).

However, many accountability relationships do not share these features. An agent may be accountable to many stakeholders. It is also an uncomfortable fit where there are numerous principals, such as the government's accountability to its subjects—which can be split into the government's accountability to each citizen—or the increasing insistence of NGO's accountability to its many beneficiaries. In none of these has a contract been signed, but, in all of them, the accountability is by the *agent* to a wide group of *principals*. In each, the claim is important: in his development of a normative theory of legitimacy, Raz observes that the governments' relationship to its citizens is generated through its claim of legitimate authority over the citizens (Raz, 1986), similarly, the NGOs', through its claim to benefit a particular community and the individuals represented. Each generates expectations and norms. An agent–principal relationship does not acknowledge such parallel accountability relationships to others within a group. Moreover, the agent–principal definition focuses on the relationship to the exclusion of the wider organisation context. Thus, Ebrahim (2003) notes that by focusing on a relationship between an agent and principal, the focus is taken off the range of accountabilities that an organisation like an NGO owes. The focus suggests that the responsibility to the principal is the primary driver of the agent. In fact, it may be incidental: like the accounting requirements of an NGO to the government, which are important but incidental to its key work. Lastly, the agent–principal conception tends to exclude the context to a relationship, thereby distracting from the challenges associated with the context, such as the need for an agent to balance accountability (the *multiple accountability disorder* highlighted by Koppell, 2005).

Answerability/Holding to Account (1)

The third element refers to the process of holding to account and the consequences attached to that process. It is this *answerability* and *enforceability* (see 'Enforceability/Holding to Account (2)') that distinguishes accountability from responsibility. Here, the stakeholder has the opportunity to hold the agent to account on the basis of the shared expectations, and the agent is responsible for providing answers. The nature of this process depends on the nature of the relationship involved. Bovens (2007) identifies three key elements: (a) the agent must inform the stakeholder about the manner in which their responsibility was discharged; (b) a form of debate must take place where the stakeholder can question the agent; and (c) the stakeholder must be able then to judge or evaluate the agent's behaviour against the shared expectations.

The definition proposed in the current chapter is less constrained. It requires only that the stakeholder is capable of reviewing the performance of the agent against the shared expectations, with the intention of coming to a judgement. This allows us to distinguish third-party, second-party and first-party accountability mechanisms.

- A third-party accountability mechanism allows a third party such as a court, arbitrator or tribunal to evaluate or assess adherence to an established set of expectations on behalf of the agent and stakeholders. An independent evaluation takes this form.
- A second-party mechanism is one where stakeholders review the performance themselves. This may take several forms: it may convey on the principal a power to question the agent or ask them to justify his or her actions; it may involve the agent actively reporting or publishing information at specified points which can be used by stakeholders to assess the agents' actions. Second-party mechanisms rely on the ability of the stakeholder to judge for themselves the extent to which an organisation has met the shared expectations.
- Lastly, a first-party mechanism is one in which the agent creates the mechanisms themselves: complaints handling mechanisms developed in the corporate world, and increasingly in the humanitarian sector, are examples of this.

Common to all of these accountability mechanisms is the agent's duty to answer for his or her actions, and the principal's power to evaluate or assess the agent's performance with respect to his or her responsibility. This captures the *answerability* dimension of accountability (Koppell, 2005).

This dimension also points to the role of transparency within the accountability process—particularly, the availability of accurate and timely information on the actions and intentions of an agent. In this context, stakeholders can hold the agent to account according to their *answerability*—with consequences to follow, if the expected standards are not met (see 'Enforceability/Holding to Account (2)'). Simply put, information is vital to enable a stakeholder to assess or evaluate the extent to which an agent is (or is not) behaving according to their expectations and duties. Transparency is a necessary, but not a sufficient, condition of accountability. As expectations change, so do transparency requirements. This is evident, for example, in the rise of triple-line reporting, according to which the public has access not only to the financial data and well-being of an organisation, but to the social and environmental impacts of its activities as well. The information must be sufficient for stakeholders—not necessarily the whole public, except insofar as they are stakeholders—to make a judgement on the extent to which an agent has met, or is likely to meet, the expectations.

Enforceability/Holding to Account (2)

The fourth and final element of accountability is the stakeholders' power to impose consequences on the agent in the event that they have not acted according to the shared expectations. Bovens treats this as constitutive of accountability (Bovens, 2007; Goetz and Jenkins, 2004; Newell and Bellour, 2002). Mulgan (2000) argues that 'accepting ... redirection' is an alternative to accepting consequences. The definition used in this chapter will be broad enough to include the informal withdrawal of cooperation as a sufficient consequence. This expands the definition of accountability from the traditional or *core* definition which is typified by the application of sanctions by a formal second-(stakeholder-led) or third-party (court or arbitrator) enforcement mechanism. The repertoire of possible sanctions, therefore, expands to include the withdrawal of cooperation or participation by a stakeholder, after their assessment of the agents' behaviour against the shared norms.

This definition draws on the accountability literature in the corporate sector, which goes beyond formal input/output models to include the consideration of any stakeholder affecting or affected by a company (Freeman, 1984). Subsequent research points to an *instrumental* definition of accountability which applies to situations where an agent responds to the needs and interests of their stakeholder for purely practical reasons (such as the continuation of funding), rather than for adherence to an ethical norm (Donaldson and Preston, 1995). Consider the case of a research team conducting a trial of a new community-based governance system for pasture access. As a matter of practicality, it is vital for the implementation of the project that the researchers gain the cooperation of research participants. Their withdrawal of participant cooperation from the trial would make it much more difficult to conduct or complete the research successfully, particularly if the study is longitudinal and premised on long-term cooperation. Practically, therefore, the need to meet the expectations and norms of the local population is of the first importance if the research is to be allowed to be completed. Alongside this instrumental consideration, the team is also responsible for maintaining the ethical standards expected in the conduct of action research (e.g., to inform them about the work, to treat them with respect, and so on), which may be enforced through an ethical review board in the case of university-based research.

The implies that ethical and instrumental accountability mechanisms can exist in parallel and, therefore, that the same actions can be evaluated and held to account by different stakeholders, potentially using different standards. *Traditional* accountability mechanisms allow an organisation's stakeholders to hold the organisation to account for meeting a particular ethical standard, and if necessary, to exact redress. Similarly, instrumental definitions of accountability identify stakeholders as those who can impose sanctions by withdrawing (or threatening to withdraw) cooperation or funding from an organisation. The ability to change the researcher's behaviour by making a threat to withdraw cooperation or funding entails an unambiguous form of control. The enforcement mechanism for identifying the consequences can be third, second or first person.

The definition above suggests that there is a relationship between accountability and evaluation. Understood from the perspective of accountability as the act of reviewing and appraising an agent's performance against a shared expectation (see Bovens, 2007, p. 462), evaluation is the essential element of the overall process of holding to account. The accountability perspective is not the only lens through which evaluation can be viewed: It may not even be the most appropriate one (Bunda, 1979) as the definition offered in Chapter 1 of this book makes clear. However, the process of assessment or evaluation is necessary to all the standards for which an agent, such as a researcher or research organisation, will be held to account. The adoption of a wider *account-ability* perspective does two things: First, it allows us to look at the broader set of relationships and to understand how the programme was formulated and what might be the potential consequences of the evaluation. Second, it allows us to understand how programme evaluation fits alongside other accountability mechanisms by which the researcher will be held to account.

Profiling the Accountability of Research Organisations

One implication of the *relational* nature of accountability is that multiple accountability relationships are possible—indeed, likely—whereby different people, communities or agents (known by the inclusive label *stakeholders*) are embedded within a shared web of interests. The people to whom we owe responsibilities and to whom we must give account will be shaped by the commitments we make and the context in which we find ourselves. For example: An unmarried person in their 20s will have different accountability relationships than a married mother of three. A doctor in the UK will have a different set of accountability relationships compared to a truck-driver, convict or lawyer, or a doctor in Afghanistan. A second implication is that while all accountability relationships must bear the core elements identified above—common norms accompanied by a means to hold to account—each relationship will be different. The accountability owed by a person to their employer is different than that owed to the state, friends or mother-in-law. The standards that characterise these various relationships and consequences that flow from them are different. The menu of accountabilities to different agents constitutes an *accountability profile* which is shaped by an individual's careers, personal affairs and other such choices and circumstance. A third implication is that there will be many overlapping accountability relationships, which may be formal or informal, complementary or contradictory.

Research organisations, similarly, have accountability profiles characterised by a range of relationships that will be shaped through the actions and track record of that particular organisation, as perceived by themselves and by their stakeholders. While there may be similarities between organisations, each will have its particular accountability profile. The section below identifies, first, specific stakeholders and the characteristics of accountability relationships owed to these stakeholders, and second, how these relationships are managed and balanced by research organisations *positioning* themselves differently within their contexts. This discussion is the middle level in the conceptual scaffolding. It draws on four case studies of research organisations and identifies their key stakeholders and the nature of their accountability relationships.[5] Two case studies work in VDS: ForestAction in Nepal and Centre for Governance and Development (CGD) in Kenya. Both organisations are similar in size, employing approximately a dozen professional research staff. ForestAction conducts participatory action research with a view of improving the equity of natural resource management in Nepal, while CGD mobilises coalitions to conduct citizen monitoring of government activities, amongst other governance and development research activities. The other two case studies are the *Centro Latinoamericano para el Desarrollo Rural* (RIMISP), a regional network working through partnerships on rural development in Latin America, and *Centro de Implementacion de Politicas Publicas para la Equidad y el Crecimiento* (CIPPEC) a large policy research organisation working across a number of sectors in Argentina. These cases are used in this chapter to sharpen the conceptual framework being developed here, and to highlight the distinctions between research organisations with regard to accountability profiles.

Accountability to Whom? A Research Organisation's Stakeholders

Who are the stakeholders of a research organisation? Clearly, at a programme level, the funders are vital stakeholders—indeed, so central are they to evaluation processes, as the commissioners of the evaluations, that their involvement and interests are inextricably linked. However, as the contributions to this book make clear, the interests of several other stakeholders are involved; Kevin Kelly (Chapter 6), for example, identifies the policy-makers, the users of the research and agents within the programming context. Jayawickrama/Strecker and several other contributors stress the importance of taking into account the interests and sensibilities of local communities in both the research process and the evaluation process—in addition to the formal academic community where projects use or generate research products. It is to these stakeholders and to their expectations that we will now turn our attention.

Policy-community

Researchers working in VDS, or on VDS issues, are situated within a wider policy community implicitly or explicitly,[6] which they seek to influence through their research.[7] Their influence will be affected by their ability to deploy evidence and arguments that are theoretically and empirically grounded, and that are perceived to be valid by academic, activist or policy stakeholders. To profile the accountability of these stakeholders, it is important to understand the overlap in the expectations between these groups. Caplan's *two communities* theory of research use in policy offers a helpful starting point. He proposes that there are two different groups within the policy community: researchers on the one hand, and policy-makers on the other (Caplan, 1979). Each has its own needs, requirements and standards. Choi notes that within the two communities, there are 'different views of what constitutes evidence', different timeframes and different expectations for what research is there to do. Policy-makers want specific answers to specific questions or problems, while researchers tend to give nuanced and careful analysis to more theoretically cast research questions (Choi et al., 2005, p. 634).

> Scientists are essentially accountable to editors of peer-reviewed journals and grant funders. They may be interested in policy but, at the end of the day, they are not required to focus on issues that have policy relevance or application. On the other hand, policy-makers are usually accountable to political parties, government, and taxpayers, if not the voters.

In an influential analysis of federal decision-making in USA, Kingdon identifies parallel processes or *streams*, the confluence of which is argued to determine policy: One stream is comprised of policy alternatives that emerge within a *primeval soup* of expert discourse and engagement (Kingdon, 1995). Added to this is the rise in political and social problems that are independent processes which impinge at certain points in time. The agents and the processes in each stream are very different: politicians are accountable to the public in the way the political agenda is set; those generating policy alternatives compete for resources and hold each other to account for meeting the standards at an individual and organisational level, through the stringent rules of public and academic debate.

More recently, this dichotomised view of policy communities has been challenged. Systems of knowledge production and the expectations for research are changing: increasingly, research must prove its worth (particularly, publicly funded research) and scientists must justify their value to society. Thus Gibbons et al. (1994) argue that knowledge production systems are changing; that they are increasingly becoming problem-oriented, multi-disciplinary and applied. The range of organisations using empirical research to develop, support and justify policy positions is proliferating. This includes universities, NGOs, activist organisations, commercial firms, interest groups and lobby groups (Stone, 2005, pp. 262–264).

As expectations that research will have clear and direct policy utility or impact have increased, tools and approaches are being developed to bridge potential gaps between researchers and policy-makers (Braun et al., 2004; Carden, 2009; Court and Young, 2005). As applied researchers seek to influence policy, so are political interests influencing research—in the sense that research is often framed, funded and undertaken with policy impact in mind. However, it may also become *politicised* in the sense that the framing of questions, the methods adopted and even the *desired outcomes* come to be shaped by the political interests of policy-makers, rather than empirical and theoretical interests of academics. Higgins et al. (2006) acknowledge a divide between the *citizen scientist* and the *strictly objective* researcher, where only the latter respects the rules and shared norms of scientific quality and method. At the same time, people argue that not only is science being politicised, but politicians increasingly draw on scientific language to legitimise public decisions and policies. Research is used for tactical and political usages (Weiss, 1979) and divisions are breaking down (Weingart, 1999).

Efforts have been made to make sense of the blurring of the lines between the two communities. Sabatier (1988, p. 139) employs the term 'advocacy coalitions' to refer to those groups of people with shared beliefs and complementary objectives working within policy subsystems:

> These are people from a variety of positions (elected and agency officials, interest group leaders, researchers) who share a particular belief system—i.e., a set of basic values, causal assumptions and problem perceptions—who show a non-trivial degree of coordinated activity over time.

Sabatier's advocacy coalitions are founded not only on shared moral values, but also on shared causal assumptions and policy assumptions. Advocacy coalitions are formed around a core set of beliefs and values that are stable and not easily shaken. Researchers will be evaluated and will be identified as belonging to one or other advocacy coalition by the extent to which they express specific core beliefs, which comprise their perspective towards the world and form the basis for beliefs about problems and a favoured programme of interventions in particular policy fields (Lindquist, 2001). Research is used to refine the *secondary aspects* of the belief system, which may be understood as the details of the policy narratives (Roe, 1991) or *theories of change* by which researchers propose that positive change be brought about. Advocacy coalitions, therefore, offer a set of expectations on policy beliefs that will be shared between the members of that coalition and against which a research organisation will be assessed; included in these will be the rules for valid evidence. Indeed, a key criterion binding members of Haas's epistemic community[8] is 'shared notions of validity, which is inter-subjective, internally defined, criteria for weighing and validating knowledge in the domain of their expertise' (Haas, 1992, p. 6). Membership in that community, and the legitimacy that membership affords, requires adherence to these expectations. Organisations locating themselves in these communities must meet these epistemic—and policy belief—standards in order to achieve legitimacy.

The four case studies included in this chapter position themselves differently within the different policy arenas they work in, and align themselves with different stakeholders. Thus, RIMISP in Chile works in rural development and includes a strong network of researchers producing academic-oriented research. It emphasises the importance of adherence to scientific methods and to the rules of the academic community in the field of rural development. For RIMISP, the academic community constitutes the key stakeholder along with its donors. The organisation is strongly connected to think tanks and academic policy institutes across Latin America. At the other end of the spectrum is CGD in Kenya, which does not identify the university-based academic community as one of its stakeholders. Instead, it seeks to mobilise coalitions of civil society organisations and individuals to strengthen an essentially activist position vis-à-vis the government. Somewhere between these two lies CIPPEC, which identifies policy-makers as its core stakeholders and which incorporates and institutionalises this fact in its mission. The central importance of this relationship is reflected throughout CIPPEC's processes. Its office is within the sight of the Argentine Parliament. Through an active relationship cultivation process, CIPPEC maintains strong relationships between its management and policy-makers. Its advisory board is selected with an eye to the synergistic benefits members may generate, and the organisation is extremely responsive to policy needs and cycles. While CIPPEC acknowledges the importance of the quality of its evidence, in the event of conflict, the needs of the policy-maker will be prioritised over the academic quality of work.

What does this mean for the accountability of research organisations? Under the two communities' theory, there are two relatively polarised communities, each with different ideas of the kind of knowledge needed and the standards by which this knowledge will be evaluated. Subsequent research suggests that policy communities, and the standards by which the legitimacy and authority of a research organisation are established, will be determined by a range of criteria. These are reflected in an organisation's accountability profile, including the rules of evidence and of ethics. Values and accepted theories of change will all be determined by an organisation's identification with an advocacy coalition.

Donors

Clearly, funders are key stakeholders for a research organisation. Having committed resources for a defined piece of work, the funder is interested in assessing a programme's quality, outcomes and impacts. In one way, a research organisation's accountability to funders and its use of evaluation are straightforward: Evaluation expectations are articulated in the terms of reference and in the evaluator's contract. While an evaluator can employ different evaluative techniques, approaches or lenses, the details for the evaluation are most often formally outlined in the contract. Timelines, evaluation questions to be answered and answerability/enforceability mechanisms are likewise expressly stipulated. These are enforced through both third- and second-party mechanisms: respectively, by the law courts or the potential of withdrawal of cooperation through delays in delivering further tranches of funds or payments, or by the withdrawal of future funding opportunities.

This apparently straightforward contractual relationship between the evaluator and the evaluation commissioner obscures many of the complexities addressed within the other chapters in this book. Evaluations may be used for different reasons (Weiss, 1979; Patton, 2008). Healy and Healy (Chapter 9) offer some important insights into how the commissioners of research—in their case, a philanthropic organisation—use evaluations. Two competing worldviews are argued to guide the approaches of commissioners of research evaluations—positivist and social constructivist approaches. The differences between them 'are broadly aligned with how people think about the role of social science and the quest for generalisable knowledge or rules that can inform human behaviour'. They argue that some donors use evaluations to identify specific patterns that are replicable and may be applied more broadly, while others see evaluations as an opportunity to learn and improve programming. A mixed-method approach would include a learning component and a component for tracking progress against pre-identified goals. On the other hand, evaluations may not be used at all if they are simply exercises to justify funding decisions or if they are treated as bureaucratically required box-ticking exercises. Provided that the methodology captures fairly the shared norms stated in the contract, the accountability is relatively straightforward.

The accountability of researchers to donors, on the other hand, reaches beyond contractual commitments. Practical considerations also drive the need to be responsive to the wider funding context, not least the iterative nature of funding cycles, and an acute awareness that keeping a funder happy is the basis for future funding and institutional sustainability. Even so, funding contexts vary over time as the interests and attention of donors shift geographically and by sector.

Turing our attention to Nepal, funding opportunities are relatively sparse for research in the forestry sector. ForestAction must, therefore, respond quickly and nimbly to requests for proposals and opportunities as they arise. This reality shaped their management approach to fundraising and their internal structure. An earlier experimentation with a programme structure failed: For ForestAction, a programme is a group of researchers who coalesce around allocated goals to generate resources to explore a relatively narrow set of research questions and areas that are designed to foster an ongoing system of research. ForestAction has adopted a more fluid structure where key researchers are empowered to raise funds within a relatively wide set of research questions and areas. This is in contrast to CIPPEC which capitalised on its reputation and has been successful at drawing support from a wide set of funders within Argentina, including international and corporate funds. CIPPEC has a well-defined programmatic structure operating across a wide set of thematic areas, with many donors and projects. Its internal evaluation processes monitor a range of largely output-driven, standardised indicators which are used to gauge success in projects. CIPPEC is able to shift funds between programmes to ensure that priorities are met. RIMISP funding is based on a unique niche, founded on its research quality and the network that it maintains through its organisational culture. This has enabled it to build a number of on-going relationships with established donors.

Accountability to donors, thus, takes place at two levels. First, with those who are already providing funds and where expectations are clearly articulated in the contract and accountability is likewise clear. The second-level constitutes a wider range of donors on whose support research organisations can draw to further their missions. This requires legitimacy and the ability to align with donors, who like other agents in the policy community, share rules and causal/value beliefs.

Local Communities

What accountability exists to local communities? The different organisations in the case studies examined relate to local communities in different ways. Broadly speaking, ForestAction and RIMISP both seek to gain more equitable and efficient use of resources for rural users. Their mission has prompted a modus operandi in which ForestAction works closely with resource user communities that they foster and maintain, and with whom it conducts its participatory research. It builds close links with these communities, and its legitimacy is in part founded on these links and on the quality of the findings from its work. RIMISP, in contrast, operates at both regional and national levels. It convenes and coordinates a network of research organisations and cooperates with them. This network model makes it difficult to forge direct links with the *ultimate beneficiaries*—rural resource users. Indeed, representatives from RIMISP maintained that they have no obligation of accountability to the rural poor *as such*[9] (the ultimate beneficiaries identified in their mission) and instead prioritise links with network partners and the quality and integrity of the evidence they collect. RIMISP's respect for research ethics is enforced through a strong internal culture: Staff members are recruited from academic disciplines that have been subject to and are familiar with ethical rules of academic research. The organisational culture stresses the importance of academic rigour and ethics; proposals are reviewed internally for rigour and the underlying expectations of the researchers include respect for ethics. CIPPEC represents a third model. Its mission seeks explicitly to generate change and to mobilise support from Argentine policy-makers who will in turn generate change for the citizenry. This is reflected in their mode of working, which tends to focus on policy-makers and government officials, who are their immediate beneficiaries.

The relationship between organisation and local community is, therefore, profoundly different. Each claims different beneficiaries, and aligns itself differently to local communities. ForestAction seeks to interact with its local communities, using participatory methods, as partners. RIMISP, on the other hand, interacts with local communities more as though they are *participants* in a research project. Traditional research practice recognises communities as research objects. Researchers are governed by the ethical rules that are formed with research disciplines (anthropological, medical or otherwise), as they are institutionalised within universities. Established norms are based on the notion of the Hippocratic oath, 'first, do no harm'. These are typically enforced by university research ethics boards, which essentially constitute third-party mechanisms. However, none of our case studies had formal mechanisms of this nature.

In asking the development industry 'whose reality counts?', Robert Chambers critiques this traditional stance. This challenge confronts issues of epistemology as well as research ethics. According to this critique, research is a reductive process which seeks to synthesise and process information, removing it analytically from the experience of the participants. The use of 'linguistic and textual styles, classificatory systems and particular discursive formations can be seen to empower some and silence others' (Keeley and Scoones, 1999, p. 5). Scientific discourses legitimise politics while removing the policy process from democratic politics (Fischer, 1993; Keeley and Scoones, 1999, p. 2000). Research, depending on epistemological choices, can exclude and alienate local communities. Chambers contended that nothing less than a paradigm shift was necessary, where development professionals—the *uppers*—should place power in the hands of the *lowers*, those affected by aid policy but with little opportunity to shape or challenge the development discourse. According to Chambers, a change in focus, from linear top-down thinking to recognition of the complex and the local, was necessary (Chambers, 1997).

The validity of this argument depends on the legitimising foundation of the organisation: whether in the scientific method, or the value to a specific group. In the aid sector, interventions are premised on a proximate relationship to *beneficiaries*. In research, however, the idea of *beneficiaries* carries little traction, except in cases like ForestAction where the group is identifiable and relatively specific, and where ForestAction has direct relationships with representatives of the group. For many organisations *accountability to research beneficiaries* is unrealistic for a variety of reasons: the remoteness of beneficiaries in the organisation's model of change; the indistinctness of the beneficiary group; the logistical challenges in developing accountability relationships to a potentially diverse range of individuals, sometimes with limited literacy or understanding of the research process or purpose; the need for independence; and the overriding requirements of quality and expertise.

A second critique questions the validity of traditional Western research ethics systems to non-Western contexts. Contributors in this book launch powerful critiques of the accountability mechanisms *owed to* local communities. Jayawickrama and Strecker note that the lack of ownership of the established norms is reflected in enforcement mechanisms. The processes for evaluating ethics are third-party accountability mechanisms enforced by ethics boards far removed from the local communities. Moreover, Jayawickrama and Strecker observe that the current ethics and ethical discourses are derived mainly from Western knowledge systems, over which people in non-Western societies do not have much ownership, and for whom they have little relevance.

It should also be noted that for many non-university organisations, formal mechanisms do not exist. None of our research organisations, for example, had formal systems for accepting complaints. Indeed, non-university-based research undertaken by, and in, communities (both in general, and in violently divided communities) is conspicuously bereft of any kind of *formal* ethical review.[10]

Positioning or Balancing Stakeholders

Positioning

The case study organisations in this chapter seek to position themselves differently vis-à-vis three key stakeholder groups: the research community, policy-makers and *ultimate beneficiaries* (those who are identified in the organisation's mission as benefiting from its work). Thus, while each of the case study organisations has to balance the demands of a range of stakeholders, each orients itself differently within its respective communities: CIPPEC identifies with policy-makers and government officials, and their needs, in designing and conducting research; RIMISP prioritises the academic and regional/international policy communities and academic standards of research; ForestAction builds its research and legitimacy on its close relationships with, and relevance to, the communities with whom its works; CGD builds coalitions of civil society groups and individuals to push forward an activist agenda. Each of these research organisations makes claims to the quality of their evidence, the projects they undertake and benefit they seek, and the claims made about goal or mission and the means by which the changes will occur. The claims of legitimacy by each organisation and their perceptions of the benefits of their work are therefore different.

Accordingly, each has a different accountability profile. Those who claim academic quality of the research will have their work assessed according to the standards of evidence and validity of the academic discipline. Those claiming to base their legitimacy on the relevance of their work to the policy community will be judged on that basis. That is, the legitimacy and credibility of the work they accomplish will be assessed on the basis of these claims. The accountability relationships are, therefore, informed by the claims they make about the standard of their work, which positions each organisation and defines the frame by which it is to be judged. Their credibility and ability to meet the standards must be continually managed. It is a process that requires constant nego- tiation and tending among the parties involved. An organisation must continue to generate and use evidence that propagates its credibility.

As a matter of management, the positioning of an organisation stems partly from deliberate actions of the staff, and is also partly emergent. It is deliberate in that an organisation's management can recruit staff with particular research skills, can forge a research culture and can generate a communication strategy which places it within a public context. All of these serve in managing stakeholder relationships and create a brand or image. At the same time, organisational positioning is emergent, in that the image and brand are not wholly within the control of the organisation. They emerge through the constant discussion and nego- tiation between others in the policy context. This requires active man- agement and maintenance of reputation. As such, these processes of managed and emergent positioning inform the policy communities from whom they claim legitimacy and consequently the standards by which their legitimacy and authority will be judged.

Relevance of the Type of Organisation

Research is 'no longer only [generated in] universities and colleges, but in non-university institutes, research centres, government agen- cies, industrial laboratories, think-tanks [and] consultancies' (Gibbons et al., 1994, p. 6; Stone, 2005, pp. 263–264). Each of these institutional forms has different missions, mandates, structures and accountability challenges. While the case studies in the current chapter were all non-profit organisations, similar challenges were faced by other types of research organisations, including universities. Thus, for example, an academic must negotiate the ethical and political space beyond the university in much the same way as the non-profit organisations discussed here. Traditionally, university researchers acquire external funds from research bodies on the basis of research proposals which are framed and oriented largely according to the particular needs, and world view, of the traditional (i.e., university-based) research community:

> The university has been commonly characterised as a decentralised, 'loosely-coupled' organisation, whose professors are accorded a significant degree of autonomy in their work, and where the quality of teaching and learning was maintained principally by reliance on shared norms and disciplinary traditions. (Dill, 1999, p. 128)

This model, however, no longer tells the full story. Just as the sources generating knowledge are diversifying to include *non-traditional* organisations (Gibbons et al., 1994), so too the university is being increasingly asked to demonstrate both *value for money* (Geuna and Martin, 2003, p. 277; OECD, 1997) and the *applicability* of its work (Dill, 1999). While research councils themselves still largely rely on bibliometrics to assess the value of commissioned research, they are increasingly looking for evidence of and the societal impact of the research being funded.

As universities adapt to these pressures, they are increasingly engaging in what Slaughter and Rhoades (1997, p. 6) describe as 'academic capitalism', characterised by a commodification of intellectual property, 'aggressive commercialisation of instruction' and increasing access to consultancy opportunities and commercialised service provision in the knowledge economy (Clark, 1998). Dill notes that the increasingly competitive environment for resources means that organisations have *innovated* in accountability mechanisms, seeking to monitor, evaluate and improve their internal structures—adopting, in essence, the business models of the private sector (Dill, 1999).

As the international development sector increasingly funds research, it contributes to this *academic capitalism*. In this process, universities and university research centres become key grant recipients of international aid.[11] Jones and Young identified 11 international donors who committed more than US$100 million to external research in FY 2005;

the Gates Foundation, alone, disbursed some US$450 million (Jones and Young, 2007, p. 4). This illustrates the importance of research to the international development sector as well as an erosion of the line between aid spending for on-the-ground programmes and for research. It also acknowledges the increase in university engagement in projects which seek to *make a difference.*

Balancing Stakeholders

As with many organisations, research institutions of all forms are susceptible to what Koppell describes as 'multiple accountability disorder' (Koppell, 2005) or what Bovens describes as 'the problem of many eyes' (Bovens, 2007, p. 455). While it is inevitable—and reasonable—for an individual or organisation to be accountable to more than one stakeholder, the challenge is when the accountability requirements either are contradictory or generate excessive administration costs. Both Koppell and Bovens are referring to the need to balance the expectations and demands of different stakeholders.

This was true of the organisations in the case studies included in this chapter. However, it also applies to much larger organisations such as the research units of the World Bank which are similarly faced with the need to balance a large and diverse group of stakeholders: 'We don't have a singular stakeholder and respond to a lot of people. These include people in developing countries, management, operation side colleagues, donors; we try to balance all constituencies.'[12]

There are several key tensions that arise. The first is between the policy-makers and the research community (see Caplan, 1979; Choi et al., 2005), and arises due to the differences in expectations between the two groups in terms of quality, content and availability of research. A week is famously a long time in politics. Policy-makers require findings to be available on short notice, often a fraction of the time needed for the systematic collection of robust evidence, and the subsequent analysis and drafting of research findings—whether this is related, for example, to policy on global warming or on immigration.

Further, the criteria for judging quality differ between researchers (who prioritise detail, nuance and thoroughness) and policy-makers (who privilege simplicity, brevity and clear answers to specific questions that lead to justifiable policy action). This can create problems. The management processes, the personal skills and the outputs are often different when producing a thorough, well-evidenced research paper as opposed to a punchy policy brief. This was reflected in our case studies: representatives from CIPPEC noted the challenge of ensuring the delivery of high-quality research findings in response to the demand of policy-makers. It described the difficulty in ensuring quality research products within the tight timeframes dictated by media cycles or policy processes with the Parliament of Argentina. For its part, RIMISP, who has prioritised research community standards, was undergoing a process of organisational change in an effort to improve its links to policy-makers and the media, including bolstering its communication team.

A second common tension is the need to balance the independence and credibility of academic research with membership in an advocacy coalition. Research organisations will always be positioned somewhere in the public policy firmament. Researchers will often have their own political preferences and allegiances. At the same time, research organisations make claims about the legitimacy of their recommendations. Regardless of the value beliefs of the research organisation, its legitimacy is founded on its ability to produce evidence-based recommendations. Research organisations can find themselves in an awkward balancing act between their reputation and the validity of their research on the one hand, and the need to establish or maintain working relationships with specific stakeholders who have particular advocacy goals which may be at odds with the research findings on the other.

A third tension arises between the generation of evidence that will be accepted by the policy community and the desire to work with the beneficiaries of research. Referring to theories of the sociology of science using the example of soil erosion in Zambia, Keeley and Scoones (1999, p. 8 citing Callon, 1986 and Latour, 1987) argue that research can create agent-networks that imbue certain types of knowledge—often evidence using objective evidence collection—which act to exclude *local* or *traditional* knowledge. Positivist approaches to the generation of evidence use models, theories and reductionist processes that are outside the experience of the *beneficiaries* of the research. At the same time, participatory research techniques generate evidence which may lack widespread applicability and may lack legitimacy in the eyes of policy-makers. For organisations like ForestAction, who use predominantly participatory action research, this may create challenges between the epistemological approaches they use and the desire to influence policy.

A fourth tension relates to the need to balance the requirements of funding agencies with the mission-driven priorities of the organisation. An organisation may be forced to balance applying for a grant which falls outside its mission and priorities, but that offers the possibility of much-needed funding. ForestAction, for example, was unable to string together consecutive grants into longer term programmes of research targeting the areas of concern of their partner-communities because there was a lack of consistent funding. The funding context and the availability of funds for research will, therefore, shape the context in which the organisational mission can be implemented. In difficult funding contexts, in order to remain sustainable, organisations can be faced with the challenge of accepting donor requirements, regardless of considerations such as organisation-level strategy. This can result in mission creep. Others (like CIPPEC), who have a broader mission, can be more flexible on which projects they take on. On a broader note, resource limitations, whether in the form of client timeframes or donor budgets, can entail compromises in the ability of an organisation to deliver on the quality of a project deemed necessary to effect the desired change.

These four examples are illustrative of the main challenges facing the organisations observed. Others are possible. Each result from the need to balance stakeholders, and their different accountability relationships, and the consequences attached to each. These must be constantly assessed, managed and navigated by the staff of the organisation.

Accountability and Evaluation in Violently Divided Societies

Regardless of whether they are universities, non-profits or consultancy firms, research organisations differ greatly in mandate, capacity and accountability profile. Similarly, VDS come in many shapes and sizes—in this book alone, the heterogeneity is evident in such case studies as South Africa, Afghanistan, Sri Lanka, India and Northern Ireland. Policy-makers in each may have different priorities, different capacities and interests in evidence and different belief-systems.

Drawing on 23 research case studies across the Global South, Carden (2009) identifies five *policy/political contexts* ranging from *clear government demand* to downright disinterest or hostility. Each has different consequences for the likely influence of research and the strategies of research organisations to have an impact. Without an in-depth study which is beyond the scope of this chapter, it is difficult to identify whether VDS are characterised more often by one policy/political context than another.

While ForestAction and CGD work within societies that may be described as being *violently divided*, they are as different from each other as they are from CIPPEC or RIMISP (based in societies which are not as obviously *violently divided*). It is difficult to identify whether aspects of the accountability profiles of CGD and ForestAction arise from the nature of their policy/political context as violently divided, other aspects of their context and policy environment, or the mission and institutional specificities of the research organisation itself. However, it is possible to make some statements based on what we know of VDS and the other contributions to this book.

Violent Divisions and Advocacy Coalitions

The term 'violently divided societies' gives us the entry point: political violence constitutes the division of a society into factions who are willing to use violence to pursue political aims. Regardless of whether the divisions are founded on ethnic, linguistic, class, tribal or rural/urban divisions, they share the common structural characteristic of a volatile division between society, politics and policy. Sabatier's description of policy processes unfolding within policy subsystems through the negotiation of advocacy coalitions has implications for political dynamics within VDS. In VDS, the advocacy coalitions are likely to be particularly strong, and will follow the fault-lines of the violent divisions.

Members of a political subsystem are, therefore, likely to divide in line with the factions. The advocacy coalitions will be characterised by strongly held value systems and causal beliefs between themselves, while as with other *opposing* (for such is the best term) advocacy coalitions, there will be no consensus. *Within* an advocacy coalition there will be strongly shared norms, narratives and discourses which legitimise policy recommendations. However, *between* advocacy coalitions, the level of shared discourse is typically much less. A research organisation will often be forced to make a decision, therefore, to be accepted within one or the other advocacy coalition. Since the norms, narratives and depictions of realities in a society such as Northern Ireland are likely to be shaped by the divisions, the choice to work within one or the other will, therefore, inevitably be politicised. In terms of accountability, an organisation may be faced with a choice. It may claim membership in an advocacy coalition, and thereby be associated with its policy beliefs and objectives. While this may provide solidarity and support with that particular coalition, the organisation is also publicly separating itself from other coalitions and interest groups.

Another option is to choose *not* to publicly align with an advocacy organisation—in which case the decision to remain independent carries the risk of being considered irrelevant and/or being ignored by all. Moreover, for researchers who are identifiably from one part of the community or the other, it may be difficult or even impossible to cultivate a perception of neutrality. The name, the personal appearance, the language or simply the perception may identify a researcher or an organisation as being from one or the other *side*—Catholic, Protestant, Tamil, from the city, rural areas or otherwise (Finlay, 2001). Deliberate efforts to maintain independence within the community will be difficult, as the perception of others overrides self-identification or claims (Finlay, 2001; Hermann, 2001). Maintaining the accountability profile may be difficult or impossible (see Colin Knox, Chapter 5).

Value of Evidence

A second way in which location within a VDS may affect evaluation and accountability within research organisations is by reducing the value of evidence as a legitimising force (for a case study example, see Kelly, Chapter 6). On one level, there are significant methodological difficulties in the rigid application of the scientific method within the context of VDS: 'with regard to the study of violent conflicts, both the positivistic demand for objectivity and the hermeneutic requirement for honest reflexivity are extremely difficult to meet' (Hermann, 2001, p. 79). On another level, evidence-based causal relationships may be subordinated in some circumstances to politically-based values and assumptions, based on the history of the violent divisions. Kelly (Chapter 6) illustrates how the political beliefs of policy-makers and other stakeholders buffeted HIV/AIDS research in South Africa. This was exacerbated by the absence of shared norms, such as a lack of respect for evidence and the scientific method. However, this needs to be treated with care. Twenty-three cases that underpin Carden's five-type classification of policy and political context are characterised by violence. There is no clear relationship between violence and the receptivity of the policy-maker to evidence. Of the case studies in the current chapter, both CGD and ForestAction formulated self-conscious strategies for dealing with the government: CGD, by drawing civil society organisations into wider platforms; ForestAction, by maintaining links with the government but working at a community level and seeking to target community-level policy-makers. This suggests that evidence may be more likely to have an impact at the lower or middle government tiers, rather than at higher policy levels (Thomas and Grindle, 1990).

Funding

A third key way in which location within VDS affects evaluation and accountability concerns the resources available for research. Just as the position of researchers within the wider policy community may affect their research interests, the work, and commissioning of research, by funders also risks being politicised and de-legitimised. The subordination of research to political interests and beliefs may either devalue that research or leave it without funding. Moreover, since violent divisions are normally antithetical to equitable economic growth, essential resources may be scarce for large swaths of society. Funding from outsiders may be more plentiful, but ForestAction nonetheless notes the difficulty in building sustainable programmes relevant to its core constituencies, the forest users of Nepal. RIMISP, ForestAction and CGD all relied heavily on international donor funding. While RIMISP has been able to build long-term repeat-project funding through strong links with international and bilateral donor agencies, for the former two the funding environment exercises a significant influence. Although CGD's and ForestAction's internal organisational structures are designed to be nimble and reactive to opportunities as they arise, they find that the maintenance of sustainable long-term programmes are too difficult. The nature of the funders is likely to affect both the research that is funded and the ability of organisations to balance the pursuit of their mission and the sustainability of funding.

Local Populations in Violently Divided Societies

A fourth impact of VDS affects the relationship between the researchers and their research participants, rather than the surrounding political context and policy-makers. The challenges in engaging local populations are deepened by the violent divisions, as in building accountability. Any research taking place within VDS will inevitably and unavoidably affect communities and individuals living there. Social and political violence leave legacies of disempowerment and vulnerability. However, as argued by Jayawickrama and Strecker (this book), researchers should not *pathologise* those who suffer violence; nor should research participants be stripped of dignity or agency by being cast as no more than victims. They argue that researchers must act in a way that acknowledges the legacy of the violent divisions, while not marginalising the communities or misrepresenting their experiences through the research process. The need to balance these demands can confront the researcher with intense personal and ethical challenges.

Establishing accountability relationships with local populations is undertaken in parallel with those ethical dilemmas sketched out by Jayawickrama and Strecker. For those outside the VDS, identifying or building shared expectations can be very difficult, since they are not immersed in the narratives of the violence or the political/advocacy coalitions. For researchers from within the society, they will tend to be linked with one faction or another within the schisms that characterised that society. Either way, their objectivity may be challenged. The maintenance of systems of enforceability and answerability is equally difficult. Research organisations working within such contexts, by and large, have no ethics boards to help them with their work. An alternative had been adopted by ForestAction, which is to nurture a relationship with the communities, characterised by ongoing dialogue and feedback loops.

Conclusion

Wherever they work, research organisations are complex and varied in nature. They are accountable to—and are evaluated by—many different stakeholders. The formal evaluation techniques by programme evaluators commissioned by their funders and donors offer one set of expectations by which the work of research organisations is to be evaluated; the traditional tools of research evaluation (bibliometrics and peer review) offer another set that is linked to the priorities and expectations of a community of academic peers. However, these are a few evaluation approaches amongst many, and donors are only one of myriad stakeholders. Research organisations are also evaluated by their fellow experts within the policy community, against the rules of the advocacy coalition. Each of these stakeholders is different, and while each reacts to the context, the differences within individual organisations are equally important to the differences in the society within which they work. Violent divisions in societies change the nature of politics, and, therefore, the nature of the formulation and advocacy coalitions. This, in turn, affects the manner in which organisations position and orient themselves vis-à-vis a range of specific stakeholders. Conditions of violence heighten and entrench the challenges of being accountable to the policy community; they can undermine the value of the research itself, in favour of policy beliefs and political narratives not necessarily rooted in evidence. Managing multiple accountabilities to multiple stakeholders can also entrench problems of sustainability and accountability to local communities. Balancing these stakeholders, while remaining effective, ethical and solvent, is an even more difficult job for research organisations.

Notes

1. The case studies are drawn from a One World Trust research project that examined the accountability of research organisations. See http://www.oneworldtrust.org/apro/
2. Gibelmann and Gelman (2001) list a series of scandals that found their way into national newspapers in the USA and across a range of other countries; these were chiefly concerned with various forms of theft of donations and public funds. Experiences in Rwanda and other difficult interventions have triggered a wider discussion on the quality and professionalism of the non-profit sector: Ebrahim (2003), Edwards and Hulme (1996), Spar and Dail (2002).
3. The agent–principal conception of accountability describes the situation where a principal contracts an agent by mutual agreement to act in a particular way. This empowers the principal with mechanisms to hold the agent to account for how the agent discharges this duty.
4. This is a legal doctrine which treats the company or corporation as a person in itself, capable of having rights, duties, privileges and powers. The ability to exercise these is conferred on people by virtue of their position within the management and governance of the organisation, but the organisation itself is treated as a person by the court.
5. All four organisations agreed to be part of a wider project, supported by the International Development Research Centre (IDRC), called 'Accountability Principles for Research Organisations' (see http://www.oneworldtrust.org/apro/). They were not originally identified specifically for their relevance to this chapter.
6. A concept introduced by Pross (1986), who used 'policy communities' to describe all of the agents with an interest in a broad policy area such as health or transportation. Heclo (1978) uses the term, 'issue networks'.
7. This chapter does not consider research purely for the sake of research: the researchers relevant to this book are considered as either seeking to have an influence on their field, at the least, or to make changes in policy more broadly.
8. 'An epistemic community is a network of professionals with recognised expertise and competence in a particular domain and an authoritative claim to policy-relevant knowledge within that domain or issue-area' (Haas, 1992, p. 3).

9. Although they emphasised that they are responsible for following the ethics governing a researchers' duty to their participants.

10. The one exception of which I am aware (there may be others) is a collaboration set up between Kenneth Bush of the International Conflict Research (INCORE, University of Ulster) and the Irish Peace Centres in Northern Ireland labelled the Community Based Research Ethics Review Group. This peer-based initiative undertakes ethical reviews of selected community-based projects which possess a research component. This, however, has been established on a pilot basis, and has not yet been formally institutionalised as an on-going mechanism.

11. As an example, I searched on the Research for Development database for DFID R4D spending in three countries referred to in this book: in Afghanistan, three of four project recipients were universities or university centres; in Sri Lanka it was one of two; and in South Africa seven of twelve. Link: http://r4d.dfid.gov.uk/Output/196907/ (accessed on 24 July 2015).

12. Personal communication, World Bank Development Research Group, 18 April 2008.

References

Bovens, M. (2007). Analysing and assessing accountability: A conceptual framework. *European Law Journal, 13*(4), 447–468.

Braun, M., Chudnovsky, M., Ducote, N. and Weyrauch, V. (2004). *A comparative study of policy research institutes in developing countries* (Working Paper: CS 2 component of the Phase II of Global Development Network's Bridging Research and Policy project, carried out by the Centre for the Implementation of Policies Promoting Equity and Growth (CIPPEG)). Retrieved from http://www.ebpdn.org/download/ download.php?table=resources&id=1413 (accessed on 22 April 2015).

Bunda, M. A. (1979). Accountability and evaluation, *Theory into Practice, 18*(5), 357–376.

Callon, M. (1986). Some elements of a sociology of translation: Domestication of the scallops and the fishermen of St Brieuc Bay. In J. Law (Eds), *Power, action and belief: A new sociology of knowledge?* London: Routledge and Kegan Paul.

Caplan, N. (1979). The two communities theory and knowledge utilization. *American Behavioral Science, 22*(3), 457–470.

Carden, F. (2009). *Knowledge to policy: Making the most of development research.* Ottawa and Delhi: International Development Research Centre and SAGE Publications. Retrieved from http://web.idrc.ca/openebooks/417-8/ (accessed on 27 April 2015).

Choi, B. C. K., Pang, T., Lin, V., Puska, P., Sherman, G., Goddard, M., Ackland, M. J., Sainsbury, P., Stachenko, S., Morrison, H. and Clottey, C. (2005). Can scientists and policy makers work together? *Journal of Epidemiology and Community Health, 59*(8), 632–637.

Chambers, R. (1997). *Whose reality counts? Putting the last first.* London: ITDG Publishing.

Chambers, R. and Pettit, J. (2004). Shifting power to make a difference. In L. Groves and R. Hinton (Eds), *Inclusive aid, changing power and relationships in international development* (pp. 137–162). London and Sterling, VA: Earthscan Publications Ltd.

Clark, B. R. (1998). *Creating entrepreneurial universities: Organisational pathways of transformation.* Bingley: Emerald Group Publishing Limited.

Court, J. and Young, J. (2005). Bridging research and policy in international development: Context, evidence and links. In D. Stone and S. Maxwell (Eds), *Global knowledge networks and international development: Bridges across boundaries* (pp. 18–36). Oxford and New York: Routledge.

Day P. and Klein, R. (1987). *Accountabilities: Five public services.* London: Tavistock Publications.

Dill, D. D. (1999). Academic accountability and university adaptation: The architecture of an academic learning organisation. *Higher Education, 38*(2), 127–154.

Donaldson, T. and Preston, L. E. (1995). The stakeholder theory of the corporation: Concepts, evidence and implications. *Academy of Management Review, 20*(1), 65–91.

Ebrahim, A. (2003). Accountability in practice: Mechanisms for NGOs. *World Development, 31*(5), 813–829.

Edwards, M. and Hulme, D. (1996). *Beyond the magic bullet: NGO performance and accountability in the post-cold war world.* Sterling, VA: Kumarian Press.

Finlay, A. R. (2001). Reflexivity and the dilemmas of identification: An ethnographic encounter in Northern Ireland. In M. Smyth and G. Robinson (Eds), *Researching violently divided societies: Ethical and methodological issues* (pp. 55–76). Tokyo: United Nations University Press.

Fischer, F. (1993). Citizen participation and the democratization of policy expertise: From theoretical inquiry to practical cases. *Policy Studies, 26*(3), 165–187.

Freeman, R. E. (1984). *Strategic management: A stakeholder approach.* Boston, MA: Pitman Publishing.

Geuna, A. and Martin, B. R. (2003). University research evaluation and funding: An international comparison. *Minerva, 41*(4), 277–304.

Gibbons, M., Limoges, C., Nowotny, H., Schwartzman, S., Scott, P. and Trow, M. (1994). *The new production of knowledge: The dynamics of science and research in contemporary societies.* London, New York, New Delhi: SAGE Publications.

Gibelman, M. and Gelman, S. R. (2001). Very public scandals: nongovernmental organisations in trouble. *Voluntas: International Journal of Voluntary and Nonprofit Organizations, 12*(1), 49–66.

Goetz, A. M. and Jenkins, R. (2005). Reinventing accountability: Making democracy work for human development. *International Political Economy Series.* United Kingdom: Palgrave MacMillan.

Haas, P. M. (1992). Introduction: Epistemic communities and international policy coordination. *International Organisation, 46*(1), 1–35.

Heclo, H. (1978). Issue networks and the executive establishment. In A. King (Ed.), *The new American political system* (pp. 87–124). Washington, DC: American Enterprise Institute for Public Policy Research.

Hermann, T. (2001). The impermeable identity wall: The study of violent conflicts by 'insiders' and 'outsiders'. In M. Smyth and G. Robinson (Eds), *Researching violently divided societies: Ethical and methodological issues.* London and Tokyo: Pluto Press and United Nations University Press.

Higgins, P. A. T., Chan, K. M. A. and Porder, S. (2006). Bridge over a philosophical divide. *Evidence and Policy, 2*(2), 249–255.

Jenkins, R. and Goetz, A. M. (1999). Accounts and accountability: Theoretical implications of the right-to-information movement in India. *Third World Quarterly, 20*(3), 603–622.

Kearns, K. P. (1994). The strategic management of accountability in nonprofit organisations: An analytical framework. *Public Administration Review*, *54*(2), 185–192.

Keeley, J. and Scoones, I. (1999). *Understanding environmental policy process: A review* (IDS Working Paper 89). Brighton: Institute for Development Studies, University of Sussex. Retrieved from http://www.ids.ac.uk/files/dmfile/wp89.pdf (accessed on 22 April 2015).

————. (2000). *Environmental policymaking in Zimbabwe: Discourses, science and politics* (IDS Working Paper 116). Brighton: Institute for Development Studies, University of Sussex. Retrieved from http://www.ids.ac.uk/files/Wp116.pdf (accessed on 22 April 2015).

Kingdon, J. R. (1995). *Agendas, alternatives and public policies*. New York, NY: Harper Collins College Publishers.

Koppell, J. G. S. (2005). Pathologies of accountability: ICANN and the challenge of 'multiple accountabilities disorder'. *Public Administration Review*, *65*(1), 94–108.

Latour, B. (1987). *Science in action: How to follow scientists and engineers through society*. Milton Keynes: Open University Press.

Lindquist, E. A. (2001). *Discerning policy influence: Framework for a strategic evaluation of IDRC-supported research*. Ottawa: International Development Research Centre. Retrieved from http://web.idrc.ca/uploads/user-S/10359907080discerning_policy.pdf (accessed on 22 April 2015).

Lingán, J., Cavender, A., Palmer, T. and Gwynne, B. (2010, June). *Responding to development effectiveness in the GlobalSsouth* (World Vision Briefing Paper No. 126). London: One World Trust.

Mulgan, R. (2000). Accountability: An ever-expanding concept? *Public Administration*, *78*(3), 555–573.

Newell, P. (2006). Taking accountability into account: The debate so far. In P. Newell and J. Wheeler (Eds), *Rights, resources and the politics of accountability* (pp. 37–58). London and New York, NY: Zed Books Ltd.

Newell, P. and Bellour, S. (2002). *Mapping accountability: Origins, contexts and implications for development*. Brighton, UK: Institute for Development Studies.

OECD. (1997). *Evaluation of programs promoting participatory development and good governance—Synthesis report*. Paris: OECD.

Patton, M. Q. (2008). *Utilization focused evaluation* (4th ed.). Thousand Oaks, CA: SAGE Publications.

Pross, A. P. (1986). *Group politics and public policy*. Toronto: Oxford University Press.

Raz, J. (1986). *The morality of freedom*. New York, NY: Oxford University Press.

Roe, E. M. (1991). Development narratives, or making the best of blueprint development. *World Development*, *19*(4), 287–300.

Sabatier, P. (1988). An advocacy coalition framework of policy change and the role of policy-oriented learning therein. *Policy Sciences*, *21*(2), 129–168.

Slaughter, S. and Rhoades, G. (1997). *Academic capitalism and the new economy: Markets, state, and higher education*. Maryland, MD: The Johns Hopkins University Press.

Stone, D. (2005). Knowledge networks and global policy. In D. Stone and S. Maxwell (Eds), *Global knowledge networks and international development: Bridges across boundaries* (pp. 89–105). Oxford and New York, NY: Routledge.

Thomas, J. W. and Grindle, M. S. (1990). After the decision: Implementing policy reforms in developing countries. *World Development*, *18*(8), 1163–1181.

Weiner, L. (2004). The unity of Rawl's work, *The Journal of Moral Philosophy*, *1*(3), 265–275.

Weingart, P. (*1999*). Scientific expertise and political accountability: Paradoxes of science in politics. *Science and Public Policy*, *26*(3), 151–161.

Weiss, C. H. (1979). The many meanings of research utilization. *Public Administration Review*, *39*(5), 426–431.

4

The Ethics of Evaluating Research
Views from the Field

Janaka Jayawickrama* and Jacqueline Strecker

thics, along with logic, metaphysics and epistemology, is one of the main branches of Western scientific philosophy. It corresponds, in the knowledge division of the field, to formal, natural and moral philosophy. However, there are many different—often completing—definitions, understandings and applications of ethics. The variances in conceptual understandings of ethics are, in part, due to the three interrelated meanings that have been applied to the term: (a) the principles of morality that theorise right or wrong behaviour for every individual; (b) the codes of conduct developed by and for individuals within a particular profession and (c) the scientific study of ideal human behaviour (Newman and Brown, 1996). All three of these definitions are relevant to the professional ethics that guide researchers and evaluators in violently divided societies (VDS). The application of any one dimension to the exclusion of the others tends to lead to misunderstanding or misapplication (Newman and Brown, 1996, p. 20). To avoid *doing*

---

* Since 2004, all my research activities were collaborations with communities from disaster and conflict affected countries. These collaborations are special because I encountered the best teachers in the world and they all provided ethical reviews of my research outcomes. Prof. Phil O'Keefe granted the much needed criticisms and comments. A very big thank you to all.

harm, researchers and evaluators in VDS must have a *balanced* perspective of these three ethical dimensions and a sense of their interconnections. For example, a simple action such as reporting *wrongdoing* (such as bribe taking) in a VDS could have disproportionate effects for the accused, since underdeveloped or corrupt administrative structures may set in motion events leading to consequences much more dire than in other circumstances.

There are several ethical issues that are common across all types of research, including evaluation, which in itself is a form of research. Ethical dimensions may touch upon research design, methodology, sources of funding and methods in reporting data. Unlike evaluators, university-based researchers are often required to undergo an ethical review process at their institutions before commencing a study. This process affords researchers an opportunity to think through ethical scenarios that could manifest and develop mitigation strategies to reduce risk. For the evaluator, ethical considerations are present throughout the evaluation process, including during: the entry/contracting; the design of the evaluation; the data collection; analysis and interpretation; communication of results and the utilisation of results (Morris, 2008). Importantly, although development and humanitarian agencies are increasingly supporting research and evaluation, formal, binding, systemic, ethic review mechanisms are not in place—although non-binding codes of conduct, with no enforcement mechanisms, have been developed.

Research ethics are based on the underlying principles of autonomy, beneficence and justice (Orb et al., 2000). These key ethical principles are designed to protect and respect research participants, doing good for others and fairness and preventing harm (Capron, 1989; Raudonis, 1992). Within the context of evaluation ethics, Morris adds fidelity and non-maleficence (Morris, 2008), explaining that evaluators are expected to maintain fidelity by acting in good faith and ensuring they are loyal, honest and keep their promises (Newman and Brown, 1996). Non-maleficence, or the *Do no harm* principle, exhorts evaluators to avoid inflicting injury on others (either physical or psychological), and to 'protect individuals from exposure to the *risk* of harm' (Morris, 2008, p. 5). For those situations where harm is unavoidable, the evaluator is expected to manage and reduce harm (where possible) and should maintain a reasonable expectation that the harm incurred will be compensated by the benefits of the evaluation (Morris, 2008).

The underlying principles of research and evaluation ethics are therefore similar in the sense that the core concepts of integrity and wrongdoing are used as blanket norms in both frameworks (UNEG, 2008). However, approaches to evaluation in the humanitarian field have less focus on ethical frameworks, than on the personal integrity of the evaluator.[1]

The much-cited principle of *Do No Harm* has, paradoxically, served to subsidise the lack of development of guiding ethical frameworks. This is partly because, although there are many ethical frameworks that provide strong guidelines for research practice, there are a few evaluation frameworks designed explicitly for VDS. Instead, evaluators are advised to call upon broadly articulated regional or organisational guidelines that have been developed for evaluation of all forms and contexts. Unfortunately, these frameworks often fail to provide appropriate support and guidance for evaluators working within VDS and, thus, are often not readily applied in the field. Another major issue is that evaluation commissioners and donors often have their own set of *ethical standards*, which are not adequately enforced or adhered to, creating a predicament for the evaluator trying to manage competing ethical protocols.

The aim of this chapter is to discuss critical implications of evaluation ethics and frameworks within VDS through the examination of field-based examples. We examine the ethics of evaluating research in and on violently divided contexts, through the lens of personal experiences as an evaluator and researcher.[2] We use existing ethical frameworks and guidelines to unpack the diversity of ethical dilemmas, and to highlight what additional considerations are needed for this context. This analysis is largely shaped by Jayawickrama's particular positionality (a male, Sri Lankan, evaluator/researcher, currently working in the European university setting) and by what he has learned working in the space within and between the European university system and VDS. From this particular vantage point, we are able to discern some of the central challenges to evaluators working in VDS, and the dilemmas faced by academics and policy-makers attempting to evaluate and conduct research in and on VDS. The following sections are described in a first person account from Jayawickrama's perspective.

Ethical Principles and Frameworks in VDS

Within the Western[3] academic and political traditions (two traditions that are intimately connected), ethics and ethical discourse are derived mainly from scientific knowledge systems, which have discounted and marginalised non-Western systems of knowing. The model of ethical frameworks that prominent social research councils such as ESRC (UK) was first developed in the context of medical and clinical research on patients (Dyer and Demeritt, 2008). Research councils have appropriated the medical model to ensure that all research was, and is, conducted in a manner that protects all groups involved in the research, including the participants, institutions, funders and researchers. This protection is extended throughout the entire research and dissemination process (ESRC, 2010). Similar research councils can be found in almost every country conducting research. Although the focus on research ethics is a prominent pillar of all councils, the review processes differ from country to country (Iphofen, 2009). In some countries, particularly those experiencing conflict or crisis, the ethical protocols may be weak or non-existent. In these contexts, researchers and evaluators are left with a dilemma of establishing which ethical systems should be employed. Researchers who originate from the Global North often rely on the frameworks outlined by their *home* institutions or countries, not least because their research protocols are typically governed by the legal contracts formalising financial arrangements between research institutions and funding agencies. While the guiding frameworks are deemed to be part of the research governance structures of a university within which ethics review is located, it is only by examining what happens *on the ground* that we can better understand whether this is indeed ethical in practice.

For the majority of ethics review boards, assessments of research projects within VDS are typically made by academics or policymakers who have no training in peace and conflict studies, and no on-the-ground field experience which might otherwise temper or contextualise their understandings of the impact of the ethico-political environment on research and vice versa. This difficulty is exacerbated by epistemological schisms—in particular, by institutions and researchers who *believe* exclusively in the positivist scientific processes, and, therefore, disregard different ways of knowing. This is not necessarily a problem between the Global North and Global South, but between the *believers* (of science) and *non-believers* of scientific approaches.[4] In Chapter 8 of this book, Healy and Healy examine the various ways in which the worldview of funding agencies influences the evaluation process. They maintain that the type of evaluation and learning approaches selected by non-profits often reflect the worldview of their funding agency.

Similarly, as highlighted in Chapter 2, programme evaluation methodology often reinforces a particular worldview. As Kushner (2000, as cited in Conley-Taylor, 2005, p. 7) observes:

> Evaluation methodology necessarily privileges one view of the world over another—usually selecting the view of program administrators, funding bodies and other powerful actors over that of the individuals who participate in programs. Because evaluation methodology pursues a logic of 'coherence', it necessarily selects a point of view that will deny meaning to other 'different worlds of meaning' involved.

A positivist worldview, or what Chambers refers to as Neo-Newtonian practice, posits a single knowable reality, which speaks to a universal order and suggests that ethical processes need to be standardised in order to ensure better control (Chambers, 2010). However, the notion that an externally generated set of ethical principles can be applied to local participants in the South raises a possible ethical dilemma itself. The moment externally generated ethical principles are applied to a local community of research participants, an insider–outsider, top-down power dynamic risks casting the researcher and research institution as *Others* (Said, 1978). The realities of this dilemma can be underscored in discussions I had with a researcher/practitioner in the British health care system about the ethical parameters of his work. He argued that although people in Western Darfur may not have the same opportunities or living conditions as people in the UK, they should be covered under the same ethical framework used in the UK, if the researcher is from the UK. He further explained that in a country like Sudan, ethical frameworks and processes are so poor that a researcher needs to follow, and research participants should be subject to, an advanced framework from the UK. The same tension is evident in what we call the *ideology of doing the right thing*, which does not question the assumption that what is acceptable to a professional body or research institute in the Global North is axiomatically appropriate for *researched communities* in the Global South. When a researcher begins to question the unquestioned imposition of ethical principles from the North on the South, and begins to explore the ethico-power relationships between the research community and the researched community, the legitimacy of the research process is open for discussion. This convergence of *what is right for everyone* and professional principles highlights the need for a balanced understanding of Newman and Brown's three ethical understandings.

As noted, in the field of evaluation, evaluators are not usually guided by ethical review boards and processes, but are still required to abide by an array of professional principles and frameworks that are articulated and updated by regional and international evaluation associations. Some of the most prominent frameworks include: American Evaluation Association (AEA) Guiding Principles for Evaluators (2004), Australasian Evaluation Society's (AES) Guidelines for the Ethical Conduct of Evaluations (2010), Canadian Evaluation Society Guidelines for Ethical Conduct (2012), African Evaluation Guidelines AfrEA (2002), French Evaluation Society's Charter of evaluation guiding principles for public policies and programmes (2003), OECD-DAC's Quality Standards for Development Evaluation (OECD DAC 2010) and United Nation Evaluation Group (UNEG) Ethical Guidelines (2008).

Many of these frameworks draw from one another, and all of them aim to promote ethical practice and improve evaluation theory and use, by providing guidance and awareness to ethical issues prominent in evaluation. These frameworks have been proven to provide a useful warning of ethical dilemmas in evaluation, but they do not provide a *blue print* for how to approach and respond to particular situations (Morris, 2008). Several of the frameworks have also been criticised for this degree of ambiguity. One review of the AEA's Guiding Principles suggested 'the Principles in particular seem so open to interpretation that a wide range of values, preferences, and opinions can be projected onto them' (Datta, 2002, p. 195—as cited in Morris, 2008). While this critique is valid, it is this same openness that enables these principles to be transferred from one context to another. The usefulness of these ethical frameworks is therefore variable, depending on appropriate interpretation and implementation by the evaluator. If these principles are not applied through an appropriate mechanism, they contain the same risk as ethics boards: imposing externally generated principles onto local participants and projects, which may actually cause harm, by subordinating local needs and realities, or by creating Southern subservience to Northern research or ethical agendas.

Within violently divided contexts, the concept of codifying a strict set of unified ethical principles is simply unrealistic. This is because each situation in VDS provides social, political and cultural challenges that are different to each other, and, thus, finding and applying a uniform ethical framework is extremely challenging. There are two reasons for this: one is the social, political and cultural differences between the violently divided context and the evaluator; and the second relates to the requirements of the organisation that commissioned the evaluation.

For example, within the OECD-DAC's evaluation criteria (OECD DAC, 2010)—impact, efficiency, effectiveness, relevance and sustainability—the evaluator faces this two-prong challenge. To evaluate a research project through these criteria requires time; time to learn the local social, political and cultural situation, as well as time to cultivate engagement from the community or project beneficiaries. In most cases, this is not possible, due to tight time scales or budget limitations, constraints that plague most evaluations. The evaluator walks in and out of the project community; at best, he or she can only hope to gather good quality data; however, the quality, validity or utility of this data may be questionable if the necessary relationships of trust do not exist between the evaluator and the evaluation's *subject* or stakeholder.

Evaluators working in VDS are, therefore, faced with a difficult task of negotiating the ethical line within a fractured context and against ethical frameworks that propose a distant ideal. The following sections unpack different ethical dilemmas faced by evaluators and researchers working in VDS. The sections highlight the limitations of the available frameworks within these contexts, and provide guidance on what additional considerations are needed to increase the chances of achieving good ethical decisions and practice. While it is not within the scope of this chapter to deconstruct and address all ethical issues that arise from the cases, the following discussion chronicles some of the prominent challenges we have faced as both researchers and evaluators.

Knowing Your Values and Respecting Those of Others

The first lesson an evaluator must learn is that it is imperative to start with what one knows and recognise one's inherent values and bias. Understanding the deeper values that underpin personal actions and cultural practices is a difficult, but important, prerequisite to demonstrate cultural competency or humility. According to the AEA's guiding principles, part of cultural competence is seeking awareness of your own culturally based assumptions, and then seeking to understand the worldviews of culturally different participants and stakeholders in the evaluation (AEA, 2004). Various other scholars, including Humberto

Reynoso-Vallejo (2012), the Director for Programme Evaluation with the Center for Health Policy and Research at the University of Massachusetts Medical School, highlight the need for *cultural humility*, as opposed to cultural competency, because it takes into account the political power imbalances inherent within evaluation processes.

> Cultural humility assumes that individuals' life experiences and multiple affiliations (e.g., racial/ethnic group, gender group, age cohort, region, religion, and leadership roles) interact in complex ways to shape their views. This approach assumes that the political and economic position of the group from which an individual comes, their life experiences, as well as the larger national culture shape perspectives and behavior.

Adopting a framework of cultural humility means committing oneself to on-going self-evaluation and self-critique; processes which help individuals identify their own values. Recognising personal values is important because they can influence one's actions during a study or evaluation. House and Howe (1999) note that it is useful to think about values and facts as existing on a continuum where brutal facts are positioned at one end and bare values at the other. Evaluative statements or claims often fall somewhere towards the centre of this continuum, where facts and values blend.

Morris (2008) also contends that it is important to acknowledge this delineation because 'personal values can influence one's response to numerous features of the project—for example, ways in which specific stakeholder groups (e.g., females, youth, the elderly, ethnic minorities, religious fundamentalists, the disabled) are treated or the degree to which one feels justified in drawing generalised conclusions from evaluation data' (Morris, 2008, p. 200). In VDS, there is often a multiplicity of actors who hold different values and have played different roles, for example, those who have been the perpetrators, the victims, the bystanders and even people who may be completely unaware of the violence surrounding them. These challenging contexts can be particularly disorienting for an evaluator who is not confident and honest about his or her moral values.

The word *moral* can be confusing, as it can be used in two different senses. According to the Concise Oxford Dictionary, moral is: 'Concerned with goodness or badness of character or disposition' (1989, p. 657). Social research, in this sense, is certainly moral, because for each and every one of us, the study is about the things that we care, or are curious, about. As evaluators and researchers, we constantly negotiate and re-negotiate important relations with our participants. Through engaging with the ethical principles provided by our employers, as well as what we learnt from our religions and traditions, we create our own morals that make sense of our findings. By virtue of the evaluations we conduct, the places we travel and the people we encounter, we live according to implicitly moral bearings. However, what we frequently miss is that when we encounter people, we are dealing not only with our own moral frameworks but also with theirs. We make our judgements based on our morals, and they make their judgements based on their moral frameworks. In some instances, these can be harmonious, while in other situations quite conflicting. Conducting research and evaluations in a VDS can be complicated because of this unavoidable condition. However, acknowledging one's own moral values is an important and necessary prerequisite, which will help evaluators and researchers navigate the juxtaposition of different moral frameworks.

The journey I took to uncovering my personal values and beliefs occurred as I transitioned roles in the development field. Before I found my way to the academic and evaluation world, I was a local NGO staff member in Sri Lanka in the humanitarian field. During this time, I was asked to participate as a research subject in a study being conducted by universities (both from the Global North and South). The researchers were interested in studying the traumas faced by humanitarian workers. Again and again, I was asked to explain the links between my experiences in a conflict-affected society and how I dealt with my traumas. There were many questionnaires, and I felt that all the questions were pushing me towards a label of *being traumatised*, while I never felt that I had a special problem different from anyone else in Sri Lanka.[5] Whenever I tried to explain this contradiction, I was, and continue to be, treated as an outcast by the majority of researchers, since I do not fit in to their criteria of trauma.

This experience influenced my understanding of the difference between the *outsiders* and *insiders*. The different knowledge systems that are developed through different experiences may not necessarily agree with each other. This later served me well as I transitioned from being a local humanitarian worker to being a disaster and conflict researcher and evaluator. When I first arrived in Sudan, a representative from a UN agency said that he was surprised to see a Sri Lankan man in his early 30s leading an important research initiative on the mental health of displaced populations. I could not help but strongly suspect that he was expecting a middle-aged white European from a British University. All these challenges provided me with an opportunity to establish relationships with my research and evaluation participants. In countries such as Sudan, Malawi, Pakistan and Jordan, there was distrust towards Westerners. Being a Sri Lankan, I was not seen to be representing the coloniser. Rather I was seen to come from a country which shared similar problems to those places where I was working. Because of this, the relationships I established with communities provided me the opportunity to receive information that they regarded as precious. Not only my background, but also my value of openness and honesty, provided me with opportunities through which I could learn, for example, how an Imam in a Muslim community was dealing with mental health issues. These experiences helped me understand the importance of cultural humility. They also humbled me, and allowed me to realise that I was not a knowledgeable expert but simply a friend who accompanied them during difficult times.

During this time in the field, I spent many sleepless nights thinking about what defines good and what defines bad when we apply this moral-evaluative question to our own work. We try to live our lives in ways that *feel right* to us. We also judge people who do not appear to live the same moral lives that we think are good. In the early stages of my work, as an outsider, these juxtaposition judgements became increasingly frustrating, confusing and upsetting. As Kleinman (2006, p. 2) puts it:

> That is why, in this first sense, what is moral needs to be understood as what is local, and the local needs to be understood to require ethical review (from the outside and from those on the inside who challenge accepted local values).

Making research or evaluative judgements on issues such as gender, power relations, conflict resolution and identity have to be understood as what is local, and to understand the local requires a collaborative ethical review between the outside researcher and inside communities. Several of the ethical frameworks emphasize that 'evaluators should be aware of different cultures, local customs, religious beliefs, gender roles... and be mindful of the potential implications of these differences when planning, carrying out and reporting on evaluations' (UNEG, 2008, p. 14). While the failure to demonstrate cultural humility can corrupt any evaluation or research setting, it poses particular ethical challenges within VDS and can lead to severe implications on both the process and the product of the study or evaluation.

For example, researchers or evaluators who elect not to follow cultural practice can unintentionally distance themselves from the community. An example of this comes from my personal research during a conversation I had with a national staff member in Jordan:

> Last year, we had a research project on gender-based sexual violence among refugees here. The research project manager who came from a European country was a very nice lady. She was very good to us and helpful. But, she refused to follow the general community practices like to cover her head at the community level. She ignored our advice. She only managed to go to the community for a week. All the women refused to talk to her. They felt that this foreign lady was disrespecting their culture. (National Staff Member, Amman, Jordan [Direct discussion with the author, September 2007])

While this example might be typified as the common story of research interventions characterised by insensitivity to cultural practices, there are often deeper values being acted upon in these situations. For example, the foreign woman might have wanted to model what she felt was important feminist conduct. When interpreted in this way, it is clear that this example is not about insensitivity to cultural practices, but rather about two sets of cultural values coming into conflict. Unfortunately, the imposition of foreign concepts is often regarded as a lack of respect for community standards. In this situation, the community perceived the actions as disrespectful and demonstrated their agency by electing not to participate. Ultimately, as both a potential feminist and researcher, the woman lost sight of the larger picture, failing to seize an opportunity to re-examine her own values, and missing an important chance to learn and share the story of these women.

In an evaluation context, a similar action from an evaluator might be met with different reactions, depending on if the local community was supportive or against the project that is being evaluated. Many communities acknowledge that evaluators are employed to make judgements; this is what delineates them from researchers. However, this fact also increases the weight of their studies. An evaluator's judgements often have real and immediate consequences. As a result, if the community is supportive of the project, individuals might feel obligated to participate (in spite of their cultural beliefs) in order to ensure that the project receives a favourable evaluation and continues. In a VDS, however this act can come with grave repercussions for individuals who deviate from cultural norms and values. The evaluator who does not demonstrate cultural humility in this instance can actually be putting him/herself, the research project, and the evaluation participants at risk.

The importance of cultural humility should not be under estimated in an evaluation context. The majority of evaluation frameworks acknowledge the need for cultural competency but fail to truly engage with the politics and power dynamics inherent in the outsider-evaluator and insider-participant relationship. Evaluators need to start with where they live, but inevitably must transcend these boundaries through the processes of self-evaluation and self-critique. It is only then that the evaluator can begin to understand what is moral through a critical local lens, and thus can understand his or her limitations, as well as the unique ethical implications of the specific context. This is especially important within VDS, since evaluators working in these environments are not only challenged with understanding concepts of locality, but they must also navigate through the politics of vulnerability.

Navigating Vulnerabilities

Evaluating research in violently divided contexts often means that evaluators will be working with *vulnerable* stakeholder groups. The politics of vulnerability is such that vulnerability can be construed differently depending on the funder or evaluation association one is a part of (see Zaveri, Chapter 7). It is important to remember here that, as previously stated, evaluation is a form of research, and as such ethical guidelines in evaluation tend to build upon research ethics, which are often imperfect in violently divided contexts.

The Economic and Social Research Council (ESRC) in the UK describes vulnerable groups as potentially those involving children and young people, those with a learning disability or cognitive impairment or individuals in a dependent or unequal relationship (ESRC, 2010, pp. 8–9). Research involving vulnerable groups must undergo a full ethical review and is highlighted as having greater risk. The Research Ethical Framework (2010) also highlights the following sub-groups or subject areas that would normally be considered as involving more than minimal risk:

- Research involving sensitive topics, this would include research which discusses participants' sexual behaviour, their illegal or political behaviour, their experience of violence, their abuse or exploitation, their mental health or their gender or ethnic status.
- Research involving groups where permission of a gatekeeper is normally required for initial access to members—this includes research involving gatekeepers such as adult professionals (e.g., those working with children or the elderly), or research in communities (in the UK or overseas) where access to research participants is not possible without the permission of another adult, such as another family member (e.g., the parent or husband of the participant) or a community leader.

These identified groups are common stakeholders in VDS, and researchers and evaluators are cautioned to take particular care when engaging with these groups during a study. Unfortunately, evaluation frameworks provide little guidance for how to approach vulnerability. UNEG's (2008, p. 7) ethical principles only vaguely reference vulnerable groups, noting that all evaluations must comply with legal codes:

> Compliance with codes for vulnerable groups. Where the evaluation involves the participation of members of vulnerable groups, evaluators must be aware of and comply with legal codes (whether international or national) governing, for example, interviewing children and young people.

While it is important for codes and protocols to be followed, these guidelines provide little direction for evaluators and focus attention on the pathology of vulnerability rather than inequalities within VDS. As a result, many of the evaluators who have a background in research tend to fall back on research ethics guidelines since these are what they know best. Evaluation is, however, distinct from research in several different ways. The most pertinent being that evaluation drives decision-making and often has immediate consequences for the people and organisations involved. Consequently, the ethical dilemmas faced by evaluators are unique, despite the fact that they tend to follow the same guidelines for research ethics and vulnerability.

In Chapter 7 of this book, Sonal Zaveri highlights that mainstream research and evaluation approaches focus too heavily on the symptoms of vulnerability, rather than the sources of vulnerability, which is usually inequality. Similarly, evaluations which only deal with the legalities of working with vulnerable stakeholders and do not adopt a local lens tend to reinforce inequalities by focusing on the vulnerability of the participant rather than acknowledging the individual's knowledge and agency.

> My dear son, we may be poor, we may be illiterate and living in difficult conditions, but we are not stupid and not a bunch of idiots. (Elderly person from Peshawar, Pakistan [Personal discussion with the author, August 1998])

The quote above was from one of my first experiences with a community member, who replied to my questions about vulnerability. The harsh reply made me realise that certain terms are embedded with attitudes and approaches that pathologise and incapacitate communities. I realised that, by concentrating on negativities and vulnerabilities in their lives, I was attempting to cast them as weak and broken rather than strong and capable of dealing with uncertainty. How ethical is it to label these communities as vulnerable, when they are struggling effectively to maintain everyday life? As Kleinman (2006) argues, they may look vulnerable and fragile from an outside point of view, but in the midst of the worst horrors, they indeed continue to live, to celebrate and to enjoy.

However, one of the features of 20th century scientific knowledge systems—particularly in the last 50 years—has been the ways in which pathology has displaced religion as the cardinal referent for explaining the uncertainties and dangers of life. As illustrated in the aforementioned quote, the same pathologising tendency appears to underpin outsider perceptions of communities in VDS. It is an insidious process through which pathologised social constructions within contemporary scientific knowledge systems come to be seen as *natural* and *self-evident*, and, therefore, unquestionable. But what kind of process underpins the transformation of a person who has experienced, or is experiencing, violence to someone with pathology?

While these questions remain unresolved, there is increasing movement away from victimisation and vulnerability pathologies, and towards recognition of the structures that manifest them. The Australian Evaluation Society Guidelines for Ethical Conduct, for example, have rightly moved beyond the vulnerability rhetoric by discussing inequalities as oppose to vulnerabilities.

> Account should be taken of the potential effects of differences and inequalities in society related to race, age, gender, sexual orientation, physical or intellectual ability, religion, socio-economic or ethnic background in the design conduct and reporting of evaluations. Particular regard should be given to any rights, protocols, treaties or legal guidelines which apply. (AES, 2010, p. 9)

Unfortunately, despite the fact that this ethical framework transcends vulnerability pathology by acknowledging the inequalities that underlie it, there is still little direction provided beyond deferring to secondary texts and protocols.

Evaluators within VDS are therefore provided very little guidance on how to navigate working with inequalities or *vulnerabilities*, regardless of whether they rely on ethical protocols outlined for evaluators or researchers. Ultimately, however the evaluator has a greater responsibility to ensure that his/her evaluations do not exacerbate existing inequalities.

One of the main ways evaluations can expose individuals to further risk is by directly or indirectly associating them with the subject of the evaluation. For example, an evaluator conducting an evaluation on genital mutilation (GM) treatment in refugee camps, may unintentionally identify those who have experienced GM by simply visiting their homes to conduct private interviews. Or if a programme is cancelled as a result of an unfavourable evaluation, those who made negative statements during the evaluation's focus groups may be blamed by the community, and may be at risk of community retaliation. It is for these reasons that additional efforts should be made to maintain and protect participant confidentiality within VDS. Ford et al. (2009) emphasize the additional risk within these contexts by proposing that 'there may be a need for an increased level of confidentiality of study data in situations where even the simplest information (household composition, age of males) could provide information to support deliberate targeting of individuals/groups by perpetrators of violence'. It is therefore important that all studies, even those which propose minimal risk, ensure that extra measures are taken to protect the voice and anonymity of participants, since the politics and stability of VDS can quickly change, placing evaluation participants at increased risk. Unfortunately with the growing reliance on digital databases to store participant information, securing data has become progressively more difficult (Morris, 2008).

Another problematic frontier, which is likely to plague both evaluation and research in the coming years, is the ethical dilemma of open data. Further monitoring and research will be needed to ensure that the demands for free and public data do not compromise the security and confidentiality of participants. While it is still unknown what the impact of open data will be in the realm of evaluation, there will undoubtedly be a series of new challenges to ethical protocols.

Although confidentiality measures are important to ensure participant security, efforts to ensure confidentiality should also be balanced with local values. The following situation demonstrates that how addressing inequality and ensuring participant anonymity is often not a black and white situation:

> The female researcher who came to our camp, wanted to talk to my daughter who has been raped. When they sat down to talk, the researcher told me to leave. She said that she wants to talk to my daughter alone. I was confused and asked her why. Then she said that she wants to make sure that I will not influence my daughter's thoughts by being there. I got very upset as I am the only person who understands what my daughter is going through and how can I let a strange woman talk to my daughter alone. I asked them to leave and later I learned that this researcher has complained about me to the camp management. (A Woman from Umkher, Western Darfur [Direct discussion with the author, May 2005])

In this retelling, the researcher is faced with a difficult situation. She might in fact be correct in her assumption that the mother's presence might skew the testimony of the daughter, or the mother's presence may have a comforting effect on the daughter and allow her to open up to the researcher. In either case, the researcher has placed the daughter in a compromising situation positioned between the researcher's and the mother's intentions (be they positive or not). This situation provides an example of the power differential that is at play, and highlights that a single protocol for confidentiality maybe inappropriate within these contexts.

This example also speaks to the need for what Schwandt (2008) refers to as practical knowledge. Practical knowledge is the knowledge gained through being present and experiencing a variety of social situations. Schwandt highlights that practical wisdom is shown not articulated, and is defined by the ability to see the nuances and details in situations, which from the outside appear to be alike. The concept of practical knowledge is vital in VDS: 'practical knowledge is called for precisely in problematic situations not resolvable by solutions forthcoming from following procedures or "going by the book"' (Schwandt, 2008). In these situations, a seasoned evaluator must fall back on their experience to interpret the situations, and should be entrusted with the freedom to mediate the dilemma without being confined to follow prescribed ethical protocols.

Evaluations and research conducted in VDS have a higher potential 'for exploiting a situation of "differential power" which could lead to denying or compromising the rights of individuals' (Ford et al., 2009). This is particularly true in situations where the research or the programme being evaluated is tied to the delivery of aid or life-saving services. In these situations, power differential is a significant factor since participants often know or presume the potential consequences for future funding and their livelihood (Duggan, 2012). Given this context many individuals feel obligated to participate even if their participation would serve to disadvantage them. For example, a recent study in Darfur unintentionally scheduled interviews during the times of food distributions, which placed participants in an unfair position having to choose between one or the other (Ford et al., 2009). Participants may also be placed in compromising situations where they feel obligated to answer questions, which could lead to increased distress or the reliving of traumatic events. The failure to assess appropriate timing and methods for evaluations provides another example of where the outsider's limited contextual knowledge leads to unethical situations, which reinforce inherent power differentials and inequalities.

These examples speak of the importance of applying a critical local lens when designing and conducting evaluations. AES's guideline draws awareness to the issues of inequality and moves away from the oppressive rhetoric of vulnerability. However, as noted, it fails to provide evaluators with further direction of how to approach these potential ethical dilemmas. Scholars like Skerry (2000) have stressed the importance of thoughtfulness and creativity when involving *vulnerable* populations in studies (Skerry, 2000 as quoted in Phillips and Morrow, 2005, p. 65). However, once again these suggestions fail to account for the insider–outsider dilemma. In external evaluation, the evaluator, as the outsider, is often positioned in a place of privilege over his or her participant. It is therefore vital that evaluations are conducted in a way which is not extractive but that empowers the voice of participants, by sincerely acknowledging their agency and knowledge as insiders. In order to do this, evaluations should be designed with a critical local lens, which should take into account the layers of inequalities and the environmental structures, which reinforce the power-dynamics that the evaluator has been dropped into. This is by no means an easy task. Evaluators are often operating under severe time and resource constraints, working to a timeline set by a client in a distant capital. This places limitations on their ability to design and engage in the processes often needed to put in place respectful relationships with *evaluation subjects*.

Methodological Issues and Sampling

All evaluators acknowledge that a fundamental component of an ethical evaluation is a sound methodological process. The first guiding principle of the AEA is systematic inquiry. This principle states that evaluations should 'adhere to the highest technical standards appropriate to the methods they use' (AEA, 2004). It also highlights that systematic and rigorous evaluation methodology should be a consistent principle across all ethical frameworks. This framework stresses the importance of methodological transparency, appropriate sampling and documented consent within the evaluation process. However, these standard evaluation practices propose protocols that are often incongruent with the context of VDS.

Far too often, the ethical frameworks and approaches regimented by the professional association become part of the problem, rather than part of the solution. Although many professional frameworks state that they are trying to ensure a safe, transparent and accountable process, the protocols required in order to ensure these practices can be alienating and alarming, depending on local norms. For example, ensuring informed participant consent is important for protecting and recognising an individual's rights and antinomy. AES' guidelines stipulate that:

> [T]he informed consent of those directly providing information should be obtained, preferably in writing. They should be advised as to what information will be sought, how the information will be recorded and used, and the likely risks and benefits arising from their participation in the evaluation. In the case of minors and other dependents, informed consent should also be sought from parents or guardians. (AES, 2012, p. 12)

While it is important to ensure that participants are informed, obtaining written consent in VDS is often not appropriate and forcing individuals to sign a form that they are not comfortable with is highly unethical. Ford et al. (2009) highlights that in these contexts there is often a high degree of illiteracy and/or mistrust of authority. As a result, signing a consent form could prove to be meaningless or even dangerous for some participants. However, ignoring the process of documenting consent also raises ethical concerns. Evaluators are thus encouraged to work within local norms to try to develop a process that will appropriately ensure that participants understand their rights within the evaluation study and give willing consent to participate. In the past, this has been achieved through verbally recording consent through audiotapes or through witnesses.

Selecting appropriate participant samples can also be a challenge within VDS. The African Evaluation Association (AfrEA) guidelines state that 'data collection procedures should be selected, developed and implemented to ensure that produced information are representative of the diversity' (AfrEA, 2002). The UNEG (2008, p. 7) principles go further to state that:

Evaluators shall select participants fairly in relation to the aims of the evaluation, not simply because of their availability, or because it is relatively easy to secure their participation. Care shall be taken to ensure that relatively powerless, 'hidden', or otherwise excluded groups are represented.

Unfortunately, while the sampling of diverse and 'hidden' groups is no doubt the ideal, the context of operating within VDS presents a number of barriers that tend to prevent or delay systematic and diverse sampling. Ford et al. (2009) highlight two main factors that impact sampling in violent contexts. First, insecurity can limit mobility and access to certain populations, while also preventing the collection of data through surveys. Second, the setting's unpredictability may preclude the use of large sample sizes, or follow-up studies, since displacement of individuals or entire groups may be a regular occurrence. These sampling roadblocks force evaluators to frequently make alterations to the evaluation plan, and make judgements about which groups are priorities for inclusion and which should be involved because of availability.

The AfrEA guidelines, which were developed loosely from the AEA's Programme Evaluation Standards (Joint Committee on Standards for Educational Evaluation, 1994), also highlight a unique methodological consideration for evaluations conducted within developing regions, such as Africa (Rouge, 2004). The guidelines note that timeliness should be regarded as secondary to due process: 'the "way in which a thing is done" is often considered more important than getting it done 'on time and within the budget' (AfrEA, 2002, p. 6). This guideline speaks of the distinctive African context, and highlights the need for modifications and diverse considerations based on the setting of an evaluation.

Each of these aforementioned considerations demand significant thought into the ethical implications of: the selected sample, evaluation timing, available resources and barriers presented by local context. Since many of these considerations are made throughout the evaluation process, good practice dictates that all evaluation reports should clearly note any methodological limitations that were encountered.

While there are many other ethical methodological considerations that are discussed in other chapters of this text, these examples demonstrate the importance of not employing a prescriptive ethical framework to an evaluation design. If evaluators were to naively apply the ethical recommendations of ensuring written consent, their evaluation may be over before they are even able to ask the first question. It is thus vital that all of the ethical frameworks are critically considered within the local context, with the norms and values of the participants prioritised within the evaluation process.

Do No Harm: 'If They Can't Do Any Good, They Shouldn't Come'

No one within our community requested these International organisations to come and help us. We have been surviving the conflict since the 1980s and disasters since the 1950s. Before 1990, we were helping each other and the few organisations in our area were listening to us. Now, it is different—all these foreigners and their assistant Sri Lankans who come in Land Cruisers with questionnaires only want our information. Then they disappear and a new group comes. I think that if they can't do any good, they shouldn't come. (A farmer from conflict affected Eastern Sri Lanka [Direct discussion with the author, October 2005])

The last ethical principle that will be discussed in this chapter is the principle of non-maleficence. In the mid-1990s, the concept of *Do No Harm* became the motto of humanitarian policy and practice. Although the concept has been part of the medical field's Hippocratic Oath since the late 5th century BC, it entered the humanitarian lexicon through the work of James Orbinski, and was adapted and globally promoted by Mary B. Anderson and her Collaborative for Development Action (CDA).

The CDA *Do No Harm* project began in 1993, with the aim of recognising ways to deliver humanitarian and/or development assistance in conflict affected communities. The driving concept behind this idea is that when frontline workers understand the patterns of harmful assistance, they can create opportunities to overcome the conflict by reducing harmful practices and increasing positive effects. In this way, they can achieve their mandates to assist, avoid doing the harm that has been done in the past and add the influence of their presence and assistance to the forces within societies that re-connect people rather than separate them (CDA, 2007).

While this is the global mandate that distinguished the *do no harm* concept, at times the reality on the ground has been markedly different. During my field experience with communities in Sri Lanka, Malawi, Sudan, Jordan, Darfur and Pakistan, community members provided very different narratives from those of research and evaluation outsiders:

> A team of researchers came to our camp and wanted to gather our experience with the war. They wanted to know our losses of loved ones and properties. By that time we had enough with these researchers who just talk to us and go away. But the Agency insisted us to talk to these researchers too. So, we agreed. These researchers were very difficult—they were not interested about our current problems in the camp, but wanted us to tell all the aspects of our experiences where we felt so sad to remember them. They were very pushy to get all what they want. At the end there were crying women and upset and angry men. (Community Leader from El-Geneina, Western Darfur in Sudan [Direct discussion with the author, May 2005])

Such stories illustrate the myopia of researchers who selectively seek, and instrumentally use, information that suits preconceived notions, while ignoring the realities, problems and needs of the community within which they are working. The voices from this community suggested that researchers and evaluators who come to collect information from them should actually listen to them and address their issues rather than just focusing on pleasing their donors and accomplishing their research agendas.

> As an academic, I know how difficult it is for these researchers to understand the complicated situations the communities are in, while

formulating their research agendas. They have to make their funders happy. Then they have to follow their ethical frameworks and research objectives from their institutions. However, what they should think about is that we are also living human beings. These are our lives and making dishonest judgements about our situations is unethical and immoral. I don't know how they sleep at night. Conducting social research is not just a job, but a responsibility towards the research participants. With all the good intentions, you can still damage us. (A Rwandan Theological Professor and Refugee, Lilongwe, Malawi [Direct discussion with the author, August 2006])

It is vital that social researchers acknowledge that they are not conducting research on rocks and soil; they are engaging with human beings who have experienced conflicts or disasters. These participants trust the researcher to share their experiences and future aspirations. Although, one could argue that what is collected is simply field data from the research subjects, many communities recognise a different relationship. For them, the moment these communities share their stories, the researcher becomes part of them. This establishes an unwritten agreement that the researcher will respect and do justice to these stories. Researchers may not meet these research participants again, but their responsibility towards participant's stories remains forever.

The evaluator, who is once again also a researcher, shares this responsibility. The job of the evaluator is to uncover the contributions or strength of the project being assessed. Evaluators are, therefore, faced with a difficult task of assessing whether the responsibilities of the researchers or development worker have been adequately met, while at the same time balancing their own responsibility to the evaluation's stakeholders. This delicate balance is part of the reason why the *do no harm* mantra has been adopted into evaluations, ethical frameworks. Evaluations, to remain ethical, must protect participants from unnecessary exposure to harm (Morris, 2008). AEA's (2004) guiding principles acknowledge the evaluator's responsibility to ensure non-maleficence, stating that:

> Because justified negative or critical conclusions from an evaluation must be explicitly stated, evaluations sometimes produce results that harm client or stakeholder interests. Under this circumstance, evaluators should seek to maximise the benefits and reduce any unnecessary harms that might occur, provided this will not compromise the integrity of the evaluation findings. Evaluators should carefully judge when the benefits from doing the evaluation or in performing certain evaluation

procedures should be foregone because of the risks or harms. To the extent possible, these issues should be anticipated during the negotiation of the evaluation.

Reducing or mitigating unnecessary harm is extremely vital within VDS. Ford et al. (2009) note that within these contexts, the dissemination of sensitive findings, be they from research or evaluation, can lead to the expulsion of organisations from conflict areas or the penalisation of individuals. 'Humanitarian organisations that have reported on human rights abuses and medical/nutritional emergencies in certain countries have been forced to withdraw from those countries or have been expelled' (Ford et al., 2009). Evaluators must therefore balance their obligation to report the truth, while balancing their responsibility to stakeholders and participants to prevent harm, which may be caused from an unfavourable evaluation.

Morris (2008, p. 19) highlights that evaluators are most likely to encounter ethical conflicts during the communication of results, with pressure to misrepresent evaluation results being most common.

> This pressure usually comes from the evaluation's primary client (but occasionally from the evaluator's superior), who wants the programme portrayed in a more positive light (occasionally more negative) than the evaluator believes is warranted by the data. Sometimes disagreement focuses primarily on what the findings *mean* rather than on how positive or negative they are.

The interpretation of results is an important concern for evaluations, since different evaluators could have extremely different criteria for judging what qualifies as success. For example, a psychosocial project that I evaluated in 2007 in eastern Sri Lanka could have had very different findings, if the meaning of the results were not interpreted through a critical local lens. Although the original project objectives were geared towards traditional individualistic psychosocial care, the local NGO and the community decided to use the project money to build houses for the tsunami-affected community. After field interviews, discussions with project staff members and much contemplation, I decided it was justifiable to build houses as a psychosocial project. The reason for this justification was based on the general Sri Lankan cultural ideology: *a roof over one's head gives peace of mind*,[6] which is imbued with the idea that when there is a house, people feel better. The aim of this psychosocial project was to improve peace of mind of tsunami-affected communities, although they had different objectives and activities in mind. Based on this perspective, I could see how they justified building houses as a psychosocial project instead of conducting activities in the original project design. Building houses was helping the community, since there was a strong community involvement and beneficiaries of course felt better. Due to this angle of the evaluation process, there were no issues accessing local communities, beneficiaries and other stakeholders. However, it was a long and difficult negotiation with the donor, but at the end they accepted this argument. They even published it as one of their successful tsunami projects in Sri Lanka. Further, due to the mutual understanding cultivated through this evaluation, the donor still continues to work with the local NGO and the community within a broader development agenda.

Enabling the critical local perspective to guide evaluation findings is an important consideration within contexts of violence. Evaluators, who find it difficult to settle on a single evaluation judgement, may find it useful to acknowledge the multiple interpretations that the findings may bring. The AfrEA (2002) guidelines highlight the importance of diverse perspectives by recommending the inclusion of multiple interpretations:

> The rationale, perspectives and methodology used to interpret the findings should be carefully described so that the bases for value judgments are clear. Multiple interpretations of findings should be transparently reflected, provided that these interpretations respond to stakeholders' concerns and needs for utilisation purposes.

While the provision of multiple interpretations may provide the needed space for evaluators to articulate findings that align with the diversity of local values, evaluators should take care in adding interpretations to simply appease pressure to alter findings. Morris (2008) highlights that another common ethical challenge for evaluators is the personal and/ or professional risks that doing the right thing might create. Hendricks (2009) highlighted that

> [t]he [AEA] Guiding Principles allow me no latitude to withhold important information simply because sharing it might make my job more difficult. In fact, The Guiding Principles clearly urge me to share all relevant information without consideration of how it affects me personally. That is, however I decide to act, I should not weigh too heavily the ramification for me professionally.

In VDS, the requirement to divulge all information can place evaluators in danger and may have serious ramifications to their personal and professional lives. This is why it is important that the principles of *Do No Harm* are interpreted with a critical local lens and applied to all evaluation participants, including the evaluator. In instances, where evaluators fear personal harm, they must rely on their practical knowledge, not necessarily the prescribed ethical protocols to help mitigate the situation. In order for evaluators and researchers to apply a local lens, they must take time to acknowledge the experiences and commitments that their work is making to the local community, and must work with evaluation participants to interpret and comprehend ethical guidelines from a local perspective.

Applying a Critical Local Lens to Ethical Frameworks for VDS

What we can glean from the previous sections is that there are three types of disjunctures which tend to occur during the application of ethical frameworks within VDS. These divisions include: disjunctures in application, disjunctures in interpretation and disjunctures between insiders and outsiders. There are, of course, also interactions between these disjunctures. Disjunctures in applications depend on how two different professional and personal cultures understand the application. Disjunctures in interpretation are always an issue with different cultures, both in translating words with different values that are embodied in culture, traditions and meaning systems. Finally, the disjunctures between insiders and outsiders could complicate the process, which is also a cultural difference of understanding concepts.

These disjunctures identify critical gaps within evaluation guidelines and threaten their ability to provide guidance to evaluators, commissioners and evaluation stakeholders in VDS. Evaluators, who focus too narrowly on applying these professional codes without sufficient reflection, are often at risk of larger ethical dilemmas because they have not recognised the other important dimensions of ethics, which acknowledge that all of these protocols must be viewed in relation to local ethical norms. This does not mean that local norms should be uncritically adopted as ethical, but rather that both outsider ethical protocols and insider norms need to be reviewed together to source appropriate practice for each unique evaluation context.

What we are, therefore, emphasizing here is that in order for these frameworks to be relevant to a violently divided context, it is imperative that they adopt a critical local lens. This means that a respectful, honest, transparent and accountable relationship is built between the outside evaluator and insider community participants. These two stakeholders should be partners in ethically reviewing and acknowledging potential ethical dilemmas during the planning of an evaluation.

Applying a critical local lens is best done at the time of evaluation planning. Evaluators will benefit from early analysis of ethical considerations, since preventing ethical problems from occurring is preferable, and often easier than responding to problems that emerge. Morris (2008) recommends using the entry/contracting stage to think through and discuss potential ethical scenarios with stakeholders. 'The more thoroughly these matters are discussed at the beginning of the evaluation, the less likely they will arise in problematic fashion later on. And if they do arise, a framework for addressing them has at least been established' (Morris 2003 as quoted in Morris, 2008, p. 197).

Although it is not always possible to have these conversations with all stakeholders in violently divided contexts, there is still a clear benefit if some local stakeholders are engaged in an ethical review (either formally or informally) before commencing a study. This process not only helps to mitigate the emergence of ethical problems, but also helps to establish confidence in the evaluator's practical knowledge, and serves as a gentle reminder of the fundamental ethical principles that guide evaluation and research. Lastly, this process also helps to provide an opportunity for trust to be developed. Through this method, the aforementioned disjunctures can be overcome and the evaluation can be fruitful for both parties.

When a critical local lens approach has been adopted in the past, there have been many positive outcomes. The following example from the field helps expound the value of this approach.

Research into Long-term Collaboration: The Study Group of El-Geneina, Western Darfur

We went to Western Darfur in 2005 as part of a UN High Commissioner for Refugees contract to evaluate and build capacity on mental health programmes for displaced populations. We established this process as a participatory research initiative. During the study, we learned that most of the mental health programme planning and implementation had been conducted by international staff members who only remained in Western Darfur for two to three months. We decided to reach out to national staff members, and where able, established equal relationships with very knowledgeable and experienced colleagues.

These national colleagues helped us to identify local expertise on mental health, for example the birth attendants and traditional healers. Through our discussion, they recognised that there is a gap for long-term educational opportunities for national and local staff members to study mental health issues of displaced communities.

We discussed this issue with the United Nations High Commissioner for Refugees Community Services Team and they agreed to provide necessary support. The preliminary discussions identified writing materials as the only resource that they needed, such as books, pens, colours pencils and paper. UNICEF agreed to provide these and we found a community hall for free, where the participants agreed to bring their own lunch and refreshments.

Based on this experience, we established the Study Group of El-Geneina for national staff members and local experts. As outsiders we shared our experiences and skills on mental health interventions and they shared their expertise with us. This was a learning process for both parties and we managed to receive all the necessary information for our evaluation. We worked with each other for 10 weeks and after we left, the group continued to meet once a week.

> This was an interesting experience for us as researchers and evaluators. The evaluation's aim was not to find faults of the interventions, but to strengthen them. After all, the most important aspect of this experience, from my perspective, is that I believe the evaluation process itself empowered the participants involved. I believe we left the participants with something valuable—we did not just extract their knowledge and make promises that we were not sure could be kept. (Experience of the author, 2005)

This example shows that identifying local expertise and respecting locals as equals is an important aspect of any evaluation. Evaluation processes are not meant to necessarily find faults with interventions, but to support their strengthening. In my experience, after we left El-Geneina many UN agencies and INGOs started collaborating with this Study Group. As researchers from a European University, we had the authority and freedom to show the rest of the international staff members that they should, and indeed that they could, work closely with national and local experts.

In many ways, this example, and this chapter, has provided an opportunity to examine some of the ethical challenges encountered in VDS. Apart from the personal qualities of the researcher or evaluator, there are many institutionalised problems of ethics, which can be resolved through establishing transparent and accountable ethical and methodological processes. The following three suggestions highlight several ways to improve ethical protocols so that they can be more applicable for VDS:[7]

1. First, we should appreciate that the existence of institutional ethical frameworks, guidelines and standards does not mean that there is agreement among actors (the researchers, evaluators, and participants) about what constitutes as an ethical issue: Disagreements are common. Much work remains to be done in examining the nature of these disagreements and strategies that might be used to address them.

2. Second, it is important that researchers and evaluators prepare themselves to deal with the finale of an evaluation or a research process. There may be problems of presentation of findings, misinterpretation and misuse of results, and/or difficulties with disclosure agreements. These problems can be avoided by establishing an honest, transparent, accountable and respectful evaluation process.

3. Third, ethical frameworks, guidelines and standards should continue to be assessed systematically and periodically, and where appropriate should be reworked to reflect local values (for example, the AfrEA Guidelines). Researchers and evaluators should also understand that these ethical frameworks are part of an evolving process of self-examination by the profession within a global multicultural context and should be revisited prior to each new evaluation context to ensure they are interpreted with a critical local lens.

4. Lastly, there is a strong need for meta-evaluation (that is, the evaluation of evaluations) to play an integral part in building and reshaping evaluation standards and practice. In 2010, meta-evaluation was recognised as the fifth dimension of the AEA Programme Standards. While it is important to balance the codification of protocols with practical knowledge, meta-evaluation can be used by evaluators and evaluation commissioners to uncover lessons from the field and hold evaluators to account.

While these suggestions are only a start, these changes will help build awareness of the realities of evaluators working in VDS. In conclusion, what is clear from the participant testimony in this chapter is that VDS are dynamic arenas, where a variety of unique ethical dilemmas play out. If evaluation and research guidelines continue to be dominated by increasing universal bureaucratic frameworks, which follow only mainstream scientific approaches, they will be useless in these complex contexts. Applying these protocols without reflecting upon how they intersect with local realities can not only disrupt the evaluation process, but can also put evaluation stakeholders, participants and even the evaluator in harm's way.

Evaluation frameworks from institutions, which are not developed from a local context, should not be implemented in different societies without scrutiny from evaluation participants. Without this review of ethical frameworks by the evaluator, *and* the evaluation participants, the tension between the ethical protocols understood by foreign institutions and the local community will increase. Community ethical frameworks that have been developed through generational and lived experiences of disasters and conflict are too valuable to ignore as *unscientific*. VDS evaluations need to consider 'the legitimacy of the people's knowledge system' (Wignaraja, 2005, p. 25). Wignaraja (2005, p. 25) further states, '[t]his is also equally the knowledge system of the poor. This knowledge and traditional technology can no longer be dismissed as romantic and unscientific. It can be a critical element in sustainable cost effective development and poverty eradication [as well as in conflict transformation]'.

As a result, the evaluator as an *outsider* and the participant communities as *insiders*, need to work together to review both institutional and community ethical frameworks, in order to establish a unique and effective frame of ethics for the particular evaluation project. This has to be an honest, transparent and accountable mechanism that maintains the integrity of both the evaluator and community. This becomes the legitimate *ethics review committee* of the research outcomes; a process that may positively transform the evaluator, researcher and community participants of the study.

> We need outside help for analysis and understanding of our situation and experience, but not for telling us what we should do. An outsider who comes with ready-made solutions and advice is worse than useless. He must first understand from us what our questions are, and help us articulate the questions better, and then help us find solutions. Outsiders also have to change. He alone is a friend who helps us to think about our problems on our own. (Wignaraja, 2005, p. 1)

Notes

1. These points were reinforced in personal discussions held by one author (Jayawickrama) with colleagues at the University of Northumbria. Professor Phil O'Keefe at Northumbria University is a founding member of ALNAP and an expert evaluator of humanitarian assistance since 1970s, and Ms. Joanne Rose is a PhD student at Northumbria University studying the delivery of humanitarian assistance in Somalia. Interviews, University of Northumbria, January and April 2011.
2. Primarily that of Jayawickrama.
3. It is important to note that the real distinction is one of paradigms of inquiry and the fact that one paradigm (generally more positivist and scientific) is the dominant tradition in academic practice in the Global North and South. However, there are exceptions—appreciative inquiry, for example, is the polar opposite of what I am describing in my critique of what knowledge is valued, and *ways of knowing*.
4. Please refer Zelinsky (1974) for further discussion of science as a religion and the scientist as a demigod.
5. This leads to a separate question that is different from the question posed by the researchers: Are all Sri Lankans traumatised?
6. There was a Government campaign called 'a shelter for the head and peace of mind in 1980s'.
7. Adapted from Morris (1999).

References

African Evaluation Association (AfrEA) Secretariat. (2002, June). *The African evaluation guidelines*. Paper presented at the Second African Evaluation Association Conference, Nairobi. Retrieved from http://www.alnap.org/pool/files/AfricanEvaluation Association.pdf (accessed on 27 April 2015; as an attachment to a report).

American Evaluation Association (AEA). (2004). *Guiding principles for evaluators* (abbreviated version). Fairhaven, MA: American Evaluation Association. Retrieved from http://www.eval.org/publications/aea06.GPBrochure.pdf (accessed on 22 April 2015).

Australasian Evaluation Society (AES). (2010). *Guidelines for the ethical conduct of evaluations*. Retrieved from http://www.aes.asn.au/images/stories/files/About/ Documents%20-%20ongoing/AES%20Guidlines10.pdf (accessed on 20 June 2015).

————. (2012). *Guidelines for the ethical conduct of evaluations*. Retrieved from http://betterevaluation.org/resources/example/aes_ethical_guidelines (accessed on 27 April 2015).

Canadian Evaluation Society. (2012). *Guidelines for ethical conduct*. Retrieved from http://www.evaluationcanada.ca/site.cgi?s=5&ss=4&_lang=an (accessed on 22 April 2015).

Capron, A. M. (1989). Human experimentation. In R. M. Veatch (Ed.), *Medical Ethics* (pp. 125–172). Boston: Jones & Bartlett.

Chambers, R. (2010). *Paradigms, poverty and adaptive pluralism* (IDS Working Paper 344). Brighton: The Institute of Development Studies, University of Sussex. Retrieved from http://www.ids.ac.uk/files/dmfile/Wp344.pdf (accessed on 22 April 2015).

Datta, L. (2001). Mixed methods evaluation: The wheelbarrow, the mosaic and the double helix. *Evaluation Journal of Australasia, 1*(2), 33–40.

Duggan, C. (2012). Show me your impact: Evaluating transitional justice in contested spaces. *Journal of Planning and Program Evaluation, 35*(1), 199–205.

Dyer, S. and Demeritt, D. (2008). Un-ethical review? Why it is wrong to apply the medical model of research governance to human geography. *Progress in Human Geography, 33*(1), 46–64.

ESRC. (2010). *Research ethics framework.* UK: Economic and Social Research Council. Retrieved from http://www.esrc.ac.uk/_images/Framework_for_Research_Ethics_tcm8-4586.pdf (accessed on 22 April 2015).

French Evaluation Society (SFE). (2003). *Charter of evaluation guiding principles for public policies and programmes.* France: Société Francaise de l'Evaluation. Retrieved from http://www.sfe-asso.fr/intranet/ckfinder/userfiles/files/charter-english.pdf (accessed on 22 April 2015).

Hendrick, D. (2009). *Complexity theory and conflict transformation: An exploration of potential and implications* (Working Paper 17). Bradford: Centre for Conflict Resolution, Department of Peace Studies, Bradford University. Retrieved from http://www.brad.ac.uk/acad/confres/papers/pdfs/CCR17.pdf (accessed on 22 April 2015).

Iphofen, R. (2009). *Ethical decision making in social research: A practical guide.* Basingstoke: Palgrave Macmillan.

Joint Committee on Standards for Educational Evaluation (Sanders, J.R. [Chair]). (1994). *The program evaluation standards: How to assess evaluations of educational programs.* 2nd ed. Thousand Oaks, CA: SAGE Publications.

Kushner, S. (2000). *Personalizing evaluation.* Gateshead and Thousand Oaks, CA: SAGE Publications and Aethenaeum Press.

Morris, M. (1999). Research on evaluation ethics: What have we learned and why is it important? *New Directions for Evaluation, 1999*(82), 15–24.

———. (Ed.). (2008). *Evaluation ethics for best practice: Cases and commentaries.* New York, NY: The Guilford Press.

Newman, D. L. and Brown, R. D. (1996). *Applied ethics for program evaluation.* Thousand Oaks, CA: SAGE Publications.

OECD DAC. (2010). *DAC guidelines and reference series: Quality standards for development evaluation.* Paris: OECD. Retrieved from http://www.oecd.org/development/evaluation/qualitystandards.pdf (accessed on 21 July 2015).

Orb, A., Eisenhauer, L. and Wynaden, D. (2000). Ethics in qualitative research. *Journal of Nursing Scholarship, 33*(1), 93–96.

Raudonis, B. M. (1992). Ethical considerations in qualitative research with hospicepatients. *Qualitative Health Research, 2*(2), 238–249.

Said, E. W. (1978). *Orientalism.* London: Routledge and Kegan Paul Ltd.

UNEG (United Nations Evaluation Group). (2008). *UNEG ethical guidelines for evaluation.* Retrieved from http://www.unevaluation.org/document/detail/102 (accessed on 21 July 2015).

Wignaraja, P. (2005). Fundamentals of poverty eradication in South Asia. In *Green Movement of Sri Lanka: Conference on Good Governance, Poverty Reduction and Community Resilience* (pp. 12–13). Nugegoda: Alternative Evolutions Working Group on Good Governance, Poverty Reduction and Community Resilience.

Zelinsky, W. (1974). The demigod's dilemma. *Annals of the Association of American Geographers, 65*(2), 123–143.

PART III

Evaluation, Evidence and Policy

Introduction to Part III

The two cases in this part draw attention to the haziness and ambiguity of the term *post-conflict setting*. In Northern Ireland, the Good Friday Agreement was signed in 1998, whereby the principal armed stakeholders agreed to de-weaponise their struggles and to accept the formal political process establish ed under the Agreement. South Africa, on the other hand, entered the post-Apartheid era following elections in 1994. Yet, despite the post-conflict label applied to both cases each is characterised by significant levels of violence.

South Africa holds the dubious distinction of having one of the highest rates of violent crime in the world—with some 50 people being murdered *daily*, in addition to extraordinary levels of rape, car-jackings, home invasions, burglary and assaults. In Northern Ireland, while the main paramilitary groups have set aside their weapons, the *Dissident Terrorist* threat is considered to be at its highest in the last 12 years according to statistics of the Police Service of Northern Ireland (PSNI, 2010a, 2010b), and the Independent Monitoring Commission (IMC, 2010). Further, well-patterned and predictable forms of inter-group violence among Northern Irish youth have come to be captured in the term *recreational rioting*. In this context, we should be wary of uncritically accepting the labeling of a case as *post-conflict*, as if the past has somehow passed—even when programming and research funds are *incentivising* our research to address the *legacy of the past*.

In both cases, we see the continuation of the violence of the past in modified forms—both weaponised violence (such as political and criminal violence) and non-weaponised violence (domestic violence, rape, assault, child abuse and so on). The inclusion of both cases in this book (like the inclusion of the South Asian cases employed by Zaveri in her chapter) helps to ensure that our understanding of the term *violently divided societies* is not limited to militarised war zones. The panoply of social violence in both the Global North and South needs to be highlighted and explored within cases, despite the complexity and opacity it introduces into our analysis.

It is also worth flagging the methodological significance of including the South Africa into the mix of case studies in this book. On one level, it shares a similarity with the South Asian cases employed by Zaveri, in that it is embedded in the structural violence inherent in the tenacious poverty of the Global South (as well as in pockets in the Global North). However, South Africa is also a society living within structures of extreme violence that continue to divide people *even within political dispensations premised on the transformation and transition of those apartheid structures of injustice.* South Africa, therefore, reminds us that the term *violently divided societies* includes cases in which systemic acts of violence *in the past* may continue to have divisive impacts *in the present.*

Kelly's chapter focuses on the impact of research on a pressing global epidemiological problem. He explores an intriguing case of HIV research in southern Africa, where policies and practices for prevention have been staunchly supported *in the absence of empirical evidence,* and where solid research evidence has been ignored or overlooked in HIV policy and programming. This chapter leads Kelly into a thick forest of the obstacles, challenges, competing interests that inhabit the terrain of VDS and that affect the role and impact of research. Some of his observations and findings are counter-intuitive, if not antithetical, to our general understandings of *how research works*—specifically of the societal impacts of research. For example, he notes how impending research on HIV/AIDS in South Africa (including within institutional *gray zones* such as military establishments') stimulated vigorous public and policy debates about the ethics, politics, and practicalities of the conduct and dissemination of such research. Thus, this is an example of the *research impact* of research *outputs* that had *not yet been produced.* This is a societal impact that is *independent of the content or quality of the research.* This chapter pushes us to consider the impacts of research well beyond the narrow focus of research products.

The cases in this part of the book concern two areas of social policy which are amongst the most important that need to be addressed in societies attempting to overcome protracted militarised conflicts: education and HIV/AIDS. The history of HIV/AIDS policy is littered with examples of ideology- and value-laden policy influences. The same may be said of the education policy in Northern Ireland, which Colin Knox describes as being 'highly segregated along religious lines'—and what the First Minister of Northern Ireland described as 'a benign form of apartheid' (BBC, 2010). Both cases demonstrate that when a contentious policy area is nested within a contested socio-political environment, the need for robust, methodologically rigorous, ethically sound, evaluation can never be greater. However, the very same conditions that create such great needs are the same ones that hinder meeting them.

Both cases also offer concrete examples of efforts to harness research to social change. They are located in *post-conflict* settings where social policy is intended not only to achieve specified social or epidemiological goals. It also intended to contribute to the broader programme of societal transition from an unjust and divisive past, to a more just and shared future. Both of these chapters are based on evaluations of research initiatives intended to have these broad, constructive, societal impacts. To understand how this works requires that we pay as much attention to the contentious environment within which research is undertaken, as to the resulting research outputs. Thus, a full understanding of multi-level impacts, requires multi-layered evaluations that are able, in the broadest sense, to delineate the trajectory of influence from research to practice with a context that is politicised, unpredictable and volatile. While it may be somewhat less complicated to identify and assess the immediate outcomes (reduction in infection rates and prevalence, or enrolment rates in integrated schools), it is much more difficult to identify the higher level impacts on inter-group integration or *reconciliation*.

References

BBC. (2010). Sinn Fein rejects Robinson's comments on education. Retrieved from www.bbc.co.uk/news/uk-northern-ireland-11555984 (accessed on 18 October 2010).

Independent Monitoring Commission (IMC). (2010). Twenty-third report of the independent monitoring commission. London: The Stationary Office.

Police Service of Northern Ireland (PSNI). (2010a). Recorded crime and clearances 1 April 2009–31 March 2010 annual statistical report, Statistical Report No. 1. Retrieved from http://www.psni.police.uk/index/updates/updates_statistics.htm (accessed on 21 July 2015).

———. (2010b). Statistics relating to the security situation 1 April 2009–31 March 2010, Statistical Report No. 5. Retrieved from http://www.psni.police.uk/5._statistics_relating_to_the_security_situation_200910_final.pdf (accessed on 21 July 2015).

5

Research within Evaluation
The Case of Northern Ireland

Colin Knox*

Introduction

This chapter is written from the perspective of an evaluator of programmes in violently divided societies (VDS). As a result, the focus on the evaluation of research tends to be set within the context of an assessment of the overall impact of a programme within these societies. More specifically, this chapter looks at how an evaluator assesses the contribution of research—as a distinct cluster of activities *within* a programme, running in parallel with other programme activities—may contribute to the overall programme impact. In other words, when a body of primary research is an integral part of the programme being evaluated, it sits alongside the implementation of other multiple types of activities, and is expected to contribute to programme impact. This is somewhat different from the evaluation of research undertaken outside of the context of an intervention (e.g., as a 'stand-alone' intervention). First, in such cases, research is but one type of input into a programme. Depending on the nature of intervention, a parallel research track within a programme may be a significant component.

* The author wishes to thank Dr Kenneth Bush, Colleen Duggan, Dr Kevin Kelly, John A. Healy and John R. Healy for very helpful suggestions on this chapter.

In other cases, however, research can be a relatively small component sitting alongside a range of other kinds of activities which collectively constitute the intervention—and, ideally, contribute to the achievement of its stated and intended objectives. Second, research within an evaluation can serve different purposes. It may serve to identify, test or justify the intervention's underpinning rationale or theory of change; it could be part of a formative assessment of the process/outputs of the intervention; or it could be carried out as a means of assessing interim programme outcomes. Bearing in mind the different roles that research can play, the empirical point of reference for this chapter is an exploration of the interaction between research and evaluation.

The discussion is grounded in a case study of a particularly contentious education programme intervention in the politically volatile environment of 'post' conflict Northern Ireland. Because the emphasis is on the evaluation of research from the perspective of an evaluator, the details of the case study are less important than the questions around how evaluation featured in a cluster of research activities. The chapter provides a brief overview of the case study before moving to consider the substantive issues around the role and assessment of research as part of the wider evaluation process.

This chapter examines the following four key questions. First, how the evaluation of research influences the theory of change which provides the underlying rationale for the programme. This will be followed by reflections on the evaluation of the research conducted by the case study delivery agents to assess the formative effects of the programme with a view to checking programme delivery. The author will then discuss some of the challenges faced by the evaluator in assessing research within the context of the programme evaluation. The chapter will conclude with a discussion of the influence of research as one component in a suite of programme activities in a given context, and the contribution that research can make to overall programme objectives.

Before exploring these questions in greater detail, a brief outline of the chapter case study is given as follows.

The Case Study

The Northern Ireland education system is highly segregated along religious lines[1] with almost 95 per cent of children attending denominational schools: Maintained (Catholic) or Controlled (largely Protestant) state schools.[2] The first planned integrated school (Lagan College) was set up by parents in 1981 and the Department of Education was given a statutory duty to *encourage and facilitate* the development of integrated education under the Education Reform (NI) Order 1989. Today there are a limited number of integrated schools (approximately 62) and Irish medium/language schools (approximately 24) in Northern Ireland. In the academic year 2010/2011, there were 154,950 primary school children and 147,902 post-primary pupils in Northern Ireland, an overall school population of 302,852 pupils within some 1,200 schools (Department of Education 2011). The integrated education movement, according to its proponents, has experienced slow growth because numbers are capped within integrated schools, and requests to transform existing schools to integrated status are often refused by the minister. The Department of Education claims it is difficult to facilitate the growth of a small integrated sector which can adversely affect existing schools in the context of a falling student population and an overall declining education market. In other words, it is argued that the growth of integrated schools can simply displace children from other sectors and increase capital spending on the school estate for fewer pupils, in line with demographic trends.

In response to the slow pace of growth in integrated education—*despite an expressed demand from parents for greater mixing amongst school children from different community backgrounds*[3]—two external funders, Atlantic Philanthropies[4] and the International Fund for Ireland[5] set up the Sharing Education Programme (SEP) in 2007. The School of Education of Queen's University Belfast (QUB) began to work with 12 specialist schools[6] that work in partnership. These schools collaborate on a cross-community basis to share classes and activities (see Table 5.1) in order to improve education outcomes for pupils (Gallagher et al., 2010). The programme has an education curriculum focus, but because of its reconciliation focus it is offered on a cross-community basis, in an effort to generate benefits for participants, teachers, parents and, in the long term, the wider community. The programme aims to demonstrate that sustained and *normalised* collaborative contact will nurture substantive relationships between peers and across school communities divided by religious difference (Atlantic Philanthropies, 2006). The theory underpinning the programme is that this kind of contact creates interdependencies between the schools, which catalyses reconciliation effects: through child-to-child engagement in shared curriculum activities, through collaboration between teachers across school sectors and through the participation of parents in *school show-casing events* (see theory of change in Figure 5.1).

Table 5.1
The Range of Activities Undertaken in Schools under the SEP

- Year 14 students completing Advanced Level (or 'A' level) subjects in cross-community classes
- Year 12 students completing General Certificate of Secondary Education (or GCSE) subjects in cross-community classes
- Jointly provided and accredited vocational training courses
- Combined citizenship and personal development and mutual understanding (PDMU) classes
- Science mentoring classes—primary school children from mixed backgrounds attending science classes in a post-primary school
- Collaborative ICT projects through face-to-face contact and web-based learning

Source: Author.

Figure 5.1
Theory of Change: Sharing in Education

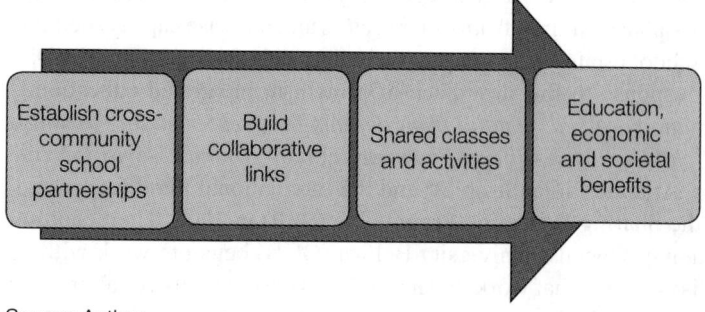

Source: Author.

The SEP of Queen's University completed its first three-year phase in June 2010. It has since been rolled out for a further three years and extended throughout Northern Ireland through two additional providers: the Fermanagh Trust (FT) and the North Eastern Education and Library Board (NEELB or PIEE).[7] Overall, the three projects of the SEP represent an investment of over £10.5 million by the International Fund for Ireland and Atlantic Philanthropies.

Although the projects are managed separately, and possess project-specific outputs and outcomes, they share common overarching goals, including:

1.   To increase the number of schools involved in shared education

2. To increase the number of pupils involved in shared education
3. To help create more positive attitudes between Protestant and Catholic communities
4. To demonstrate and raise awareness of the benefits from shared education in terms of integration and sustainability

In an effort to leverage change in education policy, the funders are collating evidence across the three areas of intended SEP impact: educational achievement, economic efficiencies and social benefits. The current chapter draws on the experience of the author as an evaluator across the three projects of the SEP. Evaluation questions for the programmes have included:

- Societal well-being: Does Sharing Education lead to greater tolerance, mutual understanding and interrelationship through significant, purposeful and regular engagement and interaction in learning? Does it lead to a reduction in barriers between school communities? Does it create greater awareness of the benefits cross-sectoral working and the potential opportunities that sharing and collaboration can create?
- Educational benefits: How has Sharing Education improved the quality of education (however measured) for those involved (if at all)? To what extent does SEP generate benefits above and beyond pre-existing single identity programmes?
- Economic considerations: Is Sharing Education more cost-effective, providing value-for-money, when set alongside existing models for the provision of education?

The remainder of the chapter focuses on the evaluation of: the theory of change for sharing education; the research conducted by the delivery agents to assess its formative impact and check ongoing delivery against programme objectives; the role of the evaluator in assessing research and, the overall influence of the research cluster within a programme which had multiple types of activities.

Evaluating Competing Theories of Change

One of the challenges confronting evaluators is the question of how to deal with existing research related to the intervention. In other words, is it the role of the evaluator to assess the substantive merits/demerits of the research (or hypotheses) informing programme design and implementation? If one accepts that the evaluator *should* have a role to play in this regard, it raises questions of the extent to which interrogation of the research underpinning any intervention or programme should feature in any evaluation of the outputs and outcomes. In addition, if one is using the logical framework approach (so often the stock-in-trade of the evaluator), then research will likely feature as *one* input to the intervention or programme of activities. How does one *weight* the contribution of research as an input relative to other inputs such as the practical experience, knowledge and skills of those delivering the activities? What role, therefore, has research played in informing the underpinning theory of change and, by extension, the evaluation? Put simply, is it the job of the evaluator to question or problematise programme theory and design? Setting aside these important questions for the moment, let us assume that the role of the evaluator is *explicit* in evaluating the research component of any evaluation. What are the key considerations?

Research in and on VDS, like many other areas of research, will often have competing theories of change. For example, in the case study topic which is the subject of this chapter, the role of integrated or shared education as a mechanism for social change is highly contested. One body of empirical research supports the whole idea of integrated schools as a way of addressing community divisions, typical of which is research by Hayes et al. (2007) who conducted a detailed quantitative study on whether religiously integrated education had a significant effect on the political outlook of the children who attend these schools (see also Hargie et al., 2008; McGlynn, 2007; Stringer et al., 2009). This research concluded that attendance at an integrated school, either a school that is formally constituted as integrated or a religious school that incorporates a proportion of pupils from the opposite religion, 'has positive long-term benefits in promoting a less sectarian stance on national identity and constitutional preferences' (Hayes et al., 2007, p. 478).

There is, however, an alternative literature which dismisses the whole idea of integrated education as a response to VDS. McGarry and O'Leary (1995), for example, cite segregation as one of five key fallacies which constitute liberal explanations of the conflict in Northern Ireland. Drawing on Bruce's work (1994), they disparagingly describe attempts to break down segregation in this way as a *mix and fix approach* espoused by the integrated education lobby who challenge stereotypes of the other religious group by tackling misconceptions and ignorance. In short, if segregation is the problem then mixing is the answer. McGarry and O'Leary reject this assertion outright. They argue that integrated education is impractical because residential segregation demands bussing children into hostile territory and mixed schools may simply exacerbate divisions on what separates groups rather than what they have in common. While McGarry and O'Leary (1995, p. 856) supported the idea that 'sufficient provision must be made for all those who wished to be schooled, live or work with members of the other community' they argued that 'many northern nationalists want equality and autonomy rather than integration'.

The key question here is whether it is the role of the programme evaluator to arbitrate on this research polemic, given that research forms the foundation of the programme theory or whether the evaluator should accept the underpinning theory of change and simply conduct the evaluation on that basis? Theories of change are a North American import into the field of policy evaluation in the United Kingdom and have been adopted as a way of addressing the problem of attribution by clearly specifying the links between inputs, activities, outputs and outcomes (Connell and Kubisch, 1998). Yet the experience of UK evaluators using the theories of change approach has been that the involvement of stakeholders in developing and evaluating a relevant theory of change for a proposed intervention has either not been entirely successful, or difficult to achieve in practice (Bauld et al., 2005). Evidence from evaluations in the UK uncovered *principal* and *elite* ownership of theories of change where theory moved closer to ideology (Sullivan and Stewart, 2006 p. 180). Gaining consensus amongst stakeholders on an appropriate theory of change in a VDS when the focus of the intervention goes to the heart of what divides that society is likely to be even more difficult, implying a role for the evaluator in interrogating the programme theory. On the other hand, Sullivan and Stewart (2006, p. 194) warn against evaluator ownership. In many cases, when beginning an evaluation, the evaluator must reconstruct or clarify the theory of change which is not always evident in the programme design. In such cases, there is a risk that the theory of change is limited to, and dominated by, the evaluator and there is 'no reference to the local agents who are responsible for delivering the policies'.

With regard to the SEP, the author took the position that it *was* his role as an evaluator to interrogate the theory of change underpinning this intervention and therefore examined secondary research evidence as a way of validating the programme design. The key sources of evidence used (Table 5.2) can be categorised as: a deliberative poll amongst parents of school children on their attitudes to cross-community sharing; a scoping study on the economic benefits of sharing; yearly public attitude surveys on whether there was a demand for more *cross-community mixing* in schools and faith-based reports on the value of separate schools. From this evidence, the evaluator concluded that the theory of change which underpinned the SEP had a sufficiently robust evidence base to warrant a practical intervention of the type described previously.

Table 5.2
Theory of Change: Research Components

Source of research	Nature of the study	Research strategy involved
Newcastle University, Stanford University and Queen's University (funded by Atlantic Philanthropies)	Deliberative poll to gauge the opinion of parents of school-aged children about school collaboration within their area	Quantitative study, deductive and positivist
Oxford Economics (funded by the Integrated Education Fund)	Scoping study to assess the potential monetary benefits which could result from greater sharing and collaboration between schools. Makes the case for a wider follow-up study	Desk-based research using secondary analysis of data
Northern Ireland Life and Times surveys (funded from a number of sources, including Office of the First Minister and deputy First Minister and Economic and Social Research Council)	NI wide surveys which track attitudes to, inter alia, reactions to 'more cross-community mixing' in primary and post-primary schools	Yearly probability surveys of around 1,200 adults: positivist
Inclusion and Diversity in Catholic Maintained Schools	Articulation of the Catholic sector's commitment to inclusion in their schools	Desk based experiential research written by School Principals in the Catholic sector

Source: Author.

Evaluating Formative Research

Research Strategies

A separate but related issue to competing theories of change is whether the evaluator *takes a position* on the type of research that: (a) informs the underpinning theory in an evaluation and, (b) is used by the delivery agents to provide a formative assessment of programme delivery/impact (Bryman, 2008). Theories of change often imply a deductive approach to research which begins with a set of theoretical assumptions, deduces a hypothesis(es), gathers data to prove or disprove the posited hypothesis and revises the original theory accordingly.

An alternative approach to research is that the relationship between theory and research is primarily inductive where theory is the outcome of empirical research. In other words, the process of induction involves drawing generalisable inferences from observations. The fluid and changing nature of context in VDS might suggest that a more inductive approach is needed for formulating or testing theories of change. For example, the OECD (2008, p. 14) argues that many of the peacebuilding interventions contemplated in VDS tend to have relatively limited theoretical foundations, 'including lack of agreed or proved strategies of how to effectively work towards peace'. Programmes may be based on little more than the hunch of programme designers and/or donors of 'what works'. Donors sometime 'hide' or 'veil' their theories of change for geo-political reasons or because the host government is hostile to donors' theories of change. But in other cases, we simply do not know what works.

There are also epistemological considerations at play here. At a general level, there is the question of whether the social world can and should be studied according to the same principles, procedures and ethos as the natural sciences (positivism), or whether one should respect the differences between people and the objects of the natural sciences which require the social scientist to grasp the subjective meaning of social action (interpretivism)—as discussed by Healy and Healy in this book. For research in VDS, the context, role of adversaries in the conflict, the political ramifications of different interventions and the need to find a resolution to the conflict, all increase the importance of adopting an appropriate research approach.

If the evaluator has a preference for the role of theory and a specific epistemological orientation, then they are more likely to favour either a quantitative or qualitative approach to the whole evaluation process: design of the evaluation, data analysis and the sort of knowledge that is valued as evidence. Quantitative methods lend themselves to a deductive approach to the relationship between theory and research or theory testing, and incorporate the norms of the natural scientific model or positivism. Qualitative methods lend themselves to inductive approaches to theory generation and an interpretivist analysis of the social world. Is it the role of an evaluator, who may have an individual preference for a particular research tradition, to make this judgement as part of their evaluation of the research underpinning the logic model and formative research on programme delivery/impact? In short, if the evaluator's own research disposition tends towards the deductive, positivist and quantitative, will it inevitably assume greater significance in their evaluation of an intervention in a VDS? Or, if another evaluator has a methodological predilection for inductive, interpretivist or qualitative approaches, how will that affect their evaluative stance and findings? The answer to such questions will hinge largely on the user of the evaluation and how evaluation findings will be used.

Research Design

An example from the evaluation case study illustrates the dilemma confronting evaluators in assessing the quality of research intended to contribute a formative evaluation on programme delivery/impact. One type of intervention in the SEP supported cross-sectoral school activities between State (Protestant) and Maintained (Catholic) schools based on sustained contact between pupils in the delivery of the education curriculum through shared classes. This approach was predicated on the *contact hypothesis* which asserts the value of inter-group contact in reducing hostility and improving inter-group relations under specified conditions (Pettigrew and Tropp, 2000). To assess the effectiveness of this approach, a questionnaire was completed by pupils on their experiences of shared classes, alongside a sample of pupils matched by age, religion and gender from the same schools but who were *not* involved in these classes. Attitudinal data were gathered on trust, anxiety, perceived comfort and positive action tendencies towards those from a different religion and the differences between the participating and non-participating students assessed (Hughes, Donnelly, Gallagher and Carlisle, 2010). See Figure 5.2.

Figure 5.2
Evaluating Programme Delivery and Formative Impact: Model A

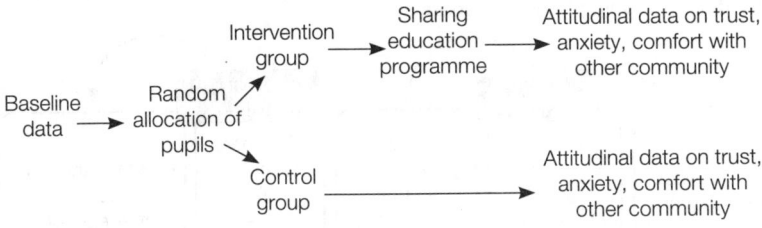

Source: Author.

This may be compared with an alternative approach adopted by a cluster of schools involved in SEP which did not wholly subscribe to pupil-to-pupil contact as the most effective way to promote reconciliation (or the reduction of hostilities and improved inter-group relations). On the hunch or intuition of programme designers, the focus of their intervention centred on school principals and teachers as education leaders. Trust, they argued, needed to be established between school leaders through shared principles, policies and practices. Thereafter, staff had to be supported and trained to work effectively in a new environment, where cross-community schools were expected to become interdependent in the delivery of the school curriculum; this, in turn, would enable contact and sharing to take place among students. Integral to this approach was securing the endorsement of school governors and parents with the long-term aim of sustaining relationships beyond the life of the intervention. Evaluating this intervention involved in-depth interviews with school principals, teachers and governors and observations of pupils involved in shared classes. The qualitative data led to the generation of a testable theory, namely, that collaboration through interdependency at the school leadership level is more likely to create the conditions for long-term sustainability of pupil-to-pupil contact (Knox, 2010a). See Figure 5.3.

In summary, one implementation approach was to see the pupils as the focus of activities (Figure 5.2) and the other was to work with school principals and teachers (Figure 5.3). Evidence gathered on the success of the former was deductive, positivist and quantitative using a quasi-experimental design. Evidence on the latter was inductive, interpretivist and qualitative, largely based on data gathered through semi-structured interviews and observations. In these examples, what was the role of

Figure 5.3
Evaluating Programme Delivery and Formative Impact:
Model B—Training School Leaders

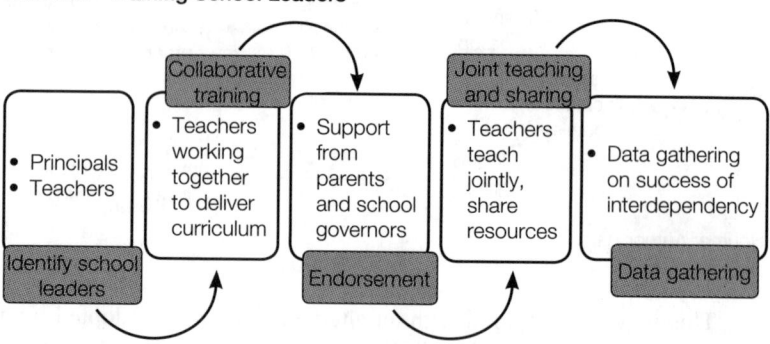

Source: Author.

the evaluator? Having interrogated the theory of change which under-pinned the programme, there are alternative implementation processes. Here, the evaluator was faced with quite different ways of attempting to deliver programme objectives and his role was to assess the quality of research conducted by the projects in their formative assessment of the programme. The evaluator needed to be wary of making judgements on the nature/quality of this formative research based on their preferred research design (either inductive or deductive). In this case, looking at the quality and usefulness of the evidence gathered, the evaluator con-cluded that the quasi-experimental approach (Figure 5.2) did not capture the complexity of attitudinal change in participating and non-participat-ing pupils with the SEP. Rather, the richness of qualitative data gathered through principals, teachers, parents and governors (Figure 5.3) offered much more useful insights into the ongoing delivery and formative effects of the programme. Table 5.3 summarises the research sources which the evaluator used in making judgements on programme delivery and formative impact.

Robustness of the Research

Directly linked to the previous discussion on different research designs, the role of the evaluator must also include some evaluation of the robust-ness of the research conducted by those delivering the programme to

Table 5.3
Formative Evaluation: Research Components

Source of research	Nature of the study	Research strategy involved
Queen's University Belfast, School of Education (part-funded by the Economic and Social Research Council and Atlantic Philanthropies)	Online survey of head teachers, face-to-face questionnaires with pupils and in-depth case studies of schools involved in collaborative activities	Mixed methods approach—interviews with teachers, classroom observations, and survey work with teachers and participating pupils: interpretivist and positivist
Schools participating in Sharing Education Programme	Views of school principals and teachers involved in delivering shared education programme alongside opinions of school governors and parents	Qualitative, inductive and interpretive
Popular press	Editorials, opinion pieces and letters to a range of local and regional newspapers	Informed popular opinion and public reactions to SEP
Hansard/Official Report	Debates, motions or parliamentary questions in Northern Ireland Assembly on shared/integrated education	Secondary research drawing on existing studies supplemented by party-political opinions. Witnesses called to give evidence to statutory education committee on the implementation of SEP

Source: Author.

assess its formative impact. Research in and on VDS poses particular problems here around reliability, replication and validity. For example, in the case study under consideration, the measures used to assess whether shared education changed the attitudes and behaviour of pupils to the *other* community may be unstable over time. There can be problems of internal reliability in attitudinal scale items used in the questionnaire administered within intervention and control schools. One important component of the research activities associated with the implementation of the intervention involved observations within schools conducted by a number of researchers. This can give rise to inter-observer consistency as to how these observations can be categorised and analysed. Because of the context of VDS, it will be difficult or impossible to replicate the findings across space and time, not least in a school setting where data are gathered from a cohort of pupils who move through the school system. Linked to the concept of reliability is the issue of measurement validity. How can we be sure that the measurements involved in testing tolerance towards the *other* community in the case study here capture that complex concept? Moreover, can we be sure that the intervention of shared education was causally linked to greater tolerance amongst young people who participated in these programmes—the whole issue of internal validity. The evaluator of the research activities associated with programme delivery must therefore exercise an explicit role in judging the quality of research[8] being evaluated. This is more important in VDS because of the contested nature of interventions normally associated with ameliorating the source of the division.

Role of Evaluator in Judging Research

If one accepts that researchers bring personal values and bias to the process of social research, then it is incumbent on the evaluator to consider the source/nature of research and the motivation of the researchers who produce the knowledge that eventually finds its way into the programme design. In VDS, this is particularly important because those issues which are the basis of division (ethnicity, religion, language, national identity, etc.) will attract the attention of different researchers with values which reflect their own biases and are likely to straddle the division(s) in question. In the case example in this chapter, for example, the Integrated Education Fund (IEF) commissioned research entitled *Developing the Case for Shared Education* whose objective was 'to assess the availability of information required to properly understand the fiscal implications (costs and savings) of alternative budget scenarios and a move towards a more shared education delivery system' (Oxford Economics, 2010, p. 2). In the assessment of this evaluator, it was clear from the title and the objectives of the study that emergent research would favour shared education. Equally notable, the funders of the SEP have organisational values which favour a more integrated society in Northern Ireland.[9] The mission statement of International Fund for Ireland (IFI) (2010) is to 'tackle the underlying causes of sectarianism and violence and to build reconciliation between people and within and between communities throughout the island of Ireland'. This is an explicit articulation of what the organisation aims to achieve. An evaluator is, therefore, clear about the values and normative orientation of the interventions funded from this source. Such value orientations can have implications through the evaluative process, from the choice of the evaluation questions, through to the design of the evaluation and the analysis and interpretation of data.

Does this imply that an evaluator should possess substantive specialist expertise in the field being evaluated and an intimate knowledge of the context and stakeholders? If so, then the generalist evaluator becomes obsolete. Equally, should an evaluator have some affinity with the funders' values? What, for example, are the implications if the evidence suggests that shared education actually divides communities and increases violence? These questions are related to a discussion on the independence of the evaluator: Is a generalist evaluator more likely to be independent than a specialist evaluator when making judgement on the programme rationale? This is a question which has received attention in the evaluation literature. Michael Scriven (1996), for example, is unequivocal in his views that the evaluator must be completely independent when making judgements within an evaluation and guard against being incorporated as an advocate of the programme they are evaluating.

Patton (2008, pp. 500–501), on the other hand, adopts an alternative position which includes two different roles for the evaluator: (a) the evaluator as a facilitator who 'facilitates others' interpretation, judgements and recommendations' and (b) the evaluator who renders their own interpretation 'either separately of as part of the interactive process'. The evaluator can move back and forth between these roles in the active-reactive-interactive-adaptive model of utilisation-focused evaluation pioneered by Patton. Although this polemical strand in the literature is interesting, it offers limited normative guidance on whether the theory of change and assessing formative research findings are best evaluated by a specialist or generalist evaluator—except to imply that the former may be less likely to adopt an 'evaluator-facilitator' role given their knowledge of 'what works'.

One of the simplest approaches to evaluation is the linear model: inputs → processes → outputs → outcomes (with this last element being seen as the ultimate rationale for a programme of activities). In most traditional or mainstream approaches to evaluation, the determination of whether an outcome has been achieved, involves the evaluator simply tracing a line from the goals, as originally specified in the log frame analysis, to programme outcome measures.[10] If the evidence based on the outcome measures supports the attainment of programme goals, then intervention is deemed successful (Dahler-Larsen, 2005). The generalist evaluator requires good research skills to gather and interrogate data consistent with this approach, rather than a specialist knowledge of the substantive topic of the evaluation. On the other hand, VDS are a very different evaluation milieu where the *normal* processes of data gathering, analysis and interpretation may be less than straightforward. Interventions in these contexts may often be funded by external and well-intentioned donors (as is the case in the case study in this chapter) who require a specialist evaluator capable of both dealing with the challenges of working within a violent context and applying their particular research expertise to an assessment of the quality of the intervention.

The Influence of Research

As mentioned in the introduction to this chapter, the defining role of any evaluator is to assess the impact of a selected intervention. It is, therefore, necessary to consider what contribution research may have on the impact of an initiative; and, in the context of the focus of the current book, what difference the VDS context has for evaluation (if any)? It is here that the attribution dilemma (that the achievement of an outcome can be directly and solely attributed to a single intervention) and counterfactual evaluative logic become even more salient—not least because there is limited evidence of what works.

There are other dilemmas for the evaluator of research. The evaluation may uncover robust and compelling research, but find that it has been poorly used within the intervention (or that it may not have been used). In the case study example in this chapter, advocacy skills in promoting social change in Northern Ireland are still underdeveloped. This is because, until recently, locally elected representatives had limited public policy leverage. During direct rule from Westminster (1972–1999, save for a short interlude), British Ministers and unelected civil servants made the major policy decisions (Knox, 2010b). Although powers were devolved to the Northern Ireland Assembly in 1999, this arrangement was highly unstable until 2007 when a mandatory power sharing coalition was established. Hence, although a robust body of research may exist, the distance from research production to research uptake may be considerable. Convincing policy-makers and ultimately, effecting social change, requires a different and broader skill set. The consideration of how knowledge production is linked to policy formulation raises a question of the extent to which/whether the impact of an intervention is necessarily informed by evidence or research.

This chapter discusses an intervention in a highly segmented system of education aimed at promoting greater sharing and collaboration between schools from different community backgrounds. The ultimate test of the programme's effectiveness is whether there are better education outcomes for pupils and, more generally, whether strong positive reconciliation effects have resulted. This suggests changes at the system level which require politicians to endorse a fundamental change in the way in which schools are structured, funded and operated. In October 2010, the First Minister created significant political momentum for change when he described the education system in Northern Ireland as a 'benign form of apartheid which is fundamentally damaging to our society', and argued for a carefully planned and 'staged process of integration' (Robinson, 2010, p. 1). This statement came on the back of comments by the Secretary of State for Northern Ireland telling Conservative Party members that the British taxpayer should not have to foot the bill for a system of parallel schools. He argued that separate schooling 'is a criminal waste of public money. We cannot go on bearing the cost of segregation and I don't see why the British taxpayer should go on subsidising segregation' (Paterson, 2010, p. 4).

These two important statements by the Secretary of State and the First Minister opened the door for a political debate on the topic. On 22 November 2010, the Northern Ireland Assembly debated (under Private Members' business) the topic of integrated and shared education and as a result of the debate passed the following motion:

> This Assembly…believes that the current system of education is unsustainable, recognises the economic, educational and social benefits that can come from integrated and shared education; and calls on the Minister of Education to actively promote a system of integrated and shared education throughout Northern Ireland. (Hansard, Official Report, 2010)

During the debate in the Assembly, reference was made by several MLAs to the SEP as a successful model of sharing which should be considered by the Minister and her Department of Education.

The previous discussion highlights the critical importance of context when considering the influence of research. The political context of Northern Ireland and other VDS is such that all policy interventions could be viewed as zero-sum. For example, an increase in integrated or shared education can be interpreted as an attack on the Catholic faith-school tradition. The evaluator needs to be acutely aware when conducting evaluations that their findings will be viewed within this win/lose framework. There is a risk that the evaluator can become personally associated as an exponent or critic of the central intention of any intervention. As an evaluator from a Catholic community background, this evaluation presented some moral struggles for the author: Could I be sufficiently dispassionate when evaluating a programme which espouses a more integrated or shared schooling sector when I myself had been educated in a system which promoted the Catholic school ethos? Of no less importance is the question of whether the evaluation stakeholders would perceive me as sufficiently dispassionate. On a more general political level, this type of education programme challenges the huge influence which the churches (Catholic and Protestant) have historically exerted on the school system in Northern Ireland.

All of this suggests that programme evaluation, in a setting like Northern Ireland, is extremely bounded by context and is wrapped in multiple layers of historical, social, political, cultural and religious complexity. In fact, context mattered enormously in this case study because of the changing political and education policy environment. Key political antagonists (the Democratic Unionist Party [DUP] and Sinn Féin)[11] had reached political accommodation to share power in a devolved government and were looking for policy areas in which they could achieve consensus. A reduction in public sector spending had become a key economic priority for the UK Government, one element of which was a significant cut to block grant assistance to Northern Ireland. The school population was in decline, there was an over-supply of school estate, and the system of parallel education provision (Controlled and Maintained schools) could no longer be sustained. In addition, the Catholic Church had been suffering from bitter criticism over the role its senior clerics had played in concealing child abuse by priests and, as a result, the whole idea of a distinctive Catholic school ethos was coming under scrutiny. This confluence of events offered a more receptive political and public policy context for, at the very least, new ideas of how education could be delivered. In short, single identity education provision was ripe for reform.

The key question for the evaluator is whether the intervention in shared education had simply caught the wider political tide or whether it was instrumental in creating it. Not surprisingly, politicians in the Assembly debate described earlier were not particularly interested in the detail of the research evidence but rather that the evidence bases were available and broadly supportive of shared education. It seems reasonable to suggest that the wider political environment which led to a consociational model of power sharing created a context in which *bold* policy interventions could flourish. Was the evidence from the evaluation of the shared education intervention simply waiting for political endorsement or was the emerging political commitment awaiting empirical support? It is difficult to assess the direction of association or indeed whether such a simple relationship exists exclusively between these two factors or variables. Collaboration between schools may have more to do with the retrenchment in public expenditure on education and the excess of school places (empty desks) rather than any cross-community or reconciliation motives. This evaluator had the difficult task of assessing the influence that research might have in the context of significant political momentum for change in the way in which education is delivered. The evaluator also accepted that research is but one component within multiple activities which comprise the SEP and recognises that social change is influenced in many different ways through advocacy, media campaigns, opportunism, political support, random events, etc. Importantly, research can often be far down the results chain and its direct association with the aspiration of a reconciled community in Northern Ireland seems tenuous. We summarise the key elements of the narrative in Table 5.4.

Conclusions

What are the challenges confronting an evaluator when tasked with evaluating research in a VDS? It is precisely because of the contested nature of the interventions being evaluated in divided societies that there is a particular need for reflexivity on the part of the evaluator. This will demand a number of things. The evaluator should, as a matter of course, self-consciously articulate their own values and biases. The author of this chapter is from a Catholic community background, attended a single sex Catholic voluntary grammar school in Northern Ireland, sent his children to a mixed gender State (Protestant) grammar school and has conducted research which espouses a more integrated society in Northern Ireland. This should be made clear in any evaluation.

Table 5.4
Evaluating Research in Programme Evaluation

Evaluating theory of change	Evaluating formative research on programme delivery/impact	Role of evaluator in judging research	Influence of research on programme impact
Role of evaluator in questioning theory of change: • Shared schooling • 'Mix and fix' approach • Separate but equal communities Validate programme design from secondary research evidence	Evaluator makes an assessment of formative research evidence based on the following: Choice of research strategies: deductive, inductive Choice of research design: quasi-experimental, qualitative Robustness of the research—reliability, replication and validity	Transparency around values and biases of programme commissioning body Generalist or specialist evaluator? Independence of evaluator—openness in personal values and biases	'Weight' of research relative to other programme inputs Importance of political context and endorsement Relationship between research and policy change. Direction of association—is policy change evidence informed?

Source: Author.

Beyond self-reflection, and because of the contested nature of interventions in VDS, the evaluator should also indicate explicitly their research values, and the particular research traditions to which s/he subscribes. The author of this chapter has a predisposition for quantitative methods, deductive research and favours positivism. Such reflexivity, by stripping bare the essential values and biases of the evaluator, will also make clear their starting point in an evaluation. This is particularly important because of the evaluator's role in interrogating the theory of change in most evaluations. Even where an intervention is based on the hunch or intuition of programme designers working in the field, the role of the evaluator is to take this as the starting point and to interrogate it, as part of the making explicit of an unstated or unformulated theory of change. To do otherwise would be to bring a normative stance to policy evaluation which simply reinforces the values and biases of the evaluator. In the circumstances of already contested interventions in VDS, this simply limits the scope for evaluation and supports the notion that we are unclear about *what works* in peacebuilding.

If, as argued, it is the role of evaluators to interrogate the theory of change which underpins an intervention, they *also* have a role in judging the robustness of the research which seeks to operationalise it. Notwithstanding the difficulties within the context and field of enquiry (VDS), the evaluator should not accept lower standards of research. Perennial research issues of measurement, replication, causality and the counterfactual, for example, are challenging whatever the field of evaluation. The fact that these are more demanding in VDS should not be a reason to lower the standards of research. Indeed, this is an opportunity to be imaginative and creative about ways in which measurement issues might be improved. In fact, the role of the evaluator should be to press for higher standards of research precisely because evaluation stakeholders are often highly sceptical about evaluation and equally critical of judging *what works* in these societies. The evaluator can play an important role in judging the quality of research conducted by those delivering programmes and aimed at making a formative assessment of impact and checking against delivery targets. Their role is to interrogate this research which may influence programme delivery in the first instance but ultimately contributes to better programme impacts.

A key challenge for the evaluator is to assess the *weight* ascribed to research as one amongst several inputs in any intervention process. If research is a key component, then it drives the process of evaluation, and may demand someone with specialist expertise in the intervention. Such a high degree of specialisation might: be difficult to justify, push up the costs of evaluation and reduce the pool of specialist evaluators. What is clear, however, in evaluating research in VDS is that, because the interventions are often about those issues which are the source of the division, there is a need to strive for the highest levels of transparency in the evaluation process. To summarise, this should include: listing the nature, source and funding for the research, articulating personal values and biases on the part of researchers and evaluators and a clear articulation of the contested political context in which the intervention takes place. In short, there should be greater and transparent interaction between research and evaluation.

Notes

1. Definitions of Catholic and Protestant (McGarry and O'Leary, 1995, pp. 508–509): Catholic is a short-hand expression for a believer in the doctrines of the Holy Roman Catholic and Apostolic Church; it is a synonym for an Irish nationalist. Protestant is

a short-hand expression for somebody who is a believer in the doctrines of one of the many Protestant (including Presbyterian) churches in Northern Ireland; it is not a synonym for a unionist, although most Protestants are unionists; cultural Protestants are those who have Protestant religious backgrounds.

2. The Northern Ireland Education system is highly segregated along religious lines denoted by various school management types as follows: Controlled schools (mainly attended by Protestants) are managed by the Education and Library Boards through the Boards of Governors which comprise representatives of transferors (Protestant churches), parents, teachers and the education and library boards. Voluntary (maintained) schools are managed by the Boards of Governors which comprise representatives of trustees (Catholic churches), parents, teachers and the Education and Library Boards. Responsibility for Catholic maintained schools rests with the statutory body, the Council for Catholic Maintained Schools (CCMS). Voluntary (non-maintained) schools are mainly voluntary grammar schools managed by the Boards of Governors and represented by a cross-community umbrella organisation the Governing Bodies Association (GBA).

   Integrated schools are schools which include pupils from both the Protestant and Catholic communities. The Department of Education accepts a balance of 70:30 (with 30 per cent coming from whichever is the smaller religious group in the area) as the minimum required for a new school to be recognised as integrated. There are also a number of Irish Medium schools (mostly in the primary sector) where children are taught through the medium of the Irish language. These are managed by the Boards of Governors and supported by Comhairle na Gaelscolaiochta (CnaG).

3. In the Northern Ireland Life and Times Survey 2010, some 86 per cent of respondents said they would like to see 'a bit more' or 'much more' mixing in primary schools; and 85 per cent said they would like to see 'a bit more' or 'much more' mixing in post primary schools. The survey is based on a systematic random sample involving 1205 face-to-face interviews with adults 18 years or over.

4. Atlantic Philanthropies is a philanthropic organisation funded by American Charles Feeney which aims to bring about lasting changes in the lives of disadvantaged and vulnerable people. For more details on the work of Atlantic Philanthropies, see John A. Healy and John R. Healy, Chapter 8.

5. The International Fund for Ireland was established as an independent international organisation by the British and Irish Governments in 1986. With contributions from the United States of America, the European Union, Canada, Australia and New Zealand, the total resources committed to the Fund to date amount to £628m/€753m, funding over 5,800 projects across the island of Ireland.

6. The specialist school programme was initiated by the UK government to encourage schools to specialise in certain sub-fields of the curriculum, such as technology, sports, music, mathematics and computing, and so on. Schools were required to raise funds from the private sector, to qualify for further public funding. Responses to the scheme were divided between those who argued that it reinforced a two-tier schools system, and those who argued that it forms part of a drive to raise educational standards.

7. PIEE is the Primary Integrating/Enriching Education Project.

8. Research quality is understood as research that is methodologically sound, scientifically valid and evidence-based.

9. See John A. Healy and John R. Healy, Chapter 8, for more details on the work and organisational values of Atlantic Philanthropies.

10. Goal-free evaluation is an exception to this practice. Goal free evaluation focuses on the actual outcomes rather than the intended outcomes of a programme. The evaluator has limited contact with the programme stakeholders and is unaware of the programme's stated goals and objectives. In the absence of this information, the evaluator focuses on looking for the effects of the programme, including any side effects.

11. The DUP or Democratic Ulster Party, shares power with Sinn Fein, the Republican political party, in a formal power-sharing arrangement in the Northern Ireland Assembly. The First Minister and Deputy First Minister are equal in constitutional status and are drawn from the respective political parties.

References

Atlantic Philanthropies. (2006). *Promoting an inclusive education system*. Belfast: PA Consulting Group.

Bauld, L., Judge, K., Barnes, M., Benzeval, M., Mackenzie, M. and Sullivan, H. (2005). Promoting social change: The experience of health action ones in England. *Journal of Social Policy, 34*(3), 427–445.

Bryman, S. (2008). *Social research methods* (3rd ed.). Oxford: Oxford University Press.

Connell, J. P. and Kubisch, A. C. (1998). Applying a theory of change approach to the evaluation of comprehensive community initiatives: Progress, prospects and problems. In K. Fulbright-Anderson, A. C. Kubisch and J. P. Connell (Eds), *New approaches to evaluating community initiatives: Vol. 2. Theory, measurement and analysis* (pp. 15–44). Washington, DC: The Aspen Institute.

Dahler-Larsen, P. (2005). Evaluation and public management. In E. Ferlie, L. Lynn and C. Pollitt (Eds), *The Oxford handbook of public management* (pp. 615–642). Oxford: Oxford University Press.

Gallagher, T., Stewart, A., Walker, R., Baker, M. and Lockhart, J. (2010). Sharing education through schools working together. *Shared Space* (6), 65–74.

Hansard (Northern Ireland Assembly). (2010, November 22). *Private members' business: Integrated and Shared Education* (Official Report, Hansard), Vol. 58, Issue 1. Retrieved from http://archive.niassembly.gov.uk/record/reports2010/101122.pdf (accessed on 22 April 2015).

Hargie, O., Dickson, D., Mallet, J. and Stringer, M. (2008). Communicating social identity: A study of Catholics and Protestants in Northern Ireland. *Communication Research, 35*(6), 792–821.

Hayes, B.C., McAllister, I. and Dowds, L. (2007). Integrated education, intergroup relations, and political identities in northern Ireland. *Social Problems, 54*(4), 454–482.

Hughes, J., Donnelly, C., Hewstone, M., Gallagher, T. and Carlisle, K. (2010). *School partnerships and reconciliation: An evaluation of school collaboration in Northern Ireland*. Belfast: Queen's University, School of Education.

International Fund for Ireland. (2010). Mission statement. Retrieved from http://www.internationalfundforireland.com/strategy (accessed on 22 April 2015).

Knox, C. (2010a). Peace building in Northern Ireland: A role for civil society. *Social Policy and Society, 10*(1), 13–28.

———. (2010b). *Sharing education programme: Views from the white board*. Jordanstown: University of Ulster.

McGlynn, C. (2007). Rhetoric and reality: Are integrated schools in Northern Ireland really making a difference? *Irish Educational Studies*, *26*(3), 271–287.

McGarry, J. and O'Leary, B. (1995). Five fallacies: Northern Ireland and the liabilities of liberalism. *Ethnic and Racial Studies*, *18*(4), 837–861.

OECD. (2008). *Guidance on evaluating conflict prevention and peace building activities.* Paris: OECD.

Oxford Economics. (2010). *Developing the case for shared education: Scoping paper.* Belfast: Integrated Education Fund.

Patton, M.Q. (2008). *Utilization focused evaluation* (4th ed.). Thousand Oaks, CA: SAGE Publications.

Paterson, O. (2010, October 6). Schools strategy is a criminal waste of public money. *Belfast Telegraph*, p. 8.

Pettigrew, T. and Tropp, L. (2000). Does intergroup contact reduce prejudice: Recent meta-analytic findings. In S. Oskamp (Ed.), *Reducing prejudice and discrimination* (pp. 93–114). Mahwah, NJ: Lawrence Erlbaum Associates Publishers.

Robinson, P. (2010, October 15). First minister argues for a single education system in Northern Ireland. *Address to Castlereagh Council.* Retirieved from http://www. welbni.org/uploads/file/pdf/First%20Minister%20argues%20for%20a%20single %20education%20system%20for%20N_050623.pdf (accessed on 22 April 2015).

Scriven, M. (1996). Types of evaluation and types of evaluators. *Evaluation Practice*, *17*(2), 151–161.

Stringer, M., Irwing, P., Giles, M., McClenahan, C., Wilson, R. and Hunter, J. A. (2009). Intergroup contact, friendship quality and political attitudes in integrated and segregated schools in Northern Ireland. *British Journal of Educational Psychological Society*, *79*(2), 239–257.

Sullivan, H. and Stewart, M. (2006). Who owns the theory of change? *Evaluation*, *12*(2), 179–199.

6

Evaluation of the Influence of Research on Policy and Practice in a Post-conflict Society

HIV/AIDS Research in South Africa

Kevin Kelly

The current chapter develops a case study of the influence of HIV/AIDS research in contemporary South Africa. While its central empirical reference is an evaluation of a research funding programme, its scope examines the political, economic and social environment within which research is undertaken. The HIV/AIDS research and policy terrain in South Africa has, in many respects, been a symbolic battleground where post-colonial economic, political and social discourses have played out at the national and international level. This makes it a particularly interesting field in which to evaluate research impact. The chapter begins with a brief introduction to the case of South Africa, before moving into an examination of the ambivalent use of HIV/AIDS research in prevention policy in southern Africa—in particular, South African President Mbeki's vehement rejection of antiretroviral therapy (ART) in the face of overwhelming scientific evidence. The chapter then turns its attention to an evaluation of a seven-year grant programme for HIV/AIDS research in South Africa which sought to assess the influence of HIV/AIDS research on policy and practice from 2002 to 2009.[1]

Introduction

The case of South Africa is a good fit for this book. It is the epitome of a violently divided society (VDS). From early colonial times to the era of apartheid, South African policies and laws enforced geographic, economic, associative and even reproductive divisions. The apartheid system allocated resources and opportunities in ways that entrenched division—these were sustained violently through political, social and security structures designed to maintain racist socioeconomic privilege and political domination.

However, since the collapse of apartheid in the mid-1990s, South Africa has attempted to radically reconstruct the legal and policy foundation of the relationship between state and society. Nonetheless, many policy areas are far from settled, for example, land reform and ownership of natural resources. Despite the new political dispensation, racial and economic divisions persist, held in place by structural forces that have been slow to yield to new policy and socioeconomic initiatives.

In South Africa, and most other societies emerging from violent conflict, efforts to move towards more democratic futures open up virtually all areas of policy to critical review and possible overhaul. Such momentous political changes create significant pressure to rapidly achieve commensurate social changes. Under normal (i.e., non-post-conflict) conditions, it is reasonable to expect processes of research and evaluation to feed into a gradual process of policy development and change. In South Africa, however, the speed and scale with which many new policies and implementation strategies were adopted, bypassed processes of research and evaluation that might be more evident in societies where the pace and scale of change were more delimited and gradual.

Societal and political pressures are driving policy changes, in many cases, faster than they can be informed by research and evaluation—although South Africa possesses relatively strong research institutions for a developing country, and is fairly hospitable to the idea that research must be used to influence policy. Yet in South Africa there have been some dramatic turns in a number of areas which had purportedly been well researched, most notably education policy. In other areas, efforts to guide policy through research have been a dismal failure, including land reform and HIV/AIDS policy.

The Use of Evidence in HIV/AIDS Programme Development in Southern Africa

Before turning our attention to the specific case study which constitutes the core of this chapter, it is necessary to get a sense of how HIV/AIDS research in Southern Africa has been undertaken, and evidence employed. There have been a number of efforts to assess the impact of AIDS research in Africa through bibliometric and infometric studies. These have focused largely on peer-reviewed journal articles whose influence is measured through metrics such as the volume of published articles, publication type and date, institutional affiliation, size of publication, gender, levels of citation, degrees of collaboration and, to a limited extent, the content of co-occurrence of topics in research publications (Onyancha, 2006; Onyancha and Ocholla, 2004, 2009). While these particular assessments may provide a sense of the impact of research on research, they offer very little insight into how HIV/AIDS research may affect the development and implementation of programmes and policy. The discussion below examines a number of evaluations that were focused specifically on the impacts of HIV research on HIV/AIDS programming and policy.

In 2005, Swaziland was the country with highest HIV prevalence in the world; with over 43 per cent of pregnant women testing HIV positive (WHO, 2005). The first phase of the study entailed building a bibliographic database of all research conducted on HIV/AIDS in Swaziland. This amounted to 290 research reports and articles. Despite this research base, it was found that those working on the ground in Swaziland did not generally have access to, or even knowledge of, much of this work. There were a number of reasons for the low levels of research use: there was no national repository of research, key journals were not subscribed to, opportunities for access to research resources were not known or pursued and new research studies were often not cross-referenced in other relevant research. These factors led to significant unmet research needs, as noted in the national strategic plan for HIV/AIDS and in the national monitoring and evaluation *roadmap*.

The challenges of developing and employing evidence-based approaches rooted in robust research are daunting in many countries in the region. This is made more difficult by the fact that HIV response requires cultural specificity and relevance, and what works in one context may not be effective in another. It is common to hear statements like these: 'The information campaigns are not working, mainly because they are not tailored to our diversity. They do not speak to us. They are not friendly. And they do not also focus on our different cultures, our different sexual diversity or different sexual orientation, our different gender, and that is pretty basic for these campaigns to have success' (Fadul, 2008, p. 1).

It is also notable that 'Reductions in HIV transmission in entire countries or regions or in specific risk groups inevitably result from a complex combination of strategies and several risk-reduction options with strong leadership and community engagement that is sustained over a long time' (Coates et al., 2008, p. 670). This means that the adoption of only one element of a multi-pronged strategy may prove quite unsuccessful when applied in isolation elsewhere.

From an evaluative perspective, it is a big challenge to delineate the unique impact of a particular research intervention. This is particularly so in environments which are saturated with: research on multi-component interventions; numerous, independent, separate interventions and trace effects of past interventions. Such environments are characterised by a degree of equivocacy about what works and what does not work. Methodological challenges abound: distinguishing the marginal effects of new interventions, establishing comparable control groups and the vagaries of determining the motivations for changes in individual behaviours (Padian et al., 2008).

Clearly, there are formidable challenges in any attempt to take stock of the prevention programme environment at a country level; and to understand how this environment affects the efficacy of interventions. Nonetheless, there have been some notable successes, most recently in Zimbabwe (Gregson et al., 2011; Halperin et al., 2011). However in that case, as well as in the earlier and much feted case of Uganda, the evaluative role played by research was to explain the observed changes understood to indicate the success of past interventions. The focus was not (as it is in this chapter) on the impact of research in shaping or scaling up programmes or in building on successes. Beyond the exceptional cases of Uganda and Zimbabwe, investments in HIV/AIDS programmes are characterised as follows: 'The largest investments in AIDS prevention targeted to the general population are being made in interventions where the evidence for large-scale impact is uncertain' (Potts et al., 2008, p. 279).

One illustration of Potts et al.'s conclusion is the all-out campaign currently underway in South Africa to test people for HIV. While this is being described as a prevention activity in AIDS response plans, there is, in fact, little evidence to suggest that when an HIV-negative person discovers their status that he or she will be motivated to practice prevention. Stated bluntly, the output of an HIV test is not a prevention response—although it is an important part of a combination of responses required for various programme outputs to affect prevention outcomes and to reduce HIV incidence.

Every year, more than $10 billion of international aid is allocated to AIDS. And, after 20 years of intensive HIV/AIDS work, there is an understandable sense of exasperation at the limited success in rolling back HIV infections. To this day, for every two people starting antiretroviral therapy (ART), five others are being infected. Growing concern about the shortfall in AIDS funding, and about competing funding priorities, have animated a new call to *follow the evidence*. Despite the enthusiasm behind this renewed call, there is an under-appreciation that the undergirding of prevention efforts over the years has been an amalgam of science, untested assumptions and competing belief systems.

The call for evidence-based health development has been a refrain in the international health field over many years. Numerous initiatives have sought to promote the *translation of research into policy and practice* (TRIPP) and [get] research into policy and practice (GRIPP). The most recent initiatives in the HIV/AIDS field have been attempts to promote responses based on better knowledge of country epidemics (know your epidemic) and on better understanding of responses (know your responses). These are undoubtedly important initiatives that have already led to the implementation of relevant research findings—for example, new understandings of the discrepancies between where resources are going and where new infections are occurring.

It is arguable whether we are in the throes of a *new game*, but it remains to be explained why research has not been more deliberately used in shaping AIDS responses. A simple explanation is that the research has not been compelling or strong enough. This explanation is illustrated by the case of research on male medical circumcision. Evidence has accumulated over the last 20 years that male circumcision (MC) reduces the risk of men acquiring sexually transmitted HIV (Siegfried et al., 2005). But for such evidence to acquire the *power of proof*, a series of three randomised control trials (RCTs) was undertaken (Bailey et al., 2008) using medical circumcision on the treatment group to motivate the introduction of male circumcision as a surgical intervention in HIV prevention. The perceived strength of this evidence led to rapid policy formulation and adoption of implementation strategies in many African countries.

This exception aside, the translation of research into policy and practice has been inefficient and not always appropriate to the urgent need to curb HIV infections. For example, as far back as 1997, the science of infection was well understood, along with compelling evidence for a focus on concurrent partnerships as a driving force of the epidemic (Morris and Kretzschmar, 1997). But only in the last two to three years—with not much new evidence to support the idea—did this prevention avenue begin to appear as a main—if not *the* main—focus of HIV prevention in sub-Saharan Africa.

This raises questions about why research is not utilised, why evidence may be overlooked and why programmes have been supported for years with little supportive evidence. In trying to understand why this is the case, it is worth noting that social science research has tended to be trailed along behind the medical sciences in the HIV/AIDS research. That is, it has followed, not led, the way. It has been used at critical junctures to enrich discussions introduced by the medical sciences, and often to justify predetermined paths of action. However, if we can harness social science research in the current chapter, we are better positioned to examine what else drives decision-making about HIV/AIDS responses.

Politics and Ideology at Play in AIDS Response

Pisani's book *The Wisdom of Whores: Bureaucrats, Brothels, and the Business of AIDS* (2008) shows how politics, money and ideology have taken centre stage in the multi-billion dollar AIDS industry. The author describes her own experience working as a UN epidemiologist at the centre of this industry, showing how these prerogatives have in some instances set aside or skewed evidence as a basis for priority setting and programme support.

The book should come as no surprise. The role of ideology has been evident throughout the history of AIDS. There are many examples where values and ideological persuasions have conflicted with the exigencies of HIV prevention. This includes the US government's AIDS response programme in hyper-epidemic countries, which, for some years, focused on a narrow band of behavioural interventions, while denying funds to programmes and agencies which supported sex workers or the termination of pregnancy. This resulted in the marginalisation of many programmes working in areas that are essential for HIV prevention. For example, seasoned and effective organisations working in reproductive health were precluded from US government support because of their policy on pregnancy termination, thereby weakening efforts to prevent mother-to-child transmission of HIV.

But perhaps the most notorious failure to follow the lead of evidence was in South Africa, where the government delayed the implementation of ART. The struggle for ART in South Africa is an extreme case of the battle between scientific evidence and other, non-scientific, influences on policy formation and implementation. The result was, depending on your perspective, either the delaying or denying of life-saving treatment. Scientific evidence was effectively ignored in policy-making for a number of years.

A body of research evidence had been amassed to support the global roll-out of ART. However, to the bewilderment of the world, then-South African State President Mbeki strenuously argued the case against ART, challenging or discounting a considerable body of scientific evidence for its safety and efficacy. For the government to sustain its policy of inaction on ART, it is 'first of all required victory in a battle between fiction and fact. To perpetuate a fiction, Mbeki and his allies needed to withhold and dispute evidence about the impact of AIDS on the South African population' (Heywood 2010, p. 15). This was achieved in part through denying access to information and through interfering with and delaying the publication of scientific reports on adult mortality (Nattrass, 2007). Mbeki also convened a panel of experts which included international figures known for the belief that it was treatment rather than HIV that was killing people. Latent cultural narratives about the Western origins of HIV conferred a degree of political and popular support to Mbeki's position. One legacy of this episode is that specious debates about the aetiology of AIDS and methods of treatment were a subject of vigorous popular debate for years afterwards.

Civil society lobbied vigorously against the government's position, including a constitutional challenge in the courts. Eventually such advocacy coerced the government to make ART a priority health service concern. In human terms, however, it is estimated that government delay resulted in over 330,000 deaths, that might otherwise have been averted (Chigwedere et al., 2008).The Mbeki AIDS story has been widely written about and there is a range of interpretations (Feinstein, 2007; Gevisser, 2007; Gumede, 2005; Kenyon, 2008) about what lay behind his denial of the connection between HIV and AIDS and then his attempts to refute the efficacy of ART. Whatever Mbeki's motives were, it is apparent that his ideas were allowed to hold sway for a few years with deadly consequences. A full understanding of this episode, however, requires us to look beyond the role of a single policy-maker, even when the policy-maker is the president. Equally important is the need to understand the context within which Mbeki was operating. What was the environment of HIV/AIDS policy formulation and the prevailing culture of evidence-based policy development? And, how did this affect the nature and duration of the situation? One answer, explored in greater detail later, is that a culture of using science and evidence—supported by social, political and economic institutions—was meagre in South Africa. This absence, as much as the role of Mbeki, created an environment ripe for *policy-based evidence making* (Boden and Epstein, 2006) as opposed to evidence-based policy-making.

The next section of this chapter turns its attention to an evaluation of an AIDS research grant programme to demonstrate how the processes of translating evidence into policies and practices require a range of preconditions. While such conditions are absent in South Africa, they are present in societies with long histories of social policy debate within environments of relative stability, where institutions and processes associated with research to policy transitions have become regularised and are managed in ways that allows research to have due influence.

Case Study: Evaluation of an HIV/AIDS Research Grant-making Programme

In this section, we move from a broad discussion of HIV research and policy in South Africa to a specific case of an evaluation of a specific HIV/AIDS research grant-making programme. The seven-year programme was funded by a philanthropic organisation, which sought to support research which identified the social impacts of HIV/AIDS and explored ways of mitigating them. It funded a range of organisations, from a national statutory research council to small NGOs. Up to that point in time, not much attention had been paid to this area of research in South Africa. Thus, an evaluation study was commissioned by the funder with the aim of identifying and understanding the intended impacts of the research funding programme.

At the inception of the programme in 2002, it was well known that there was a critical lack of empirical research documenting the social impacts of HIV/AIDS in South Africa. Reliable data were needed in strategic areas which could be understood and used by policy-makers, government leaders and those setting policy and programming priorities. It was recognised that this would involve a twofold process of first developing a research agenda and building the capacity of key institutions to conduct this research; and then, supporting policy and practices that optimised social impact. The latter task was relatively a new territory. While the programme sought to optimise the social impact of HIV/AIDS research, there was no clear or predetermined strategy to increase the likelihood of this occurring. It was hoped that researchers would be in a position to take their findings into domains of policy and practice.

The programme consisted of four areas: democracy and governance, sustainable development, peace and security and basic education and vulnerable children. Forty-five research grants were provided to 24 grantee organisations, including NGOs, university research units and statutory research organisations. Since the evaluation sought to assess and understand the impact of the research grant programme on policy and practice processes, it needed to document how the policy and practice environment had changed as a result of project activities and outputs. As part of the evaluation, a number of standard output and outcome level indicators were developed, and information was gathered to populate them. These included, for example, the proportion of projects achieving their planned research outputs, the number of policy briefs and peer-reviewed publications produced, the percentage of organisations that completed their research, reported their findings to stakeholders *and* continued their involvement with the research team in the field, and the proportion of projects showing evidence of continuing or likely future work in the field. The source of evidence for the evaluation included: interviews with funders, research programme records and outputs, interviews with research teams and sectoral experts, interviews with partners and beneficiaries, literature reviews and finally, interviews with policy-makers.

At the level of outcomes, the grant programme achieved some notable successes in meeting its aims. These included:

- production of the first generation of research on HIV/AIDS and political processes, which led directly to significant additional support on the part of international bilateral and multilateral donors for programme work in this area;
- development of a *caring schools* concept, which led to the formation of regional and national networks of organisations working in this area;
- completion of seminal work promoting a human-settlements approach to HIV/AIDS, and creation of a national forum on local government and HIV/AIDS;
- new thinking about how to measure rural livelihoods and improved indicators and measures in this area and
- the focusing of national and regional attention on the need for HIV/AIDS programmes in armed and peacekeeping forces.

But beyond these achievements, it was apparent from interviews with stakeholders that there was much more to be learned and harvested from the research projects funded through the programme. However, the positive impacts were not tied directly to research results or evidence-generation, so much as to the research processes themselves. It became apparent that, independent of research outputs, the research process itself (i.e., the formulation and conduct of research projects) can have significant effects for organisations unaccustomed to conducting research, in relatively new research environments. It was decided that these should be captured as indirect, if not always intended, consequences of the funding programme. This led to the development of the working understanding of research influence in the evaluation as follows: 'the influence of research processes and products is often indirect, non-tangible, occurs over time, interacts with a dynamic political and policy-making context, and is variously influenced by formal and informal communication processes'. The broad scope of this understanding needed to be reflected in the scope of the evaluation. Thus, five-point progress marker scales were developed to grade policy and practice outcomes flowing from research processes at four stages:

1. Assessment of research environment/planning/engagement
2. Research implementation
3. Research dissemination and advocacy
4. Use of research products

This framework helped to tease out some of the less evident successes of the funding programme, and to illustrate how and why the research *made a difference.*

Obstacles on Knowledge to Action Pathways

Despite these achievements, and as discussed further, the programme was, in some respects, barely successful. The most notable reasons for poor performance of some grantees were: failure to develop utilisation constituencies; poor understanding of policy and planning cycles and processes; and lack of preparation and capacity for actively promoting findings beyond the publication of reports. Some grantees assumed that their research would realise social returns simply by being placed in the public domain. It was evident that the environment in which the research was conducted was constricted and controlled by social and political forces affecting the access to, and impact of, research—including the need for official authorisation of research, gate-keeping and the usual tensions and suspicion around research on socially and politically important topics.

Adding to the challenges of evaluation was the fact that the policy environment was not well defined. It was found to be unpredictable and unaccommodating to researchers. The wide range of actors and the complex dynamics of their interrelationships made it difficult to discern policy influences.

It was also evident that most researchers and research organisations did not have the skills, capacity or interest to *activate* their research products on a larger stage, despite having generated findings with relevance to policy and practice. In many instances, policy change occurs through the work of coalitions and networks of like-minded groups who pursue a common strategy over time (Sabatier and Jenkins-Smith, 2003; Sabatier, 1988)—yet many research institutions were not adequately engaged with such coalitions. They were often not attuned to the dynamics of policy-making, or the processes through which policies are translated into practices.

The likelihood of achieving the desired outcomes was further hindered where institutions lacked oversight committees for approving research or for engaging with findings. In some cases, researchers found that the focus and timing of their research was out of step with their current priorities and development processes.

The Overseas Development Institute (ODI) (2004) points to three overlapping sets of factors at play in such situations—political context, evidence and links between policy and research communities—in addition to the broader external environment.

Figure 6.1 identifies the three spheres of activity that influence the efficacy and impact of research. More specifically, it highlights the importance of the *intersection* of these spheres. It is possible that a research intervention may generate a number of research outputs, but that they do not influence advocacy, media or politics and policy-making. That is, the research outputs do not travel from the *Evidence* sphere to the *Links* or *Political Context* sphere. Such research outcomes are condemned to inconsequentiality or, at best, weak societal influence through academic citations or some pallid form of *knowledge creep*. However, to the extent that the research moves from the *Evidence* sphere into the vectors of intersection with the *Political Context* or *Links* spheres, then its impact potential increases—whether, for example, due to the increased visibility or accessibility of being picked up in the popular media, or due to its placement in policy debates, proposals or legislation. The *sweet spot* for research impact is that vector where all three spheres intersect. This is marked by the combination of correctly reading and strategically

Figure 6.1
The RAPID Framework

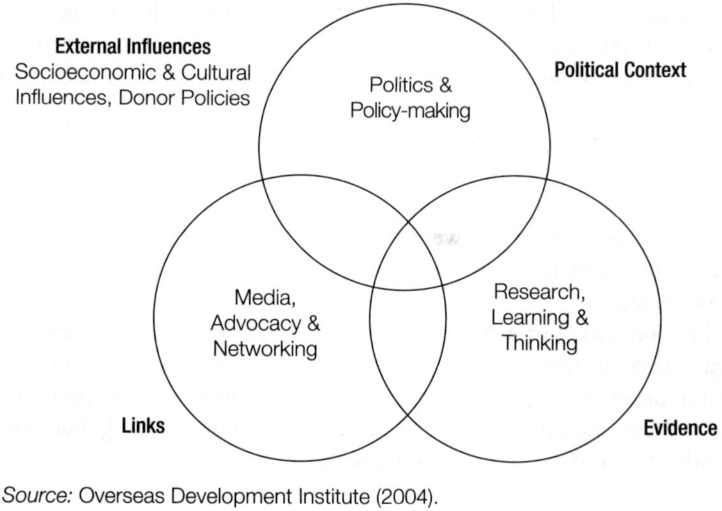

Source: Overseas Development Institute (2004).

engaging political actors, policy-making processes, the media and the channels for advocacy and networking.

Carden (2009) describes a taxonomy of policy contexts relevant to research influence on policy. These are distinguished by characteristics such as government demand and interest in research, government capacity to engage with research, perceived policy relevance of research and readiness to introduce research into policy processes. For each policy context, suggestions are made about optimising research influence. Implicit in this thinking is the idea that processes of policy change require research products, or findings; and that successes at the level of policy influence thereafter rest on what is done with the findings, or how they are managed.

In light of this characterisation of policy environments, it was surprising, during the evaluation, to hear respondents flag a range of quite notable policy and practice changes that were essentially by-products of research processes rather than trajectories of evidence or research outputs per se. In recounting his organisation's research story, one respondent commented, 'the research was a disaster, but' there was a range of positive unintended consequences that had taken place in spite of an otherwise less than satisfactory research process, some of which occurred soon after the commencement of the research.

Such outcomes were evident at four levels. The examples listed below are intended to characterise the substantive impacts and achievements of research processes, *prior to evidence produced*.

1. Outcomes related to the conceptualisation, formulation, and framing of research:

   • Research was used as a rallying or mobilising point around particular social concerns, which have now become well-established *issues* in AIDS impact mitigation. Examples are:

     ◦ A broad range of new areas of social research was initiated, many of which have become well recognised as important areas of AIDS programme research.
     ◦ Organisations that had not previously had to approve research were led to developing protocols for approving research.

2. Outcomes related to the conduct of research:

   • A number of new researchers built research careers in new fields of research, and some research institutions developed ongoing programmes of new research which endured well beyond the period of the research grant.

- Research was used to form coalitions and alignments around key issues, and developed new clusters of specialists and opinion-leaders.
- Having conducted research in particular fields, some research organisations secured significant funding for programme implementation.

3. Outcomes related to the management of research within organisations:

- The practice of research by some organisations who had previously not conducted research greatly enriched their understanding of their own fields of practice, leading to a number of ground-breaking innovations.
- Research bridged divides and led to communication between organisations that should have been working together but were not.
- *Researched organisations* developed policies and processes around management of research leading to institutionalisation of research functions and cultures of research management.
- High levels of collaboration developed between regional military leaders on HIV/AIDS, and practical training tools were developed and are being widely applied.

4. Outcomes related to the communication and dissemination of research:

- Although evidence and *science* had limited direct impacts at a policy level, the outcomes achieved through communicating and disseminating research was notable.
- The most direct policy and practice outcomes were often achieved prior to peer-reviewed publication.
- Research was used as a pretext or opportunity for engaging in policy dialogue, which was in some cases more important than actual findings.
- Research dissemination events were used as opportunities for funding new joint projects, rather than only for sharing evidence.
- Obtaining permission for dissemination led to institutional policies on knowledge management.
- Discussion of research dissemination issues led to resolution of research–policy-maker divides; for example, between department of prisons officials and researchers who had conducted research in prisons, which created understanding of how research could and should be conducted in prisons in future.
- The involvement of ministers and especially parliamentarians strongly contributed to the South African Development Community's (SADC) increased involvement in HIV/AIDS issues.
- The grant programme created some bridges between researchers and practitioners/policy-makers that look set to continue at institutional and individual levels.

This could be described as being the result of research processes rather than the impact of research outputs per se; and this is the key point in this chapter: the assessment of research through the use of bibliometrics and related approaches, at best, only reveals the tip of the impact iceberg. It only identifies the most obvious of tangible outputs. In other words, the impact of research on research may be evident in both research structures and processes, as well as in the content or methodology of subsequent research outputs. As addressed by Bush and Duggan in the introductory chapter, the evaluation of the societal and political impacts of research requires the broadening and refocusing of the analytical lens yet again.

One of the biggest challenges for researchers is gaining access to environments which have historically been *no go areas*. Security establishments are prime examples of such environments. Within such gray institutional space, outside researchers are confronted with challenges regardless of the specific topic or nature of research. In the case of AIDS research in South Africa, questions about its dissemination sparked and animated debates which led to institutional processes to manage and disseminate research. What is particularly noteworthy, in light of the themes of this book, is that these debates around the ethics, politics and practicalities of dissemination of AIDS-related information took place *independently of the research products themselves*. There was no data in the picture, no substantive questions about the veracity of the research—although questions about representativeness or generalisability of the (prospective) results featured in the public debates. The debates around the research (not the results of the research) led to a recognition of the need to address HIV/AIDS within many *institutional gray zones*. As a result of the high level of collaboration between regional military leaders on HIV/AIDS and the development of practical training tools for engagement of the military, systematic responses were developed and applied.

These incidental events should not be discounted simply as fortuitous by-products of research projects. In many cases, intended research products would have no entry point into the policy space in the absence of these *accidental* research impacts. They are, in a very real sense, literally path-breaking. They create the possibility of more predictable and better managed *research to policy* spaces. This process of increasing the awareness of and receptivity for, research is particularly important in VDS lacking strong traditions of research and knowledge management. It is a kind of induction into more evidence-based forms of public debate and policy formulation.

Thus far, our discussion has not addressed the question of the content or quality of research, in terms of the traditional standards of *good* research. Where and how does this fit into the current discussion?

The content and quality of a piece of research is more likely to be more conspicuous when it seeks to address specific research questions. In the case of the research grant programme, the questions driving research projects were, generally speaking, broadly cast—often seeking to define the most pressing and essential issues in the AIDS epidemic. That is, research sought to identify those issues that warranted further research. It was as much about defining the field of issues to be researched as it was about answering specific questions. At the time, for example, data on the effects of AIDS morbidity and mortality on electoral processes were endlessly debated and publicly contested. The research funding programme supported a number of projects that generated data which *fed into* the refinement of the understandings of this dimension of the epidemic. In this context, the legitimacy and *usability* of the research were closely tied to the perception of it having been carefully conducted following established standards of social scientific enquiry.

This opens the gate for a host of problems, not least of which is the influence of shoddy or bogus research. This risk is inevitable in all environments and particularly so in environments with under-developed research capacities. Within such environments, the presence of bogus research may have a negative collateral impact by nurturing suspicious or dismissive attitudes towards all research—the good, the bad and the indifferent—thereby reducing the influence of the findings of rigorous research. The example of AIDS denialism discussed previously is a strong case in point.

In an environment where there are well-established research traditions and rigorous studies using RCTs and the like, there may be ready opportunity for research results to decisively influence policy directions. As noted above, the question of male medical circumcision is a case in point where RCTs turned the tide on the issue. But this was only possible after a systematic history of empirical studies and hypothesis-generating research. But, in societies where research has not had a strong hand in policy formation, as in VDS, the very fact that research is being done may, itself, be catalytic. So, for example, in South Africa, when there was little research on imprisoned populations, the recommendations of preliminary studies on how to better sample imprisoned populations, were a significant outcome. They lead directly to knowledge about how

to conduct better science in this area and more openness to research—
without the empirical research having yet been conducted.

Factors Promoting Research Influence

The success of the research funding programme was assisted by its support to grantees for *non-research* activities, such as advocacy and the
building of communities of practice. This required a highly flexible
approach on the part of the funder, as well as willingness to provide
supplemental grants intended to promote research, policy and practice
interaction. Such an approach helped to avoid the *project trap* whereby
research outputs mark the termination of the research trajectory.

The approach developed and deployed by the research funding
programme served to amplify the *research influence* of the work of its
recipients. Important features of this approach included:

- *Building on Existing Engagement:* Funding was directed towards projects conducted by organisations which were knowledgeable about key
  policy questions, and already engaged in substantive research or advocacy programmes aimed at influencing policy in particular thematic
  areas.
- *Linked-Up, Synergistic Approaches:* Funding sought to build or reinforce linkages and associations between grantees and other agencies,
  thereby increasing the momentum, scale and cross-fertilisation of the
  projects. The resulting impacts were greater than would have been
  achieved had the projects been undertaken in isolation from one another.
  An inter-disciplinary social science approach further supported the
  broadening of interest in particular social problems across traditional
  research boundaries.
- *Community of Practice Approaches:* Provision of additional grants to
  support interaction of researchers and policy-makers and purposefully
  developing communities of practice that engaged involved researchers,
  policy-makers and practitioners.
- *Flexibility and Responsivity:* Flexibility regarding changes in direction
  allowed projects to refocus attention, or change research plans, in keeping with changes within policy and practice environments.
- *Matching Research Grants to Organisational Skill Sets:* Research
  grants and intended outcomes that were matched to existing organisational skills and capacities for conceptualising and managing research
  processes.

- *Dissemination and Capacity-building Support:* Research projects could draw on further funds to support the dissemination of findings, advocacy work and research capacity building.

It is also worth noting those instances where funded research was less successful in efforts to influence policy and practice. Such cases generally lacked a clear understanding of how to broker relationships between the worlds of research and social action. This should not be too surprising since research programmes are often mute on such important questions. As illustrated in the ODI RAPID framework (Figure 6.1), the likelihood of policy influence increases where there is an understanding of the political environment, policy-making processes, as well as the possession of robust evidence. Further, however, engagement with the media, networking and advocacy efforts increase the efficacy of efforts to shape policy.

Unfortunately, it was late in the programme when the funders realised that success in influencing policy could be increased by systematically educating researchers about how to connect research with policy development and other decision-making processes. A project was introduced to educate the grantees about research advocacy. While this was a good idea, the evaluation found that would likely have had a greater impact had it been introduced at the outset.

In the case of societies without strong traditions of research influence on policy, the processes through which research can influence policy may need to be created anew, rather than discovered and strengthened. Indeed, this may be true to some extent in all contexts, hence the need for advocacy. In the funding programme discussed previously in the text, research processes helped to identify and, to some extent, overcome divisions that stood in the way of policy development. They helped to build communities of practice that went beyond researchers to include influential people from the full spectrum of stakeholders, such as senior military officials and opinion shapers.

Research processes broached sensitive and guarded topics, serving to create greater openness and policy dialogue in otherwise neglected and hidden issues of critical societal importance. This included, for example, the consideration of the impact of HIV/AIDs in the armed services; the idea of using conditional cash grants to support childhood development goals; and, as noted above, the influence of AIDS morbidity and mortality on democratic processes. The scale of many of the research projects was too small to generate robust, generalisable findings. In many cases, however, this did not seem to unduly affect the various catalytic processes whereby research trundled from early meetings with the *guardians of research* to disseminating the results.

This has implications for how policy- and practice-oriented research should be funded and conducted in societies emerging from violent conflict and division. In particular, the *by-products* of research *processes* should be recognised and given much greater prominence through purposeful research conduct and support. Processes of consultation around the framing of research questions, for example, have the opportunity in, and of, themselves to set in motion different ways of thinking about a problem—as well as build support constituencies and accountability structures for the subsequent research project.

The essential lesson to be learned from the evaluation of the research grant project is this: research *outputs* are not the only result—nor, necessarily, the most important result—of a research project. Research *findings*, however robust, do not on their own *win the day* in terms of their influence on: the research environment; social, political and economic institutions; and attitudes and behaviours within society. Further, as suggested immediately above, even methodologically weak research findings may exercise important influence on the way research is undertaken, on the identification and definition of the research issues to be addressed, and on policies and attitudes.

At the same time, we should not be politically naïve. There are certainly policy issues which are so acute and politically sensitive, that even well-grounded, methodologically rigorous, evidence cannot make a difference. This was certainly the case with the research demonstrating that ART prolongs life. However, the evidence could not withstand the other forces at play.

In societies where there is already a well-established conduit between research and policy formulation, the type of evidence needed to affect change is more pointed because there is a greater awareness among policy-makers of the importance of methodological rigour—not least because opponents may capitalise on any weaknesses to rally opposition to the policy. Where the policy issue is more about identifying the need to tackle an emerging problem and exploring solutions, the facts and scientific rigour of research do not make or break the case. So, for example, what mattered in South Africa was that a group of high-ranking military officials agreed to meet to discuss research on HIV/AIDS in the military. Without downplaying the importance of the quality of the research, it was the excellent opportunity that the research provided, rather than the excellence of the research itself, that made the research *work*.

Discussion and Conclusions

The history of the responses to HIV/AIDS is littered with examples of ideology and socio-political persuasions interpolated into policy and practice. It has been argued previously that in South Africa HIV/AIDS responses have been only weakly led by research evidence—although currently there is a promising drive towards a greater use of evidence in intensifying HIV treatment and prevention.

In some respects, HIV/AIDS is an exceptional case, both because of the immediate consequences of inaction and because it took as long as it did to yield to the weight of evidence in favour of new policies and approaches. However, the obduracy of the government and the policy environment illustrates that the knowledge-to-policy process in South African society is susceptible to inertia in the face of inconvenient truths.

The case also illustrates that much more needs to happen before evidence can start to affect decision-making—beginning with the very basic issue of the policy—relevant framing of research questions; and the inclusion of strategic stakeholders in a research-to-policy community of practice. Yet, few of these issues figure in the training of researchers or in, many cases, in their own understanding of their roles. Moreover, the *research to action* flow has many tributaries, not all of which begin in research institutions.

Singularly considered, research results are inert. However, there is much that can be done to activate their catalytic potential. To influence policy formulation, the institutional provenance of the research and the way in which it was authorised and conducted have to be deemed trustworthy and non-tendentious to those involved in policy-making. The implications of research need to be appropriately, clearly and convincingly extrapolated and articulated. The limits of the generalisability of findings need to be specified, along with areas for further testing and research. Endorsement and peer review is required from the community of researchers and practitioners. This, itself, may require the formation of new communities of researchers in novel areas of research. The implications of research need to be communicated in accessible language to policy-makers who are not themselves researchers; and it needs to be done in a policy environment which is penetrable and open to the inputs of researchers. This requires timing and opportunity for input into active policy processes.

Sumner et al. (2009) stress the value of tracking outcomes of developmental research, beyond the instrumental realities of delivering results into decision-making processes. The conceptual influence of research may have quite unpredictable outcomes beyond immediate and predictable effects. But also important is the influence of the processes of knowledge generation and the *connecting* processes leading to change, including the building of coalitions. These often have effects in developmental research, and this is particularly so in VDS.

There are points in time when the policy environment is more open to new ideas, and more open to critique and contestation of orthodoxies. In South Africa, this was the case in the immediate post-apartheid period. However, the next phase (the current phase) is one in which research is more likely to be harnessed to the consolidation and refinement of policy implementation, rather than its formulation. This does not mean that critique and new ideas are not able to influence policy in this, the post-post-apartheid, period. But it does mean that different environmental conditions influence the research-to-policy process. Such a political and policy climate must be understood and engaged, for research to realise its value.

What Are the Implications of the Case of South Africa for Other Violently Divided Societies?

Processes of policy-making in VDS are likely to be evolving and complex, making it difficult to predict or pre-emptively engage with those formative forces. Researchers will need to discover—or more likely create—research-to-action structures and processes. This process takes place within the given political, social, and economic conditions, which is very far from a *tabula rasa*.

Government and social institutions are likely not to have clear processes for commissioning, approving and engaging constructively with independent research. There is likely to be limited experience and expertise for evaluating and utilising research evidence. In new areas of research, there are unlikely to be tried and tested traditions of practice or accepted conceptual and methodological foundations from which to work. There is likely to be an environment of suspicion about motives of researchers, and tendencies towards politicised interpretations of findings. The very idea that objective evidence could supersede the beliefs and convictions that have fuelled liberation struggles may generate conflict. Pressures created by research findings for political authorities to take action in areas which may not be considered to be pressing concerns, may be seen as being bothersome, or contradictory to other programmes premised on other priorities.

The key point here is that VDS will likely not have the institutional resources or political climate necessary for progress at a rate commensurate with the challenges they confront. It was evident in the evaluation case study that many of the factors needed to enable and support research-to-action processes were either non-existent or inadequately developed. This ranged from lack of systems for approving the conduct of research to managing its dissemination, allowing multiple opportunities for research influence to run to a dead end. Using traditional metrics of research utilisation, evaluation of research in such contexts is likely to come up with meagre impacts. But looking more broadly at what is achieved in research processes; there is much to be found in the wake of research which would not ordinarily be counted as research impacts.

While this may generate tensions—such as further souring of relations between institutions—the risks may be manageable when they are flagged in monitoring and evaluation processes. The prospects for successful, positive, research impacts are greater when such tensions are anticipated and well-managed, and when there is an emphasis on building the capacity to understand and work within evolving research environments. Then, these *by-products* of research enquiry may become the building blocks for evidence-based policy and practice. However, research may have the most far-reaching impact, when combined with the creation of communities of practitioners and policy-makers engaged collectively in generating, conducting and discussing research. There is no question that a culture of research-informed policy and practice must be nurtured in VDS. It is hoped that this case study has both demonstrated the need for, and the ways in which, the evaluation of research in such environments must pay attention to its contribution to this end.

Note

1. This is some years after the adoption of an interim new constitution in 1993 and the country's first democratic elections in 1994, marking the political end of the apartheid era.

References

Bailey, R. C. et al. (2007). Male circumcision for HIV prevention in young men in Kisumu, Kenya: A randomised controlled trial. *Lancet*, *369*, 643–656.

Boden, R. and Epstein, D. (2006). Managing the research imagination? Globalization and research in higher education. *Globalization, Societies and Education*, *4*(2), 223–236.

Carden, F. (2009). *Knowledge to policy: Making the most of development research*. Ottawa and Delhi: International Development Research Centre and SAGE India. Retrieved from http://web.idrc.ca/openebooks/417-8/ (accessed on 27 April 2015).

Chigwedere, P., Seage, G. R., Gruskin, S., Lee, T. H. and Essex, M. (2008). Estimating the lost benefits of antiretroviral drug use in South Africa. *J. Acquir Immune DeficSyndr*, *49*(4), 410–415.

Coates, T., Richter, L. and Caceres, C. (2008). Behavioural strategies to reduce HIV transmission: How to make them work better. *Lancet*, *372*, 669–684.

Fadul, E. (2008). *Plenary: State of the epidemic and young people*. Presented at XVII International AIDS Society Conference. Mexico City, 4 August.

Feinstein, Andrew. (2007). *After the party: A personal and political journey inside the ANC*. Cape Town: Jonathan Ball Publishers.

Genisser, M. (2007). *Thabo Mbeki: The dream deferred*. Cape Town: Jonathan Ball Publishers.

Gumede, W. (2005). *Thabo Mbeki and the battle for the soul of the ANC*. Cape Town: Zebra Publishers.

Heywood, M. (2010). *African needs and U.S. interests*. Presentation to the IOM committee on envisioning a strategy to prepare for the long-term burden of HIV/AIDS. Pretoria, South Africa, 12 April 2010.

Kenyon, Chris. (2008). Ognitive dissonancce as an explanation of the genesis, evolution and persistence of Thabo Mbeki's HIV denialism. *African Journal of AIDS Research*, *7*(1), 29–35.

Morris, M. and Kretzchmar, M. (1997). Concurrent partnerships and the spread of HIV. *AIDS*, Apr *11*(5), 641–648.

Nattrass, N. (2007) *Mortal combat: AIDS denialism and the struggle for antiretrovirals in South Africa*. Scottsville, South Africa: University of KwaZulu-Natal Press.

Onyancha, O. B. (2006). Empowering the South African community in the AIDS war: An informetric-case study of HIV/AIDS research projects, with special reference to masters and doctoral dissertations and theses. *South African Journal of Libraries and Information Science*, *71*(2), 56–71.

Onyancha, O. B. and Ocholla, D.N. (2004). A comparative study of the literature on HIV/ AIDS in Kenya and Uganda: A bibliometric study. *Library & Information Science Research Volume*, *26*(4), 434–447.

———. (2009). Is HIV/AIDS in Africa distinct? What can we learn from an analysis of the literature? *Scientometrics*, *79*(2), 277–296.

Overseas Development Institute, Research and Policy in Development (RAPID) programme. (2004, October). *Bridging research and policy in international development: An analytical and practical framework* (Briefing Paper). London: ODI. Retrieved from http://www.odi.org/sites/odi.org.uk/files/odi-assets/publications-opinion-files/198.pdf (accessed on 17 April 2015).

Padian, N., McCoy, S., Balkus, J. and Wasserheit, J. (2010). Weighing the gold in the gold standard: Challenges in HIV prevention research. *AIDS, 24*(5), 621–635.

Pisani, E. (2008). *The wisdom of whores: Bureaucrats, brothels, and the business of AIDS.* London: Granta.

Potts, M. et al. (2008). Public health: Reassessing HIV prevention. *Science, 320*(5877), 749–750.

Sabatier, P. (1988). An advocacy coalition framework of policy change and the role of policy-oriented learning therein. *Policy Sciences, 21*(2–3), 129–68.

Sabatier, P. and Jenkins-Smith, H. C. (2003). *Policy change and learning: An advocacy approach.* New York, NY: Westview Press.

Siegfried, N. et al. (2005). HIV and male circumcision: A systematic review with assessment of the quality of studies. *Lancet Infect. Dis., 5*, 165–173.

Sumner, A., Ishmael-Perkins, N. and Lindstrom, J. (2009). *Making science of influencing: Assessing the impact of development research* (IDS Working Papers 335). Brighton: University of Sussex, November.

WHO. (2005). *Swaziland: Summary country profile for HIV/AIDS treatment scale-up.* Retrieved from http://www.who.int/hiv/HIVCP_SWZ.pdf (accessed on 18 June 2015).

PART IV

Roles and Perspectives

Introduction to Part IV

Chapter 7. Evaluation and Vulnerable Groups: Forgotten Spaces
by *Sonal Zaveri*
Chapter 8. Interpreting and Evaluating a Non-profit Organisation
in a Divided Society: A Funder's Perspective by *John A. Healy*
and *John R. Healy*

The two chapters in this part are tied together by the themes of
roles and *perspectives*. Each chapter draws directly from cases
and experiences within violently divided societies (VDS): one
written by a producer of evaluations (Zaveri), the other written by a commissioner and a user of evaluations (Healy and Healy). Zaveri offers a
bottom-up perspective—from the vantage points of the *intended beneficiaries* of external interventions in South Asia. Healy and Healy, on
the other hand, develop an analysis from the *funders* perspective; one
that begins by sketching out a continuum of world views—including
activism, constructivism and social engineering—that shapes the perspectives and decisions of funders regarding funding, programming,
evaluation needs and, importantly, evaluation use.

In the context of other themes within this book, it is worth contrasting the Zaveri chapter with that by Knox (Chapter 5). While both
draw on experiences as evaluators, Knox focuses on the evaluation of a
research component within a larger social project in VDS. Zaveri, however, focuses on the ethical, political and methodological challenging
issues for evaluators in VDS. In other words, Knox addresses the *evaluation of research*, while Zaveri identifies issues to be addressed by those
who undertake *research on evaluation*—but in the process of doing so,
the chapter also demonstrates the way in which evaluation itself is a form
of empirically grounded research. Zaveri's empirically grounded and
methodologically rigorous evaluations of development programmes in
brothel districts assess not just the impact of selected interventions, but
the socio-political context and dynamics of the exploitation–vulnerability
dynamic in a way that has more ground than many of the top-down, foreign researcher-led, formal research projects.

Zaveri highlights the importance and utility of the concept of vulnerability as a focal point for evaluating the impact of interventions. Some of the cases used to illustrate her chapter make for uncomfortable reading because they point to the ways in which interventions designed ostensibly to decrease vulnerability within such populations have, in fact, had the opposite result—the project, for example, which actually increases, rather than decreases, the risk of children being pulled into the sex trade.

Healy and Healy sketch out a case from Northern Ireland to illustrate how evaluation, learning and research have been used by Atlantic Philanthropies (AP) to inform funding and programming decisions in a VDS at a time of great instability and uncertainty over whether a teetering peace agreement would hold. The story told in this chapter is one that deserves to be more widely known. The AP-funded projects were as innovative as they were risky. They involved working locally with both loyalist and republican paramilitary leaders—whose community-level justice included knee capping (with hand guns and power tools), intimidation, expulsion and murder. By supporting community restorative justice initiatives within both sides of the sectarian divide, the projects sought to find alternatives to paramilitary punishments. As they write: 'The funding of such programmes, which were viewed with extreme hostility inside the Northern Ireland Office, explicitly recognised that certain communities within Northern Ireland required alternative methods (i.e., outside the criminal justice system) for dealing with intra-community violence.' In other words, AP programming challenged existing authority structures from above (the Northern Ireland Office) and from below (communities, paramilitaries and paramilitary supporters). It is precisely within such volatile environments that monitoring and evaluation is essential for ensuring that a project or programme continues to move in the right direction.

On the question of roles, we see in these two chapters that the roles of an activist and advocate can be assumed by both the evaluator and the user of the evaluation.

7

Evaluation and Vulnerable Groups

Forgotten Spaces

Sonal Zaveri

Research on violently divided societies (VDS) has largely focused on the extent to which initiatives have promoted *peace* or have addressed the divisions that caused, or resulted from, violent conflicts (see Bush and Duggan, Chapter 1). Such research, however, has focused on *militarised* forms of violence. Much less attention has been paid to other forms of violence that are rampant in *normal* (i.e., non-militarised) societies, such as social violence. This affects a wide range of populations: sex workers, child labourers, migrant workers, pavement dwellers, children of sex workers, street children, people suffering from HIV, leprosy, etc., and backward castes and tribes. The types of violence inflicted on these groups are more insidious than what is found in overt war zones: economic violence, social violence, discrimination, injustice in policing and legal systems, and so on (Schepper-Hughes and Bourgois, 2004).

However, while these forms of violence may be less visible to the mainstream, they are both conspicuous and pervasive forces for large parts of society. In this sense, the affected groups may be categorised as being *violently divided*—not by militarised violence, but by social and structural violence. These groups face violence in their day-to-day lives and are victims of explicit and implicit abuse. By and large, however, these groups have not been recognised as a critical subset of research in either evaluation research or in the study of VDS. By expanding the scope of our understanding of what constitutes a VDS, we are challenging evaluation research to enter into an important, but ignored, area of inquiry. The point of analytical access employed in the current chapter is the concept of vulnerability, as it applies to *vulnerable populations*.

Populations who experience systemic violence within *non-militarised* societies are *vulnerable*—in the sense that they lack the resources (broadly defined) to avoid or alleviate the direct or indirect effects of predatory behaviour. The response of local, governmental and inter-governmental actors is typically a broad range of programmes and initiatives designed and implemented to reduce or manage such vulnerabilities. The key challenge for evaluation research in these settings is the same as that in militarised conflict zones: to develop and apply the appropriate methods and tools to identify and assess the relationship between intervention and outcomes.

If an initiative decreases vulnerability, then one would expect to see a reduction in the nature and magnitude of violence experienced by these people.

Although the interventions (in health, education, livelihood, habitat, food security, life skills and human rights) clearly focus on inequities, the evaluation of such programmes tends to be narrowly limited to the determination of whether project objectives were achieved, whether the intervention was cost effective, and whether outputs were delivered and outcomes achieved. Although a context-sensitive evaluation may describe how interventions reshape to adapt to prevailing conditions, it tends not to *assess the conditions in which the intervention is itself implemented.* For example, programmes for children in Sonagachi (a large brothel area in Kolkata, east India) provide early childhood education and some mobilization activities, but have difficulty addressing the actual sources of vulnerability.[1] That is, they may observe the impact of the prevailing conditions of the project, but not the impact of the project on prevailing conditions causing the vulnerability. This chapter explores this problem by drawing on a range of cases in South Asia. It concludes that the next step for evaluation research is to develop the means to systematically explore both the origins and logistics of programmes as the starting point to understand not only the efficiency and effectiveness of the project, but how it intends to reduce vulnerability.

I should make it clear that the orientation of this chapter may differ somewhat from that of the others in this book. Rather than focusing on the evaluation of research, this chapter draws on my experience as an evaluator *for* vulnerable populations in VDS as a means of pointing to essential issues for researchers of evaluation. In effect, the evaluations which constitute the central points of reference in the chapter represent a form of research that might be called evaluative research, that is, an approach to applied research which employs evaluation methodologies to explore social problems.

Understanding Vulnerability and Empowerment

Vulnerabilities are the consequence of deep-rooted inequities that divide societies. They may be caused or exacerbated by both extrinsic and intrinsic forces. Numerous development interventions attempt to alleviate these vulnerabilities. This chapter will argue that that mainstream development approaches focus on the experience of, rather than sources of, vulnerability. Or, put another way, they focus on the symptoms (vulnerability) rather than the causes (inequity).[2] Thus, for example, interventions may entail: the provision of goods or services to vulnerable groups (e.g., drugs, health care); increasing opportunities to access and utilise them (mobile clinics, mobile libraries, improved transportation and communication links); and increasing the capabilities of the marginalised to benefit from them (e.g., education and training). Typically, the evaluation of such programmes would focus (respectively) on: whether or not goods and services were provided; whether or not opportunities were increased or expanded; and whether or not capabilities were developed. But the deeper societal and *ethical* question remains unasked: How did the initiative affect the deep-rooted inequities, and was there an impact on a group's experience of violence? If this tends not to be a feature in evaluation practice, then it needs to be placed centrally on the agenda of evaluation research, otherwise initiatives will only ever be focusing on the symptoms of vulnerability, never the causes.

Programmes working with vulnerable populations are overwhelmingly associated with *rights-based approaches*. This has become the dominant paradigm shaping the rationale, mechanics and assessment of initiatives (Appleyard, 2002). *Vulnerability* is defined in many ways depending on the context in which it is used. Underlying this particular notion of vulnerability is that people have rights, but that certain conditions (whether internal or external to themselves) prevent them from enjoying these rights. Rights-based programmes seek to create the capacities and conditions which enable individuals and groups to exercise their rights to education, economic security, health, housing, sustainable development, personal security and so on. *Rights*, in this sense, are not merely about legal entitlement. The rights discourse is infused with a moral, normative undertone: Each and every person has the right to freedom, choice and the fulfilment of their potential. Further, it becomes the moral responsibility of those who enjoy these rights to support efforts to allow them to be exercised by those who do not enjoy them.

Usually funders and donors support discrete projects, focusing on project-specific activities, outputs and indicators of success (OECD DAC, 2006). However, the effects of these projects can extend beyond targeted groups. They also exercise an impact more broadly on the environment within which they are set—including other projects or programmes that are going on simultaneously. It is difficult to unravel the respective and distinct impacts of each project despite considerable attention paid to this problem (Thomas, 2010). This is made more difficult by the fluidity, complexity and (often) volatility of the violently divided environments within which such initiatives are located.

This chapter argues that unless we expand our analysis to explore these bigger societal questions, we are left fumbling in a gray zone because we are unable to critically and systematically examine (a) the broader impact of an intervention on the structures of inequality, and more problematically, (b) the possibility that such interventions may *reinforce or exacerbate* the inequalities and injustice that underpin vulnerability. In VDS, evaluation must pay particular attention not only to *vulnerabilities* deriving from contextual conditions of injustice and inequity, but also to vulnerabilities that may be generated by the *process and outcomes* of an intervention—including the evaluation of that intervention. To be blunt, we need to be attentive to the possibility that initiatives to alleviate vulnerability may *increase* or *exacerbate* vulnerability. Evaluation research will then be able to provide further insight on how evaluation emphasis (or not) on vulnerabilities and inequities influences power differentials and violence.

Such *valuing* of realities should force evaluators to ask uncomfortable questions. What if the credit line given to sex workers is used by the brothel owner to perpetuate indebtedness? What if the support to women migrant workers results in their husbands idling, with less motivation for being employed? What if the special subsidies for HIV positive self-help groups necessitating women's disclosure leads to social ostracism? What if the income-generation project for children of sex workers provides a meagre return for a temporary period and only delays their entry into sex work? It is possible that a targeted intervention empowering one group may unwittingly reinforce discriminatory practices—sponsorship of one child in a family may lead to discrimination of others. If a boy child is sponsored, it may lead to discrimination towards girls. These are hard ethical and analytical questions derived from projects in South Asia. They were in fact, not asked and in many cases this had negative effects on the projects. When they are not asked, evaluation risks becoming a technocratic exercise unable to identify the inevitable influences (positive or negative) of interventions on the socio-political power systems within which initiatives are located—within the home, within the neighbourhood, within and between communities and classes, and so on. Evaluation research, by focusing on these complex interplay of inequities and vulnerabilities, would contribute to a more nuanced and equitable understanding of impact in VDS.

This was the point of departure in the research undertaken by CARE[3] (2001) on a benefit–harm analysis. It followed a rights-based approach and explored whether the initiative produced unintended harm while trying to do good. Fundamentally, it asked two questions: How can we take responsibility for the human rights impact of our work and what can we do to ensure that others do too? The second question seeks to/attempts to ensure that all actors involved directly or indirectly in the initiative respect and protect the rights of those affected by the initiative. In the case of VDS, we must pay particular attention to the power differentials between stakeholders. Most development workers know that projects and the introduction of resources, especially where there is conflict, can have divergent results. There may be a further marginalisation of vulnerable people and intensified conflict or an opportunity for equity and social justice and peace promotion (CARE, 2001, p. 5). Though we believe that all people share the same rights and are responsible for their own development, the self-aggrandising behaviour of some power groups in VDS may subordinate and exploit the vulnerabilities of others.

Rights-based approaches to programming recognise that vulnerabilities are multiple—social, cultural and economic—and that they must be addressed simultaneously. We know from experience that improving well-being in one sector is not enough to effect full-scale societal change. In some cases, programmes have been designed in segments, with funding only available for one sector or activity. Evaluations of such projects are confined to assessing results in a rather narrow fashion. Integrated programmes are necessarily complex not only in implementation but also in networking and governance since there are multiple actors and hierarchical layers for management and coordination. At micro, meso and macro levels, it is typically difficult to attribute particular results to particular interventions (Stame, 2004). In either of these approaches, single project or integrated, when working with highly vulnerable populations, the role of evaluation must be to ascertain the extent to which vulnerabilities have been redressed, and *more importantly*, how they have affected the sources of inequity that underlie and sustain them. This requires greater sensitivity from the evaluator, and a deeper understanding of the context in which the programme is taking place. This goes *beyond* the terms of reference (ToR) of the evaluation and suggests the need for systematic ethical questioning, at the least, by the evaluator. In such contexts, the qualities of the evaluator must include a detailed, politically informed, anthropological understanding of the social, cultural, economic and political structures and processes within the project environment—in addition to the usual set of technical evaluation skills expected of a professional evaluator.

Using a vulnerability lens in evaluation is important for analysing a single or integrated project's impact because it focuses attention on the question of whether or not an initiative concretely helped people live with dignity. This also raises an uncomfortable possibility: that a project might achieve its immediate objectives (such as rights training, education targets), but increase (perhaps in very subtle ways) vulnerabilities. For example, a project may increase migrant workers' awareness of their rights, but if this leads to the assertion of those rights by the workers, which, in turn, leads to a violent and repressive crack down by those authorities who benefit from the maintenance of a fundamentally unjust status quo (through cheap labour, non-regulation of the workplace and so on), then the outcome of the project must be considered ambivalent at best, if not unambiguously negative. This possibility (indeed likelihood) must drive both programming and the evaluation research agenda when working with vulnerable populations.

Rights-based programming is also about *self-empowerment,* or the increased capacity to cope with vulnerability, and to exercise greater control over one's own life. Yet, as illustrated by the migrant worker rights example above, programmes do not take place in a vacuum. Efforts to address the conditions of vulnerability enter into the contentious and contested arena where the empowerment of the vulnerable turns the tables on the powerful. In effect, empowerment challenges existing power relations and begins to confront the vulnerability of the powerful and increases the vulnerability of the powerful's capacity to control—who often have vested interests to resist, subvert or violently repress such efforts. Evaluating such programmes becomes quite complex. For example, an escalation of violence against migrant workers may be evaluated as an indication of the *need for* the programme, as opposed to the direct *consequence of* the programme itself. If the violence leads to the murder of the leaders of the migrant worker movement, the cessation of support for the project may be couched in terms of *inhospitable conditions*, rather than as a direct result of the project. This does not imply that such projects should not be supported—on the contrary. But it does mean that the ways in which such vulnerabilities are addressed need to be rooted in a clear-headed understanding of socio-political and economic power relationships.

Another dimension to rights-based programming refers to the *relational* (see Figure 7.1) empowering–disempowering continuum along which relationships interact and influence each other. This refers to the

Figure 7.1
Questions That Examine the Issues of Vulnerability and Power

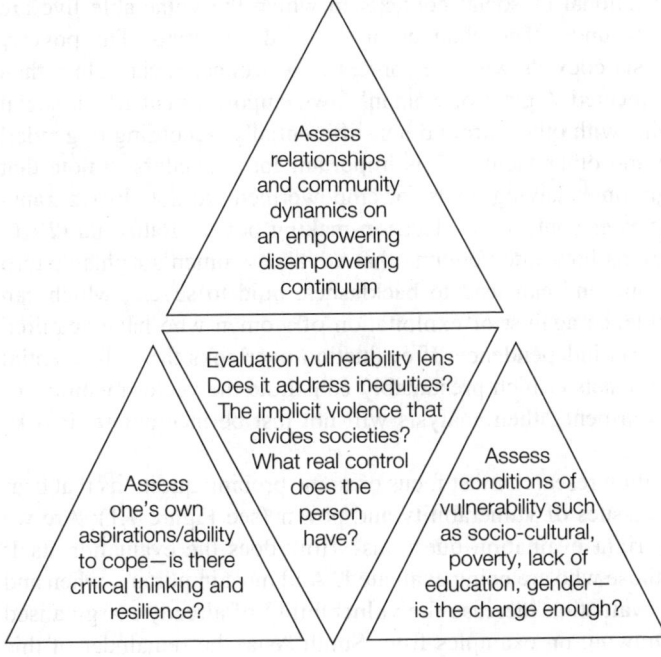

Assess
relationships
and community
dynamics on
an empowering
disempowering
continuum

Evaluation vulnerability lens
Does it address inequities?
The implicit violence that
divides societies?
What real control
does the
person
have?

Assess
one's own
aspirations/ability
to cope—is there
critical thinking and
resilience?

Assess
conditions of
vulnerability such
as socio-cultural,
poverty, lack of
education, gender—
is the change enough?

Source: Author.

interactions between different stakeholders that affect the empowered relationships between individuals. For example, within the same community, one group of children may be more vulnerable, exploited, stigmatised and ignored than another group of children. It is also possible that the different sections in the community may *pull and push* in different directions according to group-specific interests. In an examination of a sheltered home community in the Daulatia brothel in Bangladesh, which sought to create an empowering and protective environment for daughters of sex workers, access to the girls was restricted to the mothers to protect them from the larger sex worker community. But, at the same time, there was an exploitative *family* in the brothel pushing her into sex work. The girls were being coerced to join the sex trade through *emotional blackmail* mentioning that the mother was too old and not *pretty* enough to earn money through paid sex or that, being a *good* daughter, she was expected to follow the mother's (or sometimes the grandmother's!) footsteps. Underpinning this story was the grinding poverty, devaluation of girls and women and socio-political deprivation within which sex work has always been located (Zaveri, 2008).

The relational or social contexts in which the vulnerable live are a window to understand changes in power differentials. The poverty of South Asia coexists with the context of a stronger social fabric than might be expected. A girl's or woman's own empowerment affects social relationships with others around her differentially, according to gender, age, caste and other factors. It is important for evaluators to note that even programmes having goals for empowerment do not always translate into greater control and decision-making power. Batliwala (2010, p. 3) mentions how interventions that advance women's rights disturb the status quo and can lead to backlashes, mild to severe, which can include violence against or exploitation of women who have acquired new economic independence. If evaluation overlooks these differential relational impacts (which presumably constitute the vector/medium for [dis]empowerment), then analysis will not just be incomplete, it risks being skewed.

Evaluation research must focus on some probing questions that bear directly on issues of vulnerability and power (see Figure 7.1): Are we asking the right evaluation questions? How does the evaluation itself influence those who are being evaluated? And most important, when and how does evaluation increase the vulnerability of already marginalised groups? Drawing on examples from South Asia, the remainder of this chapter explores these questions.

Using the Vulnerability Lens in Evaluations

One of the most vulnerable groups in a diverse range of societies is the children of sex workers (Poudel and Carryer, 2000). As children, they are dependent. As the children of sex workers, they live in poverty, face gender violence (especially if she is a girl child), exploitation and instability. A case study of children in the Daulatia brothel in Bangladesh examined how education and a safe home might help children, especially girls, in such circumstances (Zaveri, 2008). The structure of the project was straightforward: A child-centred international NGO (INGO) worked with a local NGO and a sex worker to collectively provide rights-based programming for children of sex workers. Outside the brothel area, a primary school was set up to enable children to move from the world of brothels into the world of education, and the subsequent opportunities that may arise.

The school was established because the children of sex workers were stigmatised and ostracised, and therefore unable to gain entry into *normal* schools. The obstacles to educating children in Bangladesh are similar to those in other parts of South Asia. Although children usually drop out of school for a combination of reasons, one in particular is the poor quality of education available to this group. In this case, the INGO invested resources in curriculum development, teacher training and the creation of a child-friendly active learning atmosphere. The school was located in a community outside the brothel area. Although there was initial resistance by members of the community to sending their own children to a school that also accepted the children of sex workers, the high quality of education served as an incentive for them to register their children, and gradually the student population became more mixed. Through contact over time, the parents of community children and sex worker children learned to accept each other and even jointly attended parent–teacher meetings.

In addition to schooling, female children of sex workers were offered a sheltered home near to the school. This was to ensure that the female child not only received an education, but was protected from possible predation in the brothel environment. The rights-based approach promoted recreation rights. Children learned to dance, sing and draw, all of which provided a creative outlet to their artistic talents. As a means of ensuring that the child and mother were able to enjoy their right to belong to a family, mothers visited on occasion and the girls sometimes visited the brothel.

The INGO in this case had a history of programming in child rights and empowerment. Their national programme on life skills sought to empower children through their clubs and forums. For example, the INGO offered 'LIFE' or the Life Skills Intervention for Empowerment programme to children which includes peer leadership training and life skills sessions with peers within their own communities as well. The Shishu Parishads (child councils) received training on child rights and life skills. Together, these initiatives were meant to respond to problems of child trafficking and early marriage by establishing and supporting a network to support friends who did not want to return to the brothel.

An evaluation of the programme indicated that there were many positive changes in the lives of participants, including: an improved ability to save money; greater determination to continue with education and vocational training; increased rejection of trafficking; and an overall increase in self-esteem. Evaluation of the school programme indicated a high quality of education (a proxy indicator being community children attending school); good school performance and completion of primary education by the children of sex workers. The programme had been started in consultation with the sex workers collective and so there was a sense of ownership for a sustainable project. By these indicators, the project was cast as a success. But a broadening of the evaluative optic suggests a more mixed result.

The assessment becomes less clear-cut when our questions move from the technical to the political. Research on evaluation in this sector needs to focus more explicitly on the need for evaluations to probe whether or not vulnerabilities and inequities have been addressed. In the example above, where sex workers were marginalised and their children born and raised in a culture of deprivation and exploitation, we need to ask the right questions. Did the children's vulnerability actually decrease? Was there an increased ability to cope? Were inequities addressed and, if so, was the violence that pushed women towards sex work and exploitation diminished?

The children were mainstreamed into secondary school. However, after completion of Std. V, access to secondary school, though available, was less attractive for a variety of reasons: school fees were required, teachers were not especially child-friendly and additional coaching was not available. Consequently, although 100 per cent of the students enrolled into Std VI, almost all the children from the brothel dropped out (90 per cent) within the first year.[4] This particular experience suggests that the completion of primary education was not enough to ensure continuation along this path or to permanently address the long-term vulnerability of these particular children.

There were further ambivalent pressures on the children. For example, on the one hand, contact between the child and the mother and family is important for the nurturing of emotional and biological ties. In this case, however, this sometimes created opportunities for the family to pressure the child into the sex trade. Many mothers and grandmothers attempted to lure the children into sex work with petty gifts and emotional blackmail—'I am old and cannot work and eat, whereas you are able to do so in the shelter.' Or, 'You need to support me, I am too old/tired/sick to work.' Sometimes, the child was simply taken away by family, resulting in absence from, and failure in, school. Particularly disturbing, the value of the girls as an exploitable sexual commodity had actually increased significantly as a result of their reaching puberty (unrelated to the programme), and the range of skills they learned in the shelter (related to the programme), such as singing and dancing. This fact was not lost on the predatory nexus of ageing mothers, brothel keepers, pimps and paramours. Girls were coerced and emotionally blackmailed; some were given growth hormones; and most experienced the push and pull factors towards sex work as early as age 12. The inequities and vulnerabilities of the children that had always existed were in fact exacerbated through the programme.

Such experiences are antithetical to the intentions behind their participation in the child rights movement: to heighten their risk perception; to increase capacity for further studies; and to kindle their aspirations for a better life. Yet, when the children were interviewed, their sense of helplessness was acute. Nonetheless, evaluations of the various components of the project—education, shelter, child empowerment and community mobilisation (involving mothers and sex worker collectives)—all indicated the *success* of the initiative. The questions for evaluation research in VDS should address issues not usually framed in project evaluations such as: How can this be? What would a fully successful outcome look like? What inequities *must* be addressed—and how? How do we operationalise a broader understanding of violence and vulnerability in our thinking and programming? How can results be made sustainable?

The projects and experiences noted above underscore the need for evaluation research to look beyond the achievement of discrete outcomes. They need to be placed in the *context* in which they are implemented. While this may increase the complexity of evaluation, a more one-dimensional approach risks increasing the inequities and violence underpinning vulnerability. It is very uncomfortable to ask whether developmental interventions have *increased* vulnerability of marginalised groups. The organisation runs children's clubs that encourage children to acquire life skills in communication, risk perception, decision-making and the like. The indicators used to demonstrate that boys and girls have been empowered include their ability to discuss child marriage, poor education quality and child abuse at local, regional and national forums. The children are well aware of their risk of being exploited. But there are many factors exacerbating these risks such as lack of protected education facilities for adolescents, conflict between the rights of children towards a family (their mother and her *husband*) and possible protection risks, difficulties in obtaining jobs, and the stigma that follows these children as they grow up, to name a few. Paradoxically, the increased education, increased awareness among children (success indicators) and the evaluative process of participatory dialogue (desired evaluative practice) resulted in the heightened vulnerability of these children.

There are other examples where apparent *success stories* have, upon closer inspection, generated new vulnerabilities and placed precarious groups in even more tenuous situations. For example, in India, PWDS/ Blossoms works in South India in an area that is infamous for its child labour market. Children are employed in Sivakasi (in the state of Tamil Nadu, India) factories making firecrackers and matches. However, media exposure and community outrage ostensibly resulted in a ban on child labour in this industry. However, a more detailed situational assessment revealed that child labour had not been eradicated at all. Rather, contractors simply changed their model of exploitation by decentralising their operations. They delivered the raw material for matches and firecrackers directly to the children's homes. Children were, thus, still engaged in this activity, except that they were working from home thereby losing what little time they might previously have had to play and learn (Zaveri, 2008).This increased the difficulty of controlling child labour in this industry. The net impact of the eradication of child labour campaign was to: place the children outside the reach of the project; increase their vulnerability to HIV/AIDS; tighten control over the children by unscrupulous businessmen; and reduce, even further, the amount of time that kids had to be kids.[5]

In other cases, vulnerabilities seem to have been only superficially addressed because deep-rooted inequities have not been affected or dismantled at all. The evaluation of a migration project to combat HIV in India was designed to assess increased awareness among migrants (mostly male) regarding HIV prevention, risk perception and high-risk sexual behaviour.[6] Yet, the way this evaluation was framed, an obvious question was left unasked: 'what about the vulnerabilities of the women left behind and *their* increasing risk to HIV *because of deep rooted social expectations of faithfulness and deference to their husbands?*' (Zaveri, 2006). In fact, getting married young to a migrant male labourer was and is a major contributing factor to the wife becoming HIV positive because, generally speaking, the husband is more likely to have visited sex workers in the place to which he has migrated (Zaveri, 2006).

Increased incomes of women have led to well-documented increases in expenditure on food and education in the household. However, my own research (with sex workers, migrant workers, women living with HIV) has found that their scope for negotiation remained weak regarding household income, employment options and issues related to property. In these decisions, and others of great importance, it was still the lover, husband or father who made the decisions. Sex workers were able to negotiate condom use with clients, which is an important indicator of success in HIV/AIDS programmes. But on closer scrutiny, women had no power to do so with their own *lover* or *husband* (Ghose et al., 2008; Hoque, 2009). The evaluation of life skills programme for children affected by HIV unearthed similar contradictions. My evaluations indicated heightened awareness of rights, gender equity and risk perception, but the programme could not influence the early marriage age of girls since parents living with HIV were concerned about their own mortality and the safety of their girls. Project evaluations usually focus on outputs and outcomes as stated in project objectives which, though important, are likely to miss the opportunity to examine what inequities and vulnerabilities the project has or has not been able to affect. In such cases, the unjust status quo and inequities that sustain vulnerability are not only maintained, but perpetuated. Evaluations do not raise the issues and, therefore, they are not addressed. Evaluation research, however, can emphasize the urgency and need to address issues of vulnerability and inequities, and suggest why they are not being addressed and why they should be.

Patterns of sex work have always been influenced by economic push and pull factors, both locally and globally. Consequently, the nature—and experience—of *vulnerability* in this sector have evolved over time. This underscores the need for approaches to programming and evaluation to similarly evolve in order to take into account shifting structures and dynamics of exploitation. For example, sex workers in the Kamatipura area (a brothel area) of Mumbai were made aware of HIV risk, multi-partner sex and protection—all standard, essential, staples of HIV prevention programmes.

However, sex work itself was changing. The women involved, were not always the typical model of those lured into sex work. Increasingly, migrant women were being coerced into sex work by their husbands who essentially served as pimps. Thus, the efficacy of traditional empowerment and life skills education was limited because of the social power dynamics sustaining the practice and was tied as much to the deference and obligation of wife to husband, as anything else. The husbands themselves pushed wives into part-time sex work for a range of reasons, for example, to repay debts (due to illness, gambling or extortionate moneylenders), to pay for land and other family-related obligations. Interviews with women indicated that they felt it was their *duty* to help the family. Sex work was viewed as a means to do so, since they lacked education, skills and opportunities for work in other sectors. The HIV programme provided condoms, STI treatment, testing for HIV, crèches for the children. Thus, in a perverse way, the provision of these services made sex work even more convenient. The underlying exploitation, however, was not addressed—and may indeed have been subsidised.

If evaluations are to be useful, they need to ask how the interventions influenced lives, relationships and aspirations well beyond the narrow outputs of a project. Evaluation of an exclusive People Living with HIV (PLHIV) self-help group in a high prevalence state of Andhra Pradesh in India indicated that they were able to garner additional benefits from the government leading to greater economic security. However, unasked were such questions as: 'Did identification as a PLHIV group lead to more societal discrimination? Did this increase *self*-discrimination'? In the absence of answers for such questions, the scaling up of the programme ultimately increases negative societal impacts (Zaveri, 2004).

As the context changes, inequities and power differentials assume new forms. Paradigms of feminist rights, empowerment and inclusion, vulnerability and protection, all need to be understood in particular contexts and settings affected by these global changes. Trafficking, child labour and HIV vulnerability from migration have influenced, and have been influenced by, the growth in economies in Asia, as well as poverty and war.

Evaluation Research: Addressing the What and How in Evaluation

It has been argued that evaluations of interventions can realistically only assess direct and immediate outputs or effects, and that assessing impacts on structural inequities is beyond the scope of the evaluation (CARE, 2001). In fact, many programmes feel that an evaluative focus on an initiative's impact on deep power structures is unlikely to see success—leading instead to a focus on more immediate and tangible impacts and small differences in people's lives (CARE, 2001). But, it is erroneous to assume that in contexts like Asia—with its historical inequities—interventions do not, or cannot, have larger scale impacts. From an evaluative perspective, you cannot see what you do not look for. The current chapter argues that such impacts may be teased out using a *vulnerability lens*.

One of the areas for evaluation research that has been particularly challenging is the identification and assessment of changes in vulnerability. When someone is labelled as being *vulnerable*, we are assuming that a benchmark or threshold has been breached. However, this particular threshold is unstated. Instead, evaluations tend to substitute an output benchmark (e.g., educational achievement) for impact on vulnerability, and by extension, change in inequity, power and violence. But, in the absence of a clearly articulated *vulnerability benchmark*, we risk undertaking programmes and evaluations without clear or comparable standards or points of reference which would provide a baseline for determining project impacts—whether positive or negative. In this context, a societal-defined level of vulnerability would serve as a progress marker in each instance—in much the same way as the *poverty line* was formulated and applied in development programming.

Another problem in assessing vulnerability is that it is an evolving phenomenon, not static. Vulnerabilities are usually multiple, making it difficult to distil them down to a single measure of value. This is compounded by the likelihood that stakeholders will differ in their understandings of vulnerability. For example, the degree to which the completion of primary school is viewed as reducing the vulnerability of a child may be understood very differently by her mother compared to a development worker—not least because of the tension between the longer term perspective of the development worker, and the very short-term perspective of the mother who is likely to place greater priority on more immediate services that the child may provide such as child care, income generation (however marginal) and domestic help. Evaluators are challenged by how to obtain objective measures of such subjective concepts as powerlessness, vulnerability or the value of personal relationships. Further, as evaluators, we need to assess not just existing, but *emerging,* vulnerabilities and *potential* risks that may deepen inequities. This means that we may also need to project our assessments into the future, so that we might *anticipate and proactively address* contextual and evolving factors.

Formative evaluations lead to findings that feed into discussions of whether the intervention should be continued, and, if so, whether modifications may be required in the next stage. In these circumstances, qualitative tools are particularly useful in developing a nuanced understanding of deep rooted, and often camouflaged, inequities affecting the initiative—*and vice versa.* To understand how vulnerabilities may persist or mutate, qualitative evidence (derived, e.g., through case studies, PRA and so on) may help to shape and influence evaluation questions, approaches and use (Chambers, 1997; Catley, 2008). A number of probing, open-ended questions may help in this regard. This might include questions such as: 'What would you have done differently, and why?'; 'What did the project not address that it should have?'; and 'What are the biggest sources of vulnerability, and how has the project addressed them, or not? And if not, why not?'

By changing our evaluative *framework* of *relevance* in evaluation (OECD, 2002), evaluators can look beyond the indicators of immediate impact, towards more contextual-located and nuanced outcomes associated with the initiative. Such analysis may provide critical and relevant input into recommendations for the programme—or others like it—so as to increase the chances or scale of positive impacts, while decreasing the chances or scale of negative ones on levels of vulnerability. Such an evaluation approach would require more flexibility. This vulnerability-focused approach would also highlight the centrality of the importance of *relevant* results and the multiple accountabilities of stakeholders in programming and evaluation (see Whitty, Chapter 3).

Conflicting Rights and Their Implications for Evaluation: Views from the Field

Using a rights-based approach to evaluation may pose difficulties, since different sets of rights may come into conflict as a result of an initiative. For example, in the case of self-help groups, economic success is typically (and reasonably) used as an indicator of women's empowerment. However, a case in India illustrates how a particular women's self-help group not only succeeded in increasing incomes, but also created economic incentives for parents to pull children into family businesses and micro enterprises. Boys were pulled out of school and sent to nearby towns to sell goods. On top of the usual household chores with which girls were saddled, they were further burdened with economic chores, making them doubly *exploited*. Consequently, children, especially girls, were deprived of their rights to play, to go to school and to simply *be children*. Clearly, children's rights were compromised to achieve economic rights—and empowerment objectives—for women (Zaveri, 2008).

Case studies in Cambodia found that after-school vocational programmes for children affected by HIV were successful in nurturing new skills. But parents, looking for opportunities to capitalise on these newly acquired skills, *pushed* their children to migrate in search of work, thereby increasing their vulnerability to predation in transit, to trafficking and to HIV. The right to education fed into the *larger context of vulnerability* which incentivised the violation of their right to protection—leading to exploitation. Obviously, the answer *is not* to stop education programmes for vulnerable children. However, it is essential that such programmes—and our evaluation of such programmes—systematically examine the vulnerabilities of the children and the impacts of these programmes so as to optimise the benefits and avoid or minimise the risks of increasing vulnerabilities and exploitation.

Evaluation of an educational programme in the brothel area in Mumbai, India found that children had long absences from school. An economic downturn had pushed their mothers into sex work with the full support and encouragement of their husbands, who were motivated by the need to pay off debts, release mortgaged land and so on. Mothers would migrate back and forth in search for work, thus, uprooting their children's lives and education. The best educational support had no impact because of the migration and vulnerability faced by the mothers. Yet, in that particular case, it was not possible to recommend that children be placed in alternative care, because it was felt that family should be the first place of refuge for the child.

An evaluation of projects in Sonagachi, India and in Dhaka, Bangladesh (HIV prevention, care and support for sex workers) found that sex workers had been *empowered* regarding HIV risk perception and client negotiation over condom use, following the public health model for combating HIV.[7] But neither the project nor its evaluation examined empowerment *spillover* in the sex worker's emerging understandings of their *multiple identities and roles* as mothers, nurturers, sex workers and business women. So, while the programme was successful in its mobilisation and collectivisation objectives (including the creation of support groups and campaigns to professionalise sex *work* as legitimate work), it was found lacking by many of the women from a broader perspective. Some women in the project chose to address other concerns that they felt should have been more central, in particular, the protection of girl children through the establishment of day and night crèches, boarding schools and education support. Such initiatives were implicitly and explicitly responding to a broader set of questions: 'What impact did the project have on your life?' and 'What would you have done differently?' The project had not addressed the sex workers'/mothers' educational aspirations for their children. Thus, in their minds, the project was perpetuating a cycle of vulnerability, through the lack of viable alternative employment opportunities that would push the next generation—*their daughters*—into sex work (Zaveri, 2005).

A combination of these factors can in fact underscore, and deepen, the gender-specific inequities that were meant to be addressed by the intervention. In Bangladesh, the example of female children of sex workers completing primary education is a case in point. Sheltered, educated, trained in the arts (through various creative development courses by NGOs), and in life skills—girls were empowered and fulfilled their right to education, participation and development. On the other hand, they became prized objects for sexual exploitation by mothers and their lovers. But the girls were also acutely aware of their situation, risks and vulnerabilities and had a sense of helplessness. Boys too were part of the children's rights club but, with few marketable skills, were being pushed to become pimps or other professions related to the brothel, now acutely aware that they too will participate in the exploitation of their peers. This heightened vulnerability and feeling of *lack of empowerment* is rarely evaluated and the conventional evaluations miss evaluating the far reaching impact on inequities, which continue to persist albeit in a new garb.

The Iatrogenic Effects of Evaluation

All of these examples illustrate the ways in which the evaluation process itself may cause significant risks that need to be considered explicitly and systematically when evaluating programmes located in, or designed to address, conditions of deep inequity and power imbalance. Evaluation research can contribute to the discourse regarding safeguarding the evaluation process without compromising on addressing vulnerabilities and inequities.

While many of these examples illustrate the ways in which development programming may have iatrogenic effects, the very process of evaluation may itself be destabilising. Asking evaluative questions may challenge or threaten an unjust status quo and the power of those who benefit from it. In the course of their evaluations, evaluators may become aware of broader socio-political problems of marginalised and vulnerable groups. For the persons participating in the evaluative process, even recalling past inequities or exploitation may be traumatic. Participatory approaches to evaluation research offer scope for capacity building and empowerment (Chambers, 1994). However, such approaches require that the researcher has a well-grounded and nuanced understanding of both evaluation ethics and the local context.

More attention needs to be paid to the iatrogenic effects of evaluations, whereby participation itself may lead to unintended, unanticipated, harmful consequences. My own interviews with sex workers in Bangladesh and India sought to understand whether the creation of collectives had led to genuine *choice* and sustainable beneficial impact. One of the techniques used to specifically empower them as sex workers was a participatory-narrative tool, which forced them to retrace the trajectory of their lives. The intention of the tool was to identify milestones where the empowerment process began since the NGO had invested resources and capacity building in enabling sex workers to form collectives, to build pressure groups and to address stigma. However, in many cases, the result of this process was emotional distress as it entailed recalling (and hence, re-living) their entry into sex work (Zaveri, 2005).

Sex workers *did* mention the process of collectivisation but chose to highlight *the milestone of entering sex work.* Empowerment according to the HIV prevention programme was addressing stigma and discrimination through sex worker collectives and the intense emotional distress caused by the tool was clearly not going to be addressed by the programme. The evaluation findings were contrary to what was expected. But the more vexing problem was that the findings questioned the architecture of this and similar HIV prevention programmes for sex workers, and a fundamental shift in programming was less likely. The findings were like a *hot potato*—expressed but difficult to hold and address. From the point of view of the sex workers, how ethical is such a scenario? The question for evaluation research in VDS is how to address contrary (and not just unexpected) findings in a volatile and complex environment.

A similar experience is evident in other settings where I have evaluated programmes for children of sex workers. In assessing how children are faring in early childhood development classes or day care centres, the sex workers are interviewed using focus group discussions which stir up a sense of helplessness about the future of their children, especially girls, their ostracism from their own families and homes, and their own entry into sex work. The end result often seems puerile and distressing (Zaveri, 2003, 2004). Once again, while interviewing the children at the Daulatia Shelter home, the children were able to tell me which of their friends were forced to enter sex work, their fears of the shelter home shutting down, how someone would surely come to help them be secure in their quest for higher education with even boys mentioning that they would (without permission) enter the office premises at night to escape the brothel's pull towards being a pimp.

It is quite possible that tokenism and manipulation can inadvertently filter into the evaluation process and *use* the person being interviewed, sabotaging the intended empowerment outcomes such as the cultivation of critical thinking and independence of action (Hart, 1992; Save the Children, 2000). The evaluator, either by the way qualitative information is collected, or by the implicit viewpoint underpinning evaluative questions, may create conditions within which evaluators look for what they wish to see, and report accordingly.

Most qualitative tools engage subjects of evaluation in a process that leads to further questioning, reflection, analysis and *evaluative thinking*. However, evaluators can inadvertently create or aggravate *personal and social conflicts* (including gendered conflicts), when there are power imbalances among those involved (England, 1994). As explored in Goodhand's work (2000) and Jayawickrama's chapter in this book, evaluators and researchers working in conflict situations routinely face ethical challenges by virtue of the unique character of the environment within which they are working—although such challenges may not be recognized, or may not be recognized as being ethical in nature. This is an underdeveloped field of work. There is an urgent need to review and employ ethical frameworks of evaluation in VDS in order to ensure that interventions not only do *no harm* but may actually *do some good* (Bush and Duggan, 2013; Duggan and Bush, 2014).

Vulnerable populations deserve to be treated within the strictest ethical guidelines. In fact, a renegotiation of the ToRs for evaluation research can give voice to the less powerful, even within complex situations, and can contribute to more informed and appropriate choices by evaluation stakeholders. Unfortunately, ToRs are seldom renegotiated on these lines. The *globalisation* of research networks presents a unique opportunity for a more collaborative and equitable evaluative process rather than the too-frequent donor-driven exercise (ESRC, 2004).

Shorter funding cycles mean shorter periods of intervention.[8] The shorter cycles encourage simple quantification of effects in our evaluations. Understanding and evaluating changes in levels of inequities require attention to detail and to context. But it takes *time* for effects to become evident. In-depth evaluations require a long-term timeline if they are to be credible. For example, nascent changes in context and impact on gender inequities may go *un-noticed* if changes are too small or too subtle, or if they fall outside the epistemological scope of the ToRs of an evaluation.

A recognition that there are *multiple realities* and an acceptance that there may be *competing indicators* provide a more realistic approach to appreciating the socio-political complexities and impacts that coexist and clash within VDS (Bush, 2003). The many examples above amply illustrate the ethical, political and methodological challenges faced by ethical researchers.

In the dynamic world of VDS, ignoring context, especially in the presence of deep seated inequities, may erroneously promote strategies, policies and programmes that in the long run reinforce such inequities. The role of the evaluator becomes critical in such situations—using approaches and formulating questions that tease out these contextual changes can clearly contribute to more equitable, sensitive research in evaluation.

Notes

1. http://southasia.oneworld.net/fromthegrassroots/children-of-sex-workers-denied-a-fair-chance/. This is a report on a study of over a thousand children who continue to face stigma, lack of education and other difficulties while residing in the brothel area.
2. This particular focus is driving the development of what is being called *equity-based* evaluation. See Bamberger and Segone (2011).
3. The benefit–harm approach emerged from a review by CARE International in September 1998 of their Sudan programmes. The review recommended that there should be an assessment using this approach to better understand the humanitarian,

social and political impacts of CARE's work in Sudan. From this starting point, the approach was pilot tested over three years in Africa, the experience culminated in the development of a handbook that could be used anywhere in the world.

4. http://resourcecentre.savethechildren.se/start/countries/bangladesh (accessed on 21 July 2015). Secondary school enrolment was 45 per cent for boys and 49 per cent for girls, indicating high levels of dropout for 2007–2010.

5. When children are employed in factories or under one roof, it is easier (relatively) to access children for various development activities. Child labourers are known to be exploited by middlemen, contractors and employers, and are vulnerable to HIV risk because of child abuse. Often, these child labourers are not aware of HIV and risk factors. In Sivakasi, shutting the factories did not eradicate child labour. Instead, it went *underground*, scattered in homes and communities. They became difficult to locate and access for HIV sensitisation programmes as well as for understanding of risk and self-efficacy programmes. Being *hidden*, the chances of exploitation are also higher— it is difficult to find out who is exploiting the children and how the exploitation takes place. This phenomenon is similar to the one where brothel areas are *cleaned up*, creating sex worker diasporas that are difficult to access for various HIV risk perception programmes and placing sex workers at greater risk since they have to live and work in unfamiliar places.

6. Targeted interventions are the approaches used in combating HIV. One of the *target populations* that spreads HIV is sex workers and their clients, and most HIV prevention programmes are focused on these groups. This is a public health approach to control the vectors that spread HIV. In such an approach, less attention is paid to other populations affected by HIV. It is well documented that the AIDS infection trajectory was very different in India than that of Africa. It was only during the third five-year National Aids Control Plan in India that there was an understanding that women, who were not sexually promiscuous, were contracting HIV through their husbands (and infecting their children)—this was then described as the feminisation of the HIV epidemic.

7. HIV prevention has usually followed a public health model—identifying and targeting populations that spread HIV and building their capacities on the use of condoms, treatment of STIs and behaviour change communication. An enabling environment to ensure that the above was possible was also part of most programmes. The understanding that HIV is also a development problem gained attention in the 90s. Although there was increasing feminisation of the epidemic, the programmatic approach preference was a public health one. Empowerment of sex workers included agitating for their right to work and legalisation of the profession. The discourse was, therefore, skewed towards demanding these rights but there was a lack of attention to identifying the needs of sex workers when *they were not doing sex work.*

8. Family Health International's India Final Report (November 2007), produced at the end of the HIV/AIDS IMPACT project, mentions in its Lessons Learned, p. 53, '[t]he uncertainty of year-to-year funding obligations through global field support limited FHI's ability to develop multi-year project agreement cycles with partners. Longer programme planning cycles allow local community organisations to strategically develop long-term plans and can improve staff retention rates.' http://pdf.usaid.gov/pdf_docs/Pdack584.pdf (accessed on 23 July 2017).

References

Appleyard, S. (2002). A rights-based approach to development. Office of the High Commissioner for Human Rights (OHCHR) Background Paper. OHCHR Asia-Pacific Human Rights Roundtable No.1, 4 October 2002.

Bamberger, M. and Segone, M. (2011). *How to design and manage equity-based evaluations.* New York: UNICEF. Retrieved from http://mymande.org/sites/default/files/EWP5_Equity_focused_evaluations.pdf (accessed on 26 April 2015).

Batliwala, S. (2010). Strengthening monitoring and evaluation for women's rights: Twelve insights for donors. Association for Women's Rights in Development (AWID). Retrieved from http://www.awid.org/Media/Files/StrenghteningM-E (accessed on 27 April 2015).

Bush, K. (2003). PCIA five years on: The commodification of an idea. In Alexander Austin, Martina Fischer and Oliver Wils (Eds). *Berghof Handbook Dialogue Series No. 1. Peace and conflict impact assessment. Critical views on theory and practice* (pp. 37–51). Berlin: Berghof Centre for Constructive Conflict Management.

Bush, K. and Duggan, C. (2013). Evaluation in conflict zones: Methodological and ethical challenges. *The Journal of Peacebuilding and Development, 8*(2), 5–25.

CARE. (2001). *Benefit–Harm handbook.* Kampala: CARE. Retrieved from http://pqdl.care.org/Practice/Benefits-Harms%20Handbook.pdf (accessed on 27 April 2015).

Cately, A., Burns, J., Abebe, D. and Suji, O. (2008). *Participatory impact assessment: A guide for practitioners.* Summerville, MA: Tufts University. Retrieved from http://fic.tufts.edu/assets/PIA-guide_revised-2014-3.pdf (accessed on 18 June 2015).

Chambers, R. (1994). The origins and practice of participatory rural appraisal. *World Development, 22*(7), 953–969.

———. (1997). *Whose reality counts? Putting the last first.* London: ITDG Publishing.

Duggan, C. and Bush, K. (2014). The ethical tipping points of evaluators in conflict zones. *American Journal of Evaluation, 35*(4), 485–506.

England, Kim V. L. (1994). Getting personal: Reflexivity, positionality, and feminist research, *The Professional Geographer, 46*(1), 80–91.

ESRC. (2005). Approaches to assessing the non-academic impact of social science research. Report of the ESRC Symposium on assessing the non-academic impact of research. 12–13 May 2005. Prepared by Huw Davies, Sandra Nutley and Isabel Walter.

Ghose, T., Swendeman, D., George, S. and Chowdhury, D. (2008). Mobilizing collective identity to reduce HIV risk among sex workers in Sonagachi, India: The boundaries, consciousness, negotiation framework. *Soc Sci Med., 67*(2), 311–320.

Goodhand, J. (2000). Research in conflict zones: Ethics and accountability, *Forced Migration Review, 8,* 12–15.

Hart, R. (1992). *Children's participation: From tokenism to citizenship. Innocenti essay 4.* Florence: UNICEF International Child Development Centre.

Hoque, M. and Itohara, Y. (2009). Women empowerment through participation in micro-credit programme: A case study from Bangladesh. *Journal of Social Sciences, 5*(3), 244–250.

OECD DAC. (2002). *Glossary of terms used in evaluations and results based management.* Paris: OECD.

———. (2006). DAC evaluation quality standards: Draft for test application phase. *DAC Network on Development Evaluation.* OECD, Paris.

Poudel, P. and Carryer, J. (2000). Girl-trafficking, HIV/AIDS and the position of women in Nepal. *Gender and Development, 8*(2), 74–79.

Save the Children. (2000). *Children and participation: Research, monitoring and evaluation with children and young people.* London: Save the Children UK.

Schepper-Hughes, N. and Bourgois, P. (Eds). (2004). Introduction. In *Violence in war and peace: An anthology* (pp. 1–31). Oxford: Blackwell Publishing Ltd.

Stame, N. (2004). Theory-led evaluation and types of complexity. *Evaluation, 10*(1), 58–76.

Thomas, V. (2010). Evaluation systems, ethics and development evaluation. In L. Goodyear, (Ed.), *Ethical Challenges. American Journal of Evaluation, 31*(4), 540–558.

Zaveri, S. (2003). *Mid-term review of projects in children affected by HIV/AIDS, including children of sex workers, HIV affected children and street children.* FHI India (unpublished).

———. (2004). *Technical appraisal, care and support programs.* FHI India (Unpublished).

———. (2005). *Sex workers: Multiple identities.* Presentation, CARE, 1–5 June 2005, Bangkok, Thailand.

———. (2006). *IMPACT Evaluation of a young migrants source, destination, transit multi-state migration project.* FHI/USAID India (unpublished).

———. (2008). *Economic strengthening and children affected by HIV/AIDS in Asia: Role of communities, joint learning initiative for children affected by AIDS.* Retrieved from http://ovcsupport.net/wp-content/uploads/Documents/Economic_Strengthening_and_children_affected_by_HIV_in_Asia_Role_of_Communities_1.pdf (accessed on 18 June 2015).

8

Interpreting and Evaluating a Non-profit Organisation in a Divided Society

A Funder's Perspective

John A. Healy and John R. Healy

Introduction

This chapter explores how private funders assess the quality of the research and evaluation they fund, and the particular issues which arise when supporting evaluation-related research in the area of peacebuilding. The chapter outlines how the worldviews of funding agencies have a significant, often decisive, influence on the type of evaluation and learning approaches which non-profit organisations (NPOs) adopt.

It is suggested that evaluating non-profit activity to promote peacebuilding should draw from a palette of multiple methods in order to capture evidence and elucidate understanding of the specific social change being assessed. Similarly, in peacebuilding contexts, social constructionist approaches are needed to help understand and interpret the multiple social realities at play.

This chapter focuses on the case of an organisation in Northern Ireland supported by The Atlantic Philanthropies (*Atlantic*) to illustrate how evidence of impact and reported views of constructed social reality can help advance activists' and funders' goals. The chapter illustrates the importance, in the case of a divided society like Northern Ireland, of understanding the different, contested, perceptions of reality. It suggests that evaluation should be used to try to reach a common understanding of the design and implementation of initiatives. Practical examples indicate how evaluation-related research may contribute to:

- on-going developmental learning in peacebuilding organisations;
- development of a better understanding of the constructed reality within a conflict context; and
- assessments of progress for external audiences.

Overall, the authors contend that evaluation should help inform and ground strategic discussions as recommended in developmental approaches to evaluation (Patton, 2008).[1]

The next section of the chapter outlines briefly the origins of formal evaluations within philanthropy. It highlights how the worldview which foundations adopt strongly influences their approaches to evaluation. Two contrasting approaches to funding social change and two different philosophies of science—positivism and social constructionism—are then outlined to demonstrate this. Whether people are conscious of it or not, these different ways of funding, organising and understanding reality play a crucial role in how foundations perceive the merits of evaluation and the type of learning and evaluation strategy they adopt.

The authors believe not only that evaluation has a central role to play in helping NPOs, foundations and policy-makers to learn and to share lessons from their work but that it is vital to understand the positions where people are coming from before crafting a learning and evaluation strategy. Funding social change in a conflict setting provides a particularly rich illustration of how evaluation can inform debates which have the potential to be divisive. However, the authors believe that this applies to evaluation more widely.

One Funder's Perspective: The Atlantic Philanthropies[2]

The Atlantic Philanthropies was established by Irish-American business-man Charles F. Feeney in 1982. Its mission is to bring about lasting positive changes in the lives of disadvantaged and vulnerable people. The foundation, which does not accept unsolicited grant proposals, awards grants totalling $350 million a year. In 2002, Atlantic announced its intention to distribute all of its assets and close down prior to 2020. By that date, it is expected to have granted an estimated $7.6 billion, the largest exercise in limited-life philanthropy to date. Atlantic makes support grants in the areas of ageing, disadvantaged children, population health, reconciliation and human rights, and the foundation is active in Australia, Bermuda, Northern Ireland, the Republic of Ireland, USA and Vietnam.

Atlantic regards its grants as investments to enable its grantees to achieve specified social returns. Altlantic's approach to grantees is to respect their independence, to be supportive at all times, but to be demanding in the achievement of agreed outcomes. In recent years, Atlantic has placed more emphasis on evaluating its investments, learning from the experience of its grantees and sharing what has been learnt with the wider non-profit community.[3] This shift has influenced its approach to research and evaluation, as discussed further.

What Works and Why: The Significance of Paradigms and Funder Worldviews

Evaluation has had a long association with social reform movements. The contemporary world of organised giving is rooted in *scientific philanthropy*, an approach which builds an evidence base for solving the root causes of problems, rather than providing more traditional, charitable services (Hall, 2004). According to Orville G. Brim Jr., President of the Russell Sage Foundation, one of the pioneering institutions of evaluation in philanthropy, 'Evaluation research is the application of social science research to provide the administrator with accurate information on the consequences of his actions' (Brim, 1973).

This emphasis on evaluation as providing precise information to guide strategy and to build up an evidence base was part of a wider effort within US public policy to use evaluation in public programmes to help target resources at effective solution for social ills. The Robert Wood Johnson Foundation was one the largest and most influential foundations in the 1980s to commit to a policy of evaluation with an explicit desire to measure impact rigorously, using positivist approaches and experimental methods where possible (Hall, 2004).[4]

Within the world of foundations, the role of evaluation and research differs from funder to funder. Understanding these different interpretations is important because they shape funder's beliefs and perceptions around how social change happens and how it can best be measured or assessed. For some foundations, the role of science and scientific methods is central for achieving change; it influences what they fund and how they fund it. For others, influencing social values are the central concern, while for others, the world is seen as too chaotic and fast moving for standardised approaches to science and measurement to be of use. Some characterise these tensions as a dichotomy between an *evidence-based* approach and an *activist* approach. Debates between opposing camps often generate caricatures of each other. What we argue here is that these differences reflect diverse worldviews that are broadly aligned with how people think about the role of social science and their assumptions about generalisable knowledge or rules that can inform human behaviour. These differing worldviews are critical to how people assess the merits and usefulness of research and evaluation.

In our experience, we have encountered funders who believe that their main function is to experiment with ideas and seek social solutions that can be shared with a willing audience and then implemented widely in collaboration with others. The role of foundations with this worldview is, thus, to test out what works and then to promote the scaling up of these solutions. Whether it is envisaged that this will be done initially by foundations to demonstrate what works and then taken up by government (a progressive view), or whether it is envisaged that the scale-up is funded privately (a conservative view), the role of traditional impact evaluation and research is central in both instances. The role of a NPO is seen often as partnering with funders in search of a solution for generalisable laws or practices and many of the techniques used are imported from the natural sciences including experimental methods such as randomised control trials (RCTs). Indeed many of the foundations that have a central belief in the power of science to solve social problems focus on highly technical solutions. A current example in the field of private foundations is provided by the Gates Foundation which chooses to pursue its goal of improving the health of disadvantaged people by prioritising the development of new therapies over investing in the strengthening of the health systems which would deliver these therapies.

We have also encountered foundations who eschew traditional impact evaluation[5] and who see knowledge as contingent on specific causes or issues and would dispute whether transferable lessons (or generalisable knowledge) can be garnered from assessing a foundation's work in a standardised way. Within this worldview, there is no receptive audience for the lessons of an evaluation. Since society is seen as being shaped most primarily by powerful vested interests, there is a perception that enough knowledge exists about how to solve social problems; it is a question of garnering enough power through organising and advocating to realise your goal. Knowledge on how to do this is highly contingent and is best shared either through narratives which provide a deep understanding of context or through direct observation and mentoring by more experienced peers.

Whilst these two world views are obviously cartoons of *social engineers* on the one hand, and *activists* on the other, they do highlight the importance of understanding where on this spectrum the funder, the grantee organisation and, indeed, the evaluator are located, as this influences the conversation and expectations around which approach to assessing the merits of research and evaluation will be considered valuable and credible.

The question of world views in aid and philanthropy is related, although not parallel, to the role of paradigms within science and in turn to different schools of thought within evaluation. The school of positivism grew out of the Enlightenment and as a result places a high value on the scientific method of iterating between theory and observation. Auguste Comte in the 19th century was the first social theorist to advocate for the importation of the scientific method from the natural sciences into the social realm. Positivists see the process of research as the process of discovering reality through the identification of regularities, that is measuring phenomena that tend to move together in patterns and that may be demonstrated to be causal (Lawson, 1997). Positivists hold that experiments and measurement, often quantitative, are the best ways to uncover empirical reality. There is an emphasis on revealed phenomena rather than an emphasis on the generative structures which give rise to them. The process of research is analogous to holding up a mirror up to social reality. Therefore, it has both realist ontology (*real* objects and phenomena exist) and an epistemology which holds that it is possible for objective scientific research to discover this reality. Within this philosophy of science, the role of evaluation and research is to measure progress independently and objectively. It is a tenet of faith that the *reality* of whether a project has achieved its objectives is capable of being known with and through sufficient *proof*, which, in turn, informs generalisable laws and principles about *what works*.

Social constructionism is an alternative view of understanding social phenomena which sees meaningful reality as shaped and interpreted by individuals and groups. There are many variants of interpretative approaches but social constructionism has become one of the main alternatives to the positivist approach (Crotty, 1998). Rather than reality existing independently of social actors, meaning, norms and values are constructed and interpreted by people. How people make sense, or have sense made for them, of the world around them is key to this approach. The role of evaluation and research within this belief system is to understand better how this reality is constructed for and by the different social actors. This is not to say that everything is subjective; rather, meaning does not exist independently of either the object or the mind studying it (Crotty, 1998).

This is a social theory in which institutions exist and people have established norms and systems for making sense of the world around them which get reproduced. From this perspective, research and evaluation become less about assessing the objective impact of the project or programme to reveal a generalisable truth, and more about understanding the context within which an initiative is taking place and understanding how people are interpreting its progress. How meaning is given and is received through social rituals, rites and symbols is important for understanding perceptions within individual contexts. For the social constructivist, there is not a single objective truth to be revealed using experimental social science research methods. Rather, insights are gained which help the organisation being evaluated; the funder and others in the field understand how the initiative is being perceived during rollout and after completion. The case study is the most common approach used with a preference to use interviews and observation as data collection methods.

Scientific paradigms and their role in human thought are a much debated topic. Often it is assumed that these paradigms are incommensurate and that the individual or the organisation can only belong to one school or the other. These differing paradigms have been influential in terms of shaping or at least representing how different people understand social reality and, by extension, social change. The authors believe that it is helpful to understand the different philosophies and scientific paradigms which underpin the multiple approaches to evaluation. That said, the authors contend that this should not lead people to adopt the extreme views at either end of the spectrum.

Adopting a dogmatic approach to implementing RCTs or, at the other extreme, claiming that a finding is only relevant in the community or organisation where it is generated is unhelpful. There are many phenomena which are socially constructed (e.g., sectarianism) but which develop a reality for members of organisations or communities. There are instances in which these can be measured and where lessons or learnings can be drawn in from other similar contexts about what has worked or not worked. What is also key to this discussion is ensuring that we understand why things work or fail.

Within the world of philanthropy, decisions around funding and programme choices are based on the different political and social philosophies and upon people's understanding of what counts as evidence (scientific paradigm). While these paradigms or worldviews do not generally establish themselves in a formal way, our experience is that the approaches adopted by different foundations tend to be based on the particular worldview of the leadership. This influences funders' approach to evaluation. Some view non-profit activity as instrumental (Frumkin, 2002), that is, that the value of non-profit activity is viewed as service delivery and a means of making up for a lack of state provision of public goods (Ben-Ner, 2003).

An NPO is seen as a vehicle for achieving certain specified ends. This worldview is translated into an overtly instrumental or technical understanding of evaluation and often leads to the private or public funder placing an almost singular emphasis on *holding organisations to account* for the production and delivery of certain specified services. This view of evaluation, consciously or unconsciously, draws on positivist evaluation approaches which seek to establish the *objective truth* of the success or failure of an initiative. This positivist testing can be experimental. It can involve testing the success or failure of hypotheses in an effort to influence other organisations to adopt a model of practice, or to scale up an activity. This philosophy of science exists within a functionalist paradigm which sees organisations as instruments for achieving preordained objectives (Burrell and Morgan, 1979).

For other funders, non-profits are not solely or, indeed, primarily established to provide services. Instead they are of symbolic value to society in terms of maintaining or challenging the status quo. They enable members of society to express themselves in terms of their own values politically and socially. This expressive quality of the organisation is not instrumental in terms of producing specific outcomes. Rather it prototypes behaviours and symbolises values that its supporters believe should exist in society (Frumkin, 2002). In order to understand how these organisations are impacting society, a funder would be interested in how meaning is constructed with the specific context. Evaluations become less about objective facts and generalisable lessons which can be applied across settings, and more about understanding the nuance of each initiative and the cultural context using *thick descriptions* (Geertz, 1973) of the context so that the reader of the evaluations can draw out from them lessons about what is useful in other situations. For these funders, the *why* question is fundamental.

Most unfortunately, we have also come across a scepticism about the transferability of lessons and this results in a belief that social change is so nuanced ('it's too complex to understand' is a common refrain) that it cannot be recorded or transferred in a formal, social science sense. There is a perception that charitable resources are best spent support-ing the NPO in their struggles rather than on evaluation or research. Learning then is assumed to take place by people transferring lessons through networks or being mentored by more experienced peers.

The implications of these worldviews are paramount as they shape decisions about the types of evaluation and research that the funder will value and support. In conflict or post-conflict situations like Northern Ireland, reality—and by extension, reality testing or understanding reality—can be highly contested. In these *extreme contexts*, even seem-ingly unrelated debates can become polarised along sectarian lines. Drawing on a theoretical framework which opens up questions about how reality gets constructed and employing methods which seek to illuminate the differing interpretations of reality can help inform both the grantee organisation and the funder about progress and challenges. Whether this is called strategic learning or DE, it draws upon an understanding of social reality that focuses attention upon these social constructions. It then can help illuminate strategies for how these constructions or inter-pretations can be influenced by describing in depth both the cultural con-text and the nuanced way in which these interpretations get reproduced.

The Atlantic Philanthropies' evaluation approach focuses on gath-ering practical, useful lessons and has a very pragmatic approach to the choice of methods used in its different programmes. Atlantic has always understood that this juxtaposition of *scientific* and *values* driven approaches to philanthropy can lead to foundation executives adopt-ing doctrinaire approaches towards evaluation. For this reason, Atlantic strives to draw on aspects of the different world views. The different social change strategies (evidence-based versus activist-based) are not incompatible, rather they are often interdependent. A rigorous RCT is a waste of charitable resources if there are no activists who can advocate for the adoption and use of the findings. Funding a grassroots mobilisation of social activists can be a self-indulgent expression of values if there are not serious evaluative processes that generate evidence to track the effectiveness of the movement and the extent to which it is achieving its aims. The evaluation approach adopted and methods chosen should be designed in consultation with the activists on the ground. They should be focused on answering the questions that can help activists to learn and become more effective organisations and address funders' concerns about accountability.

The case described below highlights how evaluation, learning and research contributed to: the formation and maintenance of a community-based NPO, its policy formulation, and its capacity to attract funding from other sources. The case study focuses on a peacebuilding initiative in Northern Ireland championed by local community activists and funded by The Atlantic Philanthropies. The choice of case is justified by the fact that both research and evaluation have been used to guide and inform the work of these activists, in what at times can be very challenging circumstances.

In this sense, the role of the evaluator is close to the role described by Patton: instilling evaluation into the organisational culture (2008, p. 222). In this case, undertaking traditional impact assessments using experimental techniques would have been extremely costly, ethically risky and of limited relevance. In this scenario, the foundation opted to carryout rigorous, interview-based case research to inform strategy and to gather the different perceptions of progress from stakeholders. The case highlights how, even in very contested settings, research and evaluation can build the knowledge and strategies of both activists and funders.

The Case Study

Northern Ireland Context

It is first necessary to place the case in the context of the long-running conflict in Northern Ireland, and of the work of The Atlantic Philanthropies in that region. The area referred to as Northern Ireland is located in the north-eastern corner of the island of Ireland. With a population of 1.7 million and a total land area of just under 14,000 square kilometres, Northern Ireland is constitutionally part of the UK and is, thus, separate from the Republic of Ireland, which accounts for the rest of the island.

The conflict within Northern Ireland has its roots within the troubled history of Anglo-Irish relations.[6] Ireland was invaded by King Henry II of England in the 12th century. In the ensuing four centuries, efforts were made to extend English domination over the island and by the end of the 16th century English rule had extended to all parts of the island except the northern province of Ulster. After a hard-fought campaign, the Ulster clans were subdued and their leaders left the island for mainland Europe. Their land was confiscated and distributed to *settlers* from Britain most of whom were Protestant in contrast to the native Irish who were Catholic. So effective was this transfer of land that by the beginning of the 18th century less than 5 per cent of the land of Ulster remained in the ownership of Catholic natives. The Plantation of Ulster introduced an essentially foreign society with a different language, a different culture, different religions and a different way of life. The natives were banished to the margins, resentful of the usurpation of their land. The colonists feared that their security would be compromised by rebellious natives. The scene was, thus, set for a long-standing conflict between two ethnic groups who often identified their differences as religious and cultural over the ensuing centuries.

In 1920, independence was granted to what has become the Republic of Ireland but, crucially, the counties of what is now Northern Ireland were excluded from the arrangement and permitted to remain part of the UK. The partition of Ireland created a state with a disaffected minority who comprised about one-third of the population. Ulster's Protestants felt themselves under siege and sought to secure their position by economic discrimination against Catholics, by gerrymandering or manipulating electoral boundaries, and by ensuring the Protestant character of the police force.

A Catholic middle class emerged during the 1950s and there were signs that its members would be prepared to accept equality within Northern Ireland rather than the ending of partition. A campaign for civil rights was established, modelled on that in USA. This resulted in civil disorder and, in 1969, the British government dispatched troops to enforce order. Although welcomed initially by the Catholics, the troops provided a stimulus for the revival of extreme nationalism, and the Provisional IRA commenced a violent campaign against the British forces. This led, in 1972, to the suspension of the local administration and imposition of direct rule from London.

So began the 'Troubles'—a 25-year period of low-intensity war between the Provisional IRA and the British Army, with occasional contributions from Protestant paramilitaries. Approximately, 3,600 people were killed and 45,000 injured over this period (Hillyard et al., 2005, p. xxix). This came to an end in 1998 when the political parties, including those representing the opposing paramilitaries, and the British and Irish governments, agreed to establish a power-sharing devolved administration, on the basis that the constitutional position of Northern Ireland within the UK would be confirmed, until and unless the citizens of Northern Ireland decided to change it, and the Irish state would drop its constitutional claim to Northern Ireland.

Since 1998, there has been some change in Northern Ireland. Discrimination in housing and employment has been significantly reduced, and religiously integrated schooling encouraged.[7] However, the two communities still remain apart. Marriage across the religious divide is the exception rather than the rule. Over 90 per cent of public housing is segregated along religious lines and some areas remain separated by the so-called 'peace walls'. And the overwhelming majority of Northern Ireland's children continue to be educated apart, and to have limited opportunities to meet contemporaries from the *other* community.

The Atlantic Philanthropies and Northern Ireland

Atlantic made its first grants in Northern Ireland in the early 1990s, but from 1994 onwards Atlantic's direction in Northern Ireland centred on engaging with groups and organisations previously on the fringes of political life. At this stage in the Peace Process, the political risk element of certain interventions (e.g., working with politically motivated ex-prisoners) was relatively high and largely untested. Very few government-supported agencies were in a position to back such high-risk ventures and Atlantic sought to fill the gap at a critical time.

Between 1996 and 1998, Atlantic Philanthropies supported organisations and programmes designed to consolidate what could only be described as a fragile peace. Initiatives included support for crisis intervention work within loyalist[8] communities in North Belfast. This work, which involved engaging with local paramilitary leaders, has been credited with reducing the level of street violence in certain areas of North Belfast. Significant support was also provided for community restorative justice initiatives in loyalist and republican areas of West Belfast. These interventions were focused on finding community-based alternatives to paramilitary punishment attacks. The funding of such programmes, which were viewed with extreme hostility inside the Northern Ireland Office, explicitly recognised that certain communities within Northern Ireland required alternative methods (i.e., outside the criminal justice system) for dealing with intra-community violence.[9]

During these years, Atlantic funded organisations and projects that would not have been able to access funding from mainstream private or public sources. For example, commitments made to the provision of employment and skills training for loyalist ex-paramilitaries within East Belfast, and notably Portadown, in spite of concerns over the status of paramilitary cease-fires, were high risk funding interventions. As a funder of efforts to promote reconciliation on the island of Ireland, there are a number of reasons why Atlantic has been interested in research and evaluation. These reasons are informed in large part by Atlantic Philanthropies mission and are underpinned by Atlantic's desire to fund NPOs to assess their impact and learn from their work—both successes and failures; to inform strategic discussions amongst groups of grantees as they work towards similar objectives and deploy similar strategies, to inform Atlantic's programme reviews and strategy development, and inform choices made by public policy-makers.

Atlantic places an emphasis on encouraging learning which is directly useful for NPOs. In this way, research and evaluation are intended to feed directly into the development of strategy both internally within the foundation and, more importantly, externally amongst the NPOs and public sector agencies directly active in the field. Understanding the rationale behind Atlantic's mission and its willingness to take calculated risks is central to understanding how Atlantic evaluates the merits of research and evaluation processes and materials. Whilst in the past Atlantic funded in-depth analyses of the causes of conflict in Northern Ireland and how the conflict and efforts to promote peace and reconciliation compared to other conflicts abroad, the emphasis now is very much on utility and practical application. Over the past decade, there has been a shift towards garnering practical lessons which could help inform strategic learning.[10] This has prompted Atlantic steer away from the commissioning or funding research on the fundamental causes of conflict. Instead, it emphasises a focus on the evaluation of initiatives to promote reconciliation.

The Case: The Suffolk Lenadoon Interface Group

Civil unrest at the height of the recent conflict in Northern Ireland forced communities into sectarian strife. This often resulted in the physical segregation and demographic disruption of communities along sectarian lines. The communities of Suffolk and Lenadoon in West Belfast bifurcated into polarised communities living parallel to one another, bounded by an interface.[11] Communities in this area were violently divided by the bitter sectarian strife. Knox (2010, p. 18) outlines the polarised history of the area:

> As Lenadoon became the refuge of Catholics from other parts of Belfast, Protestant families living on the estate were forced to either move out because of sectarianism and intimidation or shift to the Suffolk estate (at the lower end of Lenadoon and the south side of the Stewartstown Road), which became an enclave for Protestants living in West Belfast. As Catholic families grew on the Lenadoon estate, Suffolk became the repository for Protestants who had chosen to remain—in effect a small commune of public houses with around 1,000 people surrounded on all sides by their Catholics neighbours. This managed 'security solution' in the early 1970s created an interface area between Lenadoon and Suffolk estates (the boundary of which is Stewartstown Road) which endures to the present day—euphemistically known as 'the peace line'.

Both communities were dedicated to their own well-being and had set up institutions to promote their advancement. The Lenadoon Community Forum was founded in 1992 and set out its mission: To provide the framework for planning and community infrastructure for planning and co-ordinated action by residents, community and voluntary groups, service providers and statutory agencies in pursuit of a shared vision. In a similar vein, The Suffolk Community Forum, established in 1994, aimed: To work towards creating a stable, secure and confident community in Suffolk. The Suffolk community—generally Protestant and Loyalist—and the Lenadoon Community—generally Catholic and Republican—in West Belfast were just one interface area of many affected by the Troubles. Much of this early work was undertaken in the shadow of the final years of sustained, organised violence by paramilitary groupings, on the one hand, and attempts to reach a political accommodation, on the other. In some ways, the area was a microcosm of the wider conflict. The two communities lived in neighbourhoods which are side-by-side but very segregated. Despite intimate proximity, there was deep-seated fear of crossing the community divide. In Northern Ireland, the wider political environment has always had an impact on community relations. Critical events like the Drumcree stand-off[12] in the town of Portadown would have had a traumatic impact at a community level across Northern Ireland. It was only when the communities decided to *park* the bigger scale differences and focus on practical, economic shared interests that progress began to be made.

In 1996, the Belfast Interface Project led a joint scoping exercise between the Suffolk and Lenadoon Community Forums. This exercise resulted in the establishment of the Suffolk Lenadoon Interface Group (SLIG). Where both Forums had broadly focused on the social and economic improvement of their respective communities, SLIG spotlighted the 'things we think we have in common, the difficulties between us and how we can be better neighbors' (Belfast Interface Project, 1999, p. 5). The joint initiative was underpinned by a common consensus that 'more could be achieved in cooperation than independently' (Knox, 2009, p. 5). Symbolically, the first SLIG project was an infrastructure regeneration initiative on the Stewartstown Road interface. By 2002, this social economy enterprise paved the way to the perception that SLIG was having success. SLIG generated new sponsors in the International Fund for Ireland and the Community Relations Council.

Building on this encouraging development, in 2006 Atlantic invested £54,928 over the space of four months to investigate and assess the potential for more formal peacebuilding initiatives in the Suffolk and Lenadoon communities. Findings suggested that there was both space and opportunity and, in December of 2006, a formal investment of £2,000,000 was guaranteed over 35 months to begin in January 2007. The grant was provided to support community-based reconciliation efforts, joint advocacy and the development of shared spaces by assisting the two communities to implement a peacebuilding plan for the Suffolk-Lenadoon area in West Belfast. In 2009, Atlantic supported a second phase of funding (of £1,100,000) for the ongoing local peace process in Suffolk and Lenadoon. This funding aimed to support peacebuilding between the Suffolk and Lenadoon communities by supporting advocacy efforts to improve public service provision and increase participation of local people in achieving social change and reconciliation.

The Role of Evaluation, Research and Learning in the Case

From the outset of its relationship with SLIG, The Atlantic Philanthropies used research to assess, against defined criteria, the most suitable site in which to finance interface work. Deloitte Consultants, who had developed a competency in the area of peacebuilding were commissioned to recommend a location for supporting an intervention that would demonstrate how tensions at interface areas could be defused and how a common cause in support of peace could be built across the sectarian divide. In 2005, Deloitte recommended that Atlantic explore the potential for financially supporting interface work in Suffolk and Lenadoon. By this stage, much progress had already been made but there was still a large degree of distrust. Atlantic initially supported the two communities to undertake separate needs assessments. As confidence grew, Atlantic then asked them to develop a joint plan.

Atlantic decided from an early stage of engagement with SLIG that the lessons from the work should be recorded and fed back into the development of the initiative. The way in which the two local communities reached across the divide was exceptional rather than typical and it was, therefore, important to share the example and to demonstrate what was being achieved, how it was being achieved and the context within which the work was taking place. Perhaps as important, there was a need to reflect back to SLIG and to both communities the emerging lessons from the work to help stimulate debate and discussion about what was working and what was not, to share any differing perceptions and to improve the implementation. This developmental approach was reflected in a series of case-studies which were commissioned by Atlantic, referred to as 'Capture the Learning' cases. The name reflects the fact that this learning was more emergent and focused on how the initiative unfolded and fitted into an ongoing, strategic learning approach (Mintzberg et al., 1998) rather than a more linear, traditional impact evaluation approach. Dr Colin Knox, a professor of public policy at the University of Ulster, was commissioned to write the case studies.

The first Capture the Learning case study focused on the development of the initiative and on how the two communities came together to develop a shared plan, how they established trust and how they dealt with the initial challenges and tensions of the funded work. This case helped each side understand the constraints that the other was working within, as various paramilitary groups were still influential in both communities, and there was a need for progress to be calibrated against what was possible in terms of what each community was willing to accept. In the early stages, there was a pervading sense of mistrust. One of the biggest contextual factors was that Lenadoon is an expanding nationalist community with an increasing need for social housing, whilst Suffolk's population is decreasing but with a strong desire not to have its physical territory encroached upon by their nationalist neighbours. The first 'Capturing the Learning' process was essentially concerned with reflecting how the initiative was constructed amid very differing interpretations of reality. It also recorded how leaders within the two communities constructed a way to recognise but *park* their political differences and not get bogged down in old arguments, and to focus on those priorities which were of immediate concern to both areas and to return to the most challenging issues as trust was established. The evaluation process involved both capturing the differing perceptions of reality and encouraging both communities to reflect on this. Also from Atlantic's perspective, recording how the communities had gone about this peacebuilding planning and the context within which it took place served as an important record that could be disseminated to other possible locations within Northern Ireland, as there might be some transportable lessons.

Whereas the first report was retrospective, the subsequent 'Capture the Learning' reports then focused on evaluating the roll-out of the initiative. These reports were used to stimulate debate and discussion about the reasons for progress or the challenges encountered, and to help each side see the constraints that the other was working within. Whilst some findings provoked disagreement, they did help surface issues in a constructive way. That said, many of the debates were heated and reflected the controversial nature of the evaluation work and the highly contested environment in which the community activists were working. The evaluator received strong challenges from one community in the face of their observations about the pace at which the community was rolling out the work. It subsequently emerged that there were strong concerns within the paramilitary groups within that community about the pace of the work. The community activists had to be careful not to move ahead of the different interest groups within their own communities. Feedback reports helped to stimulate discussion between the two communities and helped bring issues to the surface which, if left unaddressed, would have festered. This particular reality meant that the credibility and integrity of the evaluator was consistently put to the test; their legitimacy was dependent on their acceptance as being impartial.

The case study reports also helped to focus on the governance challenges and some of the operational issues encountered by SLIG. One of the challenges for the group was the management of an initiative of this scale. The strategic preparation and dissemination of reports allowed difficulties and competing perceptions to be aired, as a precursor to the holding of discussions to address them.

In terms of assessing the impact of SLIG, more positivist-type evaluation instruments were also used by the communities. They had realised the power of credible, quantitative and systematised data for advancing their interests. SLIG recognised the need to gather more evidence on the reach and breadth of the work on community attitudes, and to measure the prevalence of this impact across both communities. It, therefore, commissioned Millward Brown, a well-regarded market research firm, to survey community attitudes in Suffolk and Lenadoon. A random location sampling technique was employed to ensure that people on each street close to the interface had an equal chance of being surveyed. Four hundred questionnaires were completed. Knox (2010, p. 21) outlines that:

> [The survey found] the overwhelming support in both communities for peace building at 95.2 per cent and 82.6 per cent in Lenadoon and Suffolk, respectively. This clearly demonstrates the appetite for cross-community work in an area previously synonymous with violent conflict.

The survey was also instructive in highlighting the demographic profile of those who become engaged in peacebuilding work. In addition, an external evaluator was commissioned to assess progress towards the objectives set, to account for funds spent and to assess the quality and level of the outputs and outcomes achieved.

This diversified approach (research cases studies, randomised survey and external evaluation) yielded insights about the impact of the project and its roll out, which helped Atlantic and SLIG to interpret these findings in the light of the specific context within which the work took place. This pragmatic approach to evaluation combined rigorous assessment of impacts and rich cases studies to inform strategy. Because Atlantic was a funder, it was able to instigate certain approaches to evaluation. But, this was possible only because its partners were willing. And, it was a process that had to be nurtured and built carefully.

In the case of SLIG, the organisation discussed how research and data could strengthen their own activist and peacebuilding work as well as provide the funder with the accountability it needed. SLIG used this evidence and combined it with an adept understanding of the power of symbolism to influence policy beyond their own interface area. They approached the Parades Commission[13] and gave the first joint, cross-community submission which highlighted how they had handled the issue of parades, and outlined how they had developed a solution and had provided marshals to minimise the likelihood of trouble. The later 'Capture the Learning' reports focused on what became a concerted advocacy campaign in which SLIG drew on its strong evidence base to construct and convey compelling impact stories at times when the communities were seeking to access substantial regeneration funding, and when they were attempting to influence government policy and funding in relation to *shared facilities*. SLIG also became very adept at using symbolism to *make sense* (Weick, 2001) of the evidence contained within the reports. For example, at the launch of one report both a loyalist marching band and Irish traditional musicians performed to highlight the importance of understanding the cultural context of each community and to highlight the progress made to the guests present.

Overall, evaluation and strategic learning was used by SLIG and Atlantic to advance efforts to effect social change through the work taking place across the two communities, and to influence a wider audience. The very practical use of the case study approach was critical at certain junctures to help activists understand how others were interpreting progress and/or challenges and for each side to understand the reality of the constraints within which each community was operating. More impact-focused quantitative evaluation methods were also used to demonstrate to external audiences the impact on the communities—especially the Northern Ireland government and the European Union which in 2010 agreed to commit £4.5 million for a shared facility for the two communities, and an additional £500,000 for running costs. The 'Capturing the Learning' reports became part of the trust building process within and between the two communities, in addition to informing strategic learning about advocacy.

Conclusions

As outlined at the beginning of this chapter, funders have a significant role in encouraging helpful evaluation and learning processes in non-profit organisations. Private funders, in particular, have the flexibility to focus some of the resources they provide on organisational learning and on assessing impact to further the social causes they promote. There are many roads that a private funder can take. These are determined by paradigmatic and methodological choice. Approaches can vary from helping an organisation understand better the context and progress of its work to driving grantees to distraction by requesting formulaic, standardised reports, or by imposing unsuitable, funder-mandated, evaluation methods. As we have outlined, a foundation's world view may strongly influence its approach to evaluation. However, as our case study demonstrates, there are good reasons why the grantee organisation should play a key role in deciding the evaluation approach.

If a foundation seeks to foster understanding and to inform and influence behaviours and norms, then social constructionist approaches to research and evaluation might be better suited to informing both the work of grantees and the strategy of the foundation. This does not mean that assessments are merely subjective opinions of a single person; rather, they are efforts to understand and interpret different constructions of social reality. This may become clearer to the user of the evaluation, to the extent that there is transparency of method, which demonstrates how an evaluator (and others) understood, and interpreted differing constructions of social reality. In such cases, evaluations can spark discussion and debate in a process which is more akin to action research. In a conflict setting, where reality is so contested, the research and evaluation components of the case of SLIG highlight how the cycle of observation, feedback, reflection and deliberation can be helpful, and become part of building trust whilst at the same time constructively informing and challenging evaluation stakeholders.

Assessments should also be made of the impact of the work of the organisations. Whilst these evaluations do not provide absolute proof or truth about progress, attempts to assess rigorously and to interpret the difference an organisation has made are particularly useful for convincing sceptical audiences and other funders to support the work of that organisation. The fact that many funding agencies internationally are seeking increasing levels of evidence of impact is itself a socially constructed reality of which NPOs need to be mindful. Funders can help organisations to garner both formative evidence to influence and shape a programme, as well as credible evidence of effects and influence that can be collected in ways which contribute to community empowerment. The case of SLIG highlights that the use of evaluation to build understanding and trust is particularly important in a conflict setting. That said, using evaluation as an on-going learning process has much wider application across a range of complex, social change efforts.

In terms of the funding of evaluations by foundations, there is a need to think carefully through the costs and benefits of the evaluation itself. The authors believe that foundations should take a pragmatic approach to evaluation and avoid doctrinaire statements about the types of evaluations they fund. Foundations should consider evaluation in terms of whether it can advance their social change mission and the work of their grantees. On this basis, a choice may then be made regarding the selection of the best methods to help them advance these goals—rather than adopting an a priori position on whether or not they should fund evaluations—or the types of methods they use. The best funding strategies are those that combine concepts of effectiveness with attempts to tap into values-driven social change. This is particularly true in conflict situations where evaluation can play a key role in keeping parties to the conflict informed and in helping them to reflect on their own interpretation of the actions of others, stimulate constructive debates and provide credible evidence of progress made.

Notes

1. Developmental evaluation (DE) is emerging as an alternative to traditional model testing evaluation. DE positions the evaluator as a part of a programme's design and development process. The evaluator collects information and provides feedback to continually improve the programme. DE can be understood as *embedded evaluation* that is done in real time, has a series of short, rapid feedback loops and allows the organisation to quickly adapt its strategies and activities. See, generally, Patton (2010).
2. The views expressed in this chapter are based on the experience of the authors as senior managers in a private grant-making foundation, The Atlantic Philanthropies. They are the personal views of the authors and should not be taken to represent the views of The Atlantic Philanthropies.
3. Further information on The Atlantic Philanthropies can be found at www.atlantic philanthropies.org
4. Over time, the foundation broadened its approach with a commitment to greater methodological diversity.
5. By *traditional impact evaluation* we mean evaluation that is based on experimental or quasi-experimental design that places primary importance on the presence of a treatment group and non-treatment group (counterfactual) in order to prove or disprove the effectiveness of an intervention.
6. This summary of the historical antecedents of the modern conflict in Northern Ireland draws on John Darby's 'Conflict in Northern Ireland: A Background Essay' (Darby, 1995).

7. Colin Knox, in Chapter 5, uses a case study of integrated education in Northern Ireland to discuss the challenges and tensions surrounding the roles and responsibilities of the evaluator in a VDS.

8. One of the fundamental political divides in Northern Ireland is between Loyalist and Republicans. The former is associated with the use of violence in support of continued union with Britain, while the latter associated with the use of armed violence in favour of 'de-partitioning' or re-uniting Northern Ireland into the country of Ireland in the south of the island.

9. This recognition came from an understanding that the criminal justice system did not have the capacity, will or credibility in the eyes of the local population to deal with violence in some communities.

10. Strategic learning is the use of data and insights from a variety of information gathering approaches including evaluation to inform decision-making about strategy (Coffman and Beer, 2011, p. 1).

11. The term 'nationalist' refers to those (largely Catholic) populations in Northern Ireland who support re-unification with Ireland through political and non-violent means. In contrast, the term 'unionist' refers to those (largely Protestant) populations who support continued union with Britain through political and non-violent means. Interface area is the name given to areas where segregated nationalist and unionist residential areas meet in Northern Ireland. They have been defined as 'the intersection of segregated and polarised working class, residential zones, in areas with a strong link between territory and ethno-political identity' (Jarman, 2005, p. 9).

12. The Drumcree stand-off was a dispute about an annual parade in the town of Portadown between the Orange Order (a protestant association with close links to unionism) and nationalist residents. The Orangemen claimed the right to march on their traditional route most of which had become nationalist area. The nationalists regarded the parade as offensive and triumphalist and eventually succeeded in having it re-routed. This local conflict convulsed Northern Ireland in the late 1990s. A decade later violent confrontations have ceased but the Orange Order and the nationalist residents have not been able to agree on the route of the parade.

13. As has been seen, parades are an important and controversial part of Northern Ireland culture. One community will often interpret a parade as an assertion of control by the other community over a particular area. As a result, some parades have been highly contentious. The Parades Commission is a public body which exists to settle disputes about parades.

References

Belfast Interface Project. (1999). Inner East/outer West: addressing conflict in two interface areas. Retrieved from http://www.belfastinterfaceproject.org/sites/default/files/publications/Inner%20East%20-%20Outer%20West.pdf (accessed on 27 April 2015).

Ben-Ner, A. (2003). The theory of non-profit organisation revisited. In H. K. Anheiner and A. Ben-Ner (Eds). *The study of non-profit enterprise. Theories and approaches.* New York: Kluwer.

Brim, O. G. (1973). Do we know what we are doing? In F. F. Heinman (Ed.), *The future of foundations.* Englewood Cliffs, NJ: Prentice Hall.

Burrell, G. and Morgan, G. (1979). *Sociological paradigms and organisational analysis: Elements of the sociology of corporate life.* New Hampshire: Heinmann Educational Books.

Coffman, J. and Beer, T. (2011). *Evaluation to support strategic learning: Principles and practices.* Washington, DC: Center for Evaluation Innovation.

Crotty, M. (1998). *The foundations of social research: Meaning and perspective in the research process.* London: SAGE Publications.

Darby, J. (1995). Conflict in Northern Ireland: A background essay. In S. Dunn (Ed.), *Facets of the conflict in Northern Ireland* (pp. 15–23). Basingstoke: Macmillan Press Ltd.

Frumkin, P. (2002). *On being nonprofit: A conceptual and policy primer.* Cambridge, MA: Harvard University Press.

Geertz, C. (1973). *The interpretation of cultures: Selected essays.* New York, NY: Basic Books Inc.

Hall, P. D. (2004). A historical perspective on evaluation in foundations. In M. T. Braverman, N. A. Constantine and J. K. Slater (Eds), *Foundations and evaluation: Contexts and practices for effective philanthropy* (pp. 27–50). San Francisco: Jossey-Bass.

Hillyard, P., Rolston, P. and Tomlinson, M. (2005). *Poverty and conflict in Ireland: An international perspective.* Dublin: Institute of Public Administration/Combat Poverty Agency.

Jarman, N. (2005). Changing places, moving boundaries: The development of new interface areas. *Shared Space, 1,* 9–19.

Knox, C. (2009). Suffolk and Lenadoon peace-building plan: Capture the learning III. Jordanstown: University of Ulster.

———. (2010). Peace building in Northern Ireland: A role for civil society. *Social Policy and Society, 10*(1), 13–28.

Lawson, T. (1997). *Economics and reality.* London and New York, NY: Routledge.

Mintzberg, H., Lampel, J. and Ahlstrand, B. (1998). *Strategy safari: The complete guide through the wilds of strategic management.* London: Prentice Hall.

Patton, M. Q. (2008). *Utilization focused evaluation* (4th ed.). Thousand Oaks, CA: SAGE Publications.

———. (2010). *Developmental evaluation: Applying complexity concepts to enhance innovation and use.* NY: New York: Guildford Press.

Weick, K. (2001). *Making sense of the organisation.* Oxford: Blackwell Publishing Ltd.

PART V

Concluding Thoughts

Introduction to Part V

The final part of this book rescales its level of analysis from case-driven analyses to that of the field of evaluation writ large. Building from previous chapters, but maintaining a geographic focus on South Asia, Hay turns her attention to the question: How should we build a sub-field of the evaluation of research in VDS. On one level, the components of this process are the same as those that might be applied to strengthening the field of evaluation in non-violent settings, namely: competent and skilled evaluators and evaluation leaders; spaces and forums for sharing ideas and improving practice; a high quality knowledge base; norms, guidelines and standards; and institutional support from an engaged and open policy community. However, the VDS context is the game changer that forces us to ask how conflict context—volatility, uncertainty, high stake-high risk and so on—affects both our ability to conduct evaluations and our ability to build this particular sub-field.

Bush and Duggan similarly shift the scale of analysis in their discussion of the lessons that might be drawn from the chapters that constitute this book. Their chapter elaborates on some of the themes that have woven their way through the project, and have been explored in different ways using multiple cases.

9

Building the Field of Evaluation in Violently Divided Societies

Katherine Hay*

Introduction

This chapter examines the idea of field building in evaluation, and particularly building the sub-field of the evaluation of research in violently divided societies (VDS). The chapter identifies five elements required for a robust field of evaluation: competent and skilled evaluators and evaluation leaders; spaces and forums for sharing ideas and improving practice; a high-quality knowledge base; norms, guidelines and standards; and institutional support from an engaged and open policy community. In VDS, however, each of these elements tends to be undermined or compromised, thereby inhibiting the development of the field. Drawing from cases in South Asia, the chapter explores and maps both the challenges to, and progress towards, a vigorous sub-field of the evaluation of research in VDS.

---

* This chapter builds on a Forum on Evaluation Field Building, in the *American Journal of Evaluation*, June 2010. The views expressed are those of the author. Background research provided by Ethel Mendez is noted with thanks. Written reflections from Asela Kalugampitiya on an earlier version of the chapter have been integrated and cited within the chapter.

Governments and other development actors are constantly making decisions on policies, programmes and projects. They weigh the costs and opportunities of starting or stopping, continuing or modifying particular initiatives. Some of this decision-making is based on sound evidence or research, some on weak or faulty evidence, some on opinion, and much on a range of factors unrelated to evidence at all.

Given the focus of this book, the question is: To what extent does the context of VDS affect the evidence base of decisions? To what extent is evidence gathering or research even possible? And if so, how is that research assessed and evaluated? Do the skills needed to effectively evaluate research (a sub-field recognised as nascent and deeply specialised) exist in VDS?

While other chapters in this book explore how to evaluate research on and in VDS, this chapter starts further upstream and asks: 'What kinds of skills, capacities and systems are needed in VDS to be able to evaluate research or interventions?' and 'How does one begin to strengthen skills, capacities and systems in such contexts?' Taking the case of South Asia, this chapter attempts to describe the current state of these skills, capacities and systems; to explore how we could move forward from where we are now; and to contemplate where we might like to be in this process.

The chapter is structured as follows. First, it explores and develops a framework for evaluation field building. Next, the chapter examines the sub-field of evaluation of research and maps this against the context of VDS in South Asia. And, finally it proposes strategies for field building to support and strengthen research evaluation practice and use.

The idea of evaluation field building encompasses both the need for strengthening evaluation quality and practice and strengthening the use of research and evaluation knowledge in decision-making. It recognises that strengthening the supply of research and improving the evaluation of that research will not make decision-making transparent, technocratic, rational and linear in any context—let alone within contexts characterised by conflict. Evaluation is not value free. At the core of evaluation is the identification of relevant values or standards and their application to what is being evaluated (Scriven, 1991). Further, as Boyle et al. (1999, p. 5) note, evaluation findings may be *drowned out* by other aspects in the political context, and *often for good reason*. This chapter, thus, attempts to grapple with the complexity of both the decision-making environment and implementation systems.

The chapter suggests that there is promising work happening in evaluation field building, but that a specific focus on the building capacity to evaluate research is limited. This is even more so in VDS. In line with other authors in this book, the chapter also suggests that many of the problems of evaluation of research in VDS are similar to those in non-VDS in the same regions *but more extreme*. Consequently, it suggests that strategies for field building in VDS are likely similar to broader evaluation field building but will require more sustained effort over longer periods to bear fruit. However, the chapter also recognises that evaluation field building in VDS may require quite different approaches, and concludes with the need to evaluate and learn from efforts.

Contextual Background

In South Asia, the nature of violence is deeply contextual, historical and contentious. The section below is intended to provide the reader with a base knowledge of the South Asian conflicts which constitute the empirical foundation of the current chapter.

Afghanistan

Amalendu Misra describes the conflict in Afghanistan as one that 'has moved through several phases and might now be characterised as part regional proxy war and part civil war' (Misra, 2004). Rivalry among ethnic tribes has been common in Afghanistan and serves as backdrop to the Mujahideen and Soviet conflict of 1978–1979 and to the more recent violence involving the Taliban and US-led forces that invaded the country after the 9/11 attacks. Anti-western sentiment among extremist Islamic groups associated with the Taliban is at the heart of most of the current violence. Assassinations, ambushes and bombings, often in public areas, by Taliban insurgency have become common since 2001. The World Bank estimates that there have been over one million casualties and that approximately six million people have been displaced due to the conflict (World Bank, 2009b).

Bangladesh

The origins of conflict in Bangladesh date to the Liberation War of 1971 when Bangladesh (formerly East Pakistan) fought the Pakistani Army for independence. Casualty estimates vary from 26,000 to 3,000,000 and about 8 to 10 million people were allegedly displaced. Rape, torture and sectarian violence were widespread. The chapter includes examples of historical research, including research on events that occurred during the Liberation War.

During that period, the Pakistani army targeted Bangladeshi intellectuals, students and academics for they were the lead thinkers and promoters of ideas about independence. There are accounts of mass murders at Dhaka University residences and of researchers fleeing the country or taking refuge in other areas of the country. While the worst of the violence occurred during the months of the Liberation War (March to December 1971), political and sectarian conflict followed after independence. Disagreements among political parties on the role of Islam in the state, political and economic ideology and the state's structure led to a period of political violence characterised by assassination, violent protests, strikes and bombings. Certain areas of the country, like the Chittagong Hill Tracks in the south east and parts of the border with India and Myanmar, have also been areas of dispute and confrontation. While the situation in Bangladesh has been relatively stable since 2009, the media continues to warn about political instability (*Daily Star*, 2011).

Nepal

Nepal went through a civil war between 1996 and 2006. At the heart of the conflict was the demand from the Communist Party of Nepal (Maoist) to abolish the monarchy and convene a constituent assembly to draft a new constitution. Targeted attacks and violent clashes between the Maoist insurgents and government forces claimed over 15,000 lives, the majority of which have been blamed on the government.

A peace agreement was signed in 2006 between the Government of Nepal and the Communist Party of Nepal (Maoist) but efforts to demobilise and reintegrate Maoist insurgents have been unsuccessful and pockets of violence persist. The political climate in Nepal has remained unstable since the peace agreement.

Kashmir

Kashmir has been an area of dispute between India and Pakistan since partition in 1947. Since then, India and Pakistan have fought three wars (1947–1948, 1965 and 1971) over Kashmir. The conflict took on a different dimension in the 1990s when extremist Islamic insurgent groups infiltrated and began operating among separatist groups in the Indian-controlled Kashmir. Support from the Pakistani government to the insurgent groups heightened tensions between the two countries. Clashes between the Indian forces and the insurgent groups, targeted attacks, bombings and other acts of violence claimed between 40,000 and 80,000 lives between 1989 and 2002.

Pakistan and India signed a cease fire agreement in 2003 but there have been violent outbreaks since then between the two countries, and within Kashmir there have been ongoing protests by civil society against the sweeping powers of the Indian forces. In August 2011, mass graves were reported which many analysts argue include civilians killed by the army.

Sri Lanka

Sri Lanka experienced a 25-year civil war that ended officially in 2009 upon the government's military defeat of the militant Liberation Tigers of Tamil Eelam, better known as the Tamil Tigers. The roots of the conflict date to post-independence period when ethnic identities were mobilised by political parties in a contest for control of the government. As ethnicity was politicised, conflict escalated and became more violent leading to a heavily militarised separatist campaign seeking an independent Tamil Eelam state in the north and east of the island. The conflict was characterised by *dirty war* (human rights abuse, ethnic cleansing, disappearances, the targeting of civilians and politicians, and so on). The Tamil Tigers were labelled a terrorist organisation and became known worldwide for their suicides attacks, targeted assassinations, child soldiers and ruthless military effectiveness. Conservative estimates place the death toll at between 80,000 and 100,000; over the course of the conflict hundreds of thousands of people were forced to flee violence or become internally displaced persons and/or refugees.

Understanding and Situating Evaluation Field Building

What do we mean by 'evaluation field building'? Before attempting to answer that question, some basic definitions are required. *Evaluation practice* is the *doing* of evaluation. *Evaluation capacity* is the ability to do evaluation, and *evaluation use* is the application of evaluation to some change process. *Evaluation field building* refers to the range and diversity of efforts to strengthen practice, capacity and use (Hay, 2010). Field building includes, but is distinct from, evaluation capacity building or professionalisation. Field building encompasses an understanding that these dimensions exist in a broader context that can support or weaken efforts to strengthen practice, capacity or use. A field building view brings focus and attention on ways to shift the system of elements (whether through work on various elements or a set of interconnected elements).

The idea of field building emerged from literatures of sociology of knowledge, sociology of professions and organisational development (see for example, Bourdieu and Wacquant, 1992; Fligstein, 2001; Giddens, 1984; Sewell, 1992). Much of that work relates to building professional or organisational fields (see, e.g., Berry and Parasuraman, 1993). The idea of field building in evaluation developed in the current chapter and elsewhere (Hay, 2010) draws on that work, and also integrates ideas from research on building *fields of action* (Burns, 2007; Chambers, 2008; Ottoson et al., 1993). Groups may work to strengthen the capacity of individuals to do good evaluation, but without reshaping the larger system that surrounds evaluation, the influence of such efforts may be limited or unsustainable.

Writing about *philanthropic field building*, Hirschhorn and Gilmore note that, 'institutions surrounding the focal practice ... strengthen the practice if their goals reinforce one another' (2004, p. 32). Figure 9.1 illustrates this point drawing on a set of examples from the field of evaluation.

The example illustrates that each part of the system influences other parts of the system. While the example highlights an overly simplistic scenario of positive pull factors for the purpose of illustration, elements of the system also create drag or weaken other elements. The key point is that parts of the system co-evolve within broader contexts that are also co-evolving. Building the field of evaluation entails understanding the connections between key elements that are themselves constantly evolving. When strengthening efforts encompass the institutions and settings that surround and reinforce evaluation practice, it has shifted from evaluation capacity building to the deeper and broader effort of evaluation field building.

Building the sub-field of the evaluation of research (both within and outside VDS) is a distinct part of the broader evaluation field building. The sub-field of the evaluation of research in VDS is both positively and

Figure 9.1
Visualising Elements of the Field

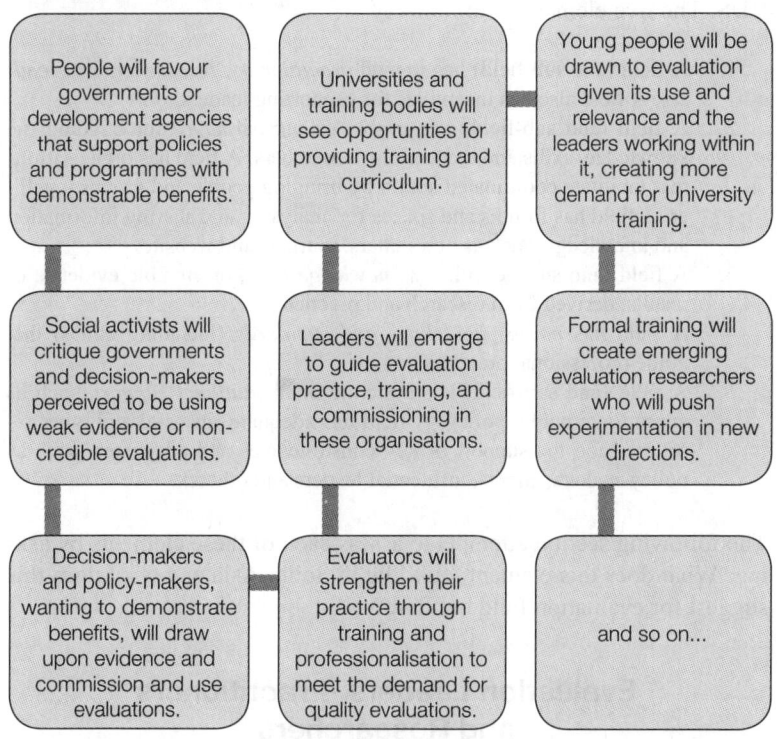

Source: Author.

negatively influenced by: the broader fields of evaluation; social science research capacities and systems; and the nature and context of policy-making. In VDS specifically, elements of the broader evaluation system may be eroded, absent or *captured* by the interests or actions of different, competing, factions. For the sub-field of evaluation of research, the additional levels of specialisation or expertise required and the systems underpinning such evaluation[1] are often weak or limited in developing countries in general, and in VDS in particular. These realities must be the foundation of any thought about field building in such sub-fields of evaluation.

The following section describes five elements of the evaluation field: people, knowledge, spaces, standards and institutions. It starts by examining each element from a broader lens of evaluation field building, and then adds the additional lens of the evaluation of research within VDS. The five elements are:

1. A field (and sub-field) has trained *practitioners, researchers and leaders*. A field also has incentives for supporting leaders.
2. A field (and sub-field) has *spaces or infrastructure* for building the knowledge, skills and credentials of members. A field has organisations that facilitate coordinated action by bringing people and groups together. A field has forums and spaces for analysing and sharing information and knowledge, such as newsletters, journals and websites.
3. A field (and sub-field) has a *knowledge base*, or credible evidence of results, derived from research and practice.
4. A field has *norms, guidelines and standards* (including ethics) that guide professional practices.
5. A field (and sub-field) has systemic or *institutional support*, such as appropriate public policy. A field has adequate financial and other resources and the support of key constituencies and advocates (such as policy-makers, clients, influential leaders and others).

The following section attempts to assess each of these elements by asking: What does this element look like in South Asia and what does this suggest for evaluation field building?

Evaluation Leaders, Practitioners and Researchers

A field has trained practitioners, researchers, and leaders. A field also has incentives for supporting leaders.

The competencies needed to be an evaluator, while connected to the competencies required for social science research, are also different and specialised. Toulemonde (1995) proposed that evaluation professionals: have mastered the range of techniques and can combine them; are specially trained in evaluation; know various conceptual frameworks underpinning evaluation; and devote the majority of their time to evaluation. Distinct from professionals, he suggested that, *craftsmen* master a range of evaluation techniques but tend to learn evaluation on the job, while *amateurs* have only a partial knowledge of evaluation theories and techniques and have the tendency to use their favourite approach (pp. 46–47).

These are useful distinctions to consider in the context of evaluation of research. Much evaluation is led by researchers who do not identify as evaluators. Because of their diverse disciplinary backgrounds, they may not be aware of, or draw from, evaluation theories and techniques, especially those from the sub-fields of evaluation of research or evaluation of research in VDS. Shiva Kumar notes, 'Professionals carrying out evaluations in South Asia...tend to be good social science researchers, not trained evaluators' (2010).

The Canadian Evaluation Society (CES) has a detailed set of competencies developed through research and consultations in 2008 and 2009. Competencies are defined as 'the background, knowledge, skills, and dispositions programme evaluators need to achieve standards that constitute sound evaluations.'[2] The domains of the CES competencies, described in detail in their report are:

1. Reflective Practice competencies focus on the fundamental norms and values underlying evaluation practice.
2. Technical Practice competencies focus on the specialised aspects of evaluation.
3. Situational Practice competencies focus on the application of evaluative thinking.
4. Management Practice competencies focus on the process of managing a project/evaluation.
5. Interpersonal Practice competencies focus on people skills.

Evaluation requires drawing concepts and approaches from multiple fields. This requires highly competent social scientists. Evaluation of research requires additional expertise, including methods for assessing the quality of research and domain expertise of the area of research. Evaluation of research in VDS also requires particularly deep competencies in several domains, including, but not limited to, conflict resolution, high sensitivity to ethical concerns, managing under particularly difficult operational conditions, diplomacy and high levels of contextual and cultural competence.

These requirements present a Catch-22. In VDS, even the presence of *good social science researchers* may be severely limited. Take Afghanistan for example, where there is limited social science research and evaluation capacity generally, and across generations, regions and sectors specifically. The total budget for the 22 universities in the country in 2009 was $35 million, a negligible $1.5 million per institution (World Bank, 2009b). According to 2008 data from the World Bank, the total number of faculty in the country with PhDs was 140, of which only four were women (World Bank, 2009b). Where are highly skilled evaluators going to come from?

Taking another example, Sri Lanka has a fairly well-established government M&E system and a solid, if small, pool of social science research capacity. But evaluation capacity and systems in the war-affected areas of the north and east and other areas of the country are completely different. According to Asela Kalugampitiya, there were no skilled national evaluators in conflict-affected areas as a result of the brain drain of qualified people fleeing the conflict.[3]

A skills audit would likely reveal that the majority of practicing evaluators in VDS lack key skills and expertise. In practice, people are often employed to count things. This devalues the field of evaluation and severely curtails the contributions that evaluation could be making in these contexts. Putting people in evaluation roles they are not equipped to do is counter-productive. It not only leads to lower quality evaluation, it also reduces the real and perceived value of evaluation to international development, reducing interest in using evaluation findings, in exploring evaluation as a career path and in investing to strengthen the system and practice of evaluation.

Taking one example, the combination of a capacity gap and the massive influx of money in the development (and to a lesser extent research) industry in Afghanistan has created a rapid movement across jobs with direct implications on evaluation field building. Depth of expertise is lacking in most areas of development programming in Afghanistan. There is a misfit between the demand and supply of skilled professionals with the necessary evaluation and sectoral skill set, the result of which, for example, leads to a person working as a *gender expert* for a year, then working in monitoring, and then working in agriculture. The culture of building and deepening skills and experience in a particular domain is generally absent. Mohammad Fahim Mehry, the Provincial Monitoring and Evaluation Officer, General Directorate of Policy, Monitoring and Evaluation in Afghanistan, has said that as soon as individuals receive some training (English language, computer skills, etc.), they move from the lowest paying jobs in the development sector (Government, local NGO) to the highest paying (INGO, Bilaterals, UN) (Hay, 2010).

This connects to the challenge of building the field of evaluation of research in VDS, namely: the reliance on foreign experts and the continuous circulation of these experts in and out of evaluations in different countries, different organisations and different sectors. Evaluation practice in VDS is often dominated by foreign experts who are parachuted in, are paid fees in recognition of the dangers they are facing and do not stay long.

As with everything in the aid industry, there are power differentials. Evaluation, as part of the aid apparatus, is not exempt. Mohammad Shah Babai, a Deputy Programme Manager at the ZOA Refugee Care Northern Program, Afghanistan, has noted that foreign experts come and design tools and processes but they move on quickly, which creates challenges such as meeting training needs, maintaining continuity and sustaining a definable field of expertise. As a consequence, an emerging set of young Afghanistan managers are struggling to replace old Russian era systems with new ideas. While their energy and youth is positive, it also carries the inherent challenge of inexperience (Hay, 2009).

One of the core elements of conventional research evaluation is peer-review processes. When strong social science researchers in various domains are already in limited supply, who is left to engage in peer review? If one focuses on evaluators from within VDS contexts, quality peer review may not be possible or at least very difficult. However, going outside of the context to review, arguably, privileges external priorities over the insights of evaluators and researchers from within VDS and may lead to gaps in the contextual understanding of the research and research use contexts.

Having said skilled evaluation *practitioners* are often absent or are in short supply, a further call for evaluation *researchers* may read as rather optimistic. It is. But a strong field of evaluation requires not only skilled evaluators, it also needs evaluation researchers. That is, it requires both (a) a pool of expertise for conducting evaluations; and (b) a pool of expertise for applied research on what works and doesn't work in evaluation, and, more importantly, on the development of new, appropriate and effective approaches to evaluation suited to the circumstances.

South Asia is an increasingly important testing ground for some types of evaluation research, particularly perhaps methodological research. For example, MIT's J-PAL Poverty Action Lab and the International Initiative on Impact Evaluation (3IE) both have offices in India and are promoting impact evaluation in different ways. Similarly, many other methodologies were tested in, and are now commonly used in, international development evaluation in South Asia (Ashford and Patkar, 2001; Chambers, 1994; Dart and Davies, 2003; Earl et al., 2001). However, most of these methodologies emerged from Northern roots, including American or British universities. Inevitably, this provokes questions. Where are the leading ideas and methodological research in evaluation in VDS? Are Southern evaluators subordinate *local members* of Northern-led evaluation teams, or are they also engaging in evaluation research and theory? While the connection between theory and practice leads to innovation in both, a lack of conceptual work on evaluation of research and evaluation of research in VDS limits the advancement of the evaluation field overall.

In addition to evaluators and evaluation researchers, a strong evaluation field needs leaders who shape evaluation research in the region through their research, publications and activities. However, in South Asia, organisations with a mandate of, and expertise in, rigorous multi-method evaluation are few or non-existent in some countries. Additionally, the published work of South Asian thought leaders is largely invisible in existing evaluation forums. This is particularly so for those specialising in evaluation in and on VDS.

Even in preparing this book, the editors' effort to find contributors from the Global South though extensive was ultimately more limited than they had hoped. If we cannot identify these individuals, is it because they do not exist or because their leadership is nascent? How can the emerging sub-field of evaluating research in VDS identify and support emerging leaders to take on increasing leadership? It is to these questions that the chapter now turns its attention. The limited leadership in evaluating research in VDS in South Asia also reflects a lack of space to: share expertise, be identified as a leader, guide others, and support and inform such evaluation. Being a leader, by definition, entails being recognised as such by others. That generally requires spaces where leadership can emerge and be exercised. Such spaces and structures are explored in the next section.

Spaces and Forums for Collaboration, Learning, Exchange and Norm-setting

A field has spaces or infrastructure for building the knowledge, skills and credentials of members. A field has organisations that facilitate coordinated action by bringing people and groups together. A field has forums and spaces for analysing and sharing information and knowledge, such as newsletters, journals and websites.

Despite variation in different countries, spaces where evaluation leadership, scholarship and practice are being strengthened globally include: universities (a site for both evaluation research and training), evaluation associations, evaluation conferences and journals. These are spaces for mentoring, sharing ideas, peer review, networking, critique and dissent. While recognising that different models may be appropriate in the evaluation of research on VDS, the next section explores the 'spaces or infrastructure for collaboration and learning' in South Asia.

Universities

There are no graduate programmes in evaluation within South Asia, although there are important developments to be noted. For example, a number of universities in Bangladesh, India and Sri Lanka are in the process of developing a post graduate diploma in evaluation.[4] Within other programmes, such as public health or development, there are also courses available with a strong monitoring and evaluation lens. IBN-Sinha in Afghanistan is building evaluation courses into their Masters in Public Health degree. BRAC University in Bangladesh offers a course on monitoring and evaluation in its Master of Development Studies programme. For many of these initiatives, one of the core challenges is the lack of availability of qualified faculty to teach the courses. For example, in 2011, BRAC noted they would not be offering the monitoring and evaluation course in part because of the absence of qualified faculty. Similar challenges underpin other efforts to offer evaluation courses in universities in the region.

Another challenge to developing strong evaluation curriculum is the absence of research in most South Asian universities. The persistent gap between research and teaching that characterises many universities weakens the quality of teaching as faculty may become disconnected from developments in the field that come, in part, through applying and conducting research. For example, as Mohammad Shah Babai of Afghanistan has noted, 'most of our systems are running with old curriculum and old ideas. There is a big need to update that system' (Hay, 2009). Evaluation teaching needs to be connected to evaluation research and practice to keep curriculum relevant, rigorous, current and grounded in the development context.

Though integrating applied research into universities is essential, it is not unproblematic, particularly in VDS. In the case of evaluation, this would entail engaging in evaluation research or doing evaluation (of policies and programmes) as part of student course work, graduate work and faculty-led research. Some governments in VDS view universities with suspicion, as spaces of dissent, and may exert controls over universities. Deeper engagement in evaluating programmes and policies particularly on and in VDS, or on research in VDS, may expose universities to pressure and scrutiny from governments or factions.

But from another vantage point, universities are looking for marketable courses. This requires that young people see evaluation as an interesting and compelling career choice amidst the other options open to them. An important factor influencing the perceptions of young people towards evaluation as a field of study is the development of a robust, engaging and relevant curriculum.

In Afghanistan in recent years, different groups have been working on curriculum development in a range of sectors, but no equivalent work has been undertaken in public universities in evaluation (Hay, 2009). The role of private sector education providers in such contexts may become more important; certain groups such as IBN-SINHA in Afghanistan are moving into evaluation training and courses in response to the growing need for graduates in these sectors. This, however, raises questions for the sub-field of evaluation of research which connects and draws from traditional social science research systems (including peer review). Many private universities may lack the base upon which new research and approaches to evaluating research quality could be founded. The market-driven focus of private universities may make them more nimble in responding to new markets for evaluation programmes. However, it may also encourage them to focus on the traditional sectors of evaluation—such as evaluating health and education programmes—where there is likely to be larger market demand. Another consideration is the possibility that they may approach evaluation *as a spending review*, following a trajectory similar to the emergence of the evaluation of public programmes in other contexts (see Chapter 2).

Evaluation Organisations

Professional associations in South Asia are starting to appear in the field and some are becoming much more active than in the past. Most, however, have limited membership, reach or influence. The Sri Lankan Evaluation Association (SLEVA) is a notable exception. Though still relatively modest, theirs is the only ongoing evaluation conference in the region and the group itself has been active for over a decade. In Bangladesh and Afghanistan, there are informal evaluation networks forming, but, as of yet, no formal evaluation associations. The Community of Evaluators Nepal has recently formally registered as a national organisation in Nepal but its membership is still small. The Development Evaluation Society of India and the Pakistan Evaluation Network have seemed largely inactive or limited to a few individuals over the past several years, though both may be showing some signs of revival.

However, if one looks at the events and public processes of associations such as SLEVA, they appear either unaware of the issues and dimensions of evaluation in VDS or are purposefully avoiding this potentially politically difficult terrain. SLEVA, for example, has chosen to work with government and has been careful to avoid criticising government policies and programmes. This has at times created tension within the group on whether the appropriate strategy in Sri Lanka is one of open critique or one of supporting change by collaborating with the government. SLEVA has existed since 2001 but at the time of writing, no evaluators from the previously rebel controlled areas of Sri Lanka were part of the association.[5] This may reflect the limited number of evaluators from such areas and/or the association's outreach or capacity to attract evaluators from these areas.

Regionally, IDRC (the organisation for which the author worked) is supporting a community of South Asian evaluators who have made efforts to connect to evaluators from VDS and to highlight issues of evaluation in VDS at their conferences and events.

Conferences and Events

The Community of Evaluators discussed earlier, held successful regional evaluation conferences in New Delhi in October 2010 and in Kathmandu in February 2013, with regional participation. These events were attempts to reach out to, and help consolidate, the community of evaluators in the region, including those working within VDS. They included, for example, presentations on the state of evaluation theory and practice in VDS. Similar events have been convened at other sites—which also may have included a focus on VDS or evaluation research.

However, such events within VDS are rare. Opportunities—indeed, incentives—to share information or collaborate are very low. In Afghanistan, for example, there is no information-sharing or collaboration on evaluations across the non-governmental organisation (NGO) sector, or between NGOs and government. The public has no knowledge that an evaluation is taking place, let alone what the content of the evaluation might be (Hay, 2009). The Afghanistan Research and Evaluation Unit has been flagged as the only NGO actively sharing their evaluations.

Within government, Asadullah Zarmalwal pointed to an informal advisory group of monitoring and evaluation experts who meet to discuss monitoring and evaluation mechanisms, methodologies and capacity (Hay, 2009). Outside of government, there is no space in Afghanistan for evaluators to come together to share experiences. According to some Afghan evaluators, this has contributed to the undermining of a sense of ownership and accountability in the field of evaluation (Hay, 2009). Mohammad Babai Shah noted that there are no donor-funded forums to share experiences across projects funded by different donors. More generally, as Babai Shah observes, the development culture is such that 'evaluation is seen as a contractual obligation—not something to learn from' (Hay, 2009). Nonetheless, there are signs of a desire for change there. Since 2011, evaluators from Afghanistan have convened both physical meetings and an evaluation list-serve.

In general, there is a lack of peer assistance, and few opportunities for on-going training of evaluators to deepen their expertise and contacts in the region. The spaces for them to connect, improve their practice and deepen their skills range from non-existent (in remote or less central locations) to inadequate. Some proponents have attempted to bring evaluators from VDS to forums in non-VDS locations. While such strategies may serve a useful function by providing a neutral, *politically decompressed* space within which evaluators from VDS may interact, it is costly and tends to exclude younger and emerging evaluators. Such approaches also limit engagement with stakeholders and policy-makers that are more likely to occur when they are undertaken within the VDS context. Informal discussions suggest that efforts to use web-based training and seminars have, until recently, had limited uptake in VDS.

Publishing Forums

In addition to having spaces for collaboration and learning, a field is characterised by forums for articulating theory, practice and knowledge. In South Asia, there is currently an absence of such forums for sharing work, publishing in general or publishing in local languages. Combined with the absence of university programmes and curricula, the result is a lack of publication by South Asian experts, based in South Asia, on evaluation research and practice. Consequently, there is a glaring absence of South Asian research in social science journals generally (Arunachalam, 2009), and almost no published research on evaluation work in VDS. The same gap is evident when we broaden our scope to include non-evaluation-specific journals (e.g., journals on development or public policy) where the results or implications of evaluation in VDS might reasonably be expected to find a receptive audience.

This book constitutes one such forum. In beginning to frame the sub-field of evaluation of research in VDS, it creates an outlet and incentives for evaluators in this sub-field to contribute and share their experiences and ideas. As other forums in evaluation begin to emerge,[6] researchers and practitioners should be supported to connect to those forums to share work on the sub-fields of evaluation research and evaluation in VDS.

Why Do Spaces Matter?

A basic criterion proposed by Toulemonde (1995, p. 47) for evaluation professionals is that 'they call their work "evaluation",' noting that 'no professionalisation can appear as long as the function of "evaluation" cannot be identified.' Put another way, people need to self-identify as evaluators for a definable field to be strengthened. Identifying oneself as an evaluator provides a starting point to connect with other evalua-tors and evaluation researchers, which may, in turn, serve to strengthen the quality and practice of evaluation through peer review and critique. Certainly, part of this process must be nested in those spaces, bodies and groupings for self-identification, and peer exchange and learning. But such spaces are also premised upon having something to share. The next section deals with this issue: the state of evaluation knowledge on evaluating research in VDS.

Evaluation as Knowledge

A field has a knowledge base, or credible evidence of results, derived from research and practice.

Is evaluation producing credible evidence and knowledge in VDS, whether through the practice of evaluation and, or, evaluation research? There are two dimensions to this question: the first is the soundness of the knowledge that is being produced; the second is the relevance of that knowledge to development questions and priorities. Rigorous evaluations on questions of little concern, or evaluations of key concerns that are not used, are of little value.

On the dimension of *soundness*, a scan of the literature identified no published research on the quality of evaluation in different countries, domains within countries or of particular commissioners of evaluation in South Asia beyond a limited number of conference power point presentations with interesting views but limited empirical backing. Writing on South Asia, Shiva Kumar (2010, p. 239) notes, 'Evaluations typically get judged as "good" or "bad" on the basis of statistical rigor—not recognising that a sound evaluation is not the same thing as a well-designed survey.' This is particularly important to keep in mind in VDS where statistical rigour may be particularly difficult to achieve given the inherent challenges of working in VDS (safety of surveyors, fear over use of data by respondents, low quality data, etc.).

Another aspect of quality has to do with the availability of data and the quality of data sets in VDS. Box 9.1 provides one such example from Kashmir India. The example illustrates how data related to VDS and conflict can be used and manipulated to suit the competing interests of different factions. While highlighting the challenges of data collection in VDS, it also illustrates how data may contribute to the creation of some common ground (empirically and politically) between competing groups when there is confidence in the quality of data.

In a meeting on the State of Evaluation in Afghanistan (Hay, 2009), several participants flagged the low quality of evaluation in all sectors. The National Risk and Vulnerability Assessment is the only basic nationwide survey in Afghanistan—and the quality of the resulting data is considered weak. Farid Ahmad pointed to the poor quality of government evaluation and reports, and noted that the reduced security within Afghanistan also results in lower quality evaluation. Commenting on his experience in an evaluation (led by an American University), Abdul Ghani noted,

> I was involved in a project in 2005 which was evaluated by a tool called (Balance Scored Card) ... After a year, the health infrastructure in the area improved as Provincial Reconstruction Teams (PRT) built clinics. But the score actually went down. I was there ... I saw so many clinics emerging—but the score went down. Why? They were hiring low capacity surveyors who were not going to the field but were filling in the surveys in the office.[7]

Box 9.1
Evaluation in Data-poor Contexts: The Census in Kashmir

In 2004, census data by religion was released in India by demographer Ashish Bose. Two figures were seized upon by politicians: that Hindus as a proportion of India's population had decreased, while the Muslim population had risen. It was later pointed out that the rates were computed without factoring in Jammu and Kashmir (conflict conditions had prohibited the 1991 census from being undertaken there). Demographically, it was understood that Muslims in Jammu and Kashmir, like all the other communities, were experiencing a declining growth rate. But many ignored this correction. Bose was quoted as saying, 'It is tragic that the census reports will be misused by various political parties when really they are inputs for researchers.' He noted that the fear of Muslim increase is exploited, when, 'The simple fact is that Muslims form a larger proportion of India's poorest states that in these states, even the Hindu growth rate is far higher than that of Hindus elsewhere.'

Separatists in Kashmir have also questioned the accuracy of census results since 1947, arguing that the demography of the predominantly Muslim region could be *misrepresented* by New Delhi to proportionally increase the number of non-Muslims, to make it difficult for the state to secede. Sheikh Showkat Hussain, a law professor at the University of Kashmir studied census trends and asked, 'Is this the real depiction of population ratio or manipulation of figures by the census department of India?' Syed Ali Shah Geelani, a hardline separatist leader, maintained that the *real motive* behind the census was to include non-locals—migrant workers and troop deployments—in the counting process, to reduce the official proportion of Muslims in the state. The controversial 1981 census has even been criticised by pro-India Kashmiri politicians, including the first chief minister, Sheikh Mohammad Abdullah, and his son Farooq (also a former Chief Minister), both of whom maintained that New Delhi was actively attempting to change the perception of the state's demography. Farooq Abdullah went so far as to order a recount of the whole census of Jammu and Kashmir in 1986, but the results were never made public.

In 2001, separatists asked Kashmiris to boycott the census, some issuing threats to census staff to stop the headcount. Enumerators faced numerous hurdles including reluctant Kashmiris who did not want to divulge information. However, in 2011 Kashmiri separatists, for the first time, encouraged locals to participate. One of the separatists advocating participation was Shakeel Bakshi, who argued that people, including those supporting succession, need to actively participate in the census to ensure that political discussions were rooted in accurate data.

Source: Hamid (2011) and Diwanji (2004).

Building on these examples, Asela Kalugampitiya notes that, before May 2009, both local and international evaluators were not willing to undertake evaluations in conflict-affected areas of Sri Lanka and UN staff, and international staff of some INGOs, were not allowed to enter the rebel-controlled areas. He reflected that,

[H]umanitarian organisations had to rely on information and data coming from field staff who were based in rebel controlled areas and were under their influence. On many occasions it was revealed that humanitarian organisations receive false reports or information from the field and development aid is used for other purposes. (Personal correspondence, 2011)

However, one should not assume that the quality of data available in divided societies will always be poor. In 2007, researcher Magnus Hatlebakk from the Chr. Michelsen Institute in Norway looked at the quality of the data collected in the second round of the Nepal Living Standard Survey (NLSS2) in Maoist-controlled areas. Contrary to his expectations, he found that while Maoists had to approve the data collection, and that approval often hinged upon bargaining, they usually allowed it, did not intervene in the interviews or try to manipulate the responses. He also found the quality of the data collected to be similar to those in the areas not under Maoist control.

A tension in VDS is often that local evaluators may be in short supply or inexperienced, while international consultants may be unaffordable for some groups (particularly NGOs) and may have limited understanding of the context. Dad Mohammad Hamdard flagged the challenges of bringing in *high profile* external people, and noted that those experts have limited understanding of the context. He argued that evaluations have been better in quality when they involved local communities in the design and ensured findings are shared in communities (Hay, 2009). Arguably, high-quality evaluation in VDS contexts should include conflict analysis, but capacities to bring in such analysis may be limited in both external and local experts.

On the dimension of *relevance* discussions and anecdotal evidence from several countries in the region suggest that, while there is general agreement on the importance of evaluation, there is also scepticism on the role evaluation is playing, perhaps particularly in VDS. This may be a function of: declining confidence in development evaluation; a growing or continued weakness of public sector evaluation institutions; poor or diminishing quality of evaluations; and limited or politicised use or uptake of evaluation (Basynat, 2009; Goyal, 2009; Khan, 2008; Pal, 2009; Tuduwe and Samranayake, 2008).

While evaluations by national institutions and groups may be struggling or limited, there has been an increase in evaluation research, including some in VDS, led by Northern academics as discussed earlier.

This trend has been driven in part by new developments in econometrics specifically of using randomised trials in development interventions. The incentives for this work include methodological advancement and have been largely driven by external incentive structures (such as publishing in academic journals in the North or external funding competitions). As Bush and Duggan flag in the introductory chapter, the incentives of university-based evaluation continue to drive even evaluation research, but are these the appropriate drivers and measures? While this research may meet standard criteria for *excellence* or *research quality*, is anyone using these findings to shape policies, programmes or change on the ground?

For evaluation to be relevant, an expanded evaluation knowledge base is required to inform which interventions are working, and whether assumptions behind development policies and programmes are valid. This is an urgent priority in VDS contexts in which perception of the nature of the problem can often be driven by the outside (as in the case of Afghanistan) or driven by the group in power of the exclusion of alternative conceptualisations of the problem (as in Sri Lanka). In both cases, applied research is inextricably linked to the conflict analysis and conflict dynamics and, thus, evaluation of who informed the research and whose questions are being addressed would seem essential to evaluating research on and in VDS. In Knox's chapter on integrated education in Northern Ireland, he wrestles with the ethical and political question of whether an evaluator should interrogate the research that underpins programme theory.

Strengthening the knowledge base is dependent, at least in part, on demand and openness from evaluation users. Unless there are incentives for improving the quality of evaluations, it will be exceedingly difficult if not impossible to do so. Key incentives would have to connect to increase the use of higher quality evaluation, itself a function of greater demand for evaluation and improved capacity to recognise and differentiate between low- and high-quality evaluation.

Evaluation Standards and Guidelines

A field has norms, guidelines, and standards (including ethics) that guide professional practices.

Groups such as the UNEG and various evaluation associations have documented guidelines, norms and standards to be followed in conducting evaluations. However, there are either no country-specific or region-specific guidelines or such standards are simply not adhered to (Shiva Kumar, 2010). One of the pressing challenges highlighted in this book is the ethical dimension of evaluation in VDS; issues of objectivity and transparency are 'heightened in the context of a VDS' and therefore require 'reflection on the reciprocal relationship between researcher and the people, and circumstances they are researching in' (see especially Chapters 3, 4 and 6). The generation of such guidelines in research on VDS is limited both by the absence of leaders and the absence of spaces for such norm setting.

Institutional Support

A field has systemic or institutional support, such as appropriate public policy. A field has adequate financial and other resources and the support of key constituencies and advocates (such as policy-makers, clients, influential leaders, and others).

A greater emphasis needs to be placed on understanding institutions or 'rules of the game' that govern evaluation use, and more broadly the use of evidence in VDS. The case of violence against women during the 1971 Liberation War in Bangladesh offers an example of how discourse and ideology underpin the promotion and use, or discredits research and non-use or misuse. In her book *Against Our Will: Men, Women and Rape*, Susan Brownmiller described the rape of hundreds of thousands of Bengali women by the Pakistani army (cited in Pistono, 1998). Her book triggered immediate criticism, most of which 'was reactionary—vitriolic and personally directed at the author' (Murdukhayeva, 2009). A few historians and scholars who did not share Brownmiller's feminist views seemed to overlook the evidence on the rapes and discredited the research on the grounds that it was extremist, a misinterpretation of events, and, in the words of Michael Novak, former US Ambassador to the United Nations Commission on Human Rights, 'a propagandistic attack on heterosexuality and marriage…a celebration of lesbianism and/or masturbation' (cited in Pistono, 1998).

The example highlights how research at the crux of divided societies is used to advance political agendas and how the integrity of the research and interests of the researchers are often questioned. The case is a historical account, but in some ways that simply makes it easier to see how politics and ideology shape discussion on research findings. Research quality does factor into the analysis but it is steeped in positionality and difficult to disentangle from ideological criticisms of the findings.

Moving from this example, what would appropriate and supportive public policy around evaluation of research in VDS look like? A supportive institutional setting would include governments that are open to evidence, particularly critical evidence. Shiva Kumar (2010) writes: 'A tradition of evaluation is yet to permeate the administrative, bureaucratic and political cultures of the South Asian countries.' This is particularly the case in VDS and by extension research on or in VDS where mechanisms both formal and informal are used to limit access, critique and evaluation of situations, processes and interventions.

Of course the particular dimensions of the setting for the evaluation of research vary greatly in South Asia. Research systems and capacities, and the traditional elements of research evaluation such as ethics committees and peer review processes vary across contexts and countries. For example, the research and evaluation landscape in Afghanistan is one of the weakest in the world. The Afghan educational infrastructure was destroyed during the Mujahideen's war against the Russians in 1979. It was never replaced or improved (Ministry of Education, Islamic Republic of Afghanistan, 2008). The establishment of the Taliban regime in 1996 exacerbated education deficiencies and enrolment in tertiary education declined sharply from 24,333 in 1990 to 7,881 by 2001 (World Bank, 2009b). The education and research infrastructure had to be built from scratch after 2001, and in doing so, Saba Gul Khattak (2009, p. 2) notes, 'priorities that promote hard sciences and business and management studies have all but destroyed rigorous social science'. To this date, data authenticity and availability is a problem as there are no national authorities responsible for collecting data and some areas of the country are inaccessible for data collection (Misra, 2004).

Elsewhere on this spectrum, in Bangladesh higher education institutions have grown significantly from having only four universities in 1971 to over 50 private universities and 1,400 colleges in 2007 (World Bank, 2007). Despite the increase in higher education institutions, the degree of academic freedom to question the government or to explore certain aspects of the historic or ongoing conflict is uncertain. Current concerns include the quality of higher education and research and the universities' focus on practical job preparation rather than analytical fields that would allow the construction of a stronger, more vibrant research and evaluation community (World Bank, 2000). Meanwhile, looking at Sri Lanka, the government arguably plans to strengthen its higher education institutions in the northern and eastern provinces that were formerly controlled by the Tamil Tigers (World Bank, 2009a). However, despite the end of the war, the International Crisis Group (ICG) reports that governance in Sri Lanka has deteriorated, and illegal detentions and harassment of academics and researchers continue to be reported. When it comes to research about the war, the ICG describes the government's efforts as 'politically motivated and predictably limited' (International Crisis Group, 2010). This begs the question of whether government efforts to reconcile ethnic differences and invest in higher education will help develop a healthy research and evaluation community if ethnic tension and fears of government repression persist.

So is the space for debate and evidence on evaluation of research in VDS growing or shrinking in South Asia? Weiss' (2009) understanding of policy windows is helpful here. Some windows are closing just as others may be opening. For example, there may be demand from government for particular types of research in VDS to address management questions (for which they may require evaluations of that research), while windows for evaluation of research that open critique of policies and programmes may be closing. Many policy-makers complain about the quality of research but also shield politically important research from the lens of evaluation. Many donors are also complicit in this.

There are visible signs of renewed or emerging emphasis (depending on the VDS) on *doing more* evaluation, though discussion does not appear to translate into system change. There is also deepening discussion on accountability to citizens, but despite massive public campaigns by citizens demanding greater accountability in some countries,[8] there is limited evidence of this being addressed.

Finally, there remains a lack of transparency, openness to negative findings, or openness to evaluating certain regions and/or schemes. Boyle et al. (1999) note that institutionalisation of evaluation in public administration, 'needs a number of years of sustained intervention ... to arrive at a position where evaluation practice is a formal, recognised, and utilised part of the decision-making process' (p. 11). In VDS, that kind of sustained institutionalisation process seems almost impossible. Boyle and Lemaire highlight four elements that they consider foundational for institutionalisation: sound data systems, social science traditions, a cadre of trained evaluators and good governance (and specifically low levels of corruption). No country in South Asia has all of these elements in place; VDS within the region are exceedingly weak in all four elements.

This suggests that evaluation of research in VDS must include, but must go beyond, government. For example, the changing role of the judiciary in pushing for evidence-based policy-making in VDS in South Asia provides new opportunities for institutionalisation efforts. It suggests a need to expand thinking on evaluation users. A movement in this direction could, for example, connect evaluation to right to information campaigns (though they notably exclude intelligence and security agencies from their provisions, limiting certain aspects of their use in VDS).

How Does a Field Get Built? Strategies for Evaluation Field Building

This section explores how to strengthen the sub-field of evaluation of research in contexts where research infrastructure, accountability systems and professional capacity have been eroded by persistent and sustained conflict. In VDS, many of the problems described in this chapter may be similar to those of non-VDS in terms of evaluation and research, but even more extreme. In that case, strengthening the evaluation of research in VDS is perhaps quite similar to efforts in non-VDS contexts but requires deeper and more sustained efforts.

Adding a further layer of complexity, in many VDS situations, the geographical area is sometimes divided into a government-controlled area and rebel-controlled area. Strategising on evaluation field building in VDS requires distinguishing between the situation in both areas. As Asela Kalugampitiya, points out: 'in most of the situations there is a huge gap between government controlled areas and rebel controlled areas, which needs to be addressed carefully', with the different elements of the evaluation field 'not functioning as well in rebel areas' (or areas that were previously held by rebels in the case of Sri Lanka) and other areas. Using elements of field building developed earlier in this chapter, Asela Kalugampitiya, an evaluator who has worked in Sri Lanka and Afghanistan, reflects on some opportunities and challenges in strengthening the different elements in VDS (see Box 9.2).

The rest of this section describes some possibilities for field building. However, there is very little systematic evaluation of what works in evaluation field building. More of the same might not work. Field building efforts need to evaluate and learn from attempts, and entertain the possibility that, in strengthening evaluation of research in VDS, we may need something quite different. Developmental evaluation (Patton, 2011)

Box 9.2
Challenges and Solutions in Evaluation Field Building in Areas Affected by
Violent Conflict or (Previously) Rebel Held Areas

Evaluation leaders	
Challenges:	Almost no evaluators.
	Outside evaluators reluctant to go to conflict-affected areas.
Solutions:	Build local capacity with community groups to gather reliable data/information by using participatory approaches.
Spaces and forums	
Challenges:	Almost no space for networking.
	Transportation/communication challenges in being part of networks outside the area.
Solutions:	Provide extra facilities for evaluators representing conflict-affected areas to be part of networks and forums.
Evaluation knowledge	
Challenges:	Low-quality evaluations.
	Skills gaps of people in conflict-affected areas.
	Use of short-term external consultants.
Solutions:	Establish standards and guidelines for evaluation in conflict-affected areas.
	Engage local expertise to work with external consultants.
Institutional support	
Challenges:	Uncertainty on who sets policy, benchmarks and guidelines in the area.
	Fear in adapting policy as that may anger the alternate groups in the conflict.
Solutions:	Let the community and evaluators from the area decide the policy/guidelines with technical support from others.

Source: Asela Kalugampitiya, who worked for EVAW Special Fund in Afghanistan as International M&E Specialist.

may provide opportunities for understanding and evaluating evaluation field building efforts.

The elements of field building are interconnected. For example, if organisations are strengthened, they can take on other aspects of field building such as developing norms. Similarly, work to develop strategies and advocate for systems changes (such as ethical review guidelines, peer review processes and incentives, etc.) would perhaps be best done by strengthened networks of evaluators and researchers. Efforts to develop norms and standards and to advocate for their use is perhaps best supported through strengthening networks of evaluators who can craft and promote those standards.

Strengthening a set of evaluators and the spaces and structures to support their work is an important starting point to which other elements of the sub-fields of research evaluation in VDS can connect. This could include capacity building programmes and curricula, identifying, engaging with and creating incentives to encourage and reward leadership, and drawing researchers and social scientists into the field of evaluation of research in VDS. Capacity building efforts in these domains would have to consider the particular mix of skills needed for the evaluation of research; an area that is in transition. It may be that in some cases there is more of a base of skills in public policy or conflict researchers than in evaluators; those looking to strengthen individual capacities would have to assess whether to build evaluation skills into social science researchers, and/or to build understanding of research processes in evaluators comfortable or experienced in working in VDS. One may imagine that the combination of approaches, that brings together leaders from research and from evaluation, would ultimately be richer than either approach individually.

Efforts would need to go beyond theory and get people evaluating research; evaluation is an applied field and building skills in this field is difficult to do without an applied component. This suggests strategies of learning by doing, internships and other field work along with other more traditional training approaches. There is a spectrum of individuals needed in the evaluation of research in VDS. At one end there is the experienced evaluator who has a large set of skills. However, there are other roles as well, such as skilled enumerators, who are critical for evaluation in VDS.

Capacity building efforts need to take a systems approach and map out the needs of the sub-field to inform capacity building initiatives. One needs to also learn from what is out there—for example many evaluation field building efforts are using webinars or Internet as a training mechanism.

There are multiple evaluators working in VDS in the region, but they are dispersed and often unconnected to each other. Similarly there are groups and individuals promoting better evaluation of research but they too are often marginalised, and/or find it difficult to get the needed traction to change systems. There is a need for networking and working in communities of practice. This could potentially include networks of evaluators working in and on VDS and/or evaluation of research specifically; initially this could be started by connecting such evaluators into broader evaluation groups not limited to VDS. Individual leaders in this sub-field will surely play a critical role, with those individuals perhaps identifying others until there are several dozen leads in this area in the North and South with several hundred more, perhaps, having this as a partial focus of their work and drawing on the work that the core group generates.

Strengthening the evaluation of research and its use should include support for open communities of practice and experimentation with ways to accelerate learning across, and from, bottom-up processes. It could also include supporting writing, exchange of ideas at events, meetings, networks and conferences, and fostering structures to support information exchange and problem solving within and across groups such as meetings, list-serves or virtual spaces. Work on these foundations of field building will help build other aspects of the field. For example, strengthening capacity of Southern evaluators through their involvement in evaluations will by extension contribute new knowledge from these evaluations.

Work on the institutional setting should be towards increasingly open cultures of evaluating and using research. Such shifts are by nature negotiated and involve responsiveness to *open windows* by policy entrepreneurs and advocates. This work is arguably one of the functions that leaders in evaluation of research in and on VDS, as they emerge, can contribute to. Field building in evaluation of research on VDS, will require astute strategising and alliance building.

It is also important to understand, in particular contexts, who is calling for strengthening the evaluation of research and why? Obviously, research and evaluation both require basic training of social scientists so that field building in either area will always be limited or strengthened by the level of research methodology skills of graduates. However, in some contexts it may be other groups pushing more actively for change in research evaluation. For example, in South Asia, it may be policy research organisations or *think tanks* who are actively engaged in debates on evaluating research quality. Policy research organisations often rely on funding from external donors who require some analysis of research quality to justify the next tranche of funds. These groups may struggle with measures that they feel are inappropriate for their research contexts (which may include VDS), potentially making them important to engage with on evaluation of research in VDS as they have an immediate use for improving such evaluation. Also, the systems within these institutions (possibly also those of private universities) are likely easier to shift than larger public social science research systems or universities which may be cumbersome and slow moving.

Support and strategies should recognise and reflect the multiple timelines involved in development and development research. There are *immediate* problems and challenges where the quality evaluation of research in VDS can help to identify what is working from what is not, and bring new evidence to bear on pressing policy and programming questions. There are complex problems of evaluating the impact of research, for example; work on building new methods to understand this can be developed in the *medium term*. Finally, building and mainstreaming structures, systems and incentives for the evaluation of research including in VDS is a *long-term* agenda that short- and medium-term work should contribute to.

In strategising on building the sub-field of evaluation of research in VDS, frameworks of evaluation supply and demand are conceptually helpful. However, they oversimplify. Field building efforts should resist a technocratic understanding of supply or demand, and instead see both as abstractions that are connected, in flux, and part of broader social settings that are themselves in flux. Integrating this systems perspective into field building work implies that instead of, for example, asking 'whether an appropriate balance means working equally on both sides of the equation or whether to focus first on one side of the equation or other' (Boyle et al., 1999, p. 13), field building should be approached developmentally, recognising that some doors will open and some will close. That is particularly true in sub-fields like evaluation of research and particularly of work in VDS, where field building efforts need to analyse how contexts are shifting and seek opportunities and quick wins while also working towards longer term, often incremental, change (see Healy and Healy, Chapter 8). Such an approach recognises that the work of institutionalisation is never complete, is not linear and is unlikely to follow a consistently positive upward trajectory. Building on this recognition strengthens our ability to plan for and learn from field building efforts more thoughtfully.

Notes

1. For university-based research, for example, this would include ethics committees, peer review processes, publishing outlets and so on.
2. Available at http://www.evaluationcanada.ca/txt/2_competencies_cdn_evaluation_practice.pdf (accessed on 24 July 2015).

3. Personal correspondence, 2011.
4. http://teachingevaluationinsouthasia.org/index.php/78-tesa (accessed on 24 July 2015).
5. Personal correspondence, 2011.
6. For example, there are ongoing initiatives to develop an evaluation journal for South Asia.
7. Remark made by Abdul Ghani of the Afghanistan Evaluation Association in the session Role of Evaluation in Conflict Settings, Evaluation Conclave 2010 'Making Evaluation Matter'. International Conference held in New Delhi, India, 25–28 October, 2010.
8. Notable has been the massive India-wide anti-corruption protests leading into and including August 2011.

References

Arunachalam, S. (2009). *Social science research in South Asia: An analysis of the published journal literature.* Paper prepared for the IDRC supported study on Policy Research Organisations and Organisations and Research Environment in South Asia, Research Councils UK.

Ashford, G. and Patkar, S. (2001). *The positive path: Using appreciative inquiry in rural Indian communities.* Winnipeg, CA: International Institute for Sustainable Development.

Basnyat, B. B. (2009). *Status and challenges of impact evaluation in Nepal.* Paper presented at the Perspectives on Impact Evaluation Conference, Cairo, Egypt.

Berry, L. L. and Parasuraman, A. (1993). Building a new academic field—The case of services marketing. *Journal of Retailing, 69*(1), 13–60.

Bourdieu, P. and Wacquant, L. J. D. (1992). *An invitation to reflexive sociology.* Chicago, IL: University of Chicago Press.

Boyle, R., Lemaire, D. and Rist, R. C. (1999). Introduction: Building evaluation capacity. In R. Boyle and D. Lemaire (Eds), *Building effective evaluation capacity* (pp. 1–19). New Brunswick, NJ: Transaction Publishing.

Burns, D. (2007). *Systemic action research: A strategy for whole system change.* Bristol: The Policy Press, University of Bristol.

Chambers, R. (1994). The origins and practice of participatory rural appraisal. *World Development, 22*(7), 953–969.

———. (2008). *Revolutions in development inquiry.* London and Sterling, VA: Earthscan Publications Ltd.

Daily Star (Diplomatic Correspondent). (2011, May 30). It's political instability, not climate: Evans' on Bangladesh's biggest threat. *The Daily Star*, Bangladesh. Retrieved from http://www.thedailystar.net/newDesign/news-details.php?nid=187816 (accessed on 24 July 2015).

Dart, J. and Davies, R. (2003). A dialogical, story-based evaluation tool: The most significant change technique. *American Journal of Evaluation, 24*(2), 137–155.

Diwanji, Amberish K. (2004). *Census: Figuring out the truth.* Retrieved from http://www.rediff.com/news/2004/sep/17spec.htm (accessed on 5 June 2015).

Earl, S., Carden, F. and Smutylo, T. (2001). *Outnbn come mapping: Building learning and reflection into development programs.* Ottawa: International Development

Research. Retrieved from http://www.idrc.ca/EN/Resources/Publications/Pages/ IDRCBookDetails.aspx?PublicationID=121 (accessed on 22 April 2015).

Fligstein, N. (2001). Social skill and the theory of fields. *Sociological Theory, 19*(2), 105–125.

Giddens, A. (1984). *The constitution of society: Outline of the theory of structuration.* Berkeley, CA: University of California Press.

Goyal, R. S. (2009). *Evaluation capacity in South Asia: Experiences, lessons learned and ways forward.* Paper presented at the Perspectives on Impact Evaluation Conference, Cairo, Egypt.

Hamid, Peerzada Arshad. (2011). Counting Kashmiris, April 2011. *Himal Southasian.* Retrieved from http://old.himalmag.com/component/content/article/4355-counting-kashmiris.html (accessed on 24 July 2015).

Hay, K. (2010). Evaluation field building in South Asia: Reflections, anecdotes and questions. *American Journal of Evaluation, 31*(2), 222–231.

Hirschhorn, L. and Gilmore T. N. (2004). *Ideas in philanthropic field building: Where they come from and how they are translated into actions.* New York: The Foundation Center. Retrieved from http://foundationcenter.org/gainknowledge/research/pdf/ practicematters_06_paper.pdf (accessed on 23 July 2015).

International Crisis Group. (2010). *Sri Lanka: After the war.* Brussels: International Crisis Group.

Khan, K. (2008). Evaluation challenges in Pakistan and establishment of Pakistan Evaluation Network (PEN). In B. Williams and M. Sankar (Eds), *Evaluation South Asia* (pp. 69–78). Nepal: UNICEF.

Khattak, S. G. (2009). Research in difficult settings: Reflections on Pakistan and Afghanistan. Ottawa: International Development Research Centre. Retrieved from http://idl-bnc.idrc.ca/dspace/bitstream/10625/40067/1/128737.pdf (accessed on 27 April 2015).

Ministry of Education, Islamic Republic of Afghanistan. (2008). The Development of Education. National Report. Retrieved from http://www.ibe.unesco.org/National_ Reports/ICE_2008/afghanistan_NR08.pdf (accessed on 24 July 2015).

Misra, A. (2004). *Afghanistan: The labyrinth of violence.* Cambridge and Malden, MA: Polity Press.

Murdukhayeva, E. (2009). Precedent, protest and politics: Changes in the prosecution of rape in England, 1810–1845. *The Columbia Undergraduate Journal of History, 2*(1), 24–79.

Pal, S. P. (2009, March 29–April 2). *Status of development evaluation in India—An overview.* Paper presented at the Perspectives on Impact Evaluation Conference, Cairo, Egypt.

Patton, M. Q. (2011). *Developmental evaluation.* IDRC Presentation. Retrieved from http://edepot.wur.nl/216077 (accessed on 5 June 2015).

Pistono, S. P. (1998). Susan Brownmiller and the history of rape. *Women's Study, 14*(3), 265–276.

Sewell, W. H., Jr. (1992). A theory of structure: Duality, agency, and transformation. *American Journal of Sociology, 98*(1), 1–29.

Scriven, M. (1991). *Evaluation thesaurus* (4th ed.). Newbury Park, CA: SAGE Publications.

Shiva Kumar, A. K. (2010). A comment on 'Evaluation field building in South Asia: Reflections, anecdotes, and questions'. *American Journal of Evaluation, 31*(2), 238–240.

Toulemonde, J. (1995). The emergence of an evaluation profession in European Countries: The case of structural policies. *Knowledge and Policy*, *8*(3), 43–54.

Tuduwe, I. and Samranayake, M. (2008). Civil society partnership in promoting an evaluation culture in the development process: Experience of the Sri Lanka Evaluation Association (SLEvA). In B. Williams and M. Sandar (Eds), *Evaluation South Asia* (pp. 61–68). Kathmandu, Nepal: UNICEF.

Weiss, C. H. (2009). Foreword. In F. Carden, *Knowledge to policy* (pp. ix–xiii). IDRC and SAGE Publications.

World Bank. (2000). *Higher education in developing countries: Perils and promise.* Washington, DC: World Bank.

———. (2007). Bangladesh: Country summary of higher education. Retrieved from http://siteresources.worldbank.org/EDUCATION/Resources/278200-1121703274255/1439264-1193249163062/Bangladesh_countrySummary.pdf (accessed on 12 April 2015).

———. (2009a). *The towers of learning: Performance, peril and promise of higher education in Sri Lanka.* Colombo: The World Bank Colombo Office. Retrieved from http://siteresources.worldbank.org/SOUTHASIAEXT/Resources/Publications/TOLreportfinal.pdf) (accessed on 12 April 2015).

———. (2009b). Expanding access to quality education. *Projects and operations, IDA at work: Afghanistan.* Retrieved from http://web.worldbank.org/WBSITE/EXTERNAL/PROJECTS/0,,contentMDK:21289161~menuPK:64282137~pagePK:41367~piPK:279616~theSitePK:40941,00.html (accessed on 12 April 2015).

10

Lessons for Researchers and Evaluators Working *in the Extreme*

Colleen Duggan and Kenneth Bush

T his book has sought to explore the ways in which research, power and politics interact and have impacts in violently divided societies (VDS). In this concluding section, we direct our attention towards two questions. First, *what should we learn* when we cast our eye back over the preceding chapters, and when we sift through the thick, rich, detail of case studies, literature reviews, theoretical and methodological debates, and discussions of how to build this field of work? Second, what are the implications for the way we think about, undertake and assess the role and impact of research in VDS?

The Variable Roles of Evaluation and Research in VDS

The first and most obvious lesson to be learned is that in the absence of *good* evaluation of research in/on VDS, policy and programming decisions may come to be based on impressions, anecdotes, or worse, opaque political, economic or particularistic interests. However, as we see in Kelly's chapter on the evaluation of HIV/AIDS research in South Africa, even research that is methodologically sound and widely accepted may be challenged, ignored or actively rejected by power-brokers when it conflicts with the cultural or social world views. So too is research likely to be rejected when it challenges entrenched political or economic interests. In such settings—regardless of evaluation—conditions are ripe for what Boden and Epstein (2006) have called *policy-based evidence making* as opposed to evidence-based policy-making.

On the other hand, we have seen in Healy and Healy's chapter that research and evaluations supported by Atlantic Philanthropies in Northern Ireland served as an important conduit for controlled communication between the divided communities of Suffolk and Lenadoon. In this case, the conduct and dissemination of research served as a bridge between violently divided communities. The evaluation of this research helped to depoliticise a politically fraught and volatile environment, and to increase the transparency—and ultimately, the legitimacy—of an innovative programme. As importantly, regular reports were produced in order to influence policy and practice in other similarly divided communities across the Northern Ireland. In other words, we see the strategic use of research, and its evaluation, to advocate for certain approaches to community relationship-building by disseminating concrete examples of real-time, good practice. In a similar way, we see that the accountability function of evaluation, if done *right*, will help to ensure that research benefits VDS while still meeting the reporting needs of funders (Whitty, Chapter 3). And finally, in Chapter 7, Zaveri illustrates how evaluation itself may constitute a form of research that challenges inequitable social structures.

In effect then, we have a number of very different examples of how research, power and politics may interact in VDS. We learn that political, economic and social interests may trump or dump research even when it has been evaluated as methodologically sound and necessary. We learn that evaluation and research may facilitate difficult conversations *and build incremental trust* in ways that bridge divided communities. We learn that evaluation may serve to challenge inequitable power structures, by shining a light on practices that sustain such imbalances implicitly or explicitly.

Thus, we find ourselves in an interesting position. To paraphrase the sociologist James Rule: We know a lot of things to be true about the inter-play of research, power and politics, but we do not know when they are going to be true. It is the second lesson to be learned from this book that helps us to better understand (and anticipate) when, why and how these phenomena interact.

The Importance of Context[1]

The second lesson of this book is the importance of integrating *context* into our understandings of, and approaches to, the evaluation of research in VDS. The risks of ignoring this fact are enormous. As Zaveri writes:

> In the dynamic world of VDS, ignoring context, especially in the presence of deep seated inequities, may erroneously promote strategies, policies, programmes that in the long run reinforce such inequities. The role of the evaluator becomes critical in such situations—using approaches and formulating questions that tease out these contextual changes can clearly contribute to more equitable, sensitive research in evaluation.

If, however, we are to put context into context, and if we are to understand the difference diverse contexts make, then we need to begin to tease out the thick details from context-specific studies—as we are attempting to do in this book.

In the introduction to this book, we identified four core domains of evaluation, namely the ethical, methodological, logistical and political (see Figure 1.2). The chapters in this book have offered a broad range of case studies and examples of how these dimensions are affected by the VDS context. What we have learned is that the relationships between the domains of evaluation and VDS context are fluid as well as interdependent. They may shift over time, particularly if conflict intensifies, which may serve to further constrain an evaluator's latitude of action. As volatility, risk, uncertainty and levels of potential harm increase—the four domains of evaluation are forced *into each other* so that decisions and actions in one domain inevitably affect all domains (see Figure 10.1).

When this happens, it becomes increasingly difficult, if not impossible, for logistical issues (for example) to be addressed independently of the ethics, politics and evaluation method. While this dynamic may also be evident in non-VDS contexts, the difference here is the acute levels of risk (and potential harm) and the speed with which relatively minor problems (or miscalculations) in one domain may trigger a catastrophic chain reaction in other domains. This begins to shed light on why the evaluation of research (or of any activity) is so much more difficult in VDS—and, as importantly, why there can be such variability in the ways in which research, power and politics interact and generate myriad impacts in VDS.

Figure 10.1
The Amalgamation of Evaluation Domains in VDS as Intensity Increases

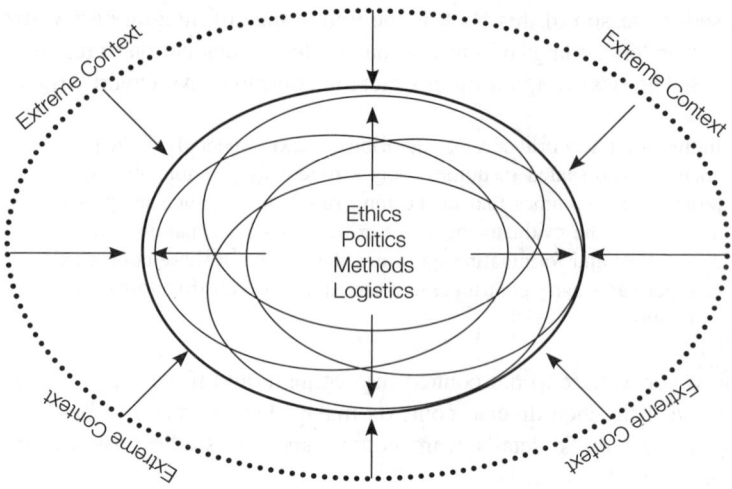

Ethics
Politics
Methods
Logistics

Source: Bush and Duggan (2013, p. 9).

Evaluation as a Fundamentally Political Activity

The evaluation of research in VDS is embedded in the political dynamics of the particular environment within which it is nested. This contextual fact unavoidably casts evaluation as a fundamentally political activity. Not because it possesses political intent or objectives (though it may), but because it will inevitably have political consequences within such an environment. Evaluators are confronted by multiple pressures emanating from diverse, intersecting, conflicts, as well as power imbalances, competing interests and their own value-systems. In this context, evaluators should be prepared for political complications and challenges throughout the evaluation process. Evaluators must, therefore, be prepared to undertake considerable (and constant) efforts to identify and understand how these various linkages are entangled with political and economic interests that interact with the conceptual, methodological, ethical and practical or logistic challenges that define this area of inquiry. This, of course, begs the question of how, exactly, evaluators should be prepared to deal with this complex uncertainty and volatility. The answer to this question is addressed in the next section.

Towards a VDS-ready Evaluator

One of the strong themes running through the chapters in this book is the question of the particular qualities needed by evaluators of research in/ on VDS. Some of these qualities may be innate and some may be learned or nurtured. The emphasis on cultural humility by Jayawickrama and Strecker is a particularly important attribute for evaluators and researchers working in/on VDS. As they note: 'While the failure to demonstrate cultural humility can corrupt any evaluation or research setting, it poses particular ethical challenges within VDS and can lead to severe implications on both the process and the product of the study or evaluation.' Both Whitty and Knox (Chapters 3 and 5, respectively) call for a complementary characteristic in evaluators in VDS: self-consciousness and reflexivity. And, at an institutional level, a similar argument is developed by Healy and Healy in Chapter 8 that funders also have their own epistemological and methodological predilections which, when made explicit, shed light on what they do, and how and why they do it. Most eloquently, Zaveri writes:

> [Making evaluation more sensitive to the vulnerabilities of stakeholders] … requires greater sensitivity from the evaluator, and a deeper understanding of the context in which the programme is taking place. This goes *beyond* the terms of reference of the evaluation and suggests the need for systematic ethical questioning, at the least, by the evaluator. In such contexts, the qualities of the evaluator must include a detailed, politically informed, anthropological understanding of the social, cultural, economic, and political structures and processes within the project environment—in addition to the usual set of technical evaluation skills expected of a professional evaluator.

When distilled into a list, the skill-set required of evaluators of research in VDS would go beyond the usual social science approaches and tools at the disposal of evaluators. In addition to the usual technical competencies of evaluators, the authors of this book have argued that they (or their team) need to possess:

- Sector-specific expertise and experience
- A well-calibrated moral compass and an appreciation of VDS-specific ethical challenges
- Political sensitivities, diplomacy and conflict resolution skills
- Peace and conflict research skills

- Anthropological, historical, political sensibilities
- In militarised zones, a technical knowledge of the structures, strategies, weapons and *behavioural patterns* of armed actors
- Knowledge and appreciation of the intersection of the political and ethnographic at local levels
- Cultural competence and cultural humility

The Ambivalent Relationship of Evaluation to Conflict

Zaveri explores the ways in which evaluative research may unearth instances where development interventions in VDS may affect harm in the name of good. The specific cases in her chapter focus on the potential increased vulnerability of children involved in child protection programmes. In both her chapter, and that of Jayawickrama and Strecker, the phenomenon of iatrogenesis enters our analytical frame of reference as a result of the application of evaluative research lenses. Recognising and responding to this pathology is particularly, and self-evidently, important for research and evaluation in VDS as a sine qua non for halting such programmes.

However, there is another less conspicuous—but no less ethically fraught—question suggested by this finding: If we recognise that such interventions may generate or subsidise corrosive structures and processes, are there instances where our research or evaluations must *necessarily* create conflict in order to problematise and change an inequitable status quo? What about that project that succeeds in increasing migrant workers' awareness of their rights, and which thus leads to the assertion of those rights by workers? But this, in turn, triggers a repressive crack down by authorities who seek to sustain their benefits from the maintenance of a fundamentally unjust status quo (through cheap labour, non-regulation of the workplace and so on). How does/should one use the findings of an evaluation or research which reveals this dynamic? Does it lead to the termination of this workers' rights project (or any self-labelled empowerment project) in the interests of stability—albeit a stability sustained through the maintenance of an exploitive economic and social system? Or does it galvanise support for workers against such practices? The answer to these questions in this case, and more generally, is rooted in what we call the final section, 'Extreme Ethics'.

Extreme Ethics

The extreme context of VDS is infused with extreme ethical implications for evaluators and for researchers—more risks, greater risks and greater potential harm inherent in all decisions and actions. It is characterised by greater ethical fog. This is partly a result of the dynamic noted earlier (Figure 10.1). However, it is possible to identify an analogous process within the realm of evaluation ethics in VDS. Under normal conditions, evaluators tend to confront ethical challenges and dilemmas in a segmented or compartmentalised fashion, as illustrated in Figure 10.2.

However, the chapters in this book point to a different dynamic in VDS. The pressure cooker context of VDS *de-compartmentalises* ethics, as they meld into each other to become increasingly and inextricably dense, complex and interconnected, as illustrated in Figure 10.3.

How do, or how should, evaluators and researchers address these particular challenges? Cultivating the personal and professional competencies listed earlier is a good place to start. However, a review of the 'ethical tipping points of evaluators in conflict zones' has highlighted the underdeveloped character of the ethical dimensions and training within the field of evaluation and, to a marginally less degree, of research (Duggan and Bush, 2014). Much work remains to be done in examining and understanding the ethical challenges confronting evaluators and researchers in VDS—and in finding strategies to anticipate and address them.

Figure 10.2
Ethical Issues in a Non-VDS Context: Segmented and Discrete

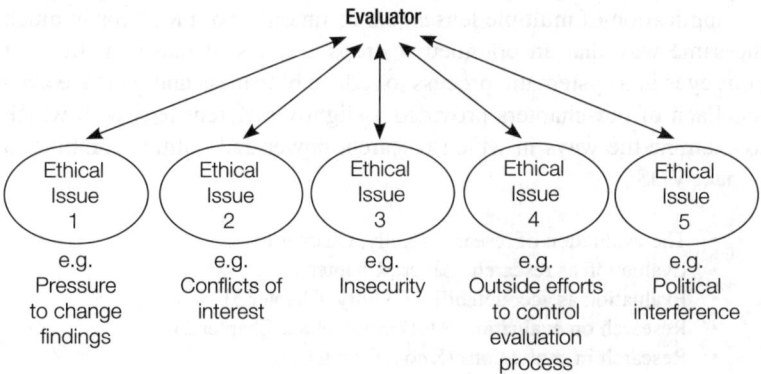

Source: Duggan and Bush (2014, p. 15).

Figure 10.3
Ethical Issues in a VDS: Conflated

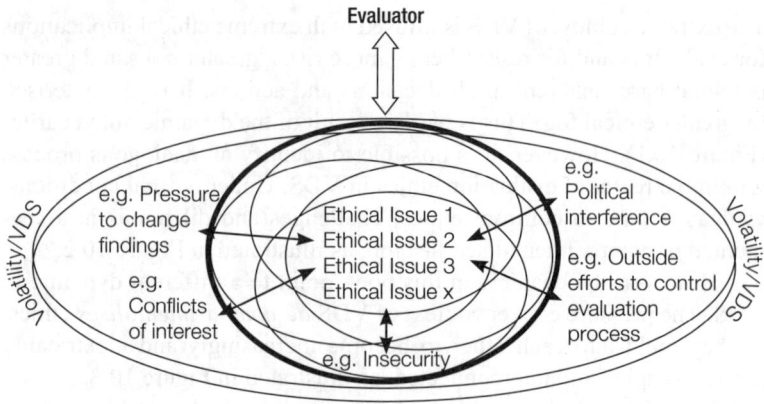

Source: Duggan and Bush (2014, p. 16).

Final Thoughts

When we started this project, we worked very hard to ensure that it focused explicitly on the evaluation *of research* in VDS. Our belief was that, in the same way that a magnifying glass concentrates the rays of the sun, we might be able to focus the analytical heat of the contributors to a point where their collective analysis might ignite greater understanding. In the course of this project, however, this metaphor shifted as we learned from each other. We realised that the project was actually about the application of multiple lenses to a common set of problems in much the same way that an optometrist drops a series of lenses in front of your eyes in a systematic process to reduce blurriness and increase clarity. Each of our chapters provided a slightly different lens with which to examine the ways in which research, power and politics combine to impact VDS:

- The evaluation of research (Kelly, Chapter 6)
- Evaluation as research (Zaveri, Chapter 7)
- Evaluation as accountability (Whitty, Chapter 3)
- Research on evaluation (McDermott et al., Chapter 2)
- Research in evaluations (Knox, Chapter 5)

- Research evaluation as ethical compass (Jayawickrama and Strecker, Chapter 4)
- Research evaluation as advocacy (Healy and Healy, Chapter 8)
- Research evaluation as institutional strengthening (Hay, Chapter 9)

Through the application of these lenses in this book, we have sought to better understand how research, power and politics interact in VDS. In so doing, we also seek to place this field of research and practice more centrally within the communities of researchers, evaluators, funders and practitioners. If there is one truth in this project—which is less contestable than others—it is this: Until there is a culture of systematic evaluation of research in and on VDS, we will limit our ability to understand the impact of research interventions—good, bad or indifferent. And, we will undermine our ability to harness research most effectively to address some of the most pressing problems confronting humankind today.

Note

1. This discussion of domains draws on our earlier work. See Bush and Duggan (2013).

References

Boden, R. and Epstein, D. (2006). Managing the research imagination? Globalization and research in higher education. *Globalization, Societies and Education, 4*(2), 223–236.

Bush, K. and Duggan, C. (2013). Evaluation in conflict zones: Methodological and ethical challenges. *The Journal of Peacebuilding and Development, 8*(2), 5–25.

Duggan, C. and Bush, B. (2014). The ethical tipping points of evaluators in conflict zones. *American Journal of Evaluation, 35*(4), 485–506.

Bibliography

Adelman, H., Suhrke, A. and Jones, B. (2006). *Study 2: Early warning and conflict management*. Odense: Steering Committee of the JEEAR.

Africa Peace Forum (APFO), Centre for Conflict Resolution (CECORE), Consortium of Humanitarian Agencies (CHA), Forum on Early Warning and Early Response (FEWER), International Alert and Saferworld. (2004, January). Conflict-sensitive approaches to development, humanitarian assistance and peacebuilding: A resource pack. APFO, CECORE, CHA, FEWER, International Alert and Saferworld. Retrieved from http://www.conflictsensitivity.org/sites/default/files/Conflict-Sensitive %20Approaches%20to%20Development,%20Humanitarian%20Assistance%20 and%20Peacebuilding%20Resource%20Pack.pdf (accessed on 27 April 2015).

Aizenman, J., Edison, H., Leony, L. and Sun, Y. (2011, May 20). Evaluating the quality of IMF research: A citation study. *IEO Background Paper*. Washington, DC: Independent Evaluation Office of the International Monetary Fund.

Ambrose, K., Earl, S., Van Ongevalle, J. and Nyangaga, J. (2008). *Outcome mapping: Frequently asked questions*. Ottawa: International Development Research Centre. Retrieved from http://www.idrc.ca/EN/Programs/Evaluation/Documents/outcome-mapping-faq-e.pdf (accessed on 27 April 2015).

American Evaluation Association. (2011). The program evaluation standards: Summary form. Retrieved from http://www.eval.org/evaluationdocuments/progeval.html (accessed on 22 April 2015).

Anderson, M. B. and Olson, L. (2003). *Confronting war: Critical lessons for peace practitioners*. Cambridge, MA: The Collaborative for Development Action, Inc.

Anderson, M. B., Chigas, D. and Woodrow, P. (2007). Encouraging effective evaluation of conflict prevention and peacebuilding activities: Towards DAC guidance. *OECD Journal on Development, 8*(3), 3–102. Retrieved from http://www.oecd.org/ dataoecd/52/3/39660852.pdf (accessed on 22 April 2015).

Anderson, M. B., Chigas, D., Olson, L. and Woodrow, P. (2004). *Reflecting on peace practice handbook*. Cambridge, MA: The Collaborative for Development Action, Inc.

ARK. (2010). *Northern Ireland life and times survey, 2010*. ARK. Retrieved from http:// www.ark.ac.uk/nilt/2010/ (accessed on 27 April 2015).

Arnold, D. (2008). Cultural heritage as a vehicle for basic research in computing science: Pasteur's quadrant and a use-inspired basic research agenda. *Computer Graphics Forum, 27*(8), 2188–2196.

Ashworth, P. and Lucas, U. (2000). Achieving empathy and engagement: A practical approach to the design, conduct and reporting of phenomenographic research. *Studies in Higher Education, 25*(3), 295–308.

Audi, R. (Ed.). (1999). *The Cambridge Dictionary of Philosophy* (2nd ed.). Cambridge: Cambridge University Press.

Austin, A., Fischer, M. and Wils, O. (Eds). (2003). *Dialogue series No. 1—Peace and conflict impact assessment: Critical views on theory and practice*. Berlin: Berghof Research Center for Constructive Conflict Management.

Australasian Evaluation Society. (2003). Evaluation ethics and quality: Results of a survey of Australasian evaluation society. Prepared by David Turner, Australian Evaluation Society. AES Ethics Committee.

Barnett, M. and Zürcher, C. (Forthcoming). The peace builders contract: How external statebuilding reinforces weak statehood. In Roland Paris and Timothy D. Sisk (Eds), *The dilemmas of statebuilding: Confronting the contradictions of postwar peace operations*. London: Routledge.

Barré, A., Shearer, D. and Uvin, P. (1999). *The limits and scope for the use of development assistance incentives and disincentives for influencing conflict situations: Case-study—Rwanda*. Paris: OECD DAC Informal Task Force on Conflict Peace and Development Cooperation.

Ben-Ner, A. and Benedetto, G. (2003). The theory of nonprofit organisations revisited. In H. K. Anheier and A. Ben-Ner (Eds), *The study of the nonprofit enterprise: Theories and approaches* (pp. 3–26). New York: Kluwer Academic/Plenum Publishers.

Boix Mansilla, V., Feller, I. and Gardner, H. (2006). Quality assessment in interdisciplinary research education. *Research Evaluation, 15*(1), 69–74.

Booth, D. (2011). *Working with the grain and swimming against the tide: Barriers to uptake of research findings on governance and public services in low-income Africa*. Africa Power and Politics Programme (Working Paper No. 18). London: Overseas Development Institute. Retrieved from http://www.dfid.gov.uk/r4d/PDF/Outputs/APPP/appp-working-paper-18.pdf (accessed on 22 April 2015).

Bordo, S. (1990). Feminist, postmodernism, and gender-scepticism. In L. J. Nicholson (Ed.), *Feminism/postmodernism*. New York: Routledge.

Bridges, D. (2009). Research quality assessment in education: Impossible science, possible art? *British Educational Research Journal, 35*(4), 497–517.

Bunde-Birouste, A. W. and Zwi, A. (2008). The peacebuilding filter. In N. Arya, J. Santa Barbara (Eds), *Peace through health: How health professionals can work for a less violent world* (1st ed., pp. 140–147). Sterling: Kumarian Press, Inc.

Bush, K. (1999). *The limits and scope for the use of development assistance incentives and disincentives for influencing conflict situations: Case-study—Sri Lanka*. Paris: OECD DAC Informal Task Force on Conflict Peace and Development Co-operation.

———. (2001). *Peace and conflict impact assessment (PCIA) of Swedish development cooperation with Sri Lanka*. Swedish International Development Cooperation Agency (SIDA). Retrieved from http://www.sida.se/Publications/Import/pdf/sv/Peace-and-Conflict-Impact-Assessment-PCIA-of-Swedish-Development-Cooperation-with-Sri-Lanka_1725.pdf (accessed on 27 April 2015).

Bush, K. (2004). Commodification, compartmentalization, and militarization of peacebuilding. In T. Keating and A. W. Knight (Eds), *Building sustainable peace* (pp. 97–123). Tokyo/Edmonton: UN University/University of Alberta Press.

———. (2009). *Aid for peace: A handbook for applying peace and conflict impact assessment (PCIA) to PEACE III projects*. Londonderry: INCORE, University of Ulster. Retrieved from http://www.incore.ulst.ac.uk/pdfs/Handbook-Aid_for_Peace-2009_Dec.pdf (accessed on 22 April 2015).

———. (2013). The politics of post-conflict space: The mysterious case of missing graffiti in 'post-troubles' Northern Ireland. *Contemporary Politics, 19*(2), 165–186.

Bush, K. and Fuat Keyman, E. (1997). Identity-based conflict: Rethinking security in a post-cold war world. *Global Governance*, *3*(3), 311–328.

Campbell, M. and Rutnik, T. (2002). *When and how to use external evaluators.* Baltimore: The Association of Baltimore Area Grantmakers. Retrieved from http://www.abagrantmakers.org/resource/resmgr/abag_publications/evaluationfinal.pdf (accessed on 22 April 2015).

Canadian Evaluation Society. (2010). *Competences for Canadian evaluation practice* (v.11.04162010). Ontario: CES. Retrieved from http://evaluationcanada.ca/txt/2_competencies_cdn_evaluation_practice.pdf (accessed on 22 April 2015).

Canadian Human Rights Mission to Sri Lanka. (1992). Report. Toronto: Author. Retrieved from http://www.kit.nl/library/documents/query.ashx?RecordID=150037 (accessed on 27 April 2015). (Cited as: Gibson, R. [1992]. *The Canadian Human Rights Mission to Sri Lanka: Report.* Toronto: CHRM.)

Carden, F. (2007, December). The real evaluation gap. *Alliance Magazine*, *12*(4). Retrieved from http://www.alliancemagazine.org/feature/the-real-evaluation-gap/ (accessed on 27 April 2015).

———. (2010). Introduction to the forum on evaluation field building in South Asia. *American Journal of Evaluation*, *31*(2), 219–221.

Carden, F. and Nielson, S. (2005). Confluence and influence: Building network capacities in research networks. In D. L. Stone and S. Maxwell (Eds), *Global knowledge networks and international development: Bridges across boundaries* (pp. 139–155). London/New York: Routledge.

Chambers, R. (2006). Transforming power: From zero-sum to win-win? *IDS Bulletin*, *37*(6), 99–110.

Chapman, J. (2004). *System failure: Why governments must learn to think differently* (2nd ed.). London: Demos. (1st ed. in 2002.)

Chen, H-T. (2005). A practical evaluation taxonomy: Selecting the evaluation approach that works. In H-T. Chen (Ed.), *Practical program evaluation: Assessing and improving planning, implementation and effectiveness* (pp. 45–70). Thousand Oaks, CA: SAGE Publications.

Chr. Michelsen Institute (CMI) and Nordic Consulting Group, Hallam, A., Halvorsen, K., Lexow, J., Miranda, A., Rebelo, P. and Suhrke, A. (1997). *Evaluation of Norwegian assistance to peace, reconciliation and rehabilitation in Mozambique* (Evaluation Report No. 4.97). Oslo: The Royal Ministry of Foreign Affairs/Norad.

Church, C. and Shouldice, J. (2002). *The evaluation of conflict resolution interventions: Framing the state of play.* Derry/Londonderry: INCORE.

———. (2003). *The evaluation of conflict resolution interventions: Part II. Emerging theory and practice.* Derry/Londonderry: INCORE.

Conflict Prevention and Post-Conflict Reconstruction (CPR) Peacebuilding Network. (2001). *Compendium of operational frameworks for peacebuilding and donor coordination.* Hull, Canada: CIDA, various dates.

Coryn, C. (Ed.). (2013). What is social science research and why would we want to evaluate it? In *Evaluating social science research: A handbook for researchers, instructors, and students* (pp. 1–32). New York, NY: Guilford.

Coryn, C. L. S., Hattie, J. A., Scriven, M. and Hartmann, D. J. (2007). Models and mechanisms for evaluating government-funded research: An international comparison. *American Journal of Evaluation*, *28*(4), 437–457.

Crotty, M. J. (2003). *The foundations of social research: Meaning and perspective in the research process*. London: SAGE Publications.

CRS SEAPRO. (2004). *Peacebuilding technical commission meeting: Learning document*. Baltimore, MD: Catholic Relief Services.

Dart, J. and Davies, R. (2003). A dialogical, story-based evaluation tool: The most significant change technique. *American Journal of Evaluation, 24*(2), 137–155.

David, M. E. (2008). Research quality assessment and the metrication of the social sciences. *European Political Science, 7*(1), 52–63.

Davies, H., Nutley, S. and Walter, I. (2005). *Assessing the impact of social science research: Conceptual, methodological and practical issues*. ESRC Symposium on Assessing Non-Academic Impact of Research, 12–13 May, London, England.

Department of Education Northern Ireland. (2011). *Enrolments at schools in Northern Ireland*. Bangor: Department of Education.

DFID. (2001) (Goodard, J., Vaux, T., and Walker, R. 2002). *Conducting conflict assessments: Guidance notes*. London: Department for International Development.

———. (2006). *Monitoring and evaluation: A guide for DFID-contracted research programmes*. London: Department for International Development. Retrieved from http://r4d.dfid.gov.uk/PDF/Publications/meguidecontractedresearch1.pdf (accessed on 22 April 2015).

Dictionary.com. (2005.). Research. *Dictionary.com* Retrieved from http://dictionary.reference.com/browse/research (accessed on 22 April 2015).

Donovan, C. (2007). The qualitative future of research evaluation. *Science and Public Policy, 34*(8), 585–597.

Downs, G. and Stedman, S. J. (2002). Evaluation issues in peace implementation. In S. J. Stedman, D. Rothchild and E. M. Cousens (Eds), *Ending civil wars: The implementation of peace agreements* (pp. 43–69). Boulder, CO and London: Lynne Rienner Publications, Inc.

EarthRights International. (2009). *Getting it wrong: Flawed 'corporate social responsibility' and misrepresentations surrounding total and Chevron's Yadana gas pipeline in military-ruled Burma (Myanmar)*. EarthRights International. Retrieved from http://www.earthrights.org/sites/default/files/publications/getting-it-wrong.pdf (accessed on 22 April 2015).

Eguren, I. R. (2011). *Theory of change: A thinking and action approach to navigate in the complexity of social change processes*. Guatemala, Panama and The Netherlands: HIVOS, UNDP, Democratic Dialogue. Retrieved from http://seachangecop.org/files/documents/2011_05_HIVOS_UNDP_-_Theory_of_Change.pdf (accessed on 22 April 2015).

Elkins, C. (2006). *Monitoring and evaluation for development in peace-precarious situations*. Paper presented at the North-South Divide and International Studies 47th Annual ISA Convention. Retrieved from http://www.rti.org/pubs/Elkins_ME_Peace.pdf (accessed on 22 April 2015).

Esman, M. (2007). *Peaceworks No. 13: Can foreign aid moderate ethnic conflict?* Washington, DC: United States Institute for Peace. Retrieved from http://www.usip.org/files/resources/pwks13.pdf (accessed on 22 April 2015).

Eyben, R. (Ed.). (2006). Introduction. In *Relationships for aid*. London, Sterling VA: Earthscan.

Fast, L. A. and Neufeldt, R. C. (2005). Envisioning success: Building blocks for strategic and comprehensive peacebuilding impact evaluation. *Journal of Peacebuilding and Development*, 2(2), 24–41.

Fast, L. A., Neufeldt, R. C. and Schirch, L. (2002). Towards ethically grounded conflict interventions: Reevaluating challenges in the 21st century. *International Negotiation*, 7(2), 185–207.

Ferlie, E., Lynn, E. L., Jr. and Pollitt, C. (Eds). (2007). *The Oxford handbook of public management*. New York, NY: Oxford University Press.

Feyen, C. and Gsaenger, H. (2003). PCIA methodology: A development practitioner's perspective. In A. Austin, M. Fischer and O. Wils (Eds), *Dialogue Series No 1: Peace and conflict impact assessment (PCIA)*. Berlin: Berghof Research Center for Constructive Conflict Management. Retrieved fromhttp://www.berghof-handbook. net/documents/publications/dialogue1_gsaenger_feyen.pdf (accessed on 27 April 2015).

Fielding, N. (2010). Elephants, gold standards and applied qualitative research. *Qualitative Research*, 10(1), 123–127.

Forman, S. and Patrick, S. (Eds). (2000). *Good intentions: Pledges of aid for postconflict recovery*. Boulder, CO and London: Lynne Rienner Publishers.

Gaigals, C. and Leonhardt, M. (2001). *Conflict-sensitive approaches to development practice*. International Alert, IDRC and Saferworld. Retrieved from http://www. conflictsensitivity.org/sites/default/files/Conflict-Sensitive_Approaches_to_ Development.pdf (accessed on 22 April 2015).

Garcé, A. and Uña, G. (Eds). (2010). *Think tanks and public policies in Latin America*. Buenos Aires: CIPPEC.

Goodhand, J. and Atkinson, P. (2001). *Conflict and aid: Enhancing the peacebuilding impact of international engagement*. London: International Alert.

Graham, L. J. (2008). Rank and file: Assessing research quality in Australia. *Educational Philosophy and Theory*, 40(7), 811–815.

Grantcraft (Mackinnon, A., Arnott, N. and McGarvay, C.). (2006). *Mapping change: Using theory of change for planning and evaluation*. Retrieved from http://portals. wi.wur.nl/files/docs/ppme/Grantcraftguidemappingchanges_1.pdf (accessed on 22 April 2015).

Gready, P. (2009). Reasons to be cautious about evidence and evaluation: Rights-based approaches to development and the emerging culture of evaluation. *Journal of Human Rights Practice, 1*(3), 380–401.

Green Network of Sri Lanka. (2002). *Bitter truths and better tomorrows: People's report on sustainable development; Sri Lanka*. Sri Lanka: Green Network of Sri Lanka.

Greene, J. C., Caracelli, V. J. and Graham, W. F. (1989). Toward a conceptual framework for mixed-method evaluation designs. *Educational Evaluation and Policy Analysis, 11*(3), 255–274.

Grob, G. F. (2010). Evaluation field building in South Asia: Insights from the rear view mirror. *American Journal of Evaluation, 31*(2), 241–245.

Groundwater-Smith, S. and Mockler, N. (2007). Ethics in practitioner research: An issue of quality. *Research Papers in Education, 22*(2), 199–211.

Gugerty, M. K. and Prakash, A. (Eds). (2010). *Voluntary regulation of NGOs and nonprofits*. Cambridge and New York: Cambridge University Press.

Guggenbuhl-Craig, A. (1971). *Power in the helping professions*. Putnam, CT: Spring Publications, Inc.

Gutman, R. and Rieff, D. (1999). *Crimes of war: What the public should know*. New York and London: W.W. Norton and Co.

Hancock, G. (1989). *Lords of poverty: The power, prestige, and corruption of the international aid business*. New York, NY: The Atlantic Monthly Press.

Hasan, K. (2005). Indian scholar sifts 1971 fact from fiction, *Daily Times*, 18 December 2005. Retrieved from http://watandost.blogspot.co.uk/2005/12/1971-different-perspective.html(accessed on 21 June 2015).

Hawe, P., Bond, L. and Butler, H. (2009). Knowledge theories can inform evaluation practice: What can a complexity lens add? *New Directions for Evaluation, 124*(Winter), 89–100.

Hay, K. and Sudarshan, R. M. (2010). Making research matter in South Asia. *Economic and Political Weekly, 45*(3), 34.

Hey, V. (2000). Troubling the auto/biography of the questions: Re/thinking rapport and the politics of social class in feminist participant observation, genders and sexualities. In G. Walford and C. Hudson (Eds), *Studies in Educational Ethnography: Vol. 3. Genders and sexualities in educational ethnography* (pp. 161–183). Bingley, UK: Emerald Group Publishing Ltd.

Higher Education Funding Council of England (Research Excellence Framework Team). (2011). *Consultation on draft panel criteria and working methods*. England: HEFCE.

Hoffman, M. (2003). PCIA methodology: Evolving art form or practical dead-end. In A. Austin, M. Fischer and O. Wils (Eds), *Berghof Handbook Dialogue Series No. 1: Peace and conflict impact assessment: Critical views on theory and practice* (pp. 11–35). Berlin: Berghof Research Center for Constructive Conflict Management.

Honea, G. E. (1992). *Ethics and public sector evaluators: Nine case studies* (Unpublished doctoral dissertation), University of Virginia, Virginia, USA.

House, E. R. (2004). The role of the evaluator in a political world. *Canadian Journal of Program Evaluation, 19*(2), 1–16.

———. (2008). Blowback: Consequences of evaluation for evaluation. *American Journal of Evaluation, 29*(4), 416–426.

Howard Ross, M. (2003). PCIA as a peacebuilding tool. In A. Austin, M. Fischer and O. Wils (Eds), *Dialogue Series No. 1—Peace and conflict impact assessment: Critical views on theory and practice* (pp. 77–81). Berlin: Berghof Research Center for Constructive Conflict Management. Retrieved from http://www.cdainc.com/cdawww/project_profile.php?pid=DNH&pname=Do%20No%20Harm; http://www.oecd.org/dataoecd/55/0/44798177.pdf (accessed on 8 June 2015).

IDEAS. (2012). *Crosswalk of evaluator and evaluation manager competencies and characteristics*. Johannesburg: International Development Evaluation Association. Retrieved from http://www.google.gr/url?sa=t&rct=j&q=&esrc=s&source=web&cd=2&ved=0CFIQFjAB&url=http%3A%2F%2Fwww.ideas-int.org%2Fdocuments%2Fdocument.cfm%3FdocID%3D588&ei=iJjQT4n_CMS98gOgv_CtDA&usg=AFQjCNFVJB-st5-gQlqqvSKRP9h7E--fbA&sig2=GCSYPKd1AAhF51Oof9yc4A (accessed on 22 April 2015).

IFRC. (2011). *Project/Programme monitoring and evaluation guide*. Geneva: International Federation of Red Cross and Red Crescent Societies. Retrieved from http://www.ifrc.org/Global/Publications/monitoring/IFRC-ME-Guide-8-2011.pdf (accessed on 8 June 2015).

International Fund for Ireland. (2010). Mission statement. Retrieved from http://www.internationalfundforireland.com/strategy (accessed on 22 April 2015).

International Labor Organisation. (2012). *Rating the quality of evaluation reports: I-Eval Resource Kits* (Checklist 6). Geneva: ILO. Retreived from http://www.ilo.org/wcmsp5/groups/public/---ed_mas/---eval/documents/publication/wcms_165968.pdf (accessed on 22 April 2015).

Jacobsen, K. and Landau, L. (2003). *Researching refugees: Some methodological and ethical considerations in social science and forced migration* (Working Paper No. 90). New Issues in Researching Refugees, UNHCR Evaluation and Policy Analysis Unit. Geneva, Switzerland: United National High Commissioner for Refugees.

Johnson, C., Whitty, B. and Hammer, M. (2008, May). *Who do you work for? Establishing a better match between justifications of research* (Working Paper). One World Trust. London, UK.

Joint Evaluation of Emergency Assistance to Rwanda (Eriksson, J.). (1996). *Synthesis report—The international response to conflict and genocide: Lessons from the Rwanda experience.* Odense: Steering Committee of the JEEAR.

Jones, H. (2011). *A guide to monitoring and evaluating policy influence: Background note.* London: Overseas Development Institute. Retrieved from http://www.odi.org.uk/resources/docs/6453.pdf (accessed on 22 April 2015).

Jones, N. and Walsh, C. (2008). *Policy briefs as a communication tool for development research: Background note.* London: Overseas Development Institute.

Jordan, L. (2005), *Mechanisms for NGO accountability* (Research Papers Series Paper No. 3). Global Public Policy Institute. Berlin, Germany.

Kaufmann, D., Kraay, A. and Zoido-Lobaton, P. (2000). Governance matters: From measurement to action. *Finance and Development, 37*(2), 10–13.

Kellogg Foundation (Ed.). (1998). *Evaluation handbook.* Michigan/Battle Creek, MI: W. K. Kellogg Foundation/Collateral Management Company. Retrieved from http://www.epa.gov/evaluate/pdf/eval-guides/evaluation-handbook.pdf (accessed on 22 April 2015).

Kenna, R. and Berche, B. (2011). Normalization of peer-evaluation measures of group research quality across academic disciplines. *Research Evaluation, 20*(2), 107–116.

King, J. A. (2010). Response to evaluation field building in South Asia: Reflections, anecdotes and questions. *American Journal of Evaluation, 31*(2), 232–237.

Kopp, S. B. (1961). *If you meet the Buddha on the road, kill him!: The pilgrimage of psychotherapy patients.* New York, NY: Bantam Books.

Kusters, C. S. L., van Vugt, S., Wigboldus, S., Williams, B. and Woodhill, J. (2011). *Making evaluations matter: A practical guide for evaluators.* Wageningen, The Netherlands: Centre for Development Innovation. Retrieved from http://dmeforpeace.org/sites/default/files/Making%20Evaluatoins%20Matter.pdf (accessed on 27 April 2015).

Lardone, M. and Roggero, M. (2008). *Study on monitoring and evaluation of the research impact in the public policy of policy research institutes (PRIs) in the region.* Argentina: CIPPEC. Retrieved from http://www.ebpdn.org/download/download.php?table=resources&id=3013 (accessed on 27 April 2015).

Laudel, G. and Glaser, J. (2006). Tensions between evaluations and communication practices. *Journal of Higher Education Policy and Management, 28*(3), 289–295.

Leaning, J. and Arie, S. (2001). *Human security: A framework for assessment in conflict and transition* (Working Paper Series No. 11[8]). Harvard Center for Population and Development Studies. Boston, Mass., USA.

Lederach, J. P. (1997). *Building peace: Sustainable reconciliation in divided societies.* Washington, DC: United States Institute for Peace Press.

———. (2003). *The little book of conflict transformation.* Intercourse, PA: Good Books.

———. (2005). *The moral imagination: The art and soul of building peace.* New York: Oxford University Press.

Lederach, J. P., Neufeldt, R. C. and Culberston, H. (2007). *Reflective peacebuilding: A planning, monitoring and learning toolkit.* Mindanao, Philippines: The Joan B. Kroc Institute for International Peace Studies and Catholic Relief Services.

Leonhardt, M. (2000). *Conflict impact assessment of EU development cooperation with ACP countries—A review of literature and practice.* London: FEWER, International Alert and Saferworld.

Leonhardt, M., Ardon, P., Karuru, N. and Sherriff, A. (2002). *PCIA and NGO peacebuilding —Experiences from Kenya & Guatemala: A briefing paper.* London/Kenya/ Guatemala: International Alert/CCR/IEPADES.

Liang, L., Wu, Y. and Li, J. (2001). Chinese use of databases: Selection of databases, indicators and models for evaluating research performance of Chinese universities. *Research Evaluation, 10*(2), 105–113.

Lindblom, C. E. (1959). The science of muddling through. *Public Administration Review, 19*(2), 79–88.

London School of Economics. (2011). *Impact of social sciences: Maximizing the impact of academic research.* Retrieved from http://blogs.lse.ac.uk/impactofsocialsciences/ (accessed on 27 April 2015).

Malterud, K. (2001). Qualitative research: Standards, challenges, and guidelines. *The Lancet, 358*(9280), 483–488.

Manenti, A. and Cassabalian, C. (2003). *Inventory of 'health as a bridge for peace' interventions in WHO: Survey conducted in WHO headquarters in December 2002– February 2003.* Geneva: WHO, Department of Emergency and Humanitarian Action.

Marsden, D., Oakley, P. and Pratt, B. (1994). *Measuring the process: Guidelines for evaluating social development.* Oxford: INTRAC.

Martí, J. and Villasante, T. R. (2009). Quality in action research: Reflections for second-order inquiry. *Systemic Practice and Action Research, 22*(5), 383–396.

Martin, B. R. (2011). The research excellence framework and the 'impact agenda': Are we creating a Frankenstein monster? *Research Evaluation, 20*(3), 247–252.

Martin, B. R. and Whitley, R. (2010). The UK research assessment exercise: A case of regulatory capture?' In R. Whitley, J. Gläser and L. Engwall (Eds), *Reconfiguring knowledge production: Changing authority relationships in the sciences and their consequences for intellectual innovation* (pp. 51–80). Oxford: Oxford University Press.

Melvern, L. (2000). *A people betrayed: The role of the West in Rwanda's genocide.* London/ New York, NY: Zed Books Ltd.

Meyer, J. and Scott, W. R. (1983). *Organisational environments: Ritual and rationality.* Beverly Hills, CA: SAGE Publications.

Ministry of Foreign Affairs of Denmark (Ed.). (2006). Evaluation questions. *Evaluation Guidelines* (pp. 46–61). Copenhagen: Ministry of Foreign Affairs of Denmark Evaluation Department. Retrieved from http://www.netpublikationer.dk/um/7571/ html/chapter05.htm (accessed on 5 June 2015).

Mintzberg, H. (2007). *Tracking strategies: Towards a general theory.* New York, NY: Oxford University Press.

Mitchell, R. B., Clark, W. C. and Cash, D. W. (2006). Information and influence. In R. B. Mitchell, W. C. Clark, D. W. Cash and N. M. Dickson (Eds), *Global environmental assessments: Information and influence* (pp. 307–338). Cambridge, MA: MIT Press.

Mitleton-Kelly, E. (2003). Ten principles of complexity and enabling infrastructures. In E. Mitleton-Kelly (Ed.), *Complex systems and evolutionary perspectives of organisations: The application of complexity theory to organisations* (pp. 23–50). Bingley: Emerald Group Publishing Ltd.

————. (2004, April 29–30). *Knowledge generation & sharing & plural rationalities.* Discussion paper and challenge prepared for the Knowledge Anywhere Anytime Workshop, Brussels.

————. (2006). A complexity approach to co-creating an innovative environment. *World Futures, 62*(3): 223–239.

————. (2007). LSE Complexity EPSRC Short Course 2007 Programme Retrieved from http://www.lse.ac.uk/researchAndExpertise/units/complexity/events/2007/shortcourse/shortcourse.aspx (accessed on 2 June 2015).

Mookherjee, N. (2008, March 3). Skewing the history of rape in 1971: A prescription for reconciliation? *Bangladesh Genocide Archive.* Retrieved from http://www.genocidebangladesh.org/skewing-the-history-of-rape-in-1971-a-prescription-for-reconciliation/ (accessed on 22 June 2015).

Morariu, J. (2012, May 31). Six pieces of advice to demystify evaluation. *CTK Blog.* Retrieved from http://www.communitytech.net/news/six-pieces-advice-demystify-evaluation (accessed on 27 April 2015).

Morris, M. (1998). Ethical challenges. *American Journal of Evaluation, 19*(3), 381–382.

Morris, M. and Clark, B. (2009, November 11–14). *You want me to do what? Pressure to misrepresent findings.* Paper prepared for the Annual Meeting of the American Evaluation Association, Orlando, Florida.

Nelson, J. (2000). *The business of peace: The private sector as a partner in conflict prevention and resolution.* London: International Alert/Council on Economic Priorities/The Prince of Wales Leaders Forum.

Nightingale, P. and Scott, A. (2007). Peer review and the relevance gap: Ten suggestions for policy-makers. *Science and Public Policy, 34*(8), 543–553.

Nyberg Sorensen, N., Stepputat, F. and Van Hear, N. (2000). *Assessment of lessons learned from SIDA support conflict management and peacebuilding—State of the art/ annotated bibliography: SIDA evaluation 00/37:1.* Stockholm: SIDA, Department for Cooperation with Non-Governmental Organisations and Humanitarian Assistance.

O'Gorman, L. (2008). The (frustrating) state of peer review. *International Association for Pattern Recognition Newsletter, 30*(1), 3–5.

O'Neil, M. (2002). We may need a new definition for research excellence. *Commentary: University Affairs.* Retrieved from http://www.idrc.ca/EN/Resources/Publications/Pages/ArticleDetails.aspx?PublicationID=560 (accessed on 27 April 2015).

OECD. (1991). *Quality standards for development evaluation.* Paris: OECD. Retrieved from http://www.oecd.org/dataoecd/31/12/2755284.pdf (accessed on March 20 2012).

————. (1997). *The evaluation of scientific research: Selected experiences.* Paris: OECD.

————. (1999). *The limits and scope for the use of development cooperation incentives and disincentives for influencing conflict situations.* Paris: OECD.

————. (2001). *The DAC guidelines: Helping to prevent violent conflict.* Paris: OECD. Retrieved from http://www.oecd.org/dataoecd/15/54/1886146.pdf (accessed on 27 April 2015).

OECD. (2007). Encouraging effective evaluation of conflict prevention and peacebuilding activities: Towards DAC guidance. *OECD Journal on Development, 8*(3), 7–106.

OECD, United Nations Development Program and Geneva Declaration. (2011). Investing in security: A global assessment of armed violence reduction initiatives. *Conflict and Fragility Series.* Paris: OECD. Retrieved from http://dx.doi.org/10.1787/9789264124547-en (accessed on 23 April 2015).

Orjuela, C. (2003). Building peace in Sri Lanka: A role for civil society? *Journal of Peace Research, 40*(2), 195–212.

Ortengren, K. (2004). *The logical framework approach: A summary of the theory behind the LFA method.* Stockholm: SIDA.

Ottoson, J. M., Green, L. W., Beery, W. L., Senter, S. K., Cahill, C. L., Pearson, D. C., Greenwald, H. P., Hamre, R. and Leviton, L. C. (2009). Policy-contribution assessment and field-building analysis of the Robert Wood Johnson Foundation's active living research program. *American Journal of Preventive Medicine (Supplement), 36*(2), S34–S43.

Outcome Mapping Learning Community. (2006). *Outcome mapping and the logical framework approach: Can they share a space?* Retrieved from http://www.outcomemapping.ca/forum/files/OM-LFA_DRAFT_165.pdf (accessed on 22 April 2015).

Oxfam. (2007). *Impact measurement and accountability in emergencies: The good enough guide.* Oxford: Oxfam GB.

Paffenholz, T. (2005). Third generation PCIA: Introducing the aid for peace approach. In B. Bloomfield, M. Fischer and B. Schmelzle (Eds), *Dialogue series no 4: New trends in peace and conflict impact assessment (PCIA).* Berlin: Berghof Research Center for Constructive Conflict Management. Retrieved from http://www.berghof-handbook.net/documents/publications/dialogue4_paffenholz.pdf (assessed on 23 April 2015).

Paffenholz, T. and Reychler, L. (2004). *Introducing the peace and conflict assessment model (PCA)* (Version of the authors, 30 June 2004). Leuven: Field Diplomacy Initiative.

———. (2005). Towards better policy and programme work in conflict zones: Introducing the 'aid for peace' approach. *Journal of Peacebuilding and Development, 2*(2), 6–23.

———. (2007). *Aid for peace: A guide to planning and evaluation for conflict zones.* Baden-Baden: Nomos.

Pasteur, K. (2006). Learning for development. In R. Eyben (Ed.), *Relationships for aid* (pp. 21–42). London/Sterling, VA: Earthscan.

Petit-Zeman, S. (2003, January 16). Trial by peers comes up short. *Guardian.* Retrieved from http://www.guardian.co.uk/science/2003/jan/16/science.research (accessed on 5 June 2015).

Phillipines-Canada Local Government Support Programme (LGSP). (2003). *Walking the path of peace: Practicing the culture of peace, and peace and conflict impact assessment.* Manila: Department of the Interior and Local Government. Retrieved from http://ulrc.smu.edu.ph/cgi-bin/koha/opac-detail.pl?biblionumber=74357 (accessed on 22 April 2015).

Prendergast, J. and Scott, C. (1996). *Aid with integrity—Avoiding the potential of humanitarian aid to sustain conflict: A strategy for USAID/BHR/OFDA in complex emergencies* (Occasional Paper No. 2). Washington, DC: USAID.

Preskill, H. and Jones, N. (2009). *A practical guide for engaging stakeholders in developing evaluation questions.* Princeton, NJ: Robert Wood Johnson Foundation Series.

Retrieved   from   http://www.rwjf.org/files/research/49951.stakeholders.final.1.pdf (accessed on 22 April 2015).

Ramalingam, B. (2006). *Tools for knowledge and learning: Guide for development and humanitarian organisations.* London: Overseas Development Institute. Rerieved from http://www.odi.org.uk/resources/docs/188.pdf (accessed on 22 April 2015).

Ramalingam, B., Jones, H., Reba, T. and Young, J. (2008, October). *Exploring the science of complexity. Ideas and implications for humanitarian and development efforts* (Working Paper No. 285). Overseas Development Institute. London, UK

RAND Corporation. (2011). Standards for high-quality research and analysis. *RAND: Quality Standards.* Retrieved from http://www.rand.org/standards/standards_high. html (accessed on 22 April 2015).

Ravallion, M. (2009). Should the randomistas rule? *Economists Voice, 6*(2). Retrieved from http://www.degruyter.com/view/j/ev.2009.6.2/ev.2009.6.2.1368/ev.2009.6.2.1368. xml?format=INT (accessed on 22 April 2015).

Reay, D. (1996). Insider perspectives or stealing the words out of women's mouths: Interpretation in the research process. *Feminist Review, 53*(Summer), 57–73.

REF. (2011). *REF 02.2011: Assessment framework and guidance on submissions.* UK: Research Excellence Framework.

Reimers, F. and McGinn, N. (1997). *Informed dialogue: Using research to shape education policy around the world.* Westport, CT: Praeger Publishers.

Roche, Chris. (1999). *Impact assessment for development agencies: Learning to value change.* Oxford, UK: Oxfam/Novib.

Rodrik, D. (2011, June 10). A rejection letter I would like to receive from a journal one day. *Dani Rodrik's Blog: Unconventional Thoughts on Economic Development and Globalization.* Retrieved from http://rodrik.typepad.com/dani_rodriks_ weblog/2011/06/a-rejection-letter-i-would-like-to-receive-from-a-journal-one-day. html (accessed on 22 April 2015).

Roebber, P. J. and Schultz, D. M. (2011). Peer review, program officers and science funding. *PLoS One, 6*(4), e18680.

Rons, R., De Bruyn, A. and Cornelis, J. (2008). Research evaluation per discipline: A peer-review method and its outcomes. *Research Evaluation, 17*(1), 45–57.

Rowland, F. (2002). The peer review process: A report to the JISC Scholarly Communications Committee. Retrieved from http://www.jisc.ac.uk/uploaded_ documents/rowland.pdf (accessed on 11 July 2014).

Russ-Eft, D. and Preskill, H. (2001). *Evaluation in organisations: A systematic approach to enhancing learning, performance, and change.* Boston: Perseus Books.

Saari, E. and Kallio, K. (2011). Developmental impact evaluation for facilitating learning in innovation networks. *American Journal of Evaluation, 32*(2), 227–245.

Said, E. W. (1993). *Culture and imperialism.* London: Random House.

Sastry, T. and Bekhradnia, B. (2006). *Using metrics to allocate research funds: Initial response to the government's consultation proposals.* Oxford: Higher Education Policy Institute (HEPI).

Schram, S. F. (1993). Postmodern policy analysis: Discourse and identity in welfare policy. *Policy Sciences, 26*(3), 249–270.

Science-Metrix, Archambault, E. and Vitola-Gagne, E. (2004). *The use of bibliometrics in the social sciences and humanities* (Final Report). Prepared for the Social Sciences and Humanities Research Council of Canada (SSHRC). Montreal: Science-Metrix.

Scriven, M. (2001). Evaluation: Future tense. *American Journal of Evaluation, 22*(3), 301–307.

Sen, A. (1990). Gender and cooperative conflicts. In H. Tinker (Ed.), *Persistent inequalities* (pp. 123–149). New Delhi: Oxford University Press.

Seymour, F. (2011, June 27). Does the pressure for impact compromise research? *Forests Blog*. Retrieved from http://blog.cifor.org/3439/does-the-pressure-for-impact-compromise-research/ (accessed on 24 July 2015).

Shapiro, J. (2001). *Monitoring and evaluation*. Johannesburg, South Africa: CIVICUS. Retrieved from https://www.civicus.org/new/media/Monitoring%20and%20 Evaluation.pdf (accessed on 22 April 2015).

SIPU International, Centre for Development Research and International Peace Research Institute. (2000). *Assessment of lessons learned from SIDA support to conflict management and peacebuilding: SIDA evaluation 00/37*. Stockholm: SIDA.

Smith, L. C. and Subandoro, A. (2007). *Measuring Food Security–Using Household Expenditure Surveys*. Washington, D.C.: International Food Policy Research Institute. Retrieved from http://www.ifpri.org/sites/default/files/publications/sp3.pdf (accessed on 22 April 2015).

Smyth, M. and Robinson, G. (Eds). (2001). *Researching violently divided societies: Ethical and methodological issues*. London: Pluto.

Spencer, L., Ritchie, J., Lewis, J. and Dillon, L. (2003). *Quality in qualitative evaluation: A framework for assessing research evidence*. UK: Government Chief Social Researcher's Office.

Sridharan, S. and De Silva, S. (2010). On ambition, learning and co-evolution: Building evaluation as a field. *American Journal of Evaluation, 31*(2), 246–251.

Stephen, C. and Daibes, I. (2010). Defining features of the practice of global health research: An examination of 14 global health research teams. *Global Health Action, 3*. doi: 10.3402/gha.v3i0.5188. Retrieved from http://www.ncbi.nlm.nih.gov/pmc/articles/PMC2903310/ (accessed on 24 July 2015).

Swiss Agency for Development and Cooperation, Bolliger, E. and Hartmann, O. (2009). *Knowledge management toolkit*. Berne: Federal Department of Foreign Affairs and Swiss Agency for Development and Cooperation. Retrieved from http://www.nwf.org.za/images/2012_Files/DEZA-Vademecum-en.pdf (accessed on 12 April 2015).

Tatavarti, R., Sridevi, N. and Kothari, D. P. (2010). On assessing the quality of university research—RT Factor. *Current Science, 98*(8), 1015–1019.

Thoms, O. N. T., Ron, J. and Paris, R. (2008). *The effects of transitional justice mechanisms. A summary of empirical research findings and implications for analysts and practitioners*. Centre for International Policy Studies Working Paper. Ottawa: University of Ottawa.

Tijssen, R. J. W. (2003). Scoreboards of research excellence. *Research Evaluation, 12*(2), 91–103.

UN Security Council. (2004, August 23). *The rule of law and transitional justice in conflict and post- conflict societies: Report by the Secretary General S/2004/616*. Retrieved from http://daccess-dds-ny.un.org/doc/UNDOC/GEN/N04/395/29/PDF/N0439529.pdf?OpenElement (accessed on 22 April 2015).

UNEG (United Nations Evaluation Group). (2005). *Standards for evaluation in the UN system*. Retrieved from http://www.unevaluation.org/unegstandards (accessed on 22 April 2015).

Unerman, J. and O'Dwyer, B. (2006). Theorising accountability for NGO advocacy. *Accounting, Auditing and Accountability Journal, 19*(3), 349–376.

Uphoff, N. (1992a). *Learning from Gal Oya: Possibilities for participatory development and post-Newtonian social science.* Ithaca/New York/London: Cornell University Press.

———. (1992b). Monitoring and evaluating popular participation in World Bank-assisted projects. In B. Bhatnagar and A. C. Williams (Eds), *Participatory development and the World Bank: Potential directions for change* (World Bank Discussion Paper No. 183, pp. 135–153). Washington, DC: The World Bank.

Uvin, P. (1999). *The influence of aid in situations of violent conflict: A synthesis and a commentary on the lessons learned from case studies on the limits and scope for the use of development assistance incentives and disincentives for influencing conflict situations.* Paris: OECD DAC Informal Task Force on Conflict Peace and Development Cooperation.

Verkoren, W. (2008, July 28). The value of complexity for development. *Broker Online: Debating Complexity.* Retrieved from http://www.thebrokeronline.eu/en/articles/ Debating-complexity (accessed on 12 April 2015).

Wagner, C. S., Roessner, J. D., Bobb, K., Thompson Klein, J., Boyack, K. W., Keyton, J., Rafols, I. and Borner, K. (2011). Approaches to understanding and measuring Interdisciplinary Scientific Research (IDR): A review of the literature. *Journal of Infometrics, 5*(1), 14–26.

Ware, M. (2011). Peer review: Recent experience and future directions. *New Review of Information Networking, 16*(1), 23–53.

Webb, C. (1993). Feminist research: Definitions, methodology, methods and evaluation. *Journal of Advanced Nursing, 18*(3), 416–423.

Weiss, C. H. (1980). Knowledge creep and decision accretion. *Science Communication, 1*(3), 381–404.

WHO (2005). Swaziland. Summary Country Profile for HIV? AIDS Treatment Scale-Up. Retrieved from http://www.who.int/hiv/HIVCP_SWZ.pdf (accessed on 18 June 2015).

World Bank Independent Evaluation Group. (2011). *Writing terms of reference for an evaluation: A how-to guide.* Washington, DC: The World Bank. Retrieved from http://siteresources.worldbank.org/EXTEVACAPDEV/Resources/ecd_writing_ TORs.pdf (accessed on 22 April 2015).

Wu, H., Ismail, S., Guthrie, S. and Wooding, S. (2011). *Alternatives to peer review in research project funding.* USA (various): RAND Corporation.

Wunderlich, J. (2012, May 31). Evaluation approaches. *DM&E for Peacebuilding.* Retrieved from http://dmeforpeace.org/discuss/dme-tip-evaluation-approaches (accessed on 12 April 2015).

Yates, L. (2005). Is impact a measure of quality? Some reflections on the research quality and impact assessment agendas. *European Educational Research Journal, 4*(4), 391–403.

Yule, M. (2010). *Assessing research quality.* Ottawa: International Development Research Centre.

About the Editors and Contributors

Editors

Kenneth Bush is Executive Director and Altajir Lecturer in Post-war Recovery Studies at the Post-war Reconstruction and Development Unit of the University of York, UK. He received his PhD in International Relations and Comparative Politics from Cornell University, New York. Throughout his career, Dr Bush has worked within and between the worlds of research, policy and practice, inside and outside conflict zones. His work seeks to bridge the gap between peace studies and evaluation—in particular, his work focuses on peace and conflict impact assessment (PCIA) and on the ethical, political, logistical and methodological challenges confronting evaluators in conflict zones. Dr Bush was a founding professor of the Conflict Studies Programme at St Paul University in Ottawa, Canada. He has published and taught courses on evaluation, methodology for peace and conflict studies, social justice, ethnicised conflict, peacebuilding, post-cold war security, international relations theory, conflict management, forced displacement, war-affected kids, foreign policy and indigenous governance. Dr Bush has worked with a broad spectrum of policy, development and humanitarian organisations in the Global North and South.

Colleen Duggan is Senior Programme Specialist in the Policy and Evaluation Division of the International Development Research Centre (IDRC), a research funder located in Ottawa, Canada. Colleen brings her expertise in human rights and the rule of law in violence-affected settings to her work as a researcher and evaluator. Between 2001 and 2005, Colleen developed IDRC's programming in Latin America on peace and conflict and women's rights. She worked for more than a decade in a programming and policy capacity with the UN High Commissioner for Human Rights and with the United Nations Development Programme in

Colombia, Guatemala, El Salvador and New York. Issues she focused on with the UN included humanitarian response, security sector reform, transitional justice, gender violence, human rights and peacebuilding. Colleen has taught evaluation internationally on four continents and has published on issues of evaluation ethics, public policy evaluation, peacebuilding, gender and transitional justice, and conflict prevention. She holds a master's degree in International Human Rights and Humanitarian Law from the University of Essex, UK, and a graduate degree in international development and economic cooperation from the University of Ottawa, Canada.

Contributors

Katherine Hay is Deputy Director of the Bill and Melinda Gates Foundation in India. She leads a portfolio of Measurement, Learning and Evaluation (MLE) grants covering multiple programmes with an emphasis on integrated delivery, reproduction, maternal and child health, immunisation, family planning and tuberculosis. Katherine has published on women's empowerment, feminist evaluation and evaluation capacity building.

John A. Healy is a doctoral candidate at the School of Business in the Centre for Nonprofit Management, Trinity College Dublin. His research is in the area of institutional theory and it focuses on how ingrained cultural beliefs and practices influence the micro-process of organisational change. He is the former Director of Strategic Learning and Evaluation at the Atlantic Philanthropies, where he led and facilitated organisational change and strategy development work within the foundation. John has published in the areas of evaluation, philanthropic strategy and systems reform.

John R. Healy was Chief Executive Officer and President of the Atlantic Philanthropies, a large international grant-making foundation, from 2001 to 2007. On his retirement, he was appointed adjunct professor in the Centre for Nonprofit Management at Trinity College Dublin. He serves on the board of the Community Foundation for Northern Ireland and of the National Development Council of Wexford Festival Opera, and chairs Alliance Publishing Trust, publisher of the international philanthropy magazine *Alliance*. John is a trustee of the Trinity Foundation and chairs its Advisory Board.

Janaka Jayawickrama is Programme Director for the MSc programme in International Humanitarian Affairs in the Post-war Recovery and Development Unit of the University of York, UK. Janaka received a PhD in Social Anthropology and an MSc in Disaster Management and Sustainable Development from Northumbria University. He is also a Visiting Lecturer at the Institute of Health and Society at Newcastle University, where he specialises in mental health and politics in humanitarian assistance.

Kevin Kelly is Director, Strategic Intelligence and M&E, at Strategic Evaluation, Advisory and Development Consulting (SEAD) in Capetown, South Africa. Kevin has a PhD in psychology and an internship in community development research from Rhodes University. He is the former Research Director of the Centre for AIDS Development, Research and Evaluation, South Africa. Kevin has published widely on issues of research, evaluation, psychology and public health.

Colin Knox is Professor of Comparative Public Policy at Ulster University, UK. His research interests include devolution in Northern Ireland and comparative public sector reform in developing countries. Colin is a Fellow of the Academy of Social Sciences (FAcSS) and a Fellow of the Higher Education Academy (FHEA).

Philip McDermott is Lecturer in the School of Sociology and Applied Social Studies at Ulster University, Northern Ireland. He has a special interest in the relationship between linguistic minority groups and the state in post-conflict societies. Philip previously worked as a researcher on the IDRC-funded 'Evaluation in Violently Divided Societies' project.

Ethel Méndez is an advisor to the Honorary Ministry of Health's HIV/AIDS/STI programme on monitoring evaluation in Honduras. She has led studies on the Honduran surveillance information system for most-at-risk populations and is a member of the Honduran Evaluation Professional Society.

Jacqueline Strecker is an ICT Innovations and Education Specialist with the United Nations High Commissioner for Refugees (UNHCR). As a communication specialist with a rich background in the field of forced migration, she is managing a series of pilot projects that leverage the use of information communication technologies to broaden educational opportunities for refugees in Africa.

Brendan S. Whitty is a researcher and consultant in international development, focusing on issues of aid effectiveness and accountability. He is presently a PhD candidate (International Development) at the University of East Anglia (UEA), UK, with a research focus on the anthropology of policy, and a particular interest in knowledge practices within bureaucratic organisations in development contexts.

Zahbia Yousuf is Peacebuilding Editor and Analyst at Conciliation Resources (CR), an NGO based in London. Prior to joining CR, she was a Teaching Fellow in Violence, Conflict and Development at SOAS, University of London, and Kings College London. She has a PhD in comparative peace processes from Kings College London.

Sonal Zaveri is an evaluator based in Mumbai who specialises in participatory, gender and equity-focused evaluation with a strong emphasis on use. She is a founding member and Secretary of the South Asian Community of Evaluators. Sonal is also an international advisor to Child-to-Child Trust, Institute of Education, London.

Index*

* 't' denotes table and 'f' denotes figure.